IN WHOSE PLACE?

First published by Jacana Media (Pty) Ltd in 2024

10 Orange Street
Sunnyside
Auckland Park 2092
South Africa
+2711 628 3200

www.jacana.co.za

© Individual contributors, 2023
© Cover photo: Pamila Gupta

All rights reserved.

ISBN 978-1-4314-3446-6

Cover design by Maggie Davey and Aimèe Armstrong
Editing by Russell Martin
Proofreading by Lara Jacob
Set in Electra LT Std 11/15.5pt
Printed and bound by ABC Press, Cape Town
Job no. 004147

See a complete list of Jacana titles at www.jacana.co.za

IN WHOSE PLACE?

Confronting Vestiges of
Colonialism and Apartheid

Edited by
Hilton Judin,
Arianna Lissoni and
Ali Khangela Hlongwane

Contents

Introduction: In Whose Place? Confronting Vestiges of Colonialism and Apartheid
Hilton Judin, Arianna Lissoni and Ali Khangela Hlongwane   1

Part One: Place of Heritage

1. 'Save Our Berea!': Whose Place? Whose Heritage?
   Adheema Davis, Sibonelo Gumede and Greer Valley   15
2. Forced Removals: Reflections on Fietas' Photographic Archive, Museum and Heritage Trail
   Ali Khangela Hlongwane   37
3. Statues Also Die: The Fortress of Cacheu as a Graveyard of the Portuguese Colonial Legacy
   Nuno Coehlo   59
4. Building as Artefact: From Prison to Museum
   Nabeel A. Essa   85
5. Bantfu Netindzawo (People and Places)
   Solam Mkhabela with Hiten Bawa   113

Part Two: Buildings as Place

6. Speculative Desire and Residential Reappropriation: Johannesburg's Ponte City from Apartheid to the Present
   Stefan Chavez-Norgaard   127

7.	Political Evolution of a Building Type: Community Centres at the End of Apartheid *Hilton Judin*	155
8.	The Rescripting of the Johannesburg West Dutch Reformed Church *Brendan Hart*	181
9.	Tropical Bungalow *Roland Gunst and Esther Severi*	201

Part Three: Residual Places

10.	Notes for a Visual Essay on the Experience of Art Deco in South Africa *Pamila Gupta*	211
11.	Garden of Ruins: The Urban Production of Colonial Bissau and the History of a Dilapidated Present *Rui Aristides Lebre*	231
12.	Reclaiming South African Railway Spaces: Ruination and Remembrance in De Aar and Usakos *Giorgio Miescher and Raffaele Perniola*	259
13.	Usakos Museum and the Re-vision of Colonial Spaces: 'Put Your Hand on Your Forehead' *Florence F. /Khaxas*	279

Contributors	295
Notes	301
Index	349

Introduction

In Whose Place? Confronting Vestiges of Colonialism and Apartheid

Hilton Judin, Arianna Lissoni and
Ali Khangela Hlongwane

Since independence, African countries have been confronted with the relics of former colonial powers and, in the south, white minority regimes. Often neglected or damaged, these remains and environments are haunted by the lingering spectre of colonial history and architecture's largely hidden yet pervasive racist presence. They are a sobering reminder of the everyday bureaucracy of colonialism and apartheid – and of how this history of subjugation and planning continues in part to shape life in postcolonial societies under global capitalism. What is being done with these remnants? Which should remain preserved, and which altered or dismantled? Which do we choose to remember, and which to forget? Postcolonial conditions have been characterised by contradictions that are in some instances referred to as a 'double consciousness'.[1] Newly independent states have often experienced a memory boom as part of which countries, streets and physical outcroppings of the symbolic and physical landscapes are renamed. At the same time, the built environment itself is often left unchanged, leaving more than remnants of the past.

In the South African context, post-apartheid legislation has called for the preservation of colonial infrastructure as part of processes of acknowledging diversity and promoting reconciliation while, in some instances, their removal has been sought for reasons of political expediency. Consequently, cities and colonial infrastructure were inherited, taken over and adapted for radically new societies that had to overcome racist divisions, violent oppression and poverty. Yet it has often been the case that only the most obvious state buildings and oppressive administrative apparatuses of power were identified for destruction; others were neglected or reimagined as historical sites, memorials and museums for memory. Lingering everyday infrastructures left behind were adapted and renovated for new groups and uses or ignored and neglected when not easily disposed of. Apartheid zoning and spatial segregation often remain in place given the enormous cost and difficulties of removal and radical reconstruction. This contradiction has inadvertently created a new reality wherein apartheid legacies are commemorated within racialised landscapes instead of ensuring that the geography of apartness is negated.

In this volume architects, anthropologists, heritage practitioners, activists and historians examine ways people are critiquing, rethinking, repurposing and reusing colonial and apartheid architecture and infrastructure in postcolonial contexts. In recent years, public awareness of the physical and environmental reminders of this past has been sharpened by sporadic campaigns such as Rhodes Must Fall and ongoing disputes around land, gentrification, repatriation and heritage, in which different and often conflicting agendas are brought to the fore. Globally, there has been a wave of public clamour and contestation about the presence of racist names and statues in public spaces, litigation over abandoned and toxic sites, with calls for removal and restitution as an integral part of decolonisation. And there has been a recognition of the lived experiences, knowledge and activities through which people and communities build their heritage. In this context, questions about the place of colonial and apartheid planning and architecture and their past acquire salience and urgency in the present. Contesting one's place remains central to confronting the lingering impact of colonisation and apartheid, emerging as it does out of the intermingling of our environments, histories, languages and experiences.

Finding and claiming one's place, rather than being put in one's place, is a way of expanding one's life, of finding and making a shared social space encompassing family and one's immediate community. In this sense, processes of reclamation and renewal move from creative representation through reconstruction to transformation of one's environment, challenging the dispossessions and displacements that severed links between community and place under colonialism and apartheid. These spaces need to be recovered as tangible places and not as souvenirs of the past, no matter the extent to which the past continues to pervade the present. Belonging may have to do with place, but equally it is about family and community, shared cultures and languages, beliefs that resisted and fought against alienation brought about through colonial conquest, slavery, labour migration, forced removals, indentured labour and segregation. As the postcolonial theorist Bill Ashcroft describes the criticality of movement and remembrance in place:

> Place is never simply location, nor is it static, a cultural memory which colonization buries. For, like culture itself, place is in a continual and dynamic state of formation, a process intimately bound up with the culture and identity of its inhabitants. Above all place is a result of habitation, a consequence of the ways in which people inhabit space, particularly that conception of space as universal and incontestable that is constructed for them by imperial discourse. The transformation of imperial conceptions of place, and imperial technologies of spatial representation, has often been carried out successfully in imaginative acts of resistance through the creative representations of place. Such place forms itself out of the densely woven web of language, memory and cultural practice and keeps being formed by the process of living.[2]

The cultural impact of colonisation and its relation to cultural consciousness and identity were pronounced in the realm of the built landscape, the infrastructure and architecture imposed on the environment. Place is the material location of the accumulated layers of history imposed and resisted on a site, continuously constructed and erased over time. At the same time, place is more than just a container or a geographical location. It can best be understood as relational and underwritten by social practices that are intimately bound up with processes of communal and self-formation.

INTRODUCTION

IN THIS BOOK, WE AIM to engage with this history to address questions of colonialism and apartheid that are partially buried within the built environment or embedded within collective cultural responses, so as to explore possibilities and challenges for the future. We seek to engage with ways in which history, art and architecture practices currently contest and subvert these protracted conditions in terms of social justice, development, conservation, heritage, land reclamation and urban renewal. We also acknowledge and grapple with new challenges manifest in decaying parts of cities, in the growth of informal businesses and the escalation of homelessness. By focusing on colonial environments in different parts of Africa, we seek to understand the history of such disputed places and responses of remembrance, communal consideration, revival and conflict. The past continues to surround us. It can be found everywhere in our built landscape. It seeps into our lives and endeavours. After apartheid and colonialism it still clogs the air, and its purchase permeates our buildings. It remains obstinate in its presence, and in buildings by brick or structure it can be defining as much as felt. While not always rotting, such a corpse refuses to lie buried beneath the surface; more than memory, it leaves a ghostly imposition that will not easily depart. History continuously seeps through our cities even as people, events and sensibilities have changed.

The exploration, organisation, control and racial ordering of space were at the heart of the colonial enterprise, the economic basis for exploiting raw materials and labour from the colonies for the benefit of European metropolitan powers. European ideas and assumptions about space were imposed as farms, properties, plantations, mines and towns were established, turning the infrastructure of railways and roads, boundaries and borders into a network of colonial power that over time transformed indigenous communities and landscapes for generations thereafter. Space was also segregated along racial lines as part of colonial strategies of indirect rule and social and political control of African populations. Colonial conquest and dispossession were often accompanied by the creation of 'native reserves' organised along ethnic lines where Africans could hold land. In South Africa, this process of dispossession was legislated by the Natives Land Act of 1913 and subsequent laws, which eventually confined the African majority to 13 per cent of the country's land. Under apartheid, the reserves system provided the basis for the development of the bantustans, which effectively stripped black South Africans of their citizenship rights, while they were presented to the outside world as South Africa's own version of 'decolonisation'. Although the bantustans are ostensibly dead on paper, their complex legacies have continued to live on post-1994.

From the start, resistance to colonisation by anti-colonial and national liberation movements included the targeting of the infrastructure on which the colonial order relied, for example through sabotage, destruction and refashioning. At the same time, colonial infrastructure also shaped the possibilities of anti-colonial struggles and protests in different contexts. In the early 1960s, African liberation movements in countries that were still under the colonial yoke or white minority rule turned to armed resistance against their oppressors. In South Africa, this strategic shift initially took the form of a sabotage campaign as a first step towards guerrilla warfare. Its targets were not people, but government buildings and infrastructure such as electricity pylons and telephone lines, symbols of apartheid's infrastructure of oppression. Following another period of strategic review in the late 1970s, armed propaganda assumed an increasingly central role as a foundation of 'people's war'. Spectacular explosions such as the bombing of the apartheid parastatal SASOL oil refinery and the Koeberg nuclear power plant near Cape Town gave inspiration and hope to the masses as resistance against the regime intensified in the 1980s. But there was also the question of how much of this state infrastructure should be destroyed, given that once the liberation movement would come to power, they would need it to provide for all of the country's people.

The postcolonial period following the dismantling of colonial regimes is discussed in the chapters below in the light of contemporary urban architectural, art, ecological and heritage projects, in which buildings, objects and the environment are being renegotiated as sites of a postcolonial heritage and resurgent public practice. This process comes mired in numerous contradictions and controversy as the longstanding spatial legacy and history of landlessness are confronted. The chapters in this volume have developed from the papers originally presented at a conference in May 2021 (which took place online because of the Covid-19 pandemic), a collaboration between the Wits History Workshop and the School of Architecture and Planning organised with the support of the European Union National Institutes for Culture (EUNIC).[3] They also build on an earlier conference that resulted in the book *Falling Monuments, Reluctant Ruins: The Persistence of the Past in the Architecture of Apartheid* (2021).

IN PART ONE, 'PLACE of Heritage', the civic organisation 'Save Our Berea' in the South African city of Durban is analysed by architect Adheema Davis, urbanist Sibonelo Gumede, and curator and writer Greer Valley in Chapter 1 to understand just whose and what heritage is being addressed. The authors study the politics of ownership, race and nostalgia in saving ruined houses in the area as opposed to the reclamation of buildings as independent community spaces outside developer-driven urban regeneration. In their chapter they reflect on the settler-colonial sense of self accompanying the perceived threat of loss related to colonial architectural heritage, as once entirely white suburbs undergo dramatic demographic changes into diverse inner-city neighbourhoods.

In Chapter 2, historian Ali Khangela Hlongwane turns to Fietas/Pageview to revisit and re-engage with the history of the struggles against forced removals in the southern suburbs of Johannesburg. He finds not only a legacy of resistance in traces of the past left lying in ruins still visible in the area, and in the photographs of David Goldblatt and Mike Feldman, but hope for the future in these resilient communities and 'new' residents. While a narrative of 'dashed hopes' remains with ongoing issues of unresolved land restoration and restitution, there are signs in the oral testimonies and archives of the Fietas Museum and Heritage Trail of another community emerging out of an unspectacular everyday life of survival and remembering.

In Chapter 3, Nuno Coehlo looks at the fortress of Cacheu in Guinea-Bissau and at the Portuguese colonial legacy. After independence in 1973, the statues left behind by the colonists were removed from their public pedestals and destroyed or taken to the fortress as a place where statues 'went to die'. Coelho describes how the scattered statues were regrouped and deposited within the rehabilitated fortress without being restored.

In Chapter 4, architect Nabeel A. Essa unpacks the heritage and spatial decisions of the Constitution Hill development from disused prison to court and museum. In demolishing some buildings and erecting new ones under an urban masterplan, the site was transformed and significant built heritage and material artefacts displaced. As a consequential act of restitution, this project needs to be assessed for the evidential, memorial and interpretative context that saw these colonial and apartheid sites used for unlocking regeneration. It also raises interesting and ongoing questions about the tensions between conservation and urban development.

In Chapter 5, a selection of panels from a graphic novel by Solam Mkhabela and Hiten Bawa's traces the history of the freehold township of Alexandra in Johannesburg from its origins, linked to the mineral revolution on the Rand in the late 19th century, to the post-apartheid period, and provides insights into the daily social and political struggles of its residents. In revealing conflicts that emerge between space designed by white city planners and urban African dwellers, and the ongoing shortage of housing and services post-1994, the exclusionary nature of a city conceived by colonial and apartheid spatial practices is exposed by the subaltern voices of those transforming the margins of the economy.

In Part Two, 'Buildings as Place', urban planner Stefan Chavez-Norgaard in Chapter 6 examines a series of residential reappropriations of Johannesburg's Ponte City apartments following the panoptic ideologies of its white-minority manifestation. The author contrasts the media representations of Ponte with its political-economic realities from its development in the 1970s through to the 2020s. Ponte can be seen to have made concrete the contested aspirations of both its architects' outmoded speculative vision and its changing residents' everyday lives in a city of massive inequality, urban dispossession and failed dreams of high-density living.

In Chapter 7, the political evolution of the community centre in South Africa is surveyed by the architect Hilton Judin. In the period from the mid-1980s through the early 1990s, the community centre became an urban precursor of a new society and an architectural type at once culturally distinctive and politically vital. White architects reimagined the multi-purpose hall and resource centre as community centre and found themselves engaged as activists in building development and support for black communities.

Architect and heritage consultant Brendan Hart, in Chapter 8, looks at the rescripting of the Mayfair West Dutch Reformed Church. Churches like this in Johannesburg, once closely linked with Afrikaner identity and nationalism of the apartheid era, have been abandoned by the dwindling congregations of formerly white inner-city suburbs. In their transformation into community halls, Hindu temples and mosques, new neighbourhoods and new residents largely from other parts of Africa are evolving and becoming visible in the city.

Chapter 9 includes stills and the transcript of a filmed lecture performance by the artist Roland Gunst and choreographer Esther Severi, demonstrating the intimate history of the tropical bungalow.[4] This housing model of colonial infrastructure in the Belgian Congo was designed to outline power relations, regulate interracial interactions and programme racial categories. Gunst proposes to reverse the function of this instrument of oppression and make it one of rehabilitation from trauma on black bodies. His polyvocal performative ritual is inspired by the Luba oral tradition called Milandu in which different parties negotiate around a historical event to solve an ongoing dispute. Using a mnemonic device, or memory board, to divide a space into zones in which memory events are encoded, these narrators activate specific zones to provoke memory reproduction – in this performance, as a stage for the recomposition of history and identities for the audience.

Finally, in Part Three on 'Residual Places', the visual anthropologist Pamila Gupta shares her notes and photographs of her experience of Art Deco in South Africa. In Chapter 10 she uses her tour of three cities in the country with architects and building planners to review heritage sites layered by ruin, repair and renovation. In seeing and thinking through architecture, Gupta wonders how people caught up in everyday life experience these buildings without thinking through them.

The dilapidated present that is now a garden of ruins is traversed by the historian of architecture Rui Aristides in Chapter 11 to explain the urban development of colonial Bissau as an empire-city and key laboratory of colonialism during Portuguese domination. In showing how present decaying infrastructure emerged from the colonial production of deteriorated landscapes, Aristides argues that the forgotten Portuguese effort to keep its colonies in ruins relied on the production of a future past and imperial fable.

In Chapter 12, the reclaiming of southern African railway spaces is brought to life by the historical geographer Giorgio Miescher and historian Raffaele Perniola. Communities in small towns, such as De Aar in South

Africa and Usakos in Namibia, once owed their existence to and depended on South African Railways, succumbing from the 1970s to the decline of the company and the gradual disintegration of railway infrastructure. In De Aar, engagement with the railway ruins and organised claims by young heritage activists clash with the municipality's attempts to redevelop the former railway yard in the town centre, while residents remain indifferent to and resentful of the decaying infrastructure. In Usakos, on the other hand, the past is drawn upon in imagining an inclusive future and remains important to residents in pursuit of a local museum.

Usakos Museum in Namibia is presented in Chapter 13 by the storyteller and cultural activist Florence F. /Khaxass as a case for the revisioning of colonial spaces in a small town. The museum speaks to the descendants of families forcibly removed from the 'Old Location' to new townships under apartheid during the 1960s. They are looking to retrieve, research and collect photographs and material for museum and memorial purposes in the places and ruins where their homes once stood. In doing so, they intend to displace memories of destruction with answers about who these people were and visions of hope for where these families are now.

WHAT REMAINS OF THIS landscape today, of these cities that were never defeated? What continues to operate and flourish? What may never be swept aside, simply rearranged and restored, or dismantled while sustaining remnants of colonialism or apartheid? Highways dividing communities or bypassing them; workplaces and factories widely dispersed and at great distances from employees' homes; health and social facilities constrained and sparse; the deprivations and discriminations dividing row upon row of 'matchbox' houses from the cultural and economic infrastructure of cities. Change is taking place despite these economic systems still in place to thwart it – resistance and struggle in all forms essential to radical transformation, protest in the streets continually demanding this accounting. After centuries of European colonialism in Africa, an occupation of control through ritual and mapping, coercion and violence, still requires today comprehensive cultural and economic reckoning and reconstruction. Through the research, performance, activities and writing of engaged practitioners around the topic, this volume seeks to create and foster dialogue between the associated artistic, cultural and architectural projects. It retains a focus on the historical infrastructure of everyday oppression under colonialism and apartheid. The chapters are presented through several interrelated, imagined and practical themes outlined above: lost buildings, damaged infrastructure, ruins and heritage reconsidered. In these chapters, the role of historical evidence and its use, or misuse, continue to be of critical importance. Questioning, challenging and refuting forms of evidence form part of the toolkit enabling the reimagination of vestiges of colonial landscapes.

The contributors to this volume continue to work with a past that is not free from colonialism and apartheid. They work in a landscape that bears witness to the violence and brutality that remain attached to the very places from which lives were uprooted and torn apart. At times distant but seldom forgotten, these events have not gone away, remaining endemic and, in their obscurity, able to perpetuate the deprivations and injustices of the past. Yet this past returns in many ways. Without careful research and continuous reconsideration, this urban landscape would seem as if it had always been this way, coming to us without the concerted tactics and enforcement of its perpetrators. Its patina has not turned a shade or to dust but remains as decay and degradation, infecting memories as much as the environment. In these chapters the contributors had to choose what to recall and research, and how to distance themselves. At the same time, they recognise that they cannot be limited by these landscapes; just as people cannot be bound to them, they need to move further in redefining them and the lives these places encapsulated. All the while these memories and places are recalled, people are looking back to unpack and understand their impact as a way of moving beyond. While the obligations of this memory are manifold, understanding the history and architecture of these places will separate what might best be abandoned as ruins from that which can be taken up in building.

Many of the contributors here follow the idea of moving beyond memorialisation, remembrance and testimony to actively engaging with and healing the contemporary landscape scorched by centuries of colonialism and apartheid. For some, reparation highlights this notion of a damaged landscape, of identifying, healing and belonging, through who gets to repair, reimagine and reconstruct this evolving topography. But for all contributors, these are places embodying the deep connections we have and share with each other in our communities and neighbourhoods. In examining buildings, ruins, sites and landscapes, we continue to ask: In what ways do these retain or have they jettisoned the formal structures of power and racism in which they once symbolically and functionally operated? In what ways can their lingering past be revealed, contested, reimagined or expunged? Even as the power of these edifices, landscapes and effigies has diminished, the embedded stories need to be told, history interrogated, the many historical gaps and silences acknowledged, and redress and recuperation take place. The words 'vestiges' and 'investigate' are cognates, pointing to the continuing examination and uncovering that surround the objects, edifices, ruins and landscapes given to us. These demand to be looked at, considered and examined in the light of their deeper historical and present everyday living contexts.

Part One

Place of Heritage

Chapter One

'Save Our Berea!': Whose Place? Whose Heritage?

Adheema Davis, Sibonelo Gumede and Greer Valley

Since the end of formal apartheid three decades ago, South African cities have undergone periods of significant social and geopolitical change. However, colonial and apartheid spatial logics continue to influence and structure how cities are utilised, experienced and negotiated. Contemporary South Africa, often considered a country in transition, is emerging from the early post-apartheid era, during which the first democratically elected state led by President Nelson Mandela emphasised racial cohesion and national reconciliation over reparatory justice for colonial violence. This attitude shown by the Mandela dispensation is sometimes referred to as 'rainbowism'.[1] In recent years, the state-sanctioned reconciliation doctrine of the 1990s has clashed with the calls for decolonisation from South Africa's youth. Some analysts also argue that the emergence of movements like Rhodes Must Fall demonstrates that South Africa can no longer be thought of as a country in transition but that it has instead settled into the 'post post-apartheid'.[2]

The notion of the 'post post-apartheid' is reflected in the recent unrest that erupted throughout the KwaZulu-Natal (KZN) and Gauteng provinces in July 2021.[3] The unrest or riots, which caused extensive destruction of infrastructure, business premises, and retail and grocery outlets, arose from the intersection of South Africa's rising socio-economic disparity, political instability, economic and social strain caused by the global Covid-19 pandemic, and growing discontent with the country's governing party, among numerous other complex factors. Notably, the KZN province was most severely affected. In the city of Durban, the nation observed, through almost uninterrupted news coverage, how armed (mainly affluent) city residents set up 'checkpoints' in reaction to the unrest to secure their properties and neighbourhoods by policing who was permitted to enter. These 'checkpoints' enabled racial profiling and violent attacks to ensue, disproportionately affecting the city's black African residents (as they have been racialised).[4] Because of the tenacity of apartheid spatial planning, the invisible walls between neighbourhoods in South Africa's segregated and racialised cities have largely remained intact, with the result that the makeshift checkpoints were organised along racial lines.

Given the political and social change that the country has experienced in the past three decades, the neo-colonial South African city is the site of production for new and transforming urban narratives. In this auto-ethnographic chapter, we turn our attention to the Berea, the oldest residential suburb in the coastal city of Durban, South Africa's third-largest city. Geographically, the Berea consists of the suburbs of Upper Glenwood, Umbilo, Musgrave, Essenwood and Morningside, located along a ridge that looks over the eThekwini bay. Its dominant mix of late Victorian and Edwardian architecture consists of remnants of the city's British colonial period when the suburb was home to Durban's most affluent settler-colonist families. Under apartheid segregationist law, the Berea was declared a white residential area, and the legacies of this legislation are evident in how this space functions in the social imaginary. From the 1990s onwards, Durban's central business district and the adjacent suburb of the Berea experienced substantial white flight and a steady increase in black African and Indian residents, resulting in a diverse inner-city demographic in the present. These demographic changes mark a significant shift away from what was then a predominantly white urban centre during apartheid. As Bill Freund says, 'the densely built-up but affluent suburban mix around Musgrave Centre on the central Berea, once entirely white, has rapidly acquired a large population of residents of Indian descent'.[5] While the changes in the racialised spatial dynamics of Durban's central city may have been welcomed and even celebrated by some, it brought to the surface feelings of fear and animosity in others, leading to white families who had the means migrating northwards, towards the suburbs of Umhlanga and Ballito and further afield. This phenomenon is not unique to the Berea, as the patterns of white flight and migration northwards have also been observed in Johannesburg, another of South Africa's most populous cities. This chapter reflects on the perceived threat of loss related to colonial architectural heritage and the settler-colonial sense of self in Durban's urban context.

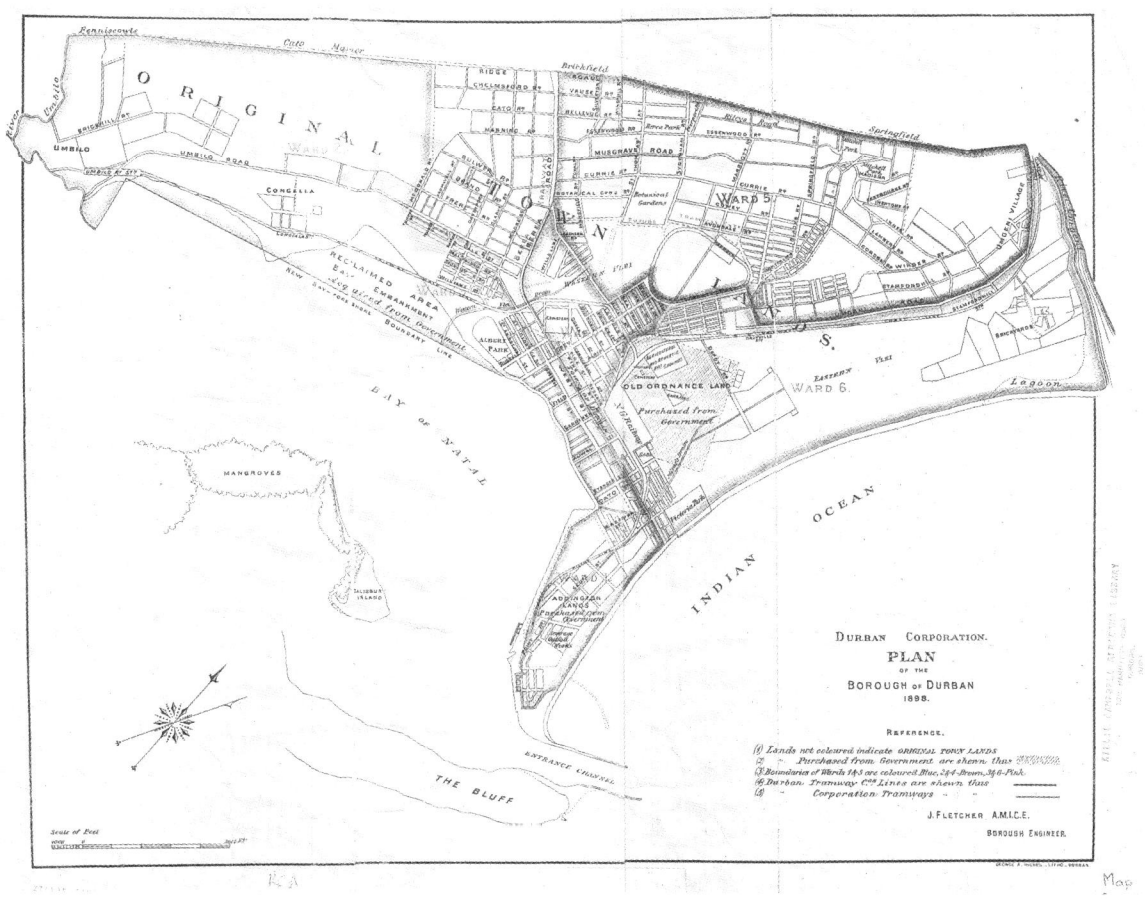

Figure 1.1: The 1898 plan of the borough of Durban by J. Fletcher, illustrating the established suburb of the Berea overlooking the original town centre layout and Bay of Natal. (University of KwaZulu-Natal Architecture Archive)

'Save Our Berea'

For some of those white residents who opted to remain in the Berea, the challenge of preserving the architectural remnants constructed during the era of British colonial rule has become a self-appointed vocation. The emergence of civic action groups and residents' associations across South Africa was a nationwide phenomenon that occurred after the country's first democratic elections in 1994, alongside socio-spatial change. Many neighbourhoods in the country now have residents groups that are typically organised through social media. Admission to the groups is usually by invitation or by approval on request. Save Our Berea (SOB), a Durban-based resident organisation operating since 2013, is an example of a civic action group acting as custodian for the built environment, having been formed in response to the real as well as imagined neglect of the suburb by city authorities and fellow city residents. The organisation describes itself as follows on its Facebook page:

> SAVE OUR BEREA FB page was created by a group of activists who have come together to form Save Our Berea Working Committee (SOBWC), specifically to PROTEST against eThekwini's lack of by-law enforcement and serial neglect of our once beautiful Berea. We hope to make a positive difference by agitating and lobbying for improvement and change – specifically by turning around the 'broken window' syndrome blighting our suburbs … We say NO to illegal building and businesses operating out of residences in our suburbs. We say NO to crime, vagrancy, self-appointed car guards and begging at traffic lights. We say NO to defecating in our streets. We say NO to corrupt building inspectors. We ENCOURAGE ratepayers to SHARE their UNRESOLVED land use issues on our FB page. Tell us about absent landlords, slum landlords, illegal businesses, abandoned houses, illegal building and alterations without approved plans as well as the illegal destruction of trees in your area. Put your stories on our FB page. If nobody else is listening to you, we will! This is YOUR Berea. YOUR investment in our city. YOUR future. We say it's time to TAKE BACK OUR STREETS, OUR SUBURBS, OUR LIVES. We say NOW IS THE TIME to SAVE OUR BEREA.

In a similar vein, a *Berea Mail* newspaper article of 2013 with the headline 'Save Our Berea!' claims: 'Once an upmarket, leafy and attractive suburb, the Berea has now plummeted into an area plagued by vagrants, street children and prostitutes. Buildings, many of which have been declared heritage sites, have been abandoned, totally neglected or renovated without proper plans or authorisation.'[6]

Whereas the frequent use of exclamation marks and capital letters conveys the urgency of the group's plight, it is unclear what Save Our Berea is attempting to save the Berea from. At first glance, the group appears to be engaged in activities that guard against what they consider to be the destruction and degradation of the Berea's 'heritage' architecture. Fuelled by anxieties around the potential disappearance of these buildings, the group created a public forum (on their Facebook page) and a collective sense of belonging whereby stakeholders with an interest in maintaining and preserving the colonial heritage of the Berea can voice their experiences and concerns, and offer information regarding the development of the suburb's built environment. In an article referring to an interview with founding members of the group, Cheryl Johnson and Kevin Dunkley, the *Berea Mail* reported that 'one of the organisation's goals was to keep the public informed and create new activists'.[7] The group also claims to be protesting against corruption in the eThekwini municipality, which they say has a culture of 'foregone conclusions, litigation, crisis management, "blacklisting" and spin', one that lacks 'honesty, competence, transparency, democracy and care'.[8]

One of Save Our Berea's most prominently publicised cases concerned building renovations by the new owners of Overdale House, a 'gracious old Victorian home in Musgrave'.[9] This home, constructed in the late 1800s, became a site of contestation in the neighbourhood because of alleged non-compliance with local heritage laws. Concerned neighbours contacted Save Our Berea to lobby on their behalf for the builders to down tools, as in their view the owners (also the first owners of the house who are not white) exhibited a 'flagrant disregard for the law'.[10] Cheryl Johnson claimed at the time: 'applications for approval for demolition and or alterations and additions to the protected structures on this site must be assessed by a consultant panel of senior architects who may or may not grant the owner a demolition order and permission to develop the site.'[11] The group took it upon themselves to organise public meetings with concerned residents and municipal officials. The screenshot taken from the Save Our Berea

Facebook page (see Figure 1.2) shows the comments made by the public in response to the post placed by the group about the case. Four years later, in 2020, Save Our Berea went to court seeking an order to review and set aside the town planning and zoning approval for an apartment building in Musgrave that the group labelled a 'monstrosity'. In 2021 the group took the matter to the High Court.

Save Our Berea's Facebook page serves as its primary public communal space. As one scrolls down the page, it becomes evident that conceptions of loss, nostalgia and longing for a specific type of city futurity – based on past and present settler-colonial privileges and entitlements – predominate. In this sense, the virtual realm that Save Our Berea forges provides a platform for reimagining and recreating what is perceived as 'lost' in the physical world. But while Save Our Berea purports to be a civic custodian of the suburb and, by extension, its residents, its online platform has also become a site for expressing racist and classist notions of architecture, heritage and space. This is antithetical to the claims made by the group in their idealist vision of the Berea as a suburb 'where different cultures could live side by side in a sought-after environment and where, through good planning, people could live, work and play near their homes'.[12]

Too many of these 'people' get away with this!!! No respect for anything - or anybody!!!! They buy these beautiful old houses, leave them to fall apart - wait for the council to declare them derelict, pull them down and replace them with a glass and chrome monstrosity??? Money does not account for taste! Uuughhh.

7y   Like   Reply

This is all a crying shame - this magnificent home was our family home from the 1950's until we sold it in 1991. The trees were planted during our time, carefully chosen cherry trees, palms etc. The embossing of 'Overdale House' lovingly put into the wall of number 10......we loved this home and respected the heritage and hereby lies the difference.....there is no respect for 'old' houses and looking around Durban (we left 26 years ago).....this area has lost all its charm, it's heritage is lost and it's all thanks to the attitude of the hopeless lot of ignorant people living there today!

6y   Like   Reply

These people have zero respect for the heritage of the area! Slowly but surely our beautiful old houses are being destroyed and replaced with tasteless glitzy monstrosities. 😒

7y   Like   Reply   6

Figure 1.2: Screenshot of comments on the Save Our Berea Facebook page in 2016.

The field of heritage conservation and its various encompassing disciplines are often positioned as a 'public good' and a neutral undertaking. As a result, the ways that heritage practice, particularly in settler-colonial nation-states, is steeped in racism and connected to histories of conquest and subjugation are largely ignored. Stuart Hall's term 'The Heritage' outlines the ways that the heritage of hegemonic groups came to be considered as 'natural' and not subject to question.[13] These were the key means through which it acquired power. According to Hall: '"The Heritage" inevitably reflects the governing assumptions of its time and context. It is always inflected by the power and authority of those who have colonised the past, whose versions of history matter.'[14] Prior to 1994 and for several years after the introduction of democracy, the field of heritage was controlled by white 'experts' with a restricted and narrow conception of what should be valued as built heritage in the African context and thus what should be preserved. Evidently, the colonial foundations of the sector have led to gatekeeping, which hinders critical scholarship, practice and legislation. Urgent action is necessary to re-evaluate present heritage legislation and, more generally, what constitutes 'heritage'.

Predominantly upper-class and middle-class white individuals claim, possess and define 'The Heritage', as exemplified by Save Our Berea. Their whiteness is naturalised by its unspoken nature and its 'invisibility', which serves to project an image of neutrality and exert authority over others.[15] In *White Innocence: Paradoxes of Colonialism and Race*,[16] Gloria Wekker reflects on the white European sense of self and employs Edward Said's concept of the cultural archive to argue that an unrecognised reservoir of information and emotions founded on four hundred years of imperial rule has played an essential but unacknowledged role in the domination of meaning-making processes in the neo-colonial world. Given Wekker's argument, we are interested in knowing how settler-colonial logic founded on the cultural legacy of Western imperialism manifests itself in Durban's heritage and preservation policies. As evidence of the past and what it symbolises, the built environment as tangible heritage can be labelled, categorised and controlled by those who own the authority to do so.

Heritage becomes one of many cultural sites and narratives through which discourses of superiority and power can be naturalised and sustained. The phenomenon of residents' associations focusing primarily on heritage is not new. In the case of Save Our Berea, there are strong parallels with the Parktown and Westcliff Heritage Trust (PWHT), which has since been renamed the Johannesburg Heritage Foundation. Also located on a ridge overlooking the Johannesburg CBD, Parktown and Westcliff are historically affluent suburbs located in central Johannesburg. The PWHT was formed in 1972 in response to the demolition of landmark historic buildings in the area to make way for what this group saw as 'uncontrolled' urban development. The PWHT's main concern was that 'without proper planning, the suburb along with other historically significant buildings in Johannesburg would disappear completely under new development enterprises'.[17]

History of the Berea

The beginnings of the settler-colonial community of Durban can be traced to 1843 when the Afrikaner republic of Natalia was annexed by the British. European settlers began arriving, mainly from Britain, under various colonisation schemes and by the 1880s Durban had become a thriving Victorian merchant city, displaying all the acquired material and institutional attributes of urban modernity.[18] According to Richard Ballard and Jeffrey Popke, European colonists began enforcing segregation of the city's black and white populations by the late 1800s. As a result, Durban was administered as if it were a European city, with its black population being seen as transient visitors whose 'real' homes were to be found in the scattered rural reserves of Natal.[19]

The European settlers who made Durban home settled along the Berea, the long ridge running across the city parallel to the bay. Settling along the ridge was desirable as it was cooled by the ocean breeze and overlooked the sea. The areas closer to the bay later became home to many workers of Indian origin who had completed their period of indenture. Soon the Berea was populated with large villas, built in the Victorian architectural style that emulated Victorian cultural values and ideas of spatial hierarchy. England was the source of many of the construction techniques and materials used in the villas, such as masonry or stone, hardwood timber windows, and ornate, custom-built wooden doors. The buildings' steeply pitched roofs were like those of comparable residences in the metropole, but the architects added broad verandas in response to the region's subtropical climate. The objective was to establish a British settlement on the south-east coast of Africa, and architecture played a crucial role in constructing this British satellite identity. Because settler-colonial towns were based on the idea of recreating the European metropole and became representations of the values and culture of the metropole, they often shared several characteristics that were based on new constructions of 'Europeanness' in the colonies.[20] Beyond the aesthetics of the façades, deeply embedded in the colonial architectural heritage of the Berea, was the display of the power of the Empire. As Fassil Demisse argues, in the British colonies architecture 'was mobilised to create a cultural environment to express the grandeur of the empire, to police social and racial borders and preserve the identity of the European settler population'.[21] Thus, architecture was used in Durban to project the authority of colonial rule and stabilise European identity at the frontiers of settlement.

The City of Durban was a pioneer in developing practices of spatial segregation, which later became central to the policies of apartheid South Africa.[22] These segregation practices grew in response to rapid urbanisation towards the end of the 19th century, which brought white settlers in increasing contact with the black and brown bodies of African and Indian labourers in the city. Labouring bodies ignited white colonial anxiety about the potential breakdown of civic order, leading to increasing attempts to contain and govern such bodies through ever-tighter forms of juridical and administrative control. This anxiety was fuelled by the racist ideologies and epistemologies that were circulated to justify colonial subjugation, such as the early 20th-century racist caricatures of Monty Wilson that were popular in Natal at the time.

The period at the turn of the 20th century was replete with European 'fears' about the 'alien' presence of black African and Indian groups and their threat to the constitution of a modern, urban order.[23] As a result settler-colonial communities sought to define and control the emerging contours of space and subjectivity in the context of a rapidly changing political economy. The Native Location Act of 1904 was an early measure to control the ordering of social space, which authorised the establishment of segregated residential locations. After South Africa became a Union in 1910, several legislative measures were taken to entrench control by demarcating the spaces where black residents could legally settle. These included the Natives Land Act of 1913 and the Native Trust and Land Act of 1936, which restricted land allocated for black occupation to the rural reserves, which were essential sources of migrant labour for the white state. Segregation laws culminated in the Group Areas Act of 1950, which led to nationwide forced removals of black people in cities and towns, and contributed to the racially segregated, inequitable urban form that characterises South African cities today.

Figure 1.3: An analysis of the segregated city map of Durban from 1951 to 1970, revealing the relegation of disproportionality and of the invisible racist mentality made visible by apartheid planning. (Adapted from Rob Davies in Rosenberg, 'A City within a City', 2023)

Berea in the Post-Apartheid Era

The early 1990s witnessed the demise of the apartheid era when the African National Congress (ANC) emerged victorious in the 1994 elections. This shift in the political terrain meant that political power was transferred to those elected by the majority. The flagship policy of the new government was the Reconstruction and Development Programme (RDP), which was designed to promote a coherent approach to urban development and provide an effective framework for urban reconstruction and development. In response to increasing urbanisation, which gave rise to inadequate housing, infrastructure deficiencies and further spatial fragmentation, the Integrated Urban Development Framework (IUDF) was developed with the aim of promoting more efficient, resilient and liveable urban areas. Despite these policy developments, issues of spatial inclusivity have not received the attention they deserve.[24]

Returning to the Berea, the census data for Ward 33 in eThekwini (Westridge, Glenwood, Carrington Heights as well as Umbilo) show that the area had a population of 28,944 in 2011, of which 44% was classified as black African, 41% as white, and less than 15% as Indian and Coloured. Many black African residents within Ward 33 live in Dalton Hostel, accommodation built by the apartheid government to house migrants who work in the factories in the industrial belt located below the Berea. This means that the suburban neighbourhoods in the Westridge, Glenwood, Carrington Heights and Umbilo areas were predominantly white in 2011 when the census was conducted.[25]

In less than fifteen years, the Berea area has evolved into a space in transition, defined by both immaterial and material markers. The material markers are the increased frequency of public transport and the occupation of previously white neighbourhoods by a growing number of black people. Taking Helen Joseph Road (formerly Davenport Road) as a specific example, we can observe that this area used to be a fine dining area, but has now become a trendy area with bars that cater to young people, especially black young professionals and students. Like Florida Road in Morningside, the road has become a hotspot for nightlife culture in Durban.

Some of the commercial buildings on Helen Joseph Road have been retrofitted to become salons and barber shops, fast-food eateries and convenience stores that offer almost any product, from cigarettes to light snacks, during the day as well as at night. Since these shops mainly depend on the patrons at the bars, they are normally busy during the afternoon until midnight and beyond. On busy days, temporary foodstalls mushroom along Helen Joseph, catering to the patrons of the popular bars where large numbers of people gather.

On a sunny afternoon, you are likely to see scores of young people walking towards Bulwer Park for recreation. There are aerobics clubs, personal training services, and people running or walking in the newly renovated park as well as on the main roads within the neighbourhood. There has also been a boom in student accommodation in the whole of the Berea, housing students who are enrolled at the University of KwaZulu-Natal, the Durban University of Technology and the many colleges found within Umbilo and in the CBD.

These forms of living that shape urban dynamics reveal the paradoxical and complex relationship between dwellers and the urban environment; through their manifold activities and the alternative spaces they create, they provide the pulse which is at the core of urban vitality.[26] By disrupting colonial spatial orderings, they also reconfigure the space through informal insurgent practices that are discernible as a disruption of the modernist apartheid urban environment.[27] As a result, black people have been participating in urban life through buying property and opening up businesses within these suburbs. This visibility is not without challenges or limitations, as there have been widespread protests within Glenwood calling for the municipality to enforce by-laws and zoning regulations. The protesters claim that the eThekwini Land Use Management by-law lacks enforcement, resulting in the deterioration of property values, which eventually leads to lower rates and less money for service delivery.[28] Furthermore, they complain about new businesses acquiring property cheaply and registering hostels, guest houses, and party venues for prostitution and drugs.[29] The rise of community groups organising within the Berea could very well be related to the activism of Save Our Berea, which was one of the first organisations to popularise these ideas.

These reflections on the residential area of Glenwood are also supported by Richard Ballard's study conducted about twenty years ago, which stated that the instinct to defend property values is indeed at the core of white resentment of the new informality in the Berea.[30] Ballard's study also demonstrates that the negative sentiments about spatial change in the Berea are longstanding; since South Africa became a democratic country, conservative elements have seen all forms of transformation in the Durban inner city and the Berea as a colossal crisis. Mpho Matsipa has explored what the notion of the city in 'crisis' overlooked when examining urban renewal in Johannesburg:[31] the departure of white-owned businesses in the CBD in fact created the conditions for the proliferation of many black-owned microbusinesses here. The same is true of the Berea.

Based on interviews that focus on perceptions of urban change among white residents of the Berea in the period after 1994, Ballard has shown that there existed an 'unambiguously racial dimension to perceived urban change'.[32] These perceptions, Ballard argues, 'are linked to the spatial imagination of the Group Areas Act, and responses to its demise. Where it was once very much "ours" under apartheid, the fear and perception in the present is that it is increasingly "theirs" since democracy.'[33] These perceptions also reaffirm obsolete ideologies, beyond the material, and operate as a plea to maintain what remains of the status quo. It is also important to note that Berea, just like many South African suburbs, has never been exclusively white. Black people, including those racialised as African, Coloured and Indian, inhabited the space as dwellers and labourers, for the suburbs in South Africa were sustained and maintained by black labour. Problems arise for some residents when black people come to participate as agents who take ownership and forge meaningful contributions to the space, ultimately changing its identity.

Kopano Matlwa's novel *Coconut* provides an interesting account of the polarisation and social differences that are still at play in suburban areas in post-apartheid South Africa. The novel also makes clear the nuances of difference, which are not easily resolved by class segmentations.[34] The story is told through the lens of two black women who, through their experience of growing up black in post-apartheid suburbia, navigate their ethnic African ideals while simultaneously being expected to assimilate to global Western values of whiteness. The book highlights that '"race" in South Africa is a spatial issue',[35] and that any form of spatial reconfiguration is bound to expose the prevailing shortcomings of not only the planning models and theories, but of the actual ailing social fabric of a society with complicated, entangled histories of subjugation and exclusion.

Daniel Schensul and Patrick Heller also depict how post-apartheid economic and social policies have preserved the class divisions of the late-apartheid distribution regime by consolidating a small fraction of the emerging black middle class who were prepared to collaborate.[36] This sedimentation of the urban space is a process that is largely driven by market mechanisms which further reproduce spatial inequalities. These reflections could be applied to the Berea post-1994 when a small group of middle-class black people began to move into the suburb.

Therefore, it is important to see preservation discourse as a kind of euphemism. Areas such as the Berea had a civilised and Western status bestowed on them in their making,[37] which was used to racialise the space. Author and activist Sizwe Mpofu-Walsh's book, *The New Apartheid*, traces how the edifice of systematic racial oppression continues to thrive in the spatiality of democratic South Africa. According to Mpofu-Walsh, apartheid did not die but was privatised through systems of markets and institutions.[38] His analysis is consistent with Ballard's notion of the racialisation of space: the book argues that there is a refashioning of urban space in contemporary South African cities into privatised islands of privilege under the pretence of safety concerns that primarily drive this kind of urban development. Yet the over-privatisation of space is emblematic of the lasting imaginaries of apartheid, which organise by means of sustained logics of race and class.

The apparent changes in the suburbs' morphology have encouraged the emergence of groupings such as Save Our Berea, through an unspoken logic of who belongs and who does not in this suburb. Their position has been to challenge certain property owners while supporting the likes of the property development company Urban Lime, which has managed to attach the idea of 'preserving' heritage to its regenerative neo-liberal projects, currently under way in Florida Road in the suburb of Morningside. In the commercial projects on Florida Road, a level of prestige and privilege is maintained while providing a sense of comfort and safety for certain groups – in contrast with the inner city or Helen Joseph Road, which has seen a different kind of overhaul in terms of functionality and the use of space.

Whose Heritage? Preserving the Myth of the Berea

Within the context of this study, what are relevant are the foundation, methodology and agenda of the structures that perpetuate exclusionary practice within the city – the myth of the Berea. According to the *Oxford English Dictionary* definition, heritage may be understood as a physical object; 'property that is or may be inherited; an inheritance', 'valued things such as historic buildings that have been passed down from previous generations', and 'relating to things of historic or cultural value that are worthy of preservation'. Critical to our understanding is the emphasis on inheritance and the implication of conservation within the context of coloniality.

> For a person who has an affinity with his fellow man and is interested in differences in cultures rather than despising all but his own, Durban is a perfect place to live and the city has a potential of becoming one of the world's greatest cities with all its diversity of inherent talent. Where else can you get such a melting pot of people who live in such harmony.[39]

In 1987 Peter Johnston and Hyacinthia Naidoo co-authored a book for the Communications Department of the Durban City Council, *Durban's Heritage Explored on Walks and Drives around the City*. It romanticised the socio-cultural diversity of Durban, acknowledging, albeit briefly, the reason for the rainbow nation, but evidently overlooking the intentionality of the apartheid regime in keeping these diverse socio-cultural groups apart. (Overlooking the politics of the day would become a common theme throughout the architectural heritage space.)[40] The selective silence on social matters, and the choice of a romanticised narrative, originate from the very inception of heritage structures in South Africa, which have focused their efforts on heritage management in particular ways connected to white settler histories. The first piece of legislation that extended protection to monuments and built structures was the National and Historical Monuments Act of 1923, which set up the first statutory body responsible for the management of heritage, the Historical Monuments Commission. This body had responsibility for the compilation of a register of monuments, and for the publication of by-laws to protect them.[41] The task of the commission was extended by an amendment to the Act in 1934, and together with the Bureau of Archaeology, it helped build the narrative of white settler identity. With the rise of apartheid in 1948, conceptions of heritage were more closely tied to Afrikaner cultural history. By the 1960s concerns around rapid urbanisation increased public awareness of heritage conservation. New legislation brought about a restructuring of the commission, now known as the National Monuments Council, serving under the Ministry of National Education, which played closer attention to the built environment. The increasing popular dissent in the 1970s and 1980s saw the heritage sector resist African nationalist currents, masking the full extent of our population's diversity, and ultimately exacerbating the disjunction between the state-driven narrative of heritage and growing popular notions.[42] This apolitical stance on architectural heritage would seep into both architectural practice and education, reinforcing notions of exclusion and the white settler-colonial myth at large.[43]

The emergence of a democratic South Africa in the 1990s saw the dismantling of separatist spatial planning, promoted for example by the Group Areas Act, and the passing of the National Heritage Resources Act of 1999 and the National Heritage Council Act.[44] Both developments sought to achieve redress for black communities post-apartheid. The notion of restitution was embedded in the Land Policy Act of 1997, informed by an understanding of what a just socio-spatial order could mean for black people.[45]

Continuing the national tradition, the heritage sector in KwaZulu-Natal consists of a number of individuals and groups with drastically different histories and motives for the practice of heritage. It includes the KwaZulu-Natal Amafa and Research Institute (Amafa) and the South African Institute of Architects KwaZulu-Natal Region (SAIA KZN) Heritage Committee, whose agenda aligns with that of groups such as Save Our Berea. The inclusion of the full histories of all South African people, and the contribution of indigenous knowledge systems in shaping and contributing to building practice, are often overlooked by the formal heritage building sector, whose main interest is in preserving white settler-colonial architecture and buildings, and thereby maintaining a firm grasp on whose heritage is protected.

Amafa is the provincial heritage resources authority for KwaZulu-

Natal, which was established under the terms of the KZN Heritage Act of 1997. Its role is 'to strive for excellence in the conservation, management, interpretation and sustainable utilisation of the heritage resources of KwaZulu-Natal for present and future generations'. Through its compliance department, Amafa is the responsible body for overseeing and authorising any applications for permits for the demolition of, or alteration to, buildings, sites and graves. According to the National Heritage Resources Act of 1999, any building over the age of sixty years is considered a historical site, and is thus subject to Amafa approval prior to the commencement of any work. Given the age of the city of Durban, and specifically the Berea, this criterion now includes an increasing number of properties, often with little or no real historical significance beyond the passage of time. Apart from buildings from the apartheid-colonial era protected from demolition by this Act, one needs to take into account those buildings and sites violently erased from the cities by apartheid-colonial legislation during the same period. As part of our heritage, we have to consider both what is present and what has been so abruptly removed.

Within SAIA KZN, the voluntary association founded in 1927 to act 'as a collective voice serving the interests of its members in pursuit of excellence and responsible design',[46] the heritage discourse is further dictated by its Heritage Committee, a preserve of whiteness. Out of growing concern for the destruction of architecture in the 1960s and 1970s as the city expanded, SAIA KZN, then known as the Natal Institute of Architects, together with the Durban City Council, produced the *First Listing of Important Places and Buildings in Durban* in 1974. While maintaining an apolitical stance, evident in the use of language, the focus was directly on the protection of architecture in the face of the expansion of Durban, and not in support of the dismantling of apartheid legislation that had led to forced removals in order to create the very space for such expansion. Professor Brian Kearney's updated catalogue, *A Revised Listing of the Important Places and Buildings of Durban* (1984), would go on to define not only the practice of architectural heritage and conservation, but the notion of excellence based on the aesthetics of the architectural heritage.

Rather than serving as a point of negotiation between social rights and heritage, the SAIA KZN Heritage Committee promotes an exclusionary agenda, as can be seen in its statement of 2011:

The committee concerns itself with the preservation and conservation of the built environment, ensuring a sustainable future for our province's heritage and environment. Its focus is on assisting our professional peers in understanding current provincial and national legislation aimed at protecting our architectural heritage. It intends to create a greater awareness of conservation principles and an improved knowledge of restoration practice through discussions, debates, education and site visits.

And in 2015 it stated its aim as 'to promote the potential of heritage in achieving a super-charged built environment and to recognise and communicate the economic, cultural and social potential of heritage resources'.[47] Devoid of any language to illustrate precisely whose heritage they refer to when using the word 'our', the SAIA KZN Heritage Committee is clear about whom it considers role players and decision-makers within the heritage space, and maintains a close proximity to Amafa to champion this. In this respect the committee is much like Save Our Berea, a collective that simply seeks to maintain nostalgic notions of the divided city.

The heritage discourse operates as potentially *the* principal site for negotiating issues of culture, identity and citizenship. It is gravely troubling, then, that organisations have been able to maintain their singular narrative of heritage; in this exercise of exclusivity, heritage has become merely a sentimental attachment to the notions of grandeur in the past,

Figure 1.4: Building a singular narrative of 'the heritage' through monumentalising documentation, Kearney's 'Revised Listing' forms part of an exclusive oeuvre of architectural heritage documentation.

a preoccupation with the spectacle of authenticity. It lacks the rigour and criticality of contemporary practice which acknowledges the rootedness and constructedness of cultural identities, and seeks to embrace decolonisation, comprehend history in its full complexity, and own up to the horrors of the past.

Instead of pursuing the national Legacy Project of redressing vernacular, intangible and living heritage, entities like the SAIA KZN Heritage Committee and Save Our Berea promote the closed, singular narrative of tangible architectural heritage, keeping us from a meaningful interrogation of what heritage means in the city of Durban post-1994. While the national Legacy Project seeks to recognise previously marginalised narratives by way of renaming places that reflect the colonial ideal, these entities persistently resist such attempts. For instance, the Itafa Amalinde Heritage Trust, the rebranded Durban Heritage Trust, noted:

> Sadly the division continues but under new masters. An example of this is the provocative way in which old street names are to be relegated to the dustbin of history by the city council and replaced by the names of persons who represent only a part of the population – recent ANC heroes and populist heroes replace the old local, nationalist or colonial ones. A new form of vengeful dispossession is taking place.[48]

What is evident here is the danger of a singular narrative, and a lack of will to embrace a holistic and reconciliatory perspective of heritage, land and belonging. The answer to the question 'whose heritage?' continues to be aligned with the settler-colonial myth.

Sanitation has a long history of use by white authorities to control the movement and engagement of black bodies within the city of Durban. The threat of 'contamination', 'the Asiatic menace' and 'plague spots', and the description of black people as 'spreading like an epidemic': this language of control, which regarded any practice outside whiteness as unsanitary, helped maintain separation between black and white in the city under the guise of sanitation.[49] Similar notions inform the efforts of community development initiatives (CDIs) like Save Our Berea and Urban Lime, in their projects for 'urban renewal'. Fears that the city will be contaminated by manifestations of black heritage are evident in calls for a return to pristine character of places like the Berea. In decrying the multi-generational living models and alterations to colonial architectural styles that have been emerging along the hills of the Berea, the proponents of the white settler-colonial myth would deny new understandings of urban density, socio-economic viability, architectural value, and belonging in the city. For the preoccupation with aspirations of excellence within the architectural heritage space denies not only its past but also its potential future in seeking an appropriate South African architecture. Yet the Natal settler-colonial residential architectural style, which is described by its devotees as the 'Natal Style' and used as a benchmark of architectural excellence, is itself 'contaminated' when one considers the elements that make it up: the Voortrekker cottage, an adaptation of the Cape Dutch dwelling; the veranda, derived from the colonial styles of the Portuguese and Spanish in the Caribbean and likely appropriated from vernacular styles there too; the central passage, roof style and pitch, french doors and sash windows, derived from French colonial styles in the Caribbean.[50]

Conclusion

What could an ideal urban futurity for Durban look like? We are in agreement that this should not involve a total erasure of the city's colonial pasts, but a willingness to search for ways of accommodating new modes of urban development that embody decolonial ideas and aspirations in the making and unmaking of the city. Hegemonic understandings of the city should be seen as limiting, as a negation of the responsibility to radically reimagine space so as to achieve the objectives of inclusivity, equity and access. There is no doubt that spatial transformation will be uncomfortable, but it is just here that the potential exists for reparation.

Figure 1.5: Transforming heritage as a crisis, the now infamous 317 Currie Road development demonstrates the problem of whitewashed agendas of the CDIs within the 'post post-apartheid' city of Durban. (Photograph by Adheema Davis)

Chapter Two

Forced Removals: Reflections on Fietas' Photographic Archive, Museum and Heritage Trail

Ali Khangela Hlongwane

Fietas, until the late 1970s a suburb of diverse communities in Johannesburg,[1] stands today partly as a monument to victorious, ongoing struggles against apartheid forced removals, a legacy of resistance that it shares with countless communities throughout the country. A poster by the Medu Art Ensemble[2] depicts women carrying children as they look at their razed homes while armed police point their guns, with smoke billowing in the background.

These images of victims and resisters of forced removals are shown in the artwork with a bold and defiant message that reads: 'In Nyanga, Kromdraai, Crossroads, Soekmekaar, the people say: No to forced removals!'[3] This kind of litany of the names of various places recorded by the artist, whose medium imposes an economical use of imagery, is also found in the work of various poets, for example that by an unnamed Black Consciousness Movement activist exiled in Botswana in the 1970s, who wrote:

> the winter wind is cutting both my hands
> The one carrying zinks to resettlement areas
> Winterveldt, Welcomwood, Majaneng, Groutville
> The other with the burden of the toddlers to their graves
> Dimbaza, Limehill, Nqutu[4]

Figure 2.1: 'Let Us All Support the Fight! No to Resettlement!' – Poster by Thami Mnyele and Judy Seidman for Medu Art Ensemble, silkscreen, 1982. (South African History Archive)

The history of these places is a history of resistance against dispossession and forced removals and against the imposed stratification of communities by the ideologues of apartheid colonialism along the lines of language and invented, fossilised 'ethnic' identities.

Today Fietas lies partly in ruins, manifested in the outcropping of buildings and other physical traces. This chapter documents and reflects on those traces as symbolic of resilient communities with a long history in the area. Through the memorialisation of these sites by a community museum, the Fietas Memory in Action Museum (opened in 2013 by a former resident, Selma Patel), and a heritage trail, we also get a sense of dashed hopes in the present as the post-apartheid bureaucratic machinery has ground to a halt in its dealings with land restitution. Fietas shares this legacy with many communities, including District Six in Cape Town, Marabastad in Pretoria,[5] and Cato Manor in Durban. These represent a growing number of places whose memorialisation focuses on forced removals.

Oral Histories of Fietas

When the area of present-day Fietas was first occupied in the 1890s, it was known as Malay Location. It was 'the overcrowded but lively home of Indians, Chinese and blacks, for decades'.[6] The so-called non-white population of Fietas was concentrated between 11th Street in the north, 24th Street in the south, Krause Street in the east, and De la Rey Street in the west. As a demarcated suburb, it occupied '17 hectares and [was] situated 2 kilometres to the northwest of the Johannesburg Central District'.[7] Whites lived across the road on 11th Street, in Vrededorp, 'the village of peace'. Lucille Davie writes that 'it was a homely community, where children would play on the streets, and people would sit on their front stoeps and talk to their neighbours across the road, also on their stoeps, making the street their outdoor living rooms'.[8] At the peak of its prosperity, in 1962, the area had 177 shops, two mosques, four churches, two cinemas, various schools, a communal hall, a sports grounds and several social clubs.[9] Former Fietas resident Selma Patel recalls, 'I had a wonderful childhood. My neighbours were Chinese and Indian families; I didn't know colour or status.'[10]

However, there was also poverty and inequality within the community. Hanifa Patel, another former resident, acknowledges the contradictions that cut across this and many other so-called freehold areas, as seen for example in the relationship between owners and tenants. His memories challenge romantic accounts that depict life in these communities as free of conflict.

> I liked living in Fietas, and also I didn't because in Fietas you were paying rent. We didn't have a very nice neighbour. They had one electricity meter for four houses, and this person was [the] one who collected the electricity, and they would never show us how much electricity we used; they just came and said so much, and we'd pay them.[11]

Hanifa Patel's account again pierces through romanticised pictures of the neighbourhood: 'We were children, and we had to go to school … we'd go to school, and our lunch was always bread, butter and jam. My parents could not afford anything else. And you have other children from Fietas there with salted meat and leg of lamb, beautiful chicken sandwiches, and you always felt a little like you did not belong there.'[12]

In 1962 Fietas was declared a white area under the 1950 Group Areas Act. The majority of its inhabitants were moved to Lenasia, designated for people classified as Indian, and Soweto, designated for Africans under the derogatory appellation of 'Bantu', between 1956 and 1977. Other residents were relocated to so-called Coloured townships such as Eldorado Park, Riverlea, Kliptown,

Orlando and Noordgesig.[13] Several shop owners were eventually forced to relocate their businesses to the Oriental Plaza in Fordsburg.

> For Selma Patel's family, Lenasia, where they were relocated to, was: 30 km away, and the commute would be crazy. At that stage, you must remember, you had a lot of job reservation, so most of the work opportunities – unless you were a wealthy business person who's got your own business maybe, or you had a business in the [Oriental] Plaza … The very important thing about why Fietas was sought after was because of its proximity to the Johannesburg CBD.[14]

Selma Patel centres her memories of Fietas on resistance: 'We joined the Save Pageview Association because we had this thing that – as a family – principles are steadfast, and I think the fact that we are still here attests to that sentiment.'[15] Hanifa Patel, on the other hand, remembers, somewhat controversially:

> so, when we were given houses in Lens [Lenasia], my parents went for it: now they could own a property. They had never owned a property in their life … There's a lot of people [who] talk about [how] they moved us from Fietas to Lens, and it was forced removal, blah blah blah; I say it's the best thing that happened to us. To my parents. Those who owned properties in Fietas collected rent; you could not buy a property.[16]

His oral account eschews resistance. He recalls his father's attitude to the resistance against forced removals.

> They wanted all the people to sign a petition to say we will not move; let's stand united. My dad felt that, I'm sorry, I'm being given a shop, I'm going to go, so he didn't sign the petition. Now you know a lot of people don't understand this, but you have to understand why he did what he did. Because he came from a certain background, that to own property was, hey, I have my own shop![17]

Nonetheless, the removals were met with fierce resistance, which continued into the 1980s. Many homes were flattened by bulldozers, and very few survived. Davie writes:

> Once the bulldozers had finished their dirty work, Fietas was left a wasteland.

The two mosques remained, and odd homes still stood where association members had refused to move. A single double-storey shop remained in 14th Street. There's a gaping, double-storey piece of a bathroom in 20th Street, a stark monument to the destruction of lives. The government built squat, discordant homes for whites on some of the empty plots, but Fietas remained largely in a time warp.[18]

This is the Fietas that the photographer David Goldblatt documented in the 1970s. Rather than describe specific photographs, I take my cue from one of Goldblatt's remarks: 'I don't often report on or photograph events.'[19]

Photographic Archives and Everyday Life in Fietas

David Goldblatt, who died on 25 June 2018, was born in Randfontein in 1930. He began taking pictures in his early school days, which appeared in the school magazine. Over the years, Goldblatt's archive has been assembled in several published works, in the vast material stored in various archival deposits locally and internationally, and curated in sites such as the Fietas Memory in Action Museum established by Selma Patel.

Before analysing Goldblatt's photographs of Fietas, I will briefly reflect on the growing body of literature on the place of the photographic archive as a tool of struggle, a visual witness to the complex histories of oppression in South Africa and a source for reimagining these in the public post-1994. This era has witnessed a memory boom characteristic of people who have emerged from centuries of uprooting and disremembering, in which photography has also been complicit. Goldblatt has been a significant player in this memory-making as a photographer and through his polemical remarks about this process.

Darren Newbury points to 'the close relationship between the development of photography and social and political issues in South Africa'.[20] This also occurred within the traditions of cultural resistance against settler colonialism and apartheid, making the large body of photographic archival material available in the country and internationally a unique source (as still images) about the liberation struggle and the everyday life of South Africans. This archive has also 'played an important role in articulating public histories of apartheid [colonialism]', as photography has the 'ability to tell stories about the past'.[21] It also can 'capture a whole repertoire of human gestures ... [to] weave violence and love, damnation and deliverance [as well as] exposing what we need to see and remember'.[22] According to Helena Pohlandt-McCormick: 'As stories, they [photographs] become part of the discourse of liberation or, in the hands of apartheid's spokesmen, part of the rhetoric of the necessity of suppression of threats to security of the state. As photographs, they become part of the inventory of public history or, in the past, material evidence or documentation for the government's investigations.'[23]

Thus, photographs can also be biased and selective, just as other sources and types of memory. As Colin Richards writes, 'artistic licence informs even photographs through selective cropping, captioning, framing and focus'.[24] Further, the notion of art – photography, poetry, theatre, visual art, dance, film – as a weapon of struggle was constantly reframed and nuanced by diverse practitioners such as Es'kia Mphahlele, Njabulo Ndebele, Ntongela Masilela and Albie Sachs,[25] to name but a few. These writers and intellectuals were particularly critical of banal work that was glorified as an aesthetic of resistance and struggle.

In the context of photography, Masilela further cautions that the politics of oppression which has reigned supreme for centuries in South Africa should not surpass 'the poetics of light, form, composition and plasticity, which should be the arbiters in matters concerning photography'.[26] This debate has also found expression in scholarly writings on public history and heritage at the intersection between the dominant authorised narrative as well as visual representation and its role in marginalising the everyday or histories from below.[27] In the context of photography, as I have pointed out elsewhere, this debate has also questioned the impact (or lack thereof) of iconic images.[28] Mark Robbins proposes that the 'iconic quality' of some photographs 'can have a freezing effect and be a barrier to truly seeing that which is depicted'.[29] The barrier tends to occur in making the non-spectacular invisible. As Njabulo Ndebele expresses his view as a creative writer:

> I became interested in exploring art beyond merely reflecting reality as it was because we are all familiar with it; we can see the evidence of oppression. I became interested in how oppression affects people in their daily lives, what it does to the fabric of family life, how it affects individual ambitions and aspirations, how it contributes to the way we rationalise things.[30]

Goldblatt made his views known on the politics of the 'creative forms of the imagination',[31] to borrow Masilela's words. 'David was very critical of people who made propaganda, and he would use that word,' says Sean O'Toole, the Cape Town-based arts writer. O'Toole goes on to say: 'He tried to directly respond to the people he photographed and to the complexity of what he saw. He was not just photographing the now. His images delivered nuance that front-line photography didn't. He wasn't shooting in that impactful way that would appeal to the hard left – what he was creating was very subtle, nuanced pictures.'[32]

As part of his subtle, if not indirect, contestation of the notion of art as a weapon of struggle, Goldblatt is on record as expressing the view that he 'did not consider himself a journalist or a polemical photographer' and further stating that 'I can't claim to be a revolutionary … and I don't like calling myself an artist … I am a craftsman of photography.'[33] In his search for a nuanced aesthetic, virtually all his work was done in black and white because, as he said, 'colour seemed too sweet a medium to express the anger, disgust and fear that apartheid inspired'.[34] In interesting practical ways, he demonstrated his quest for ways to question hegemonies of power through his ideas and photographs.

According to an obituary in *The Guardian* newspaper, 'In 1976 and 1977 [Goldblatt] pedalled the streets of Fietas, tripod on back, as the Indian township was being destroyed to make way for a white suburb.'[35] A contradiction emerges in this description of Fietas as a suburb of one 'definable' section of South African society. Do Goldblatt's photographs disrupt these imposed identities? Several of his photographs, beginning around 1965 and stretching beyond the 1970s to about 2016, are of people's homes, now empty and deserted. But the architecture, colourful walls and surviving signage are a constant reminder that people lived here. Aerial images showing graveyards and railway tracks provide the physical reminders. The landscape is softened by innocent, buoyant children across the colour line playing and posing for the photographer. The yards reflect how families lived, through mundane but telling images of toothbrushes, Colgate toothpaste or a mirror, or men making a living as backyard mechanics, or the constant presence of washerwomen. Colourful shop verandas are always remembered as one of the defining characteristics of Fietas, with wares displayed in windows, shoppers passing by but frozen by the camera with precise, sometimes faint distinctions between the worker, the security guard and the proud child of the shop owner.

Figure 2.2: From the north-east looking south-west: Fietas early in its destruction under the Group Areas Act, October 1977. (Photograph by David Goldblatt. Courtesy of the David Goldblatt Legacy Trust and Goodman Gallery)

Figure 2.3: Cleaning the car on a Sunday morning during the destruction of Fietas under the Group Areas Act, 27 June 1982. (Photograph by David Goldblatt. Courtesy of the David Goldblatt Legacy Trust and Goodman Gallery)

Children pose in their decorated bedrooms and playgrounds in religious garb or school uniforms. In many cases children had to spend whole days, weeks, months or years next to a parent – always a woman – selling cooked mealies from the brazier of her stall. Young couples with a newborn baby are shown with their worldly possessions crammed in the background though not without a sense of decor and dignity. Old people ponder the future with bottles of medication, reminding us of the years lived and the journeys travelled, which meant nothing to those who sent in the bulldozers. This reminds us of the poetic words of Don Mattera:

> Slow, painfully slow
> clumsy crushers crawled
> over the firm pillars
> into the rooms that held us
> and the roof that covered our heads.[36]

Another photographer who documented life in Fietas was Mike Feldman. Part of his collection is deposited at Museum Africa. Feldman was an optometrist and a fellow of the Royal Photographic Society and the Photographic Society of South Africa. According to Robyn Sassen, Feldman considered 'being out there with camera at hand as creatively exciting as being in the darkroom with technology and chemicals at his disposal'.[37] This is because he had a sharp eye for the social life and landscape he was documenting. Equally, he was 'creative in the darkroom and played around with solarisation [tone reversal through re-exposure of the film], with composite prints'. Sassen noted that this photographic technique 'serves to make compositional positives negative and negatives positive, lending an eerie quality. This plays with atmosphere and space and renders the photographic line moot: a solarised line is more like one drawn with a thin pencil of light.'[38]

In 2014 Museum Africa, the depository of his collection, collaborated with the Fietas Museum and the Sophiatown Heritage and Cultural Centre to present the exhibition 'Live and Let Live: Celebrating Fietas'. This exhibition featured Feldman's work documenting the forced removals in 1971. Feldman is, in his own right, a sensitive photographer with an eye for the everyday. A selection from his photographs of Fietas held by Museum

Africa reflects diverse themes. These include 'Street Football', depicting children playing soccer in the streets of Fietas, and 'The Family', in which members of a family are seen on the stoep or veranda of their home. The veranda takes on a particular significance in places that share a similar history with Fietas, such as Marabastad.

If resistance is 'the dialectical opposite of domination',[39] as the Pan-Africanist scholar and activist Tony Campbell, pointed out, defiance and social action, which characterised the experiences of dispossession and forced removal in South Africa, are, in general, missing, in fact absent, in Goldblatt's and Feldman's images of Fietas. Their 'historical imagination [does not overtly] locate even pockets of resistance,[40] a theme so well pronounced in the oral histories of the residents of Fietas. The Fietas Museum had ample opportunities to include more diverse voices in remembering Fietas and to acknowledge that people still live in the area. I now turn to the museum, where a number of Goldblatt's and Feldman's photographs are on display.

Fietas Museum: Memory in Action

Fietas Museum, described by its founder Selma Patel as a 'living museum', was officially opened in September 2013. Patel converted the lower section of her original family home in the once thriving 14th Street in the multicultural suburb of Fietas, into an interpretation centre. The display here does not follow a chronological storyline. Patel's two-roomed home is reimagined through painted walls, display cabinets and masonite boards as display spaces. Wall One features an obituary of a resident side by side with colour family photographs, that of a barber, shopkeepers, children and the Jay Cinema with the sign 'Star Cinema entertainment', and a map of the streets of Fietas. This approach was well explored by the District Six Museum in Cape Town and used by the curators of 'Marabastad: An Exhibition'.[41] The same approach is followed on all the walls, where on display are a story of a local personality, newspaper clippings, family photographs, photographs of soccer and cricket clubs, and artefacts.

This mixed medium of family photographs, newspaper clippings and artefacts donated by former residents constitutes the material culture and memories that help the visitor engage with the displays from diverse angles and points of view. Photographs by the well-known photographers we have discussed above, alongside studio photographs provided by former residents, animate the complex story of Fietas.

The core of the display gives remarkable insight into the ordinary lives and everyday experiences of Fietas residents. Narratives of community experiences also acknowledge individual persons of significance, who are viewed as role models or leading figures in particular aspects of Fietas's communal life. They are the products of the community and its social, cultural and political histories. These 'important historical personalities' are not framed as the 'big men of history'. In the context of the Fietas Museum, they are acknowledged as 'personalities who emerged/associated with Fietas who contributed to the national liberation narrative of our fledgling democracy'.[42] In the records of the museum, they are listed as Suleiman Nana, secretary of the Transvaal Indian Congress (1933–44); Dr Yusuf Dadoo, who opened his first rooms as a GP in 11th Street, Fietas; Dr Aboobaker Asvat, a Black Consciousness leader; Dr Essop Jassat, former president of the Transvaal Indian Youth Congress, and his brother Abdulhay Jassat, a Congress Movement stalwart; Molvi Saloojee, last president of the Transvaal Indian Congress; Faried Adams, a former Treason Trialist; Rebecca Mphahlele; the writer Peter Abrahams, who tells of his childhood in Vrededorp in his novel *Tell Freedom*; the photographer Peter Magubane; and the writer Ahmed Essop.[43]

There is nonetheless a contradiction in this acknowledgement. It inadvertently frames historical figures or individuals in ways that perpetuate the view that the liberation struggle rested on their shoulders only. This further supports a perception that the masses, the core and cornerstone of the liberation struggle, were mere followers or supporters of leaders. It also has implications for writing histories, in particular by unintentionally marginalising 'voices from below', whereas the stated intention of the museum is to counter the erasures of these voices.

I have quoted Selma Patel describing the Fietas Museum as a living museum. She has described the museum's purpose as including collaboration 'with the community in preserving the heritage of the historic sites of removal in the area, and by so doing promote greater understanding of pre-apartheid, non-racial communities in support of social cohesion'.[44] Through collaborative work with other partners, in Patel's view, 'we also share knowledge about the diversity of South Africa's people, using our "living treasures" – experiences/stories about culture and tradition in their times'.[45]

One of the Fietas Museum's partners is the Sophiatown Heritage and Cultural Centre, a multi-purpose centre in Sophiatown that runs tours and hosts jazz performances. The history of Sophiatown has been extensively chronicled in the autobiographies of former residents, such as Don Mattera's *Memory Is the Weapon*,[46] and in plays, such as the Junction Avenue Theatre Company's *Sophiatown*. The partnership involves collaboration 'in creating education and visitor routes about the removals in the historic western areas'.[47] Furthermore, 'the Fietas Museum and the Sophiatown Heritage and Cultural Centre work to create opportunities for affected communities to participate in writing and recording their own history, and for these histories to be available to current and future generations'.[48] Selma Patel affirms that this programme 'will promote understanding of how integrated communities existed in Johannesburg prior to the 1948 apartheid government and preserve first-hand testimony for future generations to assess and present in their contemporary setting so that these vital and diverse histories are sustained in our languages, cultural context, and images'.[49]

While the Fietas Museum is clear about its role as a living museum and about social challenges in the country in general, it has on its doorstep a challenge it has not found a way to deal with, beyond referring the problem to the local and provincial government authorities. Over the years, the two tiers of government have failed to develop an integrated strategy to deal with homelessness in the area linked to unresolved land claims. Consequently, the area has several poor and homeless people who make a living by collecting material for recycling. They also use the neighbourhood for sorting out the material, a place with no ablution facilities or access to water. The problems are further compounded by illegal construction, which threatens to undermine the heritage complex of the area. These challenges have become a source of conflict between the museum and the recyclers, as the museum sees them as people who are degrading the environment and discouraging potential tourists to the area and related sites. The heritage trail analysed in the next section has also been affected by these social ills.

To illustrate the challenges faced by the museum, we quote from correspondence between Selma Patel and various departments in the City of Johannesburg. (In this context, it is important to point out that the correspondence was first directed to the ANC-led administration and, when it was replaced by a Democratic Alliance-led coalition, Patel also wrote to them, believing that a new broom might sweep clean.) Further communication was also directed to the provincial administration. The correspondence by Selma Patel reads:

> My initial complaint regarding Erf No 92 Pageview started in 2010. At that stage, the activities and stench arising from this site was intolerable, thus forcing our tenants, 26' 10 South Architects, to terminate their lease, as the hazards from the adjacent property was harmful to their professional image. To reiterate my previous gripe, at the onset of complaints from the architects and myself, had COJ [City of Johannesburg] initiated task-specific, goal-oriented, function assessment outcomes, I am inclined to think this issue could have been rectified sooner. A reality check: seven years [2017] later, I am still in battle with COJ regarding the deplorable conditions on the adjacent site. A sad indictment of COJ's clout – I rest my case.
>
> The gravity of residents' grievances regarding their daily exposures to the dangerous effects of the recyclers' activities in sorting, burning plastic, and disposing waste materials in close proximity to their homes – incidentally, is a violation of an enshrined Constitutional right – that demand speedy resolution. Nic van Deventer's memo, 2012, bears reference.
>
> The appropriation of vacant land by recyclers and homeless, including both sidewalks in 14th Street, near the heritage plaque and behind Masjid premises is self-evident. Daily, residents, visitors and prayer congregants are vulnerable to intimidation and attack. We are mindful of the two recent interventions by COJ to seek alternative placements for the homeless, ensuring that a human rights-based approach is exercised. Equally, residents, too, are entitled to an environment conducive to their well-being.
>
> Despite various legislation and by-law enforcement instruments available to COJ, failure to prevent illegal activity/occupation of vacant land in our vicinity resulted in the escalation of environmental hazards. In an attempt to address some of these challenges, the Fietas Museum formed linkages with various stakeholders to halt the creeping squalor. Our correspondence to former Mayor Parks Tau and Premier Makhura during October/early November 2014 refers. In spite of our collective effort, we failed to elicit a response; hence Ali Khangela Hlongwane [the author, then responsible for museums in the City of Johannesburg] approached you for help. On 7 November 2014, together with your team, we conducted a site visit, the aim to mitigate the challenges. You gave us a firm undertaking to address the area's pressing needs.

In September 2016, the Heritage Association of South Africa declared the area of Pageview 'one of ten endangered heritage sites' in South Africa in recognition of the area's former glory.[50]

Fietas Heritage Trail

In addition to the museum, there has been an initiative to create a heritage trail, mapping sites of significance in Fietas. When the area was bulldozed in 1977, Boet Eshak of the *Sunday Times* wrote, 'Yesterday, Pageview was dead. Fourteen Street and Pageview were a part of Johannesburg. It was a tourist attraction. It had glamour. It had an atmosphere of its own. It can never be matched. It can never be replaced.'[51] Manfred Hermer, in his book *The Passing of Pageview*, published in 1978 shortly after the forced removals, also takes up the theme of destruction and disappearance. He writes: 'The old Vrededorp known to shoppers has disappeared forever. The narrow pavements cluttered with goods which seem to overflow from the tiny dark shops are now quiet and bare. The teeming crowds, the colourful cross-section of Johannesburg's polyglot population, have all gone, and Fourteenth Street has slipped back to take its place among all other memories of this brash city.'[52] It is equally important to state that until 1990, contrary to the narrative of a Fietas that had disappeared forever and died, 23 families held out[53] and refused to be removed.

What, then, is the agenda of these memorial initiatives in and of Fietas, which are led primarily by residents with a long history in the area? How much of the past can they re-present? And how do they grapple with the history of forced removals and homelessness in the present? That is, do the memorialisation initiatives provide space for dialogue about contemporary challenges and in the process help address the concerns of new residents?

In recalling the historically famous Pageview community, the City of Johannesburg erected two public memorials in 2002 and 2003 to commemorate the area's culture, history, forced removals and demolitions. Each memorial comprises a large, inscribed granite plaque in a frame of decorative mosaic mounted on a face-brick plinth. This memorial has since been removed by officials from the City of Johannesburg's Immovable Heritage unit, after being hit by a reversing truck. At the time of writing, a suitable home to keep it as a museum object was still under consideration.

Figure 2.4: Adam and Khatija Asvat's home, 12th Street. (Photograph by Arianna Lissoni)

In terms of built form, the area was characterised by organically developed, tight-grained structures of single- and double-storey buildings, mostly semi-detached cottages, typically with verandas or shop fronts facing onto the street. The City of Johannesburg has identified as many as 67 buildings and sites of heritage significance. These include the following.

Home of Adam Asvat

Adam Asvat and his wife moved to this house when forced removals were

Figure 2.5: Malay mosque, 23rd Street. (Photograph by Arianna Lissoni)

under way. With 66 other residents, Mr Asvat formed the Save Pageview Association. They fought the evictions and finally won a partial victory when the order was overturned in 1989. The house bears a blue plaque unveiled in about 2014 by the Johannesburg Heritage Foundation (JHF). The inscription reads:

> Asvat and his wife Khatija moved here from their home in 11th Street when forced removals were taking place. He had been driven from his birthplace in Sophiatown by the Group Areas Act and refused to let that happen

again. With sixty-six other residents, Mr Asvat founded the Save Pageview Association. They fought the evictions through the Courts, clinging to their homes while bulldozers demolished adjoining walls. Their courageous stand won, and in 1989 the eviction order was dropped.[54]

Malay Mosque, 23rd Street

The Malay community of Johannesburg settled in this area from 1895 onwards, with prayer meetings at first held in tents on this site. Between 1908 and 1910, a mosque in Ferreirastown was dismantled and moved to this site. The present mosque building dates from 1935 and was used by the Malay community, while Indian Muslims used the 15th Street Mosque. As well as holding religious and community significance, the mosques became symbols of resistance to the Group Areas Act.

St Anthony's Church, Krause Street

Erected in the early 1900s, St Anthony's Church was often the site of people seeking refuge from the onslaught of the Group Areas Act. The church gained a high political profile under the leadership of Father Sigamony, a community leader and champion of the anti-apartheid movement. Known as the 'Fighting Priest of Fietas', he championed the poor and oppressed for more than twenty years.

Dokrat Ruin

A partially demolished and ruined structure is all that remains of a building that once belonged to the Dokrat family. Today the ruin stands as a reminder of the destruction wrought by the Group Areas Act.

Figure 2.6: Ruin of the Dokrat home, 21st Street. (Photograph by Arianna Lissoni)

Figure 2.7: Fietas Museum in 14th Street. (Photograph courtesy of the City of Johannesburg)

An anchor site of the Fietas heritage trail, this double-storey shop-cum-dwelling is one of the few structures to have survived of the famous 14th Street Bazaar. The house is the best preserved and most representative building that remains. In 2012, the house was declared a Provincial Heritage Site.[55]

A blue heritage plaque was unveiled at the site by the City of Johannesburg in 2013. The inscription reads:

Surtees/Kays Fashion Building

Lined with shops on both sides, with goods spilling out onto the colonnaded pavements, the 14th Street bazaar was a bustling centre of trade. Families lived above their businesses, taking turns to help out behind the counter. By 1977, the traders were evicted by the apartheid government and moved to the Oriental Plaza. Sixty-seven households formed the Save Pageview Association, which fought for their homes through the courts, defying the bulldozers.

At ground level, the building now houses the Fietas Museum, established by Selma Patel (born 1956), whose father managed the shop next door, Surtees Silk Store.

Conclusion

In these reflections on the visual imagination of photographers like Goldblatt and Feldman and the oral testimonies of former residents, I have noted the movement, progression and intersection of the practice of documentation and artistic expressiveness. In the case of David Goldblatt, despite his protestation that he did not define himself as an artist but a craftsman, he was not content with conveying the inhumanity of apartheid colonialism. He consistently strove to relate his subjects' will to live. In his work, the landscape of Fietas is examined in its complex form in a society obsessed with dividing people. He depicted the innocence of childhood, the mutual dependency of residents and shopkeepers, and the tragic experiences of uprooting which left the gaping wounds of the ruins of Fietas. The strengths of his photographs lie in their compositional structure, the movement and projection of light in them, and the orchestration of the black-and-white photographic medium as opposed to colour images. Goldblatt explored these aesthetic devices theoretically in many of his published interviews.[56]

Using Goldbatt's and Feldman's photographs side by side with the material culture of the residents works as an interesting strategy to enrich the narrative of Fietas. So is the heritage trail, where the scars of apartheid-era demolitions are manifest in partly empty plots and the remains of demolished buildings. Many empty spaces exist where shops and houses once stood crowded side by side.[57] And these are remembered and brought to life in the oral histories of former and current residents. They are also recalled in performed activities on commemoration days.

Chapter Three

Statues Also Die: The Fortress of Cacheu as a Graveyard of the Portuguese Colonial Legacy

Nuno Coelho

Introduction

Located in northern Guinea-Bissau, the town of Cacheu was where the Portuguese first landed on this part of the West African coast in 1446. Here, they built a small fortress in 1588 to defend their first trading post in the region. In addition to securing the Portuguese military presence, the fortress supported the trade of goods, as well as the traffic of enslaved people, which accounted for more than 80 per cent of Portuguese economic profits in the region. After an 11-year-war against Portuguese colonial rule, which began in 1963, Guinea-Bissau unilaterally declared its independence in 1973, only to be recognised by Portugal one year later, after a democratic revolution in 1974 that ousted the Estado Novo, the longest European dictatorship.[1]

After independence, the statues erected over the course of this political regime in the public space of so-called Portuguese Guinea were dethroned from their pedestals, some of them destroyed. A few were taken from the capital, Bissau, to the Cacheu fortress,[2] where they can still be found today. There are currently four statues here: of Nuno Tristão, the first Portuguese navigator to reach the coast of Guinea; Diogo Gomes, the first Portuguese navigator to enter the rivers of the kingdom of Gabu; João Teixeira Pinto, a Portuguese colonial military officer and 'pacifier' of the region; and Honório Barreto, a governor of Cacheu who was of Cape Verdean origin. In 2004, the fortress was rehabilitated and the scattered statues were regrouped. Without being restored, the statues were simply deposited in the interior space of the fortress, left lying dismembered on the floor or leaning against the walls.

Figure 3.1: The dethroned and dismembered Portuguese colonial statues, once standing in Bissau, in the fortress of Cacheu today. (Photograph by Nuno Coelho, 2019)

This chapter focuses on the history of these four statues, as well as of a bust of João Teixeira Pinto, from the moment they were erected, until their dethronement and relocation, as well as their appearance in film productions, while addressing their existing presence at the fortress.[3] The statues were part of a careful and thorough programme to improve Bissau's public space, developed at the height of the Portuguese dictatorship, which included urban and infrastructure planning and architectural and monument design. Given their symbolic power, monuments are essential for understanding, articulating and confronting vestiges of the colonial landscape. Furthermore, analysing the filmed record of these monuments brings an uncommon perspective to the current debate. This chapter aims to contribute to the ongoing process of questioning these colonial vestiges.

Most research projects in Portugal, such as the portal HPIP – Património de Influência Portuguesa (Heritage of Portuguese Influence), which focuses on 'preserving the historical heritage of Portuguese origin in the world'[4] in territories once under Portuguese occupation, are almost exclusively dedicated to urban planning and architectural projects, sometimes briefly mentioning monuments, although without a specific focus on them. Tiago Castela has analysed memorials to colonialism in Portugal and Mozambique[5] while Victor Barros has examined historical commemorations, including monuments, linked to the construction of the memory of the Portuguese empire in Africa.[6] Apart from Filipa César's film *Cacheu*, analysed later, not much work has been conducted on the statues examined in this chapter.

The Fortress of Cacheu

Portuguese Guinea or simply Guinea, as Guinea-Bissau was known under Portuguese rule, was considered the oldest of the Portuguese colonies as it was the territory in the Portuguese Empire where the Portuguese first arrived.[7] According to Commander Manuel Sarmento Rodrigues, Portuguese governor of Guinea between 1945 and 1949, 'Guinea can, through the mouths of its children, announce to the whole world that the Portuguese empire has dawned here'.[8] But even though it was considered the oldest, sometimes referred to as the 'cradle of the Empire',[9] it was one of the least known by the Portuguese. Guinea was never truly a settler colony, at least in comparison with other Portuguese colonies in Africa, as it existed mainly for exploration and extractive purposes. Its current borders with Senegal and Guinea (Conakry) were defined under Portuguese rule in 1886,[10] and its entire territory is low-lying and intersected by many inlets and rivers. These made possible Portuguese penetration and invasion of the territory, at the time when Portugal had already mastered wooden shipbuilding techniques. The Portuguese Empire is considered to be the first maritime empire,[11] maintaining control over routes across the Atlantic, and later in the Indian Ocean, by setting up military and trading outposts along the African coast. Between their arrival in Guinea in the mid-15th century and the Berlin Conference (1884–5), the Portuguese never ventured inland beyond a thin strip of the coast.

One of these outposts was the fortress of Cacheu, built in 1588 by order of King João IV to defend the first Portuguese trading post in the region, known then as the Rivers of Guinea of Cape Verde, which had been established on the initiative of the Cape Verdean Manuel Lopes Cardoso.[12] The fortress of Cacheu, known then as Casa Forte (Strong House), is a square-shaped building built in adobe on the left bank of the river of the same name. Initially, the small fortress was supposed to be sturdier, but the Portuguese crown was experiencing financial problems at the time.[13] It was designed to have cannons pointed in every direction, towards the river but also facing the village inland, 'making it possible for the Portuguese authorities to anticipate being attacked by the Africans',[14] which eventually happened just two years after its erection.[15] The fortress also resisted attempts to seize it by other European powers, namely the Spanish and the Dutch.

In addition to securing the Portuguese military presence, the fortress supported the Portuguese trade in goods, with iron bars, fabrics, trinkets and alcohol being traded for gold, ivory, leather, salt, beeswax, pepper and other items,[16] but its economy was predominantly based on the slave trade.[17] It is believed that over the course of three centuries about three thousand enslaved people were taken from here every year, reaching an estimated total of one million transported to Brazil and other parts of the world.[18] The predominance of the slave system in Guinea contributed to the increasing series of wars between the Portuguese and the native peoples and reduced dramatically the native population of the region.[19]

The erection of the fortress fostered the creation of a settlement in its surroundings[20] and, almost two decades later, in 1605, Cacheu was already considered a town in its own right – 'the first genuinely Portuguese town of Guinea',[21] and became the first capital of the territory. In 1850, with about 1,800 inhabitants, Cacheu became the subject of an urbanisation scheme despite its decline after the capital was transferred to Bissau in 1834.[22] Under the Estado Novo, the fortress was restored in 1946.[23]

Figure 3.2: The Cacheu fortress seen from the Memorial da Escravatura e do Tráfico Negreiro (Memorial to Slavery and the Slave Trade). (Photograph by Nuno Coelho, 2019)

Today, inside the fortress of Cacheu, there are four statues that have been deposited here. These were erected in Bissau over the course of the 20th century, during the Estado Novo, when Guinea-Bissau was still under Portuguese rule. They were dethroned after Guinea-Bissau's independence and, a few years later, taken from Bissau to Cacheu. It is possible to tell the story of the Portuguese presence in what is today Guinea-Bissau by telling the story of the men represented by these statues. Their story will now be told in chronological order.[24] Later, questions will be raised about the importance of making these men symbols of Portuguese rule in Bissau's public space. The inauguration of these statues was part of a wave of celebrations and commemorations of five hundred years of the Portuguese Empire promoted by the Estado Novo regime in its colonies, and marked the first phase of a comprehensive programme to improve public space, which started in the 1940s and which was renewed in the second half of the 1950s.[25] In this context, the statues must be understood as an integral part of this programme, which comprised urban and infrastructure planning and architectural and monument design.

Nuno Tristão and His Statue

The first statue is of Nuno Tristão (?–1446), the first Portuguese navigator to reach the coast of Guinea in 1446. A caravel led by Tristão with 28 men on board arrived at a river mouth on the coast of Guinea[26] while looking for gold.[27] Once there, 22 men were put on two small boats, but before they could even land on shore they were attacked by men armed with bows in several boats. The Portuguese were pursued and had to immediately retreat, leaving behind 21 men dead, including Tristão.[28] Even though this incident reveals a history of resistance by local inhabitants from the very first moment of the arrival of the Portuguese in the region, Tristão's last journey is still celebrated in Portugal as a heroic feat. In 1889, the poet Augusto Casimiro asked in his poem 'Terra ardente, maravilhosa terra' (Ardent land, wonderful land): 'Nuno Tristão, where did you fall to raise the first padrão[29] of possession with your blood?'[30]

In 1945, Commander Manuel Sarmento Rodrigues ordered the construction of the monument to Nuno Tristão, saying that the task of 'erecting monuments is carrying out the Politics of the Spirit'.[31] The bronze statue was erected in Bissau five hundred years after the fatal incursion of 1446; it was designed in 1945 by the sculptor António Duarte (1912–98) and the architect Alberto José Pessoa (1919–85), after they were awarded first place in a competition; and it was unveiled two years later on 5 June 1947.[32] The statue is set on a granite plinth with the national shield in relief and the engraved words 'Nuno Tristão 1446' on its main face. Tristão is represented standing in an upright position, wearing a long cape, holding a scroll of paper in his right hand and a sword in his left hand. The statue was erected on Largo Carlos Pereira, at the beginning of Avenida da República (today's Avenida Amílcar Cabral), facing the river, indicating the direction from 'where Portugal came'.[33]

Figure 3.3: The statue of Nuno Tristão in Bissau, just before Guinea-Bissau's independence. (Photograph by António Coelho, father of the author, 1972–4)

Diogo Gomes and His Statue

The second statue is of Diogo Gomes (14??–1502?), the first Portuguese navigator to enter the rivers of the kingdom of Gabu in 1456. Gomes sailed with a fleet of three ships to the mouth of the Geba channel (where Bissau stands today), to a place known as Porto Gole,[34] in search of information about the gold trade and the routes to the trading post of Timbuktu. The result of his explorations was the permanent presence of the Portuguese in the region.[35]

Gomes's statue was erected five hundred years after he first disembarked in Guinea. It was designed in 1956 by the sculptor Eduardo Tavares (1918–91), after being awarded first place in a competition, and inaugurated two years later, in 1958. A monograph on Tavares's work states:

> The production of statuary [designed by Tavares] aimed at integrating commemorative monuments in Portugal or in the former colonies defines a way of working that intersects with portraits … We are familiar with six works in this area, two of which relate to historical figures … The first pieces – Vasco da Gama and Diogo Gomes – pose very particular problems in the field of portraits, since they require the use of documentary sources and historical records of various kinds, which sustain the correct iconography and fidelity to the accessory elements that these figures always imply. But, more than this research, which any sculptor should be able to carry out, these portraits take into account previous visual representations that convey deep-rooted traditions and nationalist values that often conflict with the data derived from the investigation. In any case, the period of great production of historical statuary, coinciding with the Estado Novo, was not very favourable to this revision and the figures ended up conforming to an established image and to a conventional model that the portraits of the two discoverers modelled by Eduardo Tavares also document.[36]

Tavares's design responds to these nationalist values, picturing Diogo Gomes standing in an upright position, wearing a long cape over his left shoulder. His right arm is raised above his head, with the palm of his right hand facing downwards, as if sheltering his eyes from the sun. He is looking into the distance, as if he is seeing something far away. His left hand is visible, holding the end of his cape, while his left leg is raised, with his left foot standing on a stone. His bodily expression is of someone still moving. The bronze statue was erected at Praça da Alfândega, by the fort of São José de Amura, overlooking the port of Pidjiguiti.[37] The pedestal in granite is an unsigned work by the Gabinete de Urbanização do Ultramar (Overseas Urbanisation Office), as it was then a standard form.[38] Engraved in stone, on its front side, can be read the words 'Diogo Gomes – Navegador ao serviço do Infante D. Henrique' (Diogo Gomes – Navigator in the service of Prince Henry) while the stone slab in front of the statue features a huge cross of the Order of Christ and a famous quote taken from *Os Lusíadas* (*The Lusiads*),[39] the epic poem by Luís Vaz de Camões: 'Se mais mundo houvera – la chegara' (If there was more of the world – we would get there).[40]

There is a small-scale model of this statue in patinated plaster on permanent exhibition in the museum dedicated to Eduardo Tavares's work in his birth town of São João da Pesqueira. A monograph published by the museum mentions that 'the statue is now in a museum in the Guinean capital dedicated to the colonial period'[41] even though this museum never existed and the statue was taken from Bissau to Cacheu several years prior to the monograph's publication.[42]

Honório Barreto and His Statue

The third statue is of Honório Pereira Barreto (1813–59), governor of Cacheu between 1834 and 1859, who was of Cape Verdean and Guinean origin. Barreto is thought to have contributed most to upholding Portuguese sovereignty in Guinea in the 19th century.[43] He was convinced that there was much good in the Portuguese methods of colonisation and realised that the abolition of slavery,[44] which he opposed,[45] would mean that new economic bases for Guinea's progress would have to be found. He promoted the settlement of European and Cape Verdean colonists despite the fact that Portugal didn't undertake any exploration of this part of Africa during the 19th century.[46] What made it difficult to effectively establish Portuguese administration in the territory was the problem of 'controlling' the local population, as well as attacks and looting conducted by Portugal's rivals, the French, Americans, English, Dutch and Spanish.[47]

Under Barreto's rule, Guinea was administered by Cape Verde under the name of 'Guinea of Cape Verde', a designation that lasted until 1879, when it became administratively independent. Guinea then became known as the 'Province of Guinea' or 'Portuguese Guinea'. Despite administrative independence, it was Cape Verdeans who formed the bulk of the colonial public administration – hence it is said that Guinea was 'a colony of a colony'.[48] The fact that Barreto was a person of colour was praised by the Estado Novo, in what we would call an act of tokenism: 'The colour of this man did not prevent Portugal from entrusting him with the government of the province in which he was born: this defines the ethics of an overseas administration policy. And in this high position, Honório Barreto rendered his homeland the highest service, as enforcer of Portuguese sovereignty in Guinea: this attests to the effectiveness of this policy.'[49]

Honório Barreto's statue, one of the very few depicting people of colour in the territories under Portuguese rule, was erected about a hundred years after his death. It was designed in 1956 by the sculptors (husband and wife) Vasco Pereira da Conceição (1914–92) and Maria Barreira (1914–2010) and inaugurated in 1958, the same year as Diogo Gomes's statue. The bronze statue pictures Barreto standing in an upright position, wearing a long coat, his left hand over a pillar where a few sheets of paper are seen. His right hand is raised above his chest as if he is waving or greeting passers-by. His right leg is leaning slightly forward as if he is about to walk. The statue was erected on top of a granite plinth, where his name was engraved in stone together with the date of his death (1859), and placed on the square bearing his name (today's Che Guevara Square).

Teixeira Pinto and His Statue

The fourth statue is of João Teixeira Pinto (1876–1917), a Portuguese colonial military officer who took part in the so-called Pacifying Campaigns[50] in Guinea between 1912 and 1915. Before the arrival of Pinto, hardly any years had passed without Portuguese military operations against resisting native populations in the last decades of the 19th century and the first decades of the 20th. Some of these operations had to be repeated against the same populations several times over. This was true of the operations against the Papéis (in 1891 and 1894), who managed to keep the capital, Bissau, under a permanent state of siege.[51] Many others followed.[52] After having served in Angola,[53] Pinto arrived in Guinea in 1912, to fulfil the requirements of the Berlin Conference for the effective occupation of African territories. The Portuguese presence and authority in Guinea were then still nominal, and Pinto began a broad military campaign to put an end to the so-called prevailing chaos, provoking great local resistance.[54] The 'pacification' wars led by Pinto, 'contrary to what the name implies, were campaigns of great violence and colonial repression against the indigenous populations. The campaigns continued until 1935, when the territories of Guinea were considered "pacified", although in practice they extended to the National Liberation Struggle.'[55]

Teixeira Pinto's statue was erected forty years after he left Guinea. It was designed by the sculptor Euclides Vaz (1916–91),[56] after being awarded first place in a competition, and was inaugurated in 1955. The bronze statue pictures Pinto standing in an upright position, wearing an uniform, with a pistol in a holster hanging on his right side, a sword hanging at his waist on his left side, and a hat placed by the sword. His bodily expression suggests strength: 'A solid body, muscled legs, broad chest, short thick neck, close-cropped hair, standing on a broadly strung forehead, and strong moustache with long upward-arched tips. A suggestion of strength and calm decision emerges from the whole, giving truth to artistic creation.'[57] His right hand is depicted as a clenched fist and his right arm is stiff, hanging alongside his body, as if ready to draw the pistol. His left hand seems to be holding his hat or else he is about to draw his sword. His legs are slightly apart, suggesting someone ready for action.

The statue was erected on top of a round granite column above a cube-shaped plinth with embossed laurel buttresses, with the bronze letters 'A Teixeira Pinto' (To Teixeira Pinto) placed below a bronze coat of arms. On the opposite surface of the plinth, bronze letters declare 'Pacificador da Guiné 1912–1915' (Pacifier of Guinea 1912–1915). Pinto's statue was erected at Alto do Crim (the Crim Heights, where the Guinea-Bissau National Assembly stands today). The statue was inaugurated by the Portuguese president General Craveiro Lopes on 4 May 1955. Official records of the event state: 'The statue of Alto do Crim, with a President of the Republic and a people at its feet, is the symbol of victory over death. Cast in bronze, men become immortal.'[58]

Prior to this full-body statue, there was another monument to Teixeira

Pinto in Bissau, a bust[59] inaugurated in 1929 by the governor, Colonel Leite de Magalhães. The bust was erected in a garden on top of a plinth, featuring a laurel wreath and lettering[60] that reads 'Vitória e Paz, 1912–1915, a Teixeira Pinto' (Victory and Peace, 1912–1915, to Teixeira Pinto). This garden once existed at the end of Avenida da República, near Largo Carlos Pereira, close to where the statue of Nuno Tristão was later erected.[61] The garden has since disappeared and its place taken by an existing building.[62]

The Urban Space of Bissau

Placed over the map of Bissau, the original locations of the statues, as well as other monuments, reveal a dense network of symbolic power. Spread as they are across the urban plan of the capital, located on major avenues and squares and visible from different angles, 'memorials [like these] can contribute to the spatial violence of unequal urban division'[63] while 'visual and sculptural representations located in urban areas are integral to urban planning, having a persistent role in a colonial tradition of memorialisation'.[64] Violence can be defined in three ways: direct (visible); structural (a set of invisible structures that materialise in the denial of people's needs); and cultural (invisible in creating a legitimising framework for violence).[65] Violence, which should not be mistaken for just the absence of peace, functions at political, institutional, physical and symbolic levels.[66] In terms of this definition, Portuguese colonial statues in Bissau can be understood as forms of cultural and symbolic violence. The dialogue established between the men represented in the statues (and the historical periods they represent) and toponymy also plays an important role in the discourse of the coloniser. We should note that, after independence, Guinea-Bissau not only toppled the colonial statues but also replaced most of the street and square names assigned by the Portuguese.

Bissau is a town with a relatively recent and geometric plan, developing from the fort of São José de Amura, built initially in 1696 and rebuilt in 1858–60. Bissau was settled in 1766 under the name of São José de Bissau (Saint Joseph of Bissau), and some urban development had already taken place by the late 19th century. The 1919 plan for the Nova Cidade de Bissau (New City of Bissau) by the engineer José Guedes Quinhones established a geometric grid, which serves as the basis for the current layout,[67] although it is much closer to a European scheme. The plan initiated the 'monumentalisation of the urban space',[68] corresponding to its expansion beyond the original perimeter, while proposing a radial square, located at the highest point, connecting through a boulevard, Avenida da República (today's Avenida Amílcar Cabral), to the lower, port area. The city limits are marked by an Avenida de Cintura (Bordering Avenue), which borders the 'suburbs', where it was proposed the African population would settle.[69]

The narrow streets of Bissau Velho (Old Bissau) near the fort, the river Geba and the Pidjiguiti port contrast with the mesh of wide, parallel and perpendicular streets, originating from the plan, with a large central roundabout known as Praça do Império (Empire Square), today's Praça dos Heróis Nacionais (National Heroes Square).[70] From the old part of Bissau, where the monuments to Diogo Gomes and Nuno Tristão once stood, all the way to Praça do Império, Avenida da República was the central, monumental axis of the urban grid in the mid-20th century.[71] It was here that the main cathedral, designed by João Simões in 1945 during the early years of the Gabinete de Urbanização Colonial (Colonial Urbanisation Office),[72] and the post office were located.[73] The Government Palace occupies the place where Quinhones imagined it would be on his 1919 plan, standing on a prominent position, at Praça do Império. This is all part of an architecture of political representation that began to be realised in the second half of the 1940s and extended from 'European Portugal' to 'African and Asian Portugal'.[74]

At the centre of this round-shaped piazza, the Portuguese built a tall obelisk called Monumento ao Esforço da Raça (Monument to the Effort of the Race). It is a commemorative work designed by Ponce de Castro in Art Deco style and built in 1934. It is monumental in size, consisting of a high base, superimposed with vertical elements, having in front a woman's bust on a plinth with a laurel wreath, flanked by stepped curved elements.[75] After Guinea-Bissau's independence, it was the only Portuguese monument that remained almost intact in Bissau, being renamed Monumento aos Heróis da Independência (Monument to the Heroes of the Independence), being topped by a star.[76] From this square, and perpendicular to Avenida da República, another large avenue (Avenida Teixeira Pinto, today's Avenida

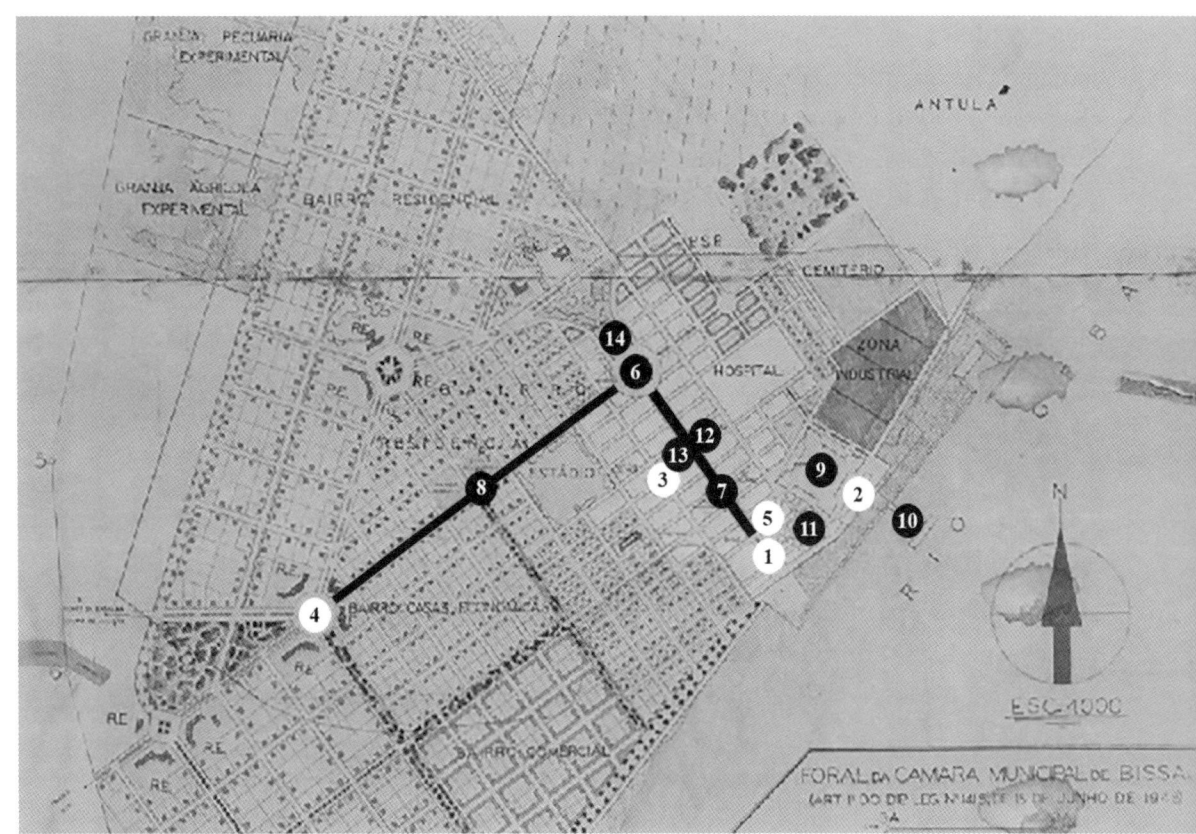

Figure 3.4: Detail of the General Urbanisation Plan for the city of Bissau (dated 12 June 1948) with superimposed identification of the location of the four statues and the bust analysed in this chapter (white circles) and other landmarks (black circles): (1) Nuno Tristão's statue at Largo Carlos Pereira; (2) Diogo Gomes's statue at Praça da Alfândega; (3) Honório Barreto's statue at the square bearing his name (today's Che Guevara Square); (4) Teixeira Pinto's statue at Alto do Crim (the Crim Heights, where the Guinea-Bissau National Assembly stands today); (5) Teixeira Pinto's bust on Avenida da República (today's Avenida Amílcar Cabral); (6) Praça do Império (Empire Square), today's Praça dos Heróis Nacionais (National Heroes Square) where the Monument of the Effort of the Race stands (today's Monument to the Heroes of the Independence); (7) Avenida da República (today's Avenida Amílcar Cabral); (8) Avenida Teixeira Pinto (today's Avenida Francisco Mendes); (9) Fort of São José de Amura; (10) Pidjiguiti port; (11) Bissau Velho (Old Bissau); (12) Cathedral; (13) Post Office; and (14) Government Palace. (Luís Pavão & Laura Guerreiro in Ana Vaz Milheiro, 'O Gabinete de Urbanização Colonial e o traçado das cidades luso-africanas na última fase do período colonial português', Urbe: Revista Brasileira de Gestão Urbana 4, no. 2 (December 2012): 6 (map) and Nuno Coelho, 2023 (superimposed identification)

Francisco Mendes) runs up to Alto do Crim, where Teixeira Pinto's statue once stood on its central visual axis. The remaining statue of Honório Barreto was located in a round-shaped piazza named after him (today's Che Guevara Square) on a crossing between two streets on the geometric grid, not far from Avenida da República. These symbolic features of the urban space (statues, monuments and toponymy) were mainly created in terms of a programme to improve public space organised by the Estado Novo regime[77] to commemorate five hundred years of the Empire, consisting of a dense network of cultural and symbolic violence. The statues that we are analysing should thus be understood as an integral part of the urban and infrastructural planning conducted by the Portuguese at the time.

The Presence of the Statues in Film Productions

It is also possible to tell the story of these four statues by looking at films that features these monuments. First, we should take into account that all these monuments were erected during the 48-year-long dictatorship in Portugal (1926–74), when there was an intensification of Portuguese colonial projections and fantasies. For this chapter, films were chosen to add another layer of meaning to the statues, either reinforcing their intended original meaning, as can be seen in the films produced during Portuguese rule of Guinea-Bissau, or offering a critical vision, as can be observed in the films produced after Guinea-Bissau's independence. The analysis of archival footage and of movie films, moreover, assumes 'the recognition of the image as a potential object of contemporary relational experiences, as well as the intrusion of silenced sources and personal files'.[78] Finally, in the sample of films produced after Guinea-Bissau's independence, we can witness the statues in different locations, as if they were wandering around, from when they were standing on their pedestals in Bissau to their final destination of Cacheu. In total, thirteen films were identified, five produced during the Portuguese rule of Guinea-Bissau, and eight produced after independence.

Films Produced during Portuguese Rule of Guinea-Bissau

The five films produced during the Portuguese rule of Guinea-Bissau reinforce the official discourse of the regime and the symbolic dimensions associated with the monuments, the represented figures and their locations. Three films were produced by directors whose body of work is closely associated with the regime, while the remaining two were produced by RTP – Radio Televisão Portuguesa (Portuguese Radio Television), the state-owned TV channel.

Guiné, berço do império 1446–1946 (Guinea, Cradle of the Empire 1446–1946) was directed in 1946 by António Lopes Ribeiro (1908–95). The film[79] is a panoramic documentary depiction of Guinea under Portuguese administration, carried out during the so-called Missão Cinegráfica às Colónias de África (Cinegraphic Mission to the Colonies of Africa). In this film we can see the bust of Teixeira Pinto only, as the other statues were yet to be erected. This is also the only film in which this bust can be seen. Over the single shot of the bust, the narrator's voice is heard saying: 'The last phase of the struggle against the battle-hardened tribe was led by one of the great figures of the national epic, Teixeira Pinto, whose memory a small monument in Bissau recalls all the time.'

The film *Viagem presidencial à Guiné* (Presidential Visit to Guinea), directed in 1955 by Ricardo Malheiro (1909–77), has several parts, of which two are of interest: the first one, 'Bissau', and the third one, 'De Farim a Bissau' (From Farim to Bissau). The film documents the first-ever visit to the colonies, in 1955, by a Portuguese president, Craveiro Lopes.[80] He is seen paying tribute to the statue of Nuno Tristão, and then goes to inaugurate the one of Teixeira Pinto (in part 1), later paying a visit to the fortress of Cacheu (in part 3). In this last scene, the narrator refers to the 'freshly whitewashed' walls of the fortress, which 'only houses old museum cannons'. The other two statues are not seen in this film, as they were yet to be erected.

When Augusto Fraga (1910–2000) directed his film *Terra ardente* (Ardent Land) in 1960,[81] all four statues were already erected. The film depicts the landscapes and cultural features of Guinea, like a series of moving postcards. Its title may have been adapted from the title of the book *Terra ardente: Narrativas da Guiné* (Ardent Land: Narratives from Guinea) by the Portuguese poet Adolfo Norberto Lopes (1900–89). The expression 'ardent land' was later reused by the Portuguese poet Augusto Casimiro (1889–1967) in his poem 'Terra ardente, maravilhosa terra' published in his book *Portugal atlântico: Poemas da África e do mar* (Atlantic Portugal: Poems from Africa and the Sea).

All four statues as well as the fortress of Cacheu featured in this movie. Over images of the statues of Diogo Gomes and Nuno Tristão, the narrator states that these 'Portuguese navigators were discovering new worlds under the inspiration of the Infant of Sagres [Prince Henry the Navigator]'. Later, over images of the fortress of Cacheu and the statues of Teixeira Pinto and Honório Barreto, the narrator mentions 'Cacheu with its venerable battlements where the frequent attacks of an embattled tough people came to break. The pacification came later when the natives understood the futility of resistance and the nobility of our intentions. Teixeira Pinto and Oliveira Muzanty were the men who carried it out. Honório Barreto, a native of the land, enjoyed prestige as governor and the indigenous chiefs collaborated in the great work that was beginning.' Over further images of the statues of Teixeira Pinto and Nuno Tristão, the narrator refers to the 'wide avenues [that] were torn open, such as the one of Teixeira Pinto, which follows from Alto de Crim, and Avenida da República, which, starting from Largo Carlos Pereira, leads to Praça do Império, where the Government Palace stands'.

The two films produced by RTP, *Cidade de Bissau* (Town of Bissau), of 1962, and *Bissau*, of 1966, show overviews of the capital, its heritage and its daily life, as if they were a series of moving postcards. All four statues were shot for both of the films.[82] At first glance, there are no substantial differences between the two films in the way both respond to their theme. However, it is important to analyse the second film for what is out of frame: despite Bissau's apparently normal life, the Independence War had already started three years before, in 1963.

Films Produced after Guinea-Bissau's Independence

After Guinea-Bissau's independence, eight films featuring the statues were produced, all of them offering a critical view of these colonial remnants, albeit at different levels and from different approaches – from fiction to documentary, from artistic films to cross-genre – by Portuguese, Guinean and French film directors. Watching the films in chronological order, we can witness the statues in different locations, as if they were wandering on their way from Bissau to Cacheu.

The feature film *Acto dos feitos da Guiné* (Act of the Achievements of Guinea), directed in 1980 by Fernando Matos Silva (1940–), mixes both fiction and documentary.[83] The film was produced six years after the end of the Colonial War (as it is known in Portugal) or the Independence War (as it is known in Guinea-Bissau), featuring images shot by the director himself when he was stationed as a soldier in Guinea during the war in 1969–70 and later in Lisbon in 1975–6. Staged in the form of a theatre play and featuring archival images from the war, the film criticises the Portuguese presence in Guinea, raising questions about the consequences of colonisation and its so-called heroes.

In this film, we can see the statue of Teixeira Pinto only. Over the shots of the statue, in combination with pictures of graphic violence from the war, a statement by a member of the PAIGC (Partido Africano para a Independência da Guiné e Cabo Verde, or African Party for the Independence of Guinea and Cape Verde) is heard, reporting on the violent attacks carried out against the civilian population of Guinea-Bissau by the Portuguese. In this way, Silva establishes a link between symbolic and real violence, and a historical comparison between the Pacifying Campaigns and the Colonial War. The movie goes on to show a speech being given by Amílcar Cabral, the leader of PAIGC, who was assassinated in 1973, just before Guinea-Bissau's independence.[84]

The French feature film *Sans soleil* (Sunless), directed in 1983 by Chris Marker (1921–2012), mixes documentary and fiction, and was filmed in several locations around the world, including Guinea-Bissau.[85] Chris Marker was a well-travelled, politicised, anti-colonial writer, photographer, multimedia artist, designer, film director and essayist who played a role in the early days of INCA (Instituto Nacional de Cinema e Audiovisual, or National Film Institute) in Guinea-Bissau, to which he travelled in 1979 after its independence from Portugal. In *Sans soleil* 'images emerge as a decolonising force'.[86] Over the images filmed by Marker, a woman reads from the reflective writings of a seasoned world traveller. A scene in this film shows the dethroned and dismembered statues, lying on the ground, after independence. One can identify parts of the statues of Honório Barreto and Teixeira Pinto, though the sequence ends with a shot of some unidentified parts. Just before and after these shots, scenes of daily life in Guinea-Bissau are shown. At this point, the narrator says:

> He [the traveller] wrote me that the pictures of Guinea-Bissau ought to be

accompanied by music from the Cape Verde Islands. That would be our contribution to the unity dreamed of by Amílcar Cabral. Why should so small a country and one so poor interest the world? They did what they could. They freed themselves. They chased out the Portuguese, they traumatised the Portuguese army to such an extent that it gave rise to a movement that overthrew its own dictatorship and led one for a moment to believe in a new revolution in Europe. Who remembers all that? History throws its empty bottles out of the window.[87]

We should note that the Portuguese revolution of 1974, known as the Carnation Revolution, was led by the Portuguese military, tired of a 13-year-long Colonial War conducted on three African fronts (Angola, Mozambique and Guinea-Bissau), in which Portugal was spending 40 per cent of its state budget.[88]

The feature film *Mortu nega* (Death Denied, or Those Whom Death Refused), directed in 1988 by Flora Gomes (1949–), was the first Guinea-Bissau independent feature film and it was premiered at the Venice Film Festival.[89] Flora Gomes is a pioneer of Guinean cinema, fusing contemporary history and African mythology in highly charged poetic films. In 1967, he and three others (Sana Na N'Hada, Josefina Lopes Crato and José Bolama Cobumba) returned from Cuba, where they were sent by PAIGC to study film. Once in Guinea-Bissau, they were given the task of filming the armed struggle against the Portuguese. For Amílcar Cabral, it was important to leave a record in film of the struggle for future generations. These images produced by them signal the birth of Guinean militant cinema.[90]

Mortu nega depicts, in an expressive and touching way, the experiences of the War of Independence by telling the story of a woman named Diminga during the last years of the war and the struggle against the drought in the early years of the newly independent country. In one scene, Diminga announces to children playing war games at the fortress of Cacheu that the war is over, which produces immediate joy among them. Later, while Diminga is searching for help for her hospitalised husband, Sako, who was once a freedom fighter against the Portuguese, two statues (of Diogo Gomes and Nuno Tristão) appear in the background, like ghosts from the past. A soft voice sings over this scene: 'Diminga, mother of guerillas, you have wept enough. Diminga, you must put up a fight. That's what "struggle" means.'[91]

The feature film *Anos da guerra, Guiné 1963–1974* (Years of War,

Guinea 1963–1974), directed in 2000 by José Barahona (1969–), features a collection of testimonies of former Portuguese combatants in the Colonial War[92] and archival footage from the CAVE (Centro de Audiovisuais do Exército, or the Portuguese Army Audiovisual Archive).[93] Two shots of the statue of Nuno Tristão, taken from archival footage, were included in the film to accompany the testimony of one combatant.

A decade later, in 2011, the Portuguese artist and film director Filipa César (1975–) started producing films related to Guinea-Bissau after a visit to the National Film Institute in Bissau, where she had access to a room that archived the hundreds of Guinean films produced in the period of armed struggle.[94] César then began a long-term collective project titled *Luta ca caba inda* (The Struggle Is Not Over Yet).

> With an artistic career anchored in the expanded concept of the moving image, the artist and filmmaker [Filipa César] explores fictions intrinsic to the image as document, the permeability of its poetic and political potential, and investigates the centrality of the image when making a shared identity and memory. Since 2011, she has dedicated herself to researching the cinema of the African Liberation Movement, in Guinea-Bissau. From this geography of resistance, several films and essays have emerged. Sometimes, those films are just the visible tip of the iceberg, the final possible enunciation for a group of meetings, readings, talks, exhibitions, performances or texts, which happen in several times and spaces, in a meeting of voices, images and narratives.[95]

According to Marquilhas, 'Filipa César's work, heir of Harun Farocki and Chris Marker, acknowledges the poetic force of images as fragments, as elements of disorder, open to citation and at the service of a history that expands until the future. Only the fragment can allow for the dialectic understanding of the work of art, in the overlapping of elements in permanent tension – a poetic, political and philosophical device.'[96] César continues to produce and direct films related to Guinea-Bissau today. In the context of her long-running project, César directed *The Embassy*, in 2011, and *Cacheu*, in 2012, in which the statues we are analysing in this chapter can be seen.

In *The Embassy* César uses one continuous shot, consisting of a guided tour by the Guinean political analyst Armando Lona through an album from the historical archives of Guinea-Bissau, inherited from the colonial period.[97] The album features images and subtitles that reveal 'a coloniser system of representation. The landscapes, people and monuments appear under the mark of domination, as if they were part of a collector's compendium.'[98] At one moment, Lona points to an image of the fortress of Cacheu; later the statue of Nuno Tristão can be seen, though he does not point to it; later he points to an image of the statue of Teixeira Pinto.

In *Cacheu*, also filmed in a single shot, the Portuguese performer Joana Barrios presents in lecture format the story of the four statues at the fortress of Cacheu.[99] In front of an audience in Berlin, images from Filipa César's *The Embassy*, Chris Marker's *Sans soleil*, and Flora Gomes's *Mortu nega* are projected on a screen behind her.[100] The lecture features four contexts in which the statues are portrayed: on a pedestal during the colonialist period, dethroned and dismembered after independence in *Sans soleil*, as ghosts of the past in *Mortu nega*; and, finally, as they are at the fortress of Cacheu, filmed at the location by César herself. 'The story of these statues, converted into images at the mercy of historical inconstancy, seems to illustrate the statement that "no image is produced naturally but according to who has the power to do it". Each time an order falls, the raised statue becomes the ruin that celebrates its fall.'[101]

Figure 3.5: A still from the film Cacheu produced in 2012 by Filipa César.

The film *Visões do império* (Visions of Empire), directed in 2020 by Joana Pontes (1960–), examines the way the Portuguese Empire and its history were imagined, documented and publicised by way of photographs, from the end of the 19th century until the Portuguese revolution of 1974.[102] The film features a single picture of the inauguration of the monument to Teixeira Pinto, which took place in 1955, from photographic archives.

The last film, *Cacheu CUNTUM*, was directed in 2020 by Welket Bungué (1988–). Bungué is an actor and director who was born in Guinea-Bissau and raised in Portugal.[103] With his smartphone, he captures images from a recent visit to Guinea-Bissau, where he went to rediscover his roots and redefine his cultural identity. The film does not intend only to make a statement but also 'to deconstruct and, at the same time, report, denounce some figures' who were part of the colonial period and who can be associated with Cacheu's history.[104] Over the images of mundane activities performed by the director, his partner and members of his family, a voice-off is heard describing the historical involvement of the Portuguese in the slave trade in Cacheu. The voice is that of the Guinean cultural guide Pascoal Gomes, recorded by Bungué during a guided tour of the Memorial da Escravatura e do Tráfico Negreiro (Memorial to Slavery and the Slave Trade) in Cacheu, a museum that opened its doors close to the fortress in 2016.

Even though Bungué mentions the four statues and the fortress in the synopsis of the film, no image associated with them is ever shown. In his words, 'this film seeks to "rub" together the memory of the past of slavery in contrast to what can be the Guinea-Bissau of tomorrow, taking into account the images we see, how the people interact with each other, how this light means vitality and, at the same time, how I myself, newly returned to the city, perceive things'.[105] He goes on to stress the importance for him of the 'performativity of the hitherto marginalised body that now occupies the centrality of the production of discourse and no longer of representation'.[106] By not showing either the fortress or the statues, Bungué has symbolically dematerialised these colonial remnants.

The Materiality of the Statues in Present Time

If these colonial statues were symbolically dematerialised by Bungué, what remains of their materiality? The bronze statues are to be found inside the fortress of Cacheu today. Various photographic records produced over time show the statues in different positions: once in Cacheu, they were placed just outside the fortress, then regrouped inside it, and then positioned in different locations, 'possibly waiting for cultural tourism'.[107] Yet, there has been no attempt to transform these statues into touristic attractions to date. A search for information about the process that took the statues from Bissau to Cacheu was inconclusive. Collected testimonies indicate that they were dethroned during the first presidency of Luís Cabral (1973–80) and stored in Bissau either in a warehouse by the port or in the open air in the town hall's gardens. The statues were then taken to Cacheu during the first presidency of Nino Vieira (1980–99) in an operation probably headed by the Ministério da Cultura/Secretaria de Estado da Cultura (Ministry of Culture/Secretariat of State for Culture). Their relocation thus precedes the rehabilitation of the fortress of Cacheu in 2004 and the inauguration of the Memorial to Slavery and the Slave Trade in Cacheu in 2016, on which the management committee had started working four years earlier.[108] While the four statues are deposited at the fortress today, the bust of Teixeira Pinto is currently kept in a storage room in the basement of the neighbouring regional government headquarters.

And if the bronze statues are located in the fortress of Cacheu (a 'graveyard', as this chapter is titled), what happened to their granite pedestals? The pedestal to the monument of Diogo Gomes can still be found in Bissau today, as well as the frontal stone slabs. Even though the name of Honório Barreto engraved in stone can still be read on its former pedestal, this block of granite acquired a new meaning. A bronze embossed profile portrait of Che Guevara and a small bronze star were placed on its surface, and it is now the monument to this revolutionary who, in 1967, visited the territories liberated from the Portuguese over the course of the Independence War. The square where it stands was also named after him.[109] At the place where the pedestal to the monument of Teixeira Pinto once stood, the Assembleia Nacional Popular (Popular National Assembly) was erected. The pedestal remained at this place until recent years but, just like the statues and the remaining pedestal (of Nuno Tristão's statue), it has now vanished from public space.

Figure 3.6: The monument to Che Guevara in Bissau using the former pedestal of Honório Barreto's statue to which a round bronze portrait of Che Guevara was added. (Photograph by Nuno Coelho, 2019)

Conclusion

This chapter focused on the history of four statues erected by the Portuguese Estado Novo regime in Bissau over the course of the 20th century. In view of their symbolic power and their involvement in a programme to improve

Guinea-Bissau's capital's public space, the analysis of these monuments and their context of production is essential for articulating and confronting colonial vestiges. In addition, the analysis of their filmed records and the process of their relocation adds another layer of understanding of their presence (or absence) to the contemporary debate on the colonial landscape.

The story of the four Portuguese colonial statues in the fortress of Cacheu, 'converted into images at the mercy of the historical inconstancy, seems to illustrate the statement that "no image is produced naturally but according to who has the power to do it". Each time an order falls, the raised statue becomes the ruin that celebrates its fall.'[110] The 'heroes' that symbolise the Portuguese presence in Guinea-Bissau, now converted into material remnants of that presence, were sent to the very same place where the Portuguese Empire began. Their relocation is thus an 'imperial sunset' – the end of an era. The fortress of Cacheu is now a graveyard of the Portuguese colonial legacy, where statues, once believed to be immortal, were sent to die.[111]

Chapter Four

Building as Artefact: From Prison to Museum

Nabeel A. Essa

The Constitutional Court, representing the new Constitution of democratic South Africa, was established in 1994. An international architectural competition was held in 1997 for a new building to house the court. The derelict colonial and apartheid Old Fort and prison complex in Johannesburg was the site selected (see Figure 4.1), in part because of the narrative it offered of a site of oppression transformed into a place of constitutional freedom. This site was layered with tangible and explicit evidence of colonial and apartheid subjugation, infrastructure and planning. Today Constitution Hill is a site with a palimpsest of contested histories – of violence, struggle, liberation and memorialisation. Layers of spatial narratives are embedded within this site. The urban fabric here has been drawn, erased and reimagined under the Zuid-Afrikaansche Republiek and British colonial rule, during apartheid and after.

The site is located in the inner city and adjacent to the high-density residential area of Hillbrow, offering central urban connections within the fragmented, sprawling and divided city of Johannesburg. The Constitution Hill precinct, which opened to the public in 2004, houses the highest court of the country and also functions as an open-air, site-specific museum. The architecture, buildings, spaces and place act as *in situ* artefacts around which content and narrative are woven and constructed. The new developments offer a potential spatial tension between past and present.

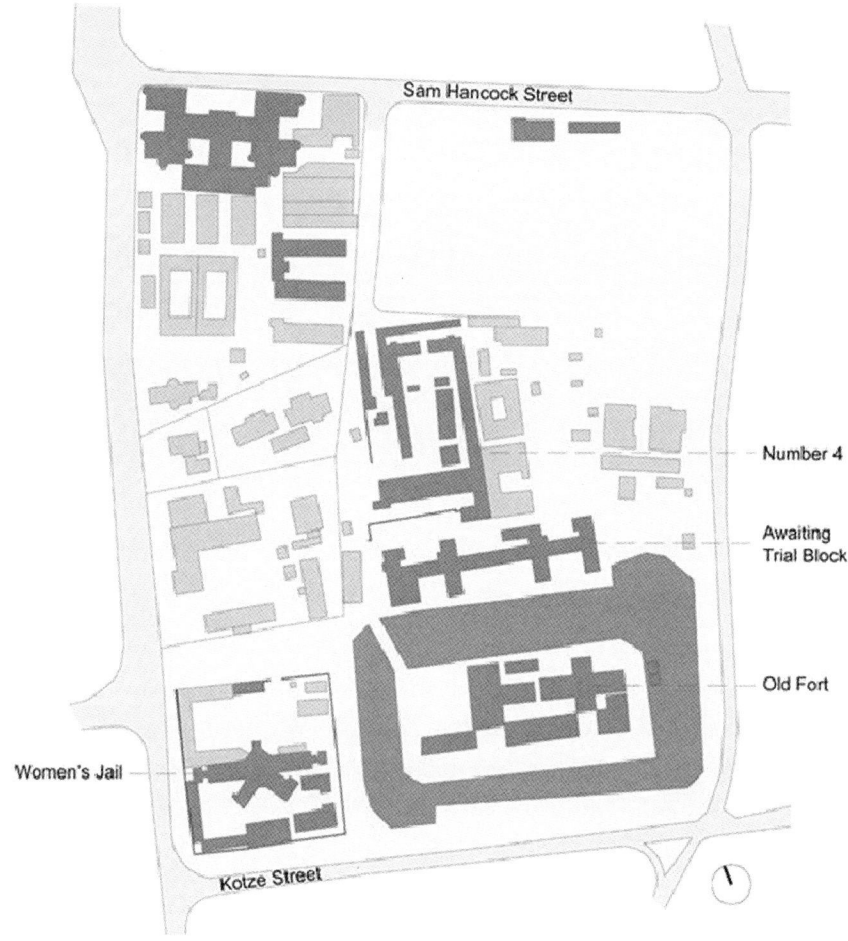

Figure 4.1: Plan of the site showing existing buildings with historical buildings highlighted based on the diagram provided in the Department of Public Works competition brief and conditions of the competition for the new Constitutional Court building of South Africa, 1997.

However, the historical buildings and spaces have been displaced and have shifted in meaning through the passage of time and through the development process. This chapter revisits the heritage conservation and spatial decisions made during the formation and development of Constitution Hill. It also considers ways of working with such toxic historical sites that allow buildings as artefacts a presence that is about a regenerative, coherent and tangible spatial layering or palimpsest and an empathetic urban strategy of unmaking boundaries and unbinding a skewed historical order. This idea of a parallel between urban reconfiguration and narrative shifts is compelling. The strategy of opening up an internalised space in the city can also be about opening up the narrative of the place from the fervour of a racist, patriarchal and Eurocentric history to a heterogeneous, complex, layered and critical historical narrative. The removal of boundary walls and the making of urban connections are the tools of urban designers and architects. It is imperative for a precinct which is inherently defined as expressive of memory and history to engage with the larger project of reinterpreting history, and that we find more nuanced and strategic tools of spatial heritage practice to enact this.

The Constitutional Court judges of the early period, through a working committee, drove the court building project in terms of site selection and architectural brief. They consulted with the Cape Town architects Vivienne and Derek Japha during the site selection processes. The South African architectural practices Urban Solutions and OMM Design Workshop were awarded the contract to design the project. Herbert Prins was the heritage consultant appointed by the Johannesburg Development Agency, which was the entity that managed the construction project.

Between 2002 and 2006, I was the spatial consultant to Constitution Hill's Heritage, Education and Tourism team. In 2017 my architectural practice, Office 24-7 Architecture, in partnership with Trace Group, was appointed as exhibition curators and designers for the Museum of the Constitution, to be housed in the new visitors' centre building on the Constitution Hill precinct. This project is to be completed in 2025. Cultural thinking, social structures and identity politics have shifted in the period between the initial development phase of the precinct and the current redevelopments. As an architect working in the heritage and museum sector at the early stages of this project and again twenty years later, I am interested in understanding how attitudes, including my own, have shifted in response to regenerative mechanisms on toxic heritage sites like this one.

This chapter seeks to unpack how spatial, architectural, heritage and urban design decisions made in the past have impacted on the authenticity and potential of the site as read today. My concern is to understand the decisions made around the nexus of heritage and regeneration at project inception, and to identify where they lacked foresight in approach and process. The lessons of hindsight can offer a more critical spatial approach to this and other heritage sites.

Within this intermediate period there were significant socio-political and cultural thinking shifts, exemplified by the Rhodes Must Fall movement; these have been explored mainly through an art-history lens in the book *Exchanging Symbols: Monuments and Memorials in Post-apartheid South Africa*. My intention is to see how cultural shifts in thinking about monuments and memorials can meaningfully impact on historical sites from a spatial, architectural and urban perspective.

Constitution Hill has been the subject of numerous heritage-related analyses and debate. There are writings on its role in heritage tourism, in its construction of post-apartheid architectural identity, its portrayal of meaning and nation-building in the realm of monument and memorialisation, and there has been analysis of how it performs and fails to perform as a public domain. Two texts were valuable in forming this spatial critique: Mark Gevisser and Sarah Nuttall's dialogue in the form of the article 'From the Ruins: The Constitution Hill Project' offered an early critique of the demolition of buildings and expressed concern about the lack of public amenity and public attraction to the site, while the architectural thesis by Ursula Rigby, 'Transforming Space and Significance: A Study of the Constitutional Court of South Africa' unpacks the processes that led to the development of Constitution Hill.

The vision of Constitution Hill as a space of collective healing is today hard to reconcile in a national context where extreme inequality persists. In the last years proactive management by the Constitution Hill Development Company, through dynamic programming and events, has redefined and extended the precinct's role in providing a platform for marginalised and disenfranchised voices around issues of social justice, identity and transformation.

The first part of the chapter examines the architectural and heritage-related decisions made in developing the Constitution Hill precinct and in particular the decision to demolish the Awaiting Trial Block. The second part reflects on alternative strategies for heritage sites like this one.

The chapter is structured around terms used by ICOMOS, the International Charter for the Conservation and Restoration of Monuments and Sites, specifically the Australian ICOMOS charter for the conservation of places of cultural significance, also called the Burra Charter (1999). This charter offers a good guiding framework for heritage sites and is used by South African heritage practitioners as an internationally accepted convention for the protection of cultural resources.

Part One

In 1996 the process commenced for the development of Constitution Hill from a disused prison complex to the site of the Constitutional Court and museum precinct. Buildings were demolished, commemorated and relocated, and new buildings were erected. The site was transformed in both its physical materiality and the way it performs in and engages with the city. If we assume a broader project vision and intention to transform the site as an act of restitution for the atrocities enacted on site, their ramifications and the systems that the site represented, then how effective were the heritage, architectural, curatorial and programming decisions made in the formation of the precinct?

The interpretative context allowed through the mechanics of museums offers the prison structures within the Constitution Hill precinct the dual role of memory and transformation.

The museum as typology is problematic in the South African context where museums were historically exclusionary and racist. Criteria around the notion of the museum and the role of heritage practice in this context need interrogation, in terms of how they are able to look beyond conservation, beyond a museum function, and unlock regeneration.

The intention of this chapter is to consider ways of intervening on toxic historical sites; ways to interpret, interrupt and transform such sites of tangible, spatial colonial and apartheid evidence.

Reconfiguring Place

In the 2020 book *Exchanging Symbols* Thabo Manetsi refers to 'expert influence and codification', and quotes a writer as saying that 'management and conservation become things that are done to sites and places but are not seen as organically part of the meaning-making process of heritage itself. This process is obscured and redefined as external to the process of heritage.'[1]

The process of heritage assessment that took place during the heady drive towards the making of the Constitutional Court project is key to understanding how the site performs today. By revisiting the heritage and spatial decisions made about Constitution Hill, we can expose issues around heritage conservation. These decisions were expedient and had far-reaching implications.

The site is significant in the physical evidence it provides of an early history of incarceration in Johannesburg that spans a period from 1893 to 1983, when prisoners were moved to Diepkloof prison and the prisons on site were closed. In 1996 a dialogue ensued between the National Monuments Council (NMC) and the judges of the Constitutional Court. The NMC, which was established as part of apartheid governance under the National Monuments Act of 1969, initially took a preservationist stance to the site. In 1998 the whole site was declared a national monument with an allowance for some demolitions. In 1999 the South African Heritage Resources Agency (SAHRA) was established under the new National Heritage Resources Act 25 of 1999, and replaced the NMC.

Today the site is configured according to a masterplan that was formed after and around the winning court design. It raises several questions: What reading, what cohesion, do the fractured components of the site offer? How in the palimpsest of the site do the prison layers emerge and to what effect? What was erased, what was left behind, partially demolished, commemorated or reconstructed? What was added and what narrative emerges? What are the new urban connections? What are the new boundaries?

The urban design and conservation decisions that were made then reconfigured and adapted the site to new use. From an architectural and sustainability perspective, the 2021 Pritzker laureates Anne Lacaton and Jean-Philippe Vassal offer an ethos of keeping and incorporating existing buildings when developing a site. Their practice begins every project with a process of discovery, which includes intensely observing and finding value in what already exists.[2] This value is considered without the weight of cultural significance, regardless of age, and involves reuse and adaptive reuse. Nostalgia for the past is absent. Rather, Lacaton and Vassal seek transparency, openness and luminosity, with a respect for what is inherited and a determination to act responsibly in the present. This ethos should be borne in mind when considering existing infrastructure at Constitution Hill and in particular the debate around the demolition of the Awaiting Trial Block (ATB).

Erasure

Cape Town architects Vivienne and Derek Japha acted as advisors to the court judges prior to the launch of the competition, and they identified the highest flat point of the site, namely the location of the ATB (see Figure 4.2), for erecting the new court. How they came to be tasked with this critical role is unclear, but it is their advice and the series of site demolition options they drafted that made the site attractive for the court.

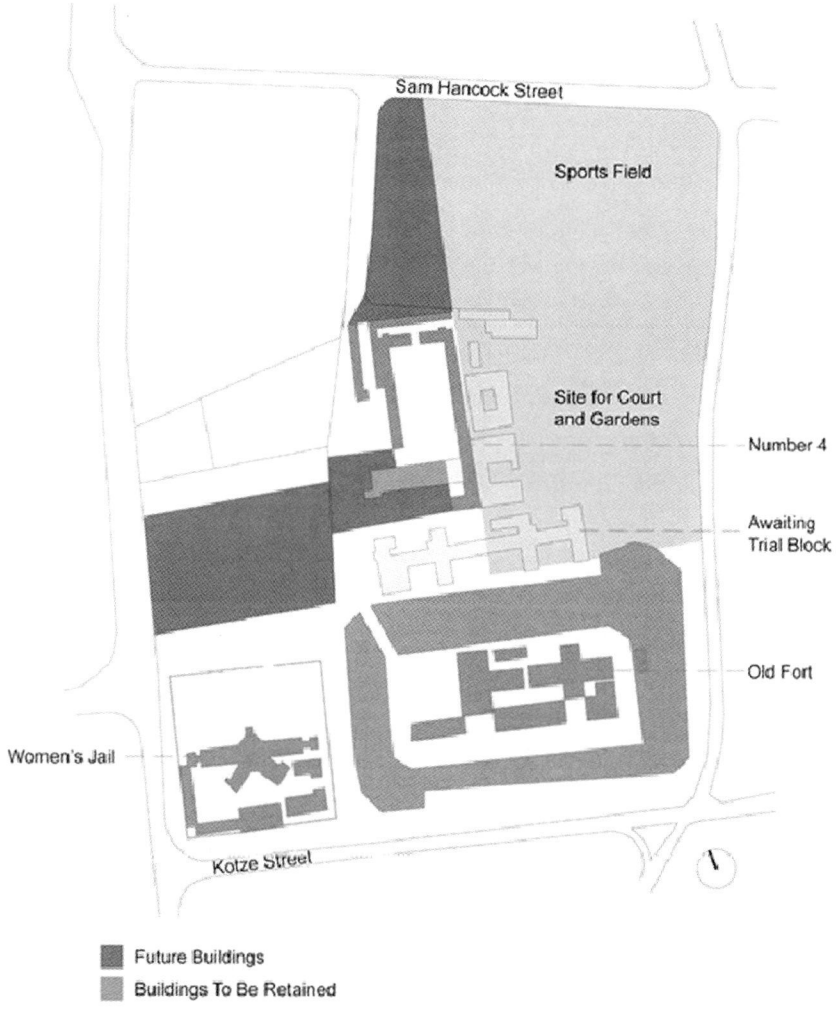

Figure 4.2: Plan of the site of the Japhas' preferred option for the competition development based on their diagram. (Rigby, 2016)

The Japhas' influence is marked in a series of layout sketches with accompanying commentary and notes, dated 13 September 1996.[3] A decision on precisely where to situate the new building had to be made in conjunction with a decision about which parts of the historical built fabric could or should be retained. The argument presented by the Japhas formed the basis of the NMC declaration for the precinct just prior to the competition.

The Japhas believed the ATB had the lowest weighting on the 'to keep' list. The ATB occupied 'an absolutely pivotal position on the site'.[4] They believed it was the most 'negotiable'.[5] Despite their immense academic, architectural and Cape heritage experience and standing, the Japhas were looking at the site from a singular perspective, that of the best architectural position for the court and not in terms of the palimpsest and narrative of the site.

Herbert Prins, the city-appointed heritage practitioner, explained that the judges had been advised by heritage experts in Cape Town that the ATB did not have particular architectural significance (see Figure 4.4), but the Regional Heritage Committee was aware of the structure's historic importance. It was a culturally significant building, as it was the place where those accused of a criminal or political offence were incarcerated pending trial. Prins's personal opinion is that if the Japhas advised the judges that the Awaiting Trial Building did not warrant conservation, this could be because of the different value placed on 19th-century buildings by conservationists in Johannesburg and Cape Town.[6] The emphasis of heritage conservation for both cities was on colonial architecture and the craft, aesthetics and detailing of buildings, and it was not particularly engaged with issues around cultural significance, especially not the cultural significance of the disenfranchised. Cape Town, with its much earlier colonial establishment, has a host of 18th-century buildings which form the basis of its heritage conservation thinking. However, this criterion does not explain the decision-making at the Hill – as the heritage practitioners and architects involved in the site assessment would have clearly understood both the micro-context of the adjacent high-density, low-income neighbourhood of Hillbrow and the macro-context of the liberation struggle and negotiated settlement in the development of the Constitution.

Prins reiterated that the Chief Justice was adamant and completely opposed to the suggestion that, as Prins put it, 'maybe we say to the competitors you can or can't, you may demolish but you may also incorporate the Awaiting Trial Block'.[7] As a result, that option was not presented in the competition brief. The judges felt that these buildings were already decaying and pushed against the conservation views of heritage agents such as Prins. The judges made the demolition of the ATB a precondition of moving onto the site (see Figure 4.3). Why they would be so adamant on issues of which they had no skill or experience is unclear. One can speculate that given the advice they were receiving they did not want this existing building to limit the creative expression of a new court that represented a new democratic South Africa.

Based on the descriptions by the jury of the four finalists of the competition, the 'symbolic formality', 'colonial classicism'[8] and monumentalism prevalent in their submissions were counter to the democratic vision embodied in the new Constitution and were hence testament to a flawed competition brief. Interestingly the massing diagram of one of the finalists, Jeff Stacey, of Design Partnership, if read simply as a massing of accommodation, offers a glimpse of a potential adaptive reuse (instead of demolition) of the ATB into the new court. If the competition brief had been brave enough to offer adaptive reuse as a potential or directive, the site could have had a better relationship across a large gathering square and a park area (see Figure 4.3) – spaces generous and welcoming enough to allow and invite varied forms of civic engagement and respite from the hard urban context. The competition should have focused on finding innovative urban strategies to deal with ways of making a closed void in the city fabric reconnect and unlock the site's potential.

In 2003 Mark Gevisser, content advisor to Constitution Hill's Heritage, Education and Tourism team, lamented that 'for an inexplicable and quite frankly unforgivable reason, the heritage consultants who originally advised the Constitutional Court said the building had to be demolished to make space for the new buildings'.[9] 'The South African Heritage Resources Agency gave permission for it to be demolished, because they understood that by giving up this building you could save the rest – by bringing the court onto the site and creating a heritage precinct around it.' But the rub was that 'in terms of heritage significance, the awaiting trial block was far away and the most important site in the complex'.[10]

BUILDING AS ARTEFACT: FROM PRISON TO MUSEUM

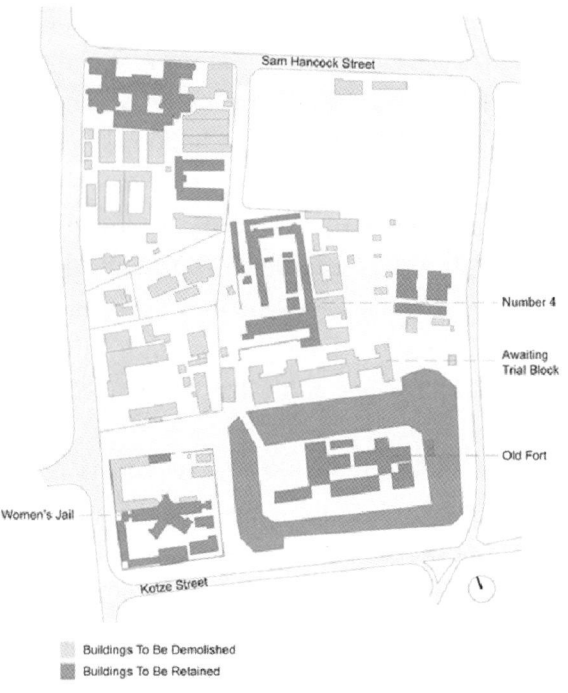

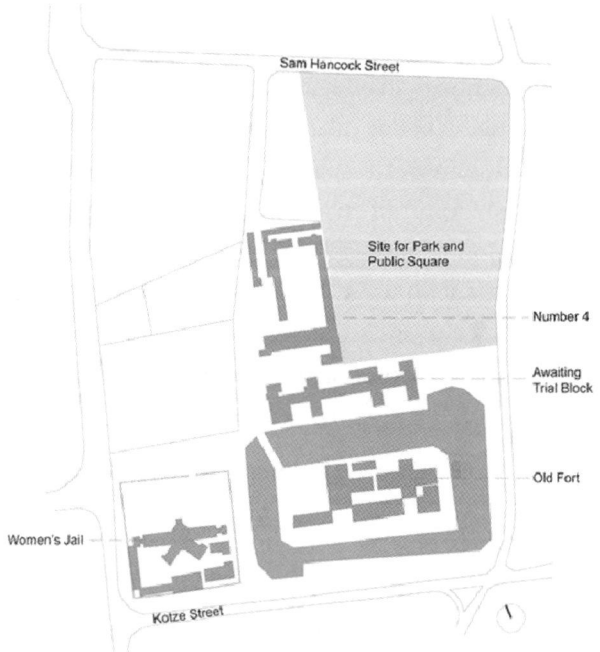

Figure 4.3: Plan of the site showing buildings to be demolished, based on the diagram provided in the Department of Public Works competition brief and conditions of the competition for the new Constitutional Court building of South Africa, 1997 (Rigby, 2016). Below is the author's own potential site development plan that keeps the ATB.

Figure 4.4: Number Four and the Awaiting Trial Block. (Bob Gosani and Bailey's African History Archive)

The ATB was built in 1928 to hold black awaiting trial prisoners (see Figure 4.4); 'tens of thousands of men passed through its large and overcrowded communal cells. Political prisoners – the treason trialists in the 1950s, the PAC pass resisters in the 1960s, the Soweto youth in the 1970s, the ANC in the 1980s – were held in special cells, separated from other prisoners'.[11]

Godfrey Moloi, an ex-prisoner, recalls: 'We went through a big iron gate to number 8 [the ATB] and were led up some stairs to Section D. This section was a big hall of a cell divided into numerous small cells of maybe two by two metres.'[12] But his description cannot reverberate within the actual walls as these no longer exist. It has been pointed out that the 'effectivity' of spaces like Constitution Hill lies largely in the power of 'oral testimony and the notion of witnessing both survivors and place.'[13]

Nelson Mandela stayed for two weeks in the ATB and observed that 'our enemy had gathered us all under one roof for what became the largest and longest unbanned meeting of the Congress Alliance in years'.[14] Through this statement Mandela intentionally shifted the perspective from a space of incarceration to a place of activism. The architects, heritage agents and judges would have been keenly aware of Mandela's description and experience at the ATB. Instead the prerequisite that the ATB be demolished in the brief was short-sighted. It is also unfortunate that this methodology of shifting perspective away from the oppressor and taking agency – adopted in Mandela's counter-narrative of this space – was not recognised and incorporated in the competition brief. When expressing narratives of oppression, it is important to shift the balance of power and highlight acts and a culture of resistance to that power.

Churchill Madikida, content advisor to Constitution Hill's Heritage, Education and Tourism team, describes one man's eloquent reaction on seeing the prison building being demolished: 'This is the place … given that the roof is gone, it no longer has the same impact it had on me when I was kept here. There is a little bit of freedom now that I can see the sky. But the anger is not gone.'[15] Justice O'Regan, a constitutional judge, explains her position: 'I am not a great fan of prisons and I don't feel this huge regret when prisons are razed to the ground … People had suffered enormously very often unjustly. That something can rise, phoenix-like from the ashes, which is the antidote to it.'[16] The architect Janina Mosojada (of OMM

Design Workshop and Urban Solutions) reinforces this idea: 'we decided that it was important to create an accessible public space at the centre of Constitution Hill that celebrated the right for people to gather, a right that had been denied to most held there'.[17]

The argument by the judges that the buildings were going to ruin is not the point, for the ruin nevertheless provides evidence and acts as a catalyst for memory. A ruin can be restored, preserved or adapted to a new use. Demolition is erasure and, in this case, the erasure of evidence of the trauma of a marginalised and oppressed group. The architecture of commemoration is a fraught concept that is often a barrier to the project of memory, as it creates another layer of design and meaning to be navigated. The argument that the new fabric that replaces the old offers the site progressive spatial transformation is valid, but the question still stands: were the intentions of liberating the space through a new urban layer necessarily in conflict with the conservation of the ATB or was the decision expedient?

In my reading of comments by the architects, heritage practitioners and the Constitutional Court judges, what I find prevalent is the idea that the problematic past should not be dwelled on too much, that the focus should be on the positive and future-thinking liberal framework of the Constitution: a kind of clean slate, with past sins symbolically adjacent (Number Four) but also somewhat washed away (ATB), to make way for a reborn, rainbow nation. The nuance and detail of spaces of black history and places of the marginalised and the oppressed became secondary to the imagined narrative of a new South Africa – through a short process of truth and reconciliation, we can forgive, forget and move forward. In hindsight the time, space and the processes required to find some healing, some repair for the depth of these traumas, are long and slow.

Heritage conservation, with its innate bias towards the quality and age of the architecture and not the meaning and memories the spaces hold, is inherently fraught and should have been, and should be, challenged. While much racial injustice is deeply embedded and inscribed in the physical urban fabric and functioning of Johannesburg, there are few spaces of symbolic potency to house a place of dialogue for remembering, overcoming and acknowledging past injustices. The prison precinct at Constitution Hill offered physical spatial evidence of the brutality of the colonial and apartheid mechanisms. In South Africa, and in Johannesburg in particular, very few accessible sites remain that provide tangible evidence of the systems of injustice that make up our history. Hence erasure within such sites earmarked for historical interpretation requires careful consideration. The demolition of the ATB had larger ramifications counter to the memory-building and history-writing project of democratic South Africa. If it had not been demolished, it could have offered the space and catalyst for narratives now lost or diminished.

We should also note the absence of black architects and heritage conservation consultants in the decision-making processes in this particular narrative. It is testimony to the demographics of the architectural profession as a white domain at this moment in time and to the very construct of architectural heritage and its protection of colonial structures, consequent to its colonial and apartheid framing. The site is tangible evidence of racial injustice – a dichotomy of black space and white space. The ATB was a space of black pain and black narratives. More concerning on this note is that one of the Japhas' layout options submitted to the judges showed the demolition of Number Four with its isolation cells (see Figure 4.5). Number Four was built as a black male prison in 1904 by the British. It had a notorious reputation for black South Africans during apartheid.[18] The very existence of this option for demolition highlights the skewed perspective offered to the judges at the time. Bob Gosani's distressing photo (see Figure 4.4) shows both Number Four and the ATB in the background – a spatial relationship and artefact of memory now lost.

A few years before the site piqued the interest of the Constitutional Court, in a very different dispensation, another significant erasure took place on this site, that of the hospital buildings that served black and white prisoners in separate sections within the Old Fort precinct. Black prisoners received lashings in the space in front of the palm tree in the hospital courtyard. This proximity was strategically used so that a doctor could be present when this punishment was meted out. These decaying buildings were demolished in 1989 to placate the demands of the Transvaal Scottish Regiment so that they could lease space and have an open area for a parade ground. The demolition permit was reluctantly approved by the very same NMC that would in 1998 make provision for the demolition of the ATB.

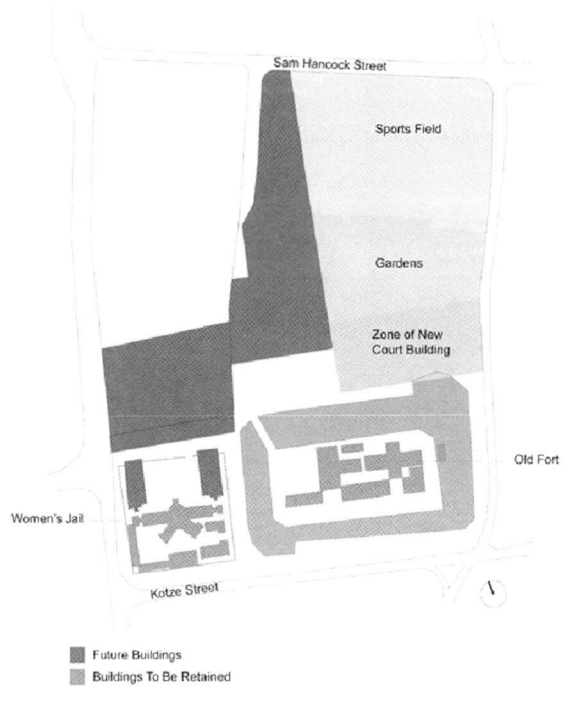

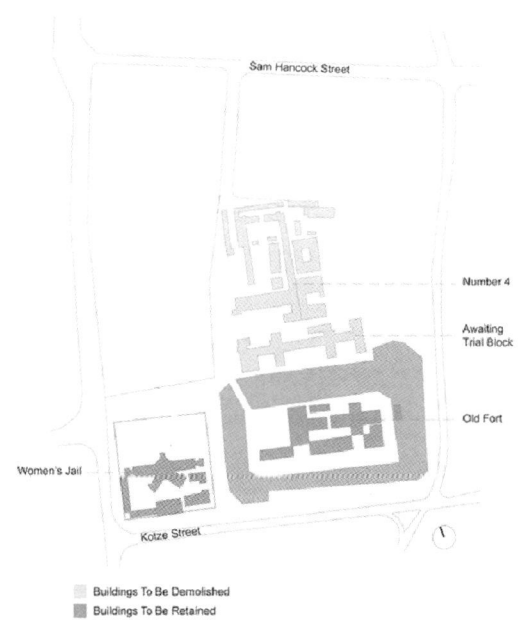

Figure 4.5: Plan of the site layout of the Japhas' option 4 for the competition development based on their diagram and the plan of buildings to be retained. (Rigby, 2016)

Commemoration

Article 24 of the Burra Charter refers to commemoration as the retaining of associations and meanings.[19] It asserts that significant associations between people and a place should be respected, retained and not obscured.

The demolition of the ATB was to be mitigated through commemoration. It was 'deemed to be of cultural value'. In cases like this, the condition of any demolition permit granted is 'that the memory of the building be commemorated by an object or volume or space or a retained fragment of the building which is identifiable as the memorial to the Awaiting Trial Building'.[20] To mitigate the impact of the demolition of the ATB, the court architects decided on two commemorative gestures. The first was to use the stair cores and extend them with tall glazed boxes, allowing for vertical landmarks. This gesture, while contributing to the presence of the new court on site, denies the narrative tangibility of the ATB. The second gesture, of using the red bricks from the demolished ATB in the court building and stepped walkway aligned to the stone wall of Number Four prison, is evocative and brings a poetic depth and texture to the material palette.

Both gestures work to support the architectural design of the new court. All conflicting narratives had to surrender to make the form of the new court work. So, the square does not fully function as a platform for civic activism, and the ATB is watered down and literally spread thin over the site. The notion of building a 'phoenix rising from the ashes'[21] became the new enforced narrative. This bombast continued with the decision to reconstruct the ATB visitors' room in a new position. While the architects' winning court design retained the visitors' room, during design development and the development of the urban plan the architects decided that the visitor room was to be dismantled (2004) and reconstructed on the east end of the site. This reconstruction, for which permission was given, was only completed in 2009.

The construct of a fragmented ATB is ambivalent. It does not express the prison processes, spaces of incarceration, and relationships between prisoners, warders and visitors. The strategy renders the ATB a mere gesture; this abstraction is watered down through the different forms of commemoration and attempts to frame the ghost of the building by keeping fragments, reusing brick, and marking the building footprint. All render the

ATB impotent. The designers were preoccupied with seeing the ATB as a bricks-and-mortar artefact rather than a place of meaning, of memories and associations between people and between people and space. The symbolic gestures are in the service of their construct, that of making a new architectural form, and ensuring the phoenix will rise from the ashes of the judges' brief, not the narrative of the prisoners.

Relocation

Article 9 of the Burra Charter refers to location. The physical location of a place is part of its cultural significance. According to the Charter, a building, work or other element of a place should remain in its historical location. Relocation is generally unacceptable unless this is the sole practical means of ensuring its survival.[22]

The visitors' room (see Figure 4.6), with its wall of wire mesh separating visitor and prisoner, was part of the ATB: it was where 'outside' met 'inside'.[23] This portion of the building was supposed to be retained as part of the court winning design. 'However, planning exigency requires that it be moved slightly to the west of its present position,'[24] explained Prins. The demolition and reconstruction of this portion of building further distorted and separated the artefact and its meaning.

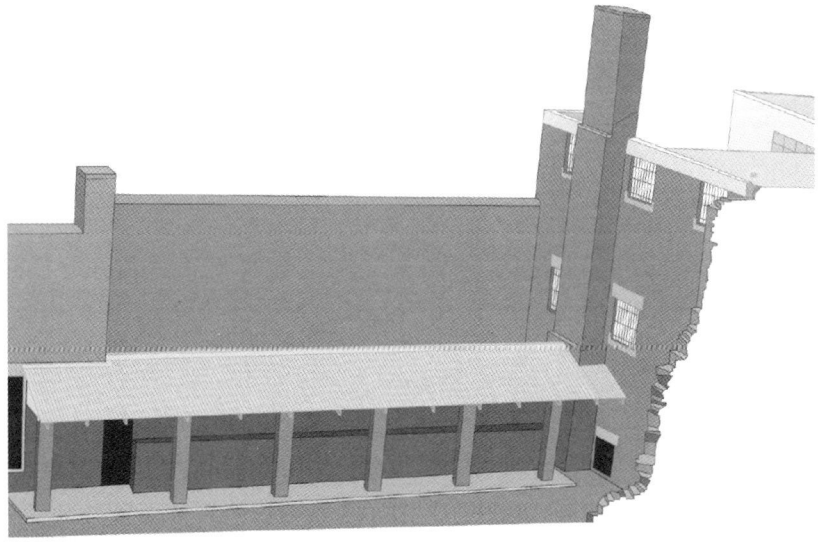

Figure 4.6: Illustration of the Awaiting Trial Block visitors' room based on a photo by Brian Orlin.

Adaptation

The development project sought a strategy of adaptive reuse of the prison site as a civic precinct housing the court, museum and square, but it does not achieve some of its intent. Neighbouring Hillbrow and Braamfontein still do not seep into the site, and there is little porosity. Children from the neighbouring schools take an ambling route after school through the site, but it is hardly a public thoroughfare.

The precinct (see Figure 4.7) seems to offer neither a space of leisure and amenity nor economic opportunity for neighbouring residents. There is no residential accommodation on site, in part because of a fear that housing would reduce the status and nature of the precinct. Softer ideas around office space have never materialised. Historically the precinct did house people: prisoners, warders, nurses in the nurses' home, and patients in the maternity hospital. Now no one sleeps on the precinct. Security is managed through an invisible boundary that manifests in the form of security guards, boom gates and cameras. The flow of the city, its buffers, road and pedestrian networks, are too entrenched to meaningfully connect with the site. The urban gestures encouraging visitor traffic are at best realised through the relatively recent decision of the sightseeing bus to stop in the square.

The Women's Jail was built in 1910. Fatima Meer's prisoner experience, quoted by Gevisser, talks about the disjunction between the oval atrium in the women's jail 'with its perfect neoclassical proportions and columns and its finely wrought iron balustrades',[25] and the atrocities carried out there. The architecture here intentionally provides a backdrop of order and control – enforcing the power of the oppressive systems and laws, first of the British, who built the structure, and later the apartheid state. Now the space sits liminally between a beautifully constructed artefact and the reminders of the trauma inflicted in these spaces that are evoked through the exhibitions. The present is aptly felt through the way the ancillary spaces are used to house offices of organisations focused on social justice. This reflects the larger project of the precinct: to rewrite over this past, allowing layers to surface as reminders and evidence of past atrocities, but also as spaces of resistance and transformation. The two new wings to the building by Kate Otten Architects create a new architectural type, an adaptive reuse hybrid that is office and museum and 'prison'. The new buildings counteract the prison building in a way that is affecting and performative.

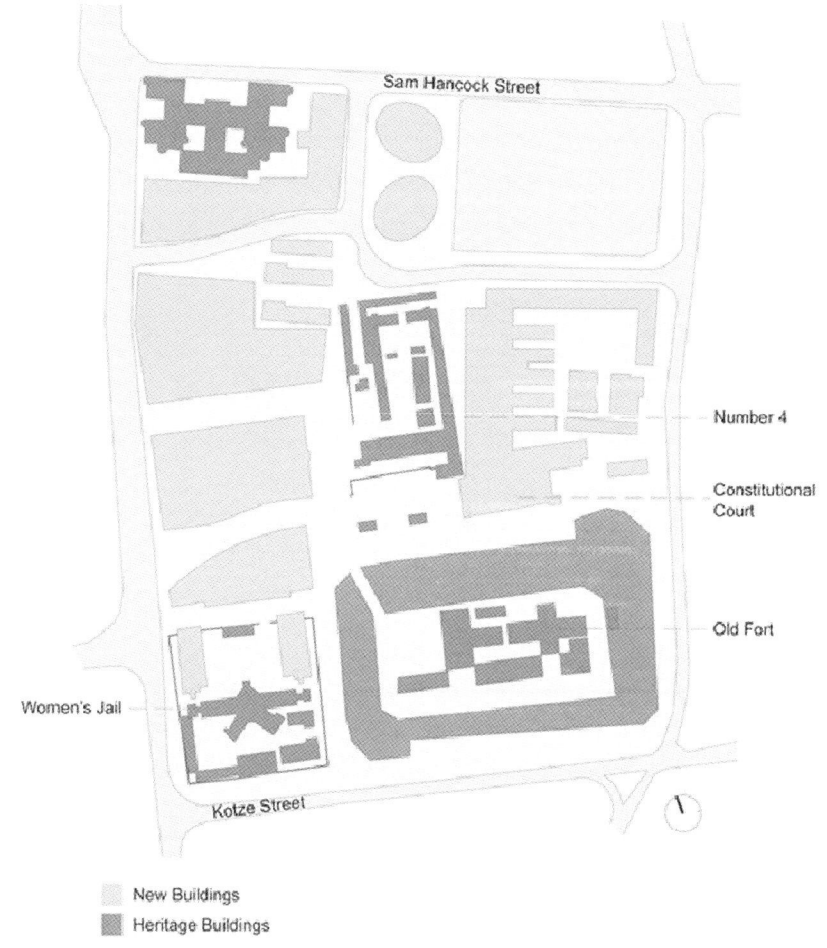

Figure 4.7: Plan of the site, 2021.

There is an automatic value associated with preservation; there is an automatic lack of value associated with demolition. Decisions have been made on what is to be inherited and what erased, and this has formed a particular and awkward spatial narrative. If there had been a more cognitive and coherent strategy in this writing of the site's palimpsest, tensions between past and present could have had more intention, with strategies to emasculate the power and monumentality these buildings enforce, through inversions and subversions of power relations, and a clear curatorial stance of framing these structures as memorials commemorating resilience through injustice, and not as historical monuments.

The palimpsest of the site does not read clearly between the dual narratives of past prison and present public precinct. There is a loss of understanding of the boundary of the prison layer. The selection and preservation of some buildings with the demolition of context and a new overlaid fabric make the preserved buildings isolated artefacts. The criteria around the notion and status of heritage practice need interrogation, in terms of how these artefacts are able to be present in a process of opening and unmaking boundaries and, in parallel, unbinding history.

Part Two

Cultural Significance

Cultural significance is embodied in the place itself, its fabric, setting, use, associations, meanings, records, related places and related objects.[26] This definition opens up the scope of a specific geographical location to wider spatial connections and socio-cultural ramifications. Article 6 of the Burra Charter refers to the cultural significance of a place, and other issues affecting its future are best understood by a sequence of collecting and analysing information before making decisions.[27] Understanding cultural significance comes first, then development of policy, and finally management of the place in accordance with the policy. This process was not followed at Constitution Hill, where development policy came before a fuller understanding of cultural significance.

The prison site is significant because the buildings are tangible evidence of oppressive systems, and the spaces have witnessed intangible histories of suffering and resistance. In order to frame the lens of cultural significance, the broader vision of the precinct must be considered. A paraphrasing of the preamble of the Constitution offers direction: 'Constitution Hill is a place for the people of South Africa to recognise the injustices of our past and honour those who suffered for justice and freedom in our land.' And, I add, Constitution Hill is a place marked through resilience and resistance to oppressive systems, a place of civic activism, of restitution, transformation and reconstruction, with the task of reorientating history in a democratic South Africa.

Achille Mbembe refers to the reorientation of history as 'a question of abolishing the moment in which the self is constituted as object of the other: only ever seeing itself in and through someone else, only ever inhabiting the name, the voice, the face, and the residence of another, and the other's work, life and language'.[28] What spatiality of place is deemed significant for a reorientation of history? How do we evaluate between tangible buildings, walls, landscaping, trees, earth mounds, courtyards and void spaces, routes, circulation and boundaries? What adjacencies, what measure of old with new, produce the tension to expose the site's layers and offer present and future trajectories?

A palimpsest is a surface on which the original writing has been erased to make way for new writing, but upon which traces of the previous layer are still legible. The identification of Constitution Hill as a palimpsest defines a methodological direction for the precinct. This identification by the Heritage, Education and Tourism team of a memorialisation of the various layers of history on the site came later in the process, after key decisions were already made. The notion of palimpsest as a driver for decisions around demolitions and interventions to avoid complete erasures could have offered, and still can offer, a fruitful reading and making of the site.

Intangible

In the Burra Charter's definition, place may have tangible and intangible dimensions.[29] The South African Heritage Resources Agency guidelines allow for the inclusion of the intangible in the process of understanding place. Events, symbolic associations, way of life, the evolution or pattern of development of our society, are all protected.[30] Uncovering the intangible is difficult to source and measure. It is an expensive and time-consuming process and requires skills not usually held by heritage practitioners. Hence the default position of focusing on the architectural artefact often prevails.

Conservation involves all the processes of looking after a place so as to retain its cultural significance. According to Article 2 of the Burra Charter, conservation is based on a respect for the existing fabric, use, associations and meanings.[31] It requires a cautious approach of changing as much as necessary but as little as possible. Heritage conservation needs to be more strategic in what it defines as requiring conservation; it cannot be a blanket approach with protection based on whether a building is over 60 years old;

public and residential buildings need to be weighted differently; and once spaces and places of significance are identified, the conservation strategy needs to be framed accordingly.

Memory

Peggy Delport refers to the District Six Museum as a place for working with memory.[32] Homi Bhabha talks of the act of rethinking the self in the company of others who have similar experiences, the building of communal memory.[33] Mbembe notes that 'Each of us needs the memory of the other. We will have to learn together, and, in so doing, to repair together the world's fabric and its visage.'[34] Framing the museum, that is Constitution Hill, as a place of making communal memory, of oral history and of embodied experience, offers the institution a vital purpose. At the Women's Jail prisoner workshop, the facilitator Audrey Brown said: 'finding out how many people had been held there made me realise how important this place was to the memory of black people. It was a fearful privilege to walk with them, to hear them scream with anguish and finally listen to their memories.'[35]

The building artefacts that make up Constitution Hill all fall into the category of structures that memorialise 'a history of specific power relations', where the past is 'constructed from an apartheid and colonial perspective'.[36] Does the preservation of these structures reinforce a system of power? The difference with buildings as artefacts in a museum realm is that they can be made to represent both power and resistance. The Hill narrative through its museum function speaks of the liberation struggle's resistance to oppression, but how does this extend to contemporary struggles?

The spaces need to be problematised, and the site's reconciliation theme risks liberal stasis where the narrative is rendered meaningless when seen in tension with the everyday and structural inequalities. The site needs to include voices of difference that do not fit the rainbow nation construct, voices that consistently contest the prevailing hegemony.

The layer of interpretation that is allowed in the context of a museum affords the potential to reinterpret, rewrite and shift the narrative from one of oppression to one of resilience. The effect of the past on the present is a process to unravel; it needs to be made, to be told so as to be shared, to be grieved. But it also needs to be unmade as an act of liberation, of envisioning a future that is better, an unmaking that is transformative.

The museum and the site need to be porous and receptive to the making and unmaking project. But how do the buildings as artefacts achieve this overwriting? Mapping loss as a process of remapping and reimagining is a challenge to those hegemonic forces that drew the maps and legislated the spaces in the first place.[37] The site acts as a bridge between an unstable past and an uncertain future.[38]

This idea of a precinct pregnant with possibilities and still alert to difference, to change, a porous architecture, a platform that allows a space for process and progress, is compelling.

Reparation

The site is seething with stories of trauma and injustice. Can the development of the site offer a form of reparation? Can it be constructed with mechanisms that make amends for the individual and collective trauma of the site? The symbolism of the Constitutional Court on this site was invoked as an act of repair and the museum as an act of healing. What amenity, what easing of trauma, does the site offer?

Gevisser states that 'what needs to be embedded into Constitution Hill's surfaces is a process rather than ideology: the belief that debate, reason, interaction, negotiation, and reconciliation will make the future happen'.[39] In order for this process to play out, the site needs prompts, platforms and facilities to allow change and transformation to be enacted here.

Mbembe asks, 'In what ways can their lingering past be revealed, contested, reimagined or expunged? How do we avoid the commodification of culture and envisage a different economy, different social relations.'[40] The need to 'demythologize that history and put it to rest' is the work of Constitution Hill. He goes on to argue:

> The decolonization of buildings and of public spaces is inseparable from the democratization of access. Such a right to belong, such a rightful sense of ownership has nothing to do with charity or hospitality. It has nothing to do with the liberal notion of 'tolerance'. It has nothing to do with me having to assimilate into a culture that is not mine as a precondition of my participating in the public life of the institution. It has all to do with ownership of a space that is a public, common good.[41]

Current and recent event programming at Constitution Hill is much more visceral in achieving this notion of a 'space of transformation'. Afropunk, the Brooklyn-based music festival that celebrates black alternative subcultures, aligns with Constitution Hill's ethos of inclusion, diversity and social justice. The Afropunk music festival of 2018 and 2019 hosted at Constitution Hill allowed the site to be a platform and safe space for difference and self-expression, and was a powerful contrast to the oppressive history of the site. The annual Constitution Hill Human Rights Festival similarly engages with the contrast between the past and present of the place, and offers a space for active citizenship where the tensions of social infrastructural inequalities meet the ideals of the Constitution. The Basha Uhuru youth festival, which commemorates the youth of the 1976 Soweto student uprising, is an annual event started in 2012, hosted and developed by Constitution Hill. Here again the synergy of place and programme has opened the site to new and young audiences, and has allowed a process of rehabilitation and unintended catharsis. It is through lived experiences like these that people build their heritage. These events are part of a largely young and black cohort with a strong voice of self-expression and identity. This is the cultural shift not accounted for during the planning of the precinct. The precinct was not designed appropriately, with the amenities, flexibilities, connections and parcels of varying space sizes to facilitate and encourage such events. The reliance of the precinct plan on the museum to satisfy cultural requirements was short-sighted, for the museum is a limited typology with limited ability for audience engagement and expression. The importance of the events and programming at Constitution Hill is the ability to tap into youth culture and engagement – bringing the site alive in ways that were not previously imagined.

Narratives of oppression are a burden to the project of renewal – the subject of tyranny risks being caught in a second exploitation and becoming a barrier to change and growth. But the erasure of the ATB and spaces of black incarceration in this context is a second act of violation. The demolition of the building and the erasure of memory are also the loss of the potential of acknowledging the pain of the past with the capacity of healing.

The spaces of the architectural design and urban framework opened up through the demolition of the ATB are problematic beyond the argument of conservation. The square in front of the court entrance connects to the larger open park space through a narrow triangular stepped walkway. The decision to turn the site of the ATB into a square and to build adjacent to the Number Four prison cuts the site into parcels that are poorly connected and further complicated by the steepness of the site. Architectural and urban design decisions in master-planning the site were driven by ideas of demonumentalising the court building and, in so doing, offered a too small and unwieldly Constitution Square. A large public square that could hold mass gatherings, events and protests and host the voice of 'We the people of South Africa' is a stark omission of the precinct. A large space of gathering and activism could have given the precinct a public identity and platform.

The open space in front of the court library cannot find synergy or connection with the other open spaces of the precinct. The idea of a consolidated site with the construction of a singular super-basement is overly prescriptive and has hampered the larger site's ability to attract development. The master-planning decisions made at the inception of the project are difficult to overturn. Renewal projects on the site are spatially complex and the difficulty is further compounded by the multiple stakeholders and the intragovernmental ownership structure.

While these constructed urban impediments make the site difficult to reimagine, there are projects under way to renew and refresh the precinct – the We the People Park, a visitors' centre and conference building, and the Museum of the Constitution. There is scope for strategic architectural and spatial insertions that can repair connections and offer adaptable infrastructures that are able to act as a platform for public engagement through programming.

How can these and future insertions shift the performativity of the site? How does the oppressive history cradled in the prison and the promise of the liberal Constitution form a hybrid – a platform that is about difference, ideas from the outside of hegemony, temporally ex-centric, interruptive and in-between?

How can the site act as a catalyst for critical engagement between the foundations of the past and an imaginary of the future, that shifts beyond a rhetoric of reconciliation and the promise of renewal? Can new narratives of leisure, culture and identity offer new performativity and visitor engagement? From an architectural perspective of programming space, and taking a cue from the recent events and programming of the

Constitution Hill Development Company, the site can offer platforms that are safe spaces to thrash out ideas, spaces to which black people and marginalised groups feel a sense of belonging, amenities that give emerging voices the space and process for both agency and leisure. One thinks here of a square to gather in, a field to perform in, an auditorium for dialogue, a new archive as resource and repository for projects of counter-narratives, recentring and transformation, a library as a medium for connectivity to information, allocation of affordable housing, infrastructure for events, fairs, conferencing, markets and concerts, allowances for entrepreneurship and economic opportunity for small and emerging enterprises, all within a clear revisioning and strategic development framework for decision-making.

The symbolic fall of Rhodes has had significant cultural resonance globally and in South Africa. In my reading as architectural critic of recent postgraduate work at the Graduate School of Architecture and the University of the Witwatersrand School of Architecture and Planning, colonial symbols in urban spaces are questioned more rigorously by students. There is a strong emerging voice critical of colonial representations of power, incensed by the narratives of exploitation, energised by the narratives of resistance, and confident in expressing black identity, culture and heritage.

Heritage practice needs to evolve and shift to allow more complex responses; to be less precious about the heritage artefact in allowing it to be adapted and reused, in ways that are transformational – an induced change and righting of the inherently problematic socio-structural conditions. Lesley Lokko, curator of the 18th International Architecture Exhibition at the Venice Biennale, refers in a reflection to the architectural canon as incomplete. 'The exhibition is a portal, a gate, a pathway, a channel, it places a non-European perspective at the heart of its story but it does not do so by overwriting the existing narrative. The story of architecture is not wrong, it is incomplete.'[42] The missing African idiom may be about working not on a clean slate but at the interstitial and through the liminal, with the capacity for duality – not about erasing but re-forming, not about façade but performance.

The lesson this exploration and critique of heritage decisions offers is the need for heritage spatial practice to confront its inherent bias and expand its framework and tool set. We need methodologies of cartography and palimpsest and instruments that challenge the reading of dominant, colonial, capitalist and segregated urban landscapes. Such counter-mapping could give marginalised narratives voice and reveal alternative histories of place as a basis for catalytic urban interventions. We can absorb from such sites of complex, contested narratives and palimpsest the impetus for imagining spatial urban transformations that redress the injustices of the past and engage with difference. Through insertions, adaptations, temporal, infrastructural and adaptable designs, and adaptive reuse, heritage projects can reconfigure the urban landscape and offer innovative, transformative, spatial and programmatic ways to intervene.

Chapter Five
Bantfu Netindzawo (People and Places)

Solam Mkhabela with Hiten Bawa

Alexandra: A Backstory *is a graphic novel about Bantfu netindzawo, from which this selection of panels that follow have been extracted. It tells how the Johannesburg suburb of Alexandra became what it is today, and how its spatial layout affects daily life. It simultaneously voices the history of the millions of black South Africans once treated as a pestilence, eyesore and nuisance when not employed for white profit or comfort. This pictorial tale unearths African voices that tell the story of Johannesburg from the 'twilight zone', the murky domain between what is official or legal and bylaw-breaching, on-the-ground operations. The voices are those of the agents who are the lifeblood of the daily street flow; they create, occupy, transform and service the zone on the margins of the economy and society. They speak of their past and present struggles, specifically their need to adapt to the spatial hostility they work in. This story is shaped by the people who breathe, work and are ultimately intrinsic to the side road of the activity street, which lies at the heart of everyday Johannesburg life. Its panels tell the turbulent and manipulated history of eGoli (Place of Gold, as the city is called in isiZulu) from the perspective of their daily life on the street in Alexandra and the road connecting it to the city CBD. Image compositions merge photographs, maps, historical documentary, memory and observation. The panels are intended to grapple with critical and complex contingencies of citizenry. They address the diversity of internal contradictions – brought into concentrated emphasis by apartheid – associated with identity, culture, ownership and belonging.*

BANTFU NETINDZAWO (PEOPLE AND PLACES)

SOLAM MKHABELA WITH HITEN BAWA

BANTFU NETINDZAWO (PEOPLE AND PLACES)

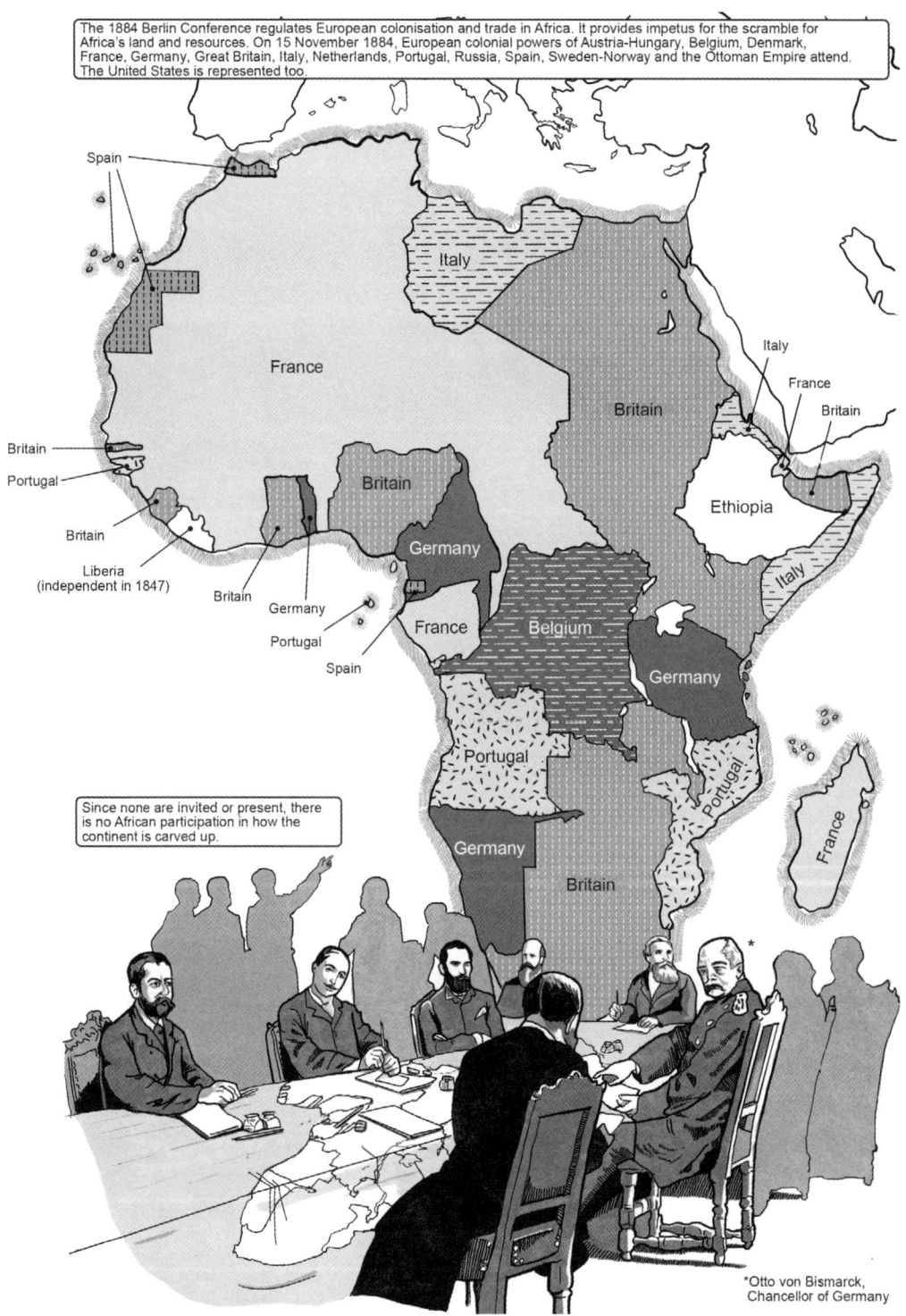

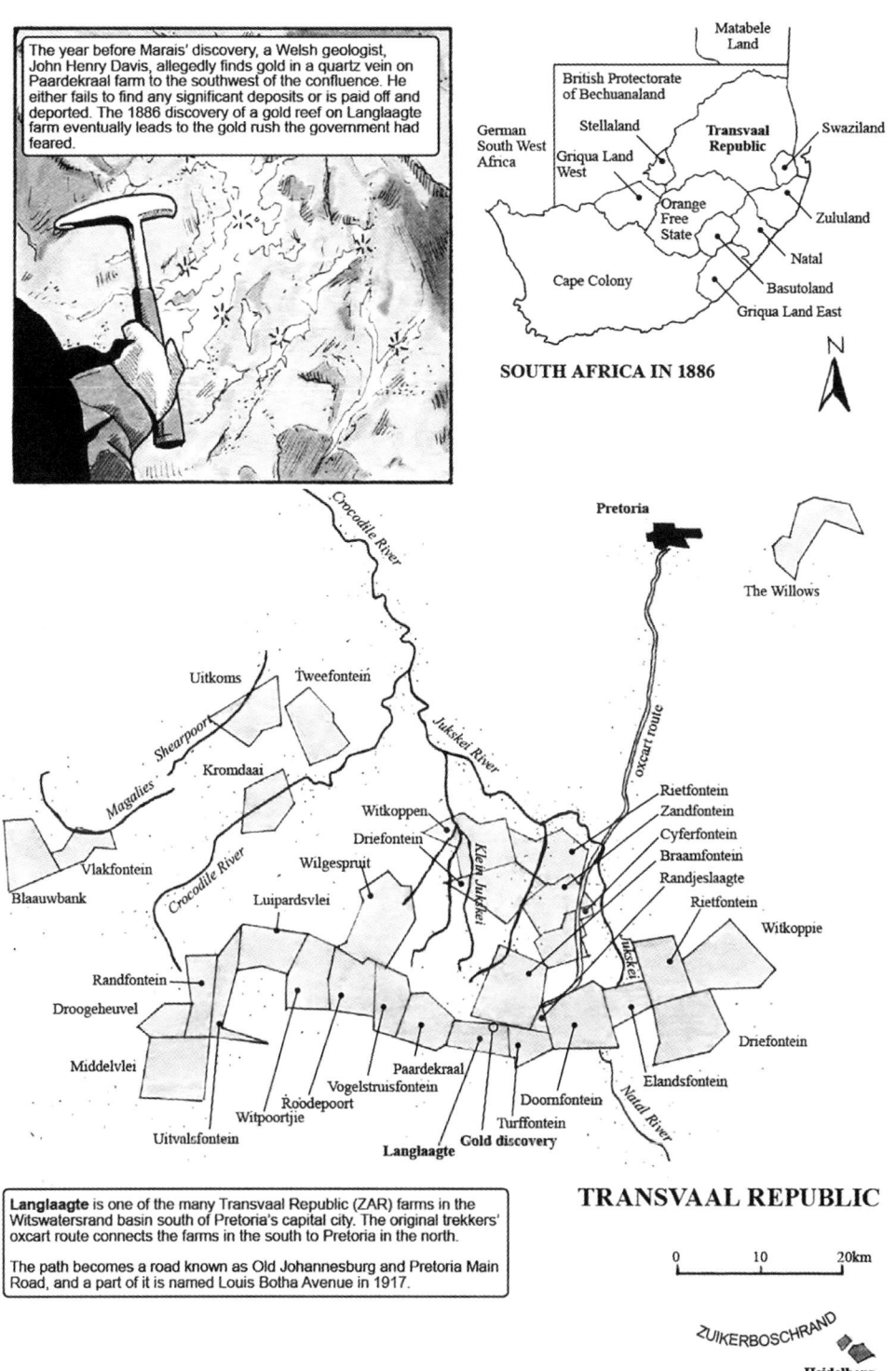

BANTFU NETINDZAWO (PEOPLE AND PLACES)

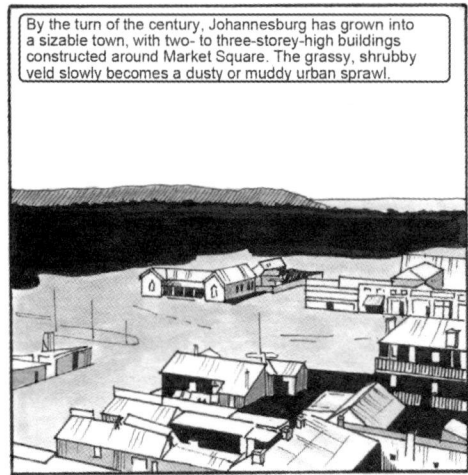

By the turn of the century, Johannesburg has grown into a sizable town, with two- to three-storey-high buildings constructed around Market Square. The grassy, shrubby veld slowly becomes a dusty or muddy urban sprawl.

Simultaneously, the mining industry is expanding with larger, towering mine shafts fitted with industrial machinery sprouting along the reef. Mining ever deeper beneath the surface, gold extraction accelerates, and mountains of mining waste transform the Johannesburg skyline.

In 1905, Herbert B. Papenfus purchases a farm called Cyferfontein 2, located 12km northeast of Market Square, and hopes to sell 338 lots to white buyers.

The plots are initially surveyed in a grid layout with two parks and a square in the centre.

Papenfus has little success selling these plots. Then, in 1911, he obtains official approval to re-divide the land into 2308 plots measuring 42 x 25m. One of his relatives, Stephanus Papenfus, begins selling the plots exclusively to black Africans and coloureds (neither black nor white).

In 1912 the area is proclaimed a Native Township and named Alexandra.

BANTFU NETINDZAWO (PEOPLE AND PLACES)

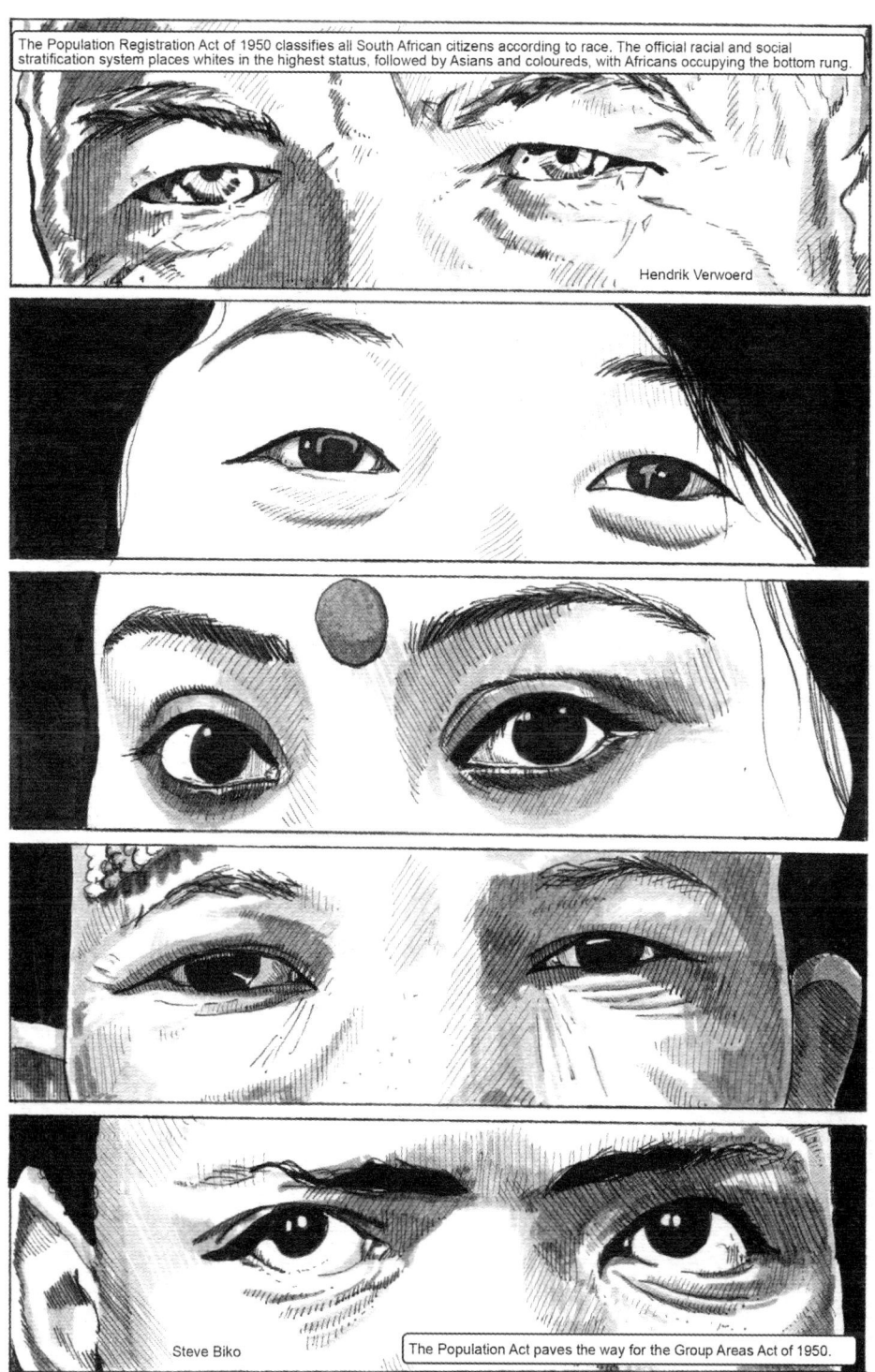

BANTFU NETINDZAWO (PEOPLE AND PLACES)

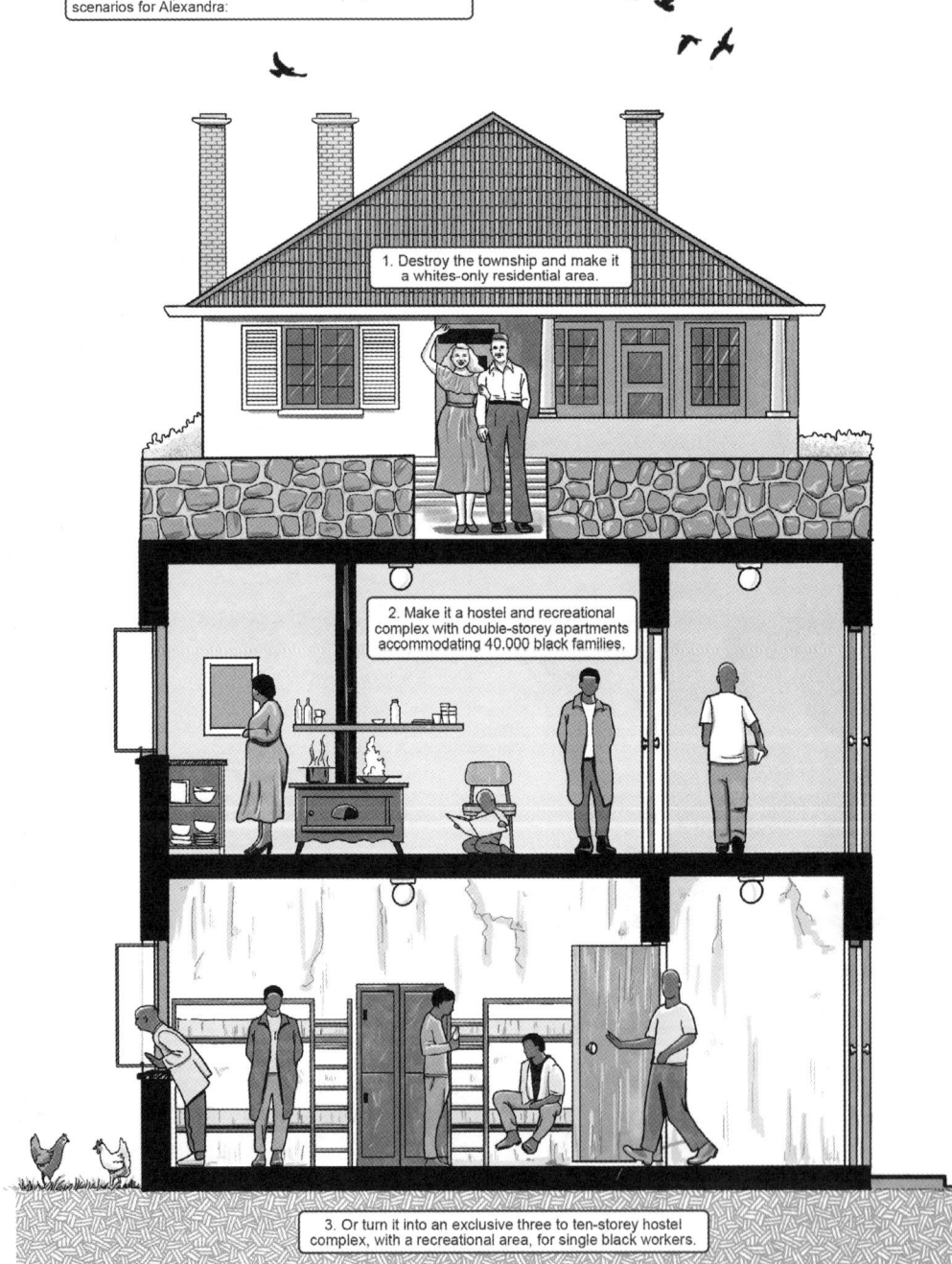

Part Two

Buildings as Place

Chapter Six

Speculative Desire and Residential Reappropriation: Johannesburg's Ponte City from Apartheid to the Present

Stefan Chavez-Norgaard

> 'We'd like to tell you a clean tall story ...'
> – *Advertisement for a custom window-cleaning service in a 1975 technical building document titled 'Ponte: The Tallest Residential Building in Africa'.*[1]

Ponte, constructed in 1975, was envisioned at the tail end of the 'grand apartheid' era. A hollow, high-modernist cylindrical tower looming over north-east Johannesburg, Ponte was framed in the technical building report, from which the epigraph above is drawn, as a building for the era's visionaries, the system's crème de la crème. Today, Ponte remains Africa's tallest residential skyscraper (see Figures 6.1 and 6.2).

The 1975 technical building report for Ponte presents itself as a banal, technical document (see Figure 6.3).[2] It notes with thoroughness the building site's dimensions, relevant access points, and myriad development, financing and investment vehicles required to construct the site. Yet visual advertisements from involved vendors buttress the report itself, and are a lens into the immensity and absurdity of the project. Vendors advertise

Figure 6.1: Ponte City Apartments loom over north-east Johannesburg. (Stefan Chavez-Norgaard, 2022)

Figure 6.2: Ponte City's hollow, cylindric, two-way panopticon includes a prominent internal security booth. (Stefan Chavez-Norgaard, 2022)

Ponte-specific custom mini-safes and 'safe door' designs, aerial communal television installation systems (likely for the building's upper floors, where the luxury units were housed), and custom window-cleaning services provided by the Riggers Steeplejacks company.

In this 1975 document, Ponte's architects, contractors and management team wanted to tell a *clean* story, one that was rational and logical, about the design choices underpinning this behemoth apartment complex. They also wanted to tell a *tall* story, one highlighting the building's sheer size, material grandeur, palatial luxury. Indeed, the racialised utopian imaginaries underpinning Ponte's design and its subsequent construction represent a concrete manifestation of the most panoptic of apartheid desires: paranoid control of space, ethno-racial homogeneity in social relations and reproduction, and an intense desire to shape South Africans' subjectivities. From a luxury penthouse apartment on the top floors of Ponte, a resident – in that era only imaged as white – would have enjoyed wine cellars, a private sauna, patio braai areas, and private roof decks, while 'servants' (service workers) living in tiny rooftop sub-units worked unseen.[3] 'Servants' was the term employed by the 1975 report and would have been, in that era, the only way black South Africans accessed the building. Yet Ponte's history is neither clean nor tall and linear. Contestations over power, dignity and livelihood in Johannesburg come to life by exploring the disjuncture between imaginative representations of Ponte – speculative, racialised fantasies of profit and largesse – and human-scale efforts to reappropriate Ponte as a site of urban living.

Existing scholarship on Ponte City has placed the building and its layered history within 20th-century architectural and social theory and associated scholarship.[4] Countless newspaper and popular press articles as well as films and artistic products have likewise documented Ponte's changing demographic composition and symbolic meaning over time.[5] South African urban theorists and social scientists have fruitfully explored the changing demographic and socio-spatial composition of the neighbourhoods surrounding Ponte, like Berea, Yeoville and Hillbrow.[6] During the 'grand-apartheid' era, from around 1948 to 1976,[7] South African architects and planners developed spatial formations in conversation with the rational, rectilinear approaches of high modernism globally, yet unique in aspects of its meticulous design for a distinctive racial-caste system.[8] Ponte, envisioned in the early 1970s and completed in 1975, drew on tropes of state-led mid-century modernism and surveillance. Though its brochures espoused luxurious living, by the time it was constructed, many of Johannesburg's wealthiest white elite had left the city for its suburbs.[9] Instead, many of Ponte's first residents were members of an aspiring new Afrikaner elite from the rural south and east of the country, newcomers to urban life and 'informally desegregated' communities.[10] Nonetheless, Johannesburg's City Council, private property managers and investors were key actors promoting Ponte's aspirational existence and form.[11] The never-realised business case for Ponte rested on public–private collaboration and a speculative desire to leverage rent gaps and cycles of devaluation to develop central Johannesburg, desires that were as ambitious as the tower itself.[12]

Just as Ponte was completed, social upheaval erupted on 16 June 1976 in Soweto, marking a turning point in the hegemonic nature of South African apartheid. In Ponte and its neighbourhoods of Hillbrow and Berea, latent racial and class mixing gave way to an official state designation as a 'grey area'.[13] By the 1980s, Alan Morris[14] and Tanja Winkler[15] document how that designation led to building and neighbourhood redlining, with dire consequences for residents: a lack of public services and bans on state-backed mortgages and financial lending. Property values plummeted. Ponte, a self-contained island, would go from housing an aspirational elite of Afrikaner nationalist society in 1975 to being declared a vacant, 'hijacked' building of squatters and informal residents by as early as 1978.[16] In short course, Ponte contained representations of both utopian imaginaries and exaggerated fears about racial hierarchy, harmony and integration, produced and reproduced through media narratives about the building. It became a symbol of South Africa's broader transition from apartheid to democracy. Because Ponte has been a site of both hubristic ambition and everyday survival, of apartheid power and resident reappropriation, studying its history affords a window into everyday struggles for dignity and voice in Johannesburg today.

In this chapter, I explore multiple reappropriations of Johannesburg's Ponte City apartment complex from its construction in the 1970s until today. Such spatial transformations involve a complex and at times contradictory mix of socio-spatial, political-economic and affective and aesthetic forces. I problematise Ponte's formal structure, its architects and the building's early reception in media and archival sources, and consider the building's multiple reappropriations from apartheid into the post-1994 period. Written, audio, visual and cinematic media narratives about Ponte from different historical periods show us the ways that Ponte's residents have adapted and repurposed the building since its modernist origins, inhabiting the building with new and layered aspirations. I conclude by situating Ponte in a contemporary Johannesburg context laden with inequality, gentrification, eviction, social-service instability, threats of real and perceived violence, and renewed postmodern dreams of high-density residential living. Through the lens of reappropriation, Ponte represents a disjointed struggle between speculative desire and resident practices of everyday dwelling, both underpinned by demographic and historical transitions.

I define reappropriation in the built environment as a reclaiming and recontextualisation of spaces originally intended for a vastly different purpose or for different inhabitants. In the context of South Africa's colonial and apartheid pasts, racist and segregated built environments were meticulously envisioned and planned at various scales from the territorial to the interpersonal.[17] There is an urgent need to confront these built sites and their histories; they are often the very container from which imaginative and more democratic alternative futures must spring. Ponte City's reappropriation is, as the term 'reappropriation' itself suggests, deeply in tune with past socio-spatial and political-economic structures. Yet that Ponte's successful reappropriations have often been led by building *users* – rather than by top-down architectural firms or professional elites – suggests that reappropriation has the potential to emerge as an alternative logic of the production of space. For Ponte, it is a logic that transgresses formally permitted circuits of capital, building codes, design guidelines and urban plans. Reappropriation gestures to a popular-democratic mode of city-making that exists in tension with enduring postcolonial legacies and unequal political-economic realities.

Scholars from South Africa and elsewhere have explored resident-led reappropriations. Using the language of 'the imaginative reclamation and reuse of city spaces',[18] 'urban re-arrangements',[19] 'building with ruins and dreams',[20] or 'planning on the edge of reason',[21] the fields of architecture and urban planning are reckoning with spatial transformations occurring at various scales *not* advanced by professional elites. Liza Cirolia and colleagues[22] use the language of 'retrofit city-making' to examine the case of residents' occupation of a vacant hospital building near the Cape Town city centre. They argue that residents have reappropriated a building originally designed for an institutional use and have transformed it into a space that fulfils material needs and acts as a space of adaptation, care and solidarity.[23]

Reappropriation at Ponte exposes a gap between speculative visions grafted onto the building and changing neighbourhood-level socio-spatial and political-economic forces. Indeed, Ponte has been viewed as a sort of aspirational yet inaccurate compass, physically and psychologically guiding long-time Joburgers and newcomers from South Africa and beyond.[24] Yet in its hulking presence, the building is also a reminder of the weight of history and of late-modernist apartheid largesse. Amid these tensions, Ponte emerges in a complex, hybridised form.

Through the lens of Ponte's multiple reappropriations, this chapter looks specifically at the complex interplay of speculative and media imaginings of Ponte, and socio-spatial and political-economic forces driving the building and its changing uses. Similarly linked processes of complex and contradictory relations in the production of space exist globally, shaping the meaning of specific buildings and surrounding neighbourhoods and cities.[25] This chapter builds on critical theoretical work about Ponte and pairs that work with a frame contrasting aspirational imaginings and vernacular form.

Methods include an analysis of official and secondary sources about Ponte; audio, visual and cinematic media engaging Ponte; and interviews and participant observation in the building and locally with artists, residents and building management. Conversations with Mikhael Subotzky and Stephen Hobbs – the former a photographer who worked with Patrick Waterhouse to photograph every apartment in Ponte, and the latter an artist whose experimental projects mirrored suicide from the building in the 1990s – bring the role and effects of artistic representations of the building to light. Time spent staying in a penthouse apartment in Ponte in March 2022 and speaking with representatives of the community group and innovative non-profit organisation Dlala Nje was invaluable for my understanding of Ponte's layered history. Dlala Nje, meaning 'Just Play' in isiZulu, runs a culture, education and youth community hub within Ponte and is led by a passionate team of guides. The organisation also leads tours and walks of Ponte and its surrounding neighbourhoods, offering their own specific narrative of reappropriation about the building and its community.

The chapter opens with a section problematising Ponte's formal structure and the intentions of its architects and design team. The next section situates Ponte's representational imaginings within a city in transition, following the socio-spatial and political-economic context underpinning and justifying the building's construction, as well as resident-centric efforts at reappropriation and the role of media in generating new, at times dystopian, meanings for the building. The final section looks at the post-apartheid era and considers renewed attempts by private developers at enlivening Ponte's speculative imaginings, and considers repurposings to enable everyday life and care in the building today. I conclude by exploring how Ponte concretises varied, contested aspirations. The building is testament to the enduring weight of South Africa's racist and colonial history yet holds the ability to generate and inspire anew.

The Structure

Ponte's original developer was Nasbou Ltd, incorporated in 1959 under CEO Charles Ferreira.[26] Insurance company Sanlam opened a merchant bank called Mercabank and in turn spun off Nasbou as a property development company in the early 1970s.[27] In the final deal through which Ponte was constructed, MDC (Miodownik Development Company) and Mercabank joined forces to finance the building for Nasbou.[28]

Ponte City's hollow, cylindric, two-way panopticon core with a prominent internal security booth – one of the key structural elements for which it became famous – was partly built by happenstance (see Figure 6.2). According to the 1975 'Architect's Report and Building Guide', site problems meant that 'although the site [was] fairly large by city standards, only a small portion of it could be used for the tower block' because portions were removed by the City Council for an aerial flyover, sparking concerns around sunlight, wind, stability and building effect on Johannesburg's cityscape.[29] That said, despite the smaller buildable footprint, architectural team member Rodney Grosskopff reflected that the zoning spatial allowances permitted for a 'colossus of a building' in terms of height.[30] The City of Johannesburg had removed building-height restrictions in previous decades, and the site's comparatively high elevation allowed for fantastic city views.[31] Other choices resulted from stringent City building regulations: 'The building regulations in Johannesburg are such that if the kitchens and bathrooms are not air-conditioned or ventilated, they must [by law] face onto natural light', which led to a 'requirement for an open core'.[32] Indeed, the architectural team led by Manfred Hermer, Mannie Feldman and Rodney Grosskopff chose a cylindrical building form partly because of the small and 'strangely shaped' plot for the building. A circular design would make the project more notable, given that it was expected to dominate Johannesburg's skyline.[33] In addition, notes Grosskopff, 'Manfred had been hankering to do a round tower building for some time'.[34]

Figure 6.3: Ponte's 'Architect's Report' includes summaries from the architects, contractors and management team. ('Ponte: The Tallest Residential Building', 1975, pp. 16–17)

Intended or not, constant and panoptic surveillance – particularly of the building's (black) service workers – became a key structural feature. White residents, by contrast, could 'perform their sophisticated lifestyles' privately, hiding the presence of their black domestic workers.[35] After the architectural team chose a hollow core, they claimed to have made deliberate efforts to account for suicide prevention and 'objects falling from the building', for example by closing and sealing windows in public spaces.[36] This is ironic given the extent to which Ponte's reputation in later years would form around the building being a locus for suicide. The team also framed the building's hollowness as a security feature. Indeed, when discussing security, the building contractors write: 'Ponte is situated … virtually on an island site … A battery of watchmen under the supervision of a Security officer are on duty day and night to protect the residents of Ponte and their possessions. Their activities are controlled by means of specially controlled "clock-in stations".'[37] In the report's 'safety' section, the architects write: 'We have colour coded the floor finishes and paint finishes so that each floor is a different colour to those above and those below it, and being round one can easily observe the access corridors on the opposite side of the circle for a large number of floors, creating a constant supervision as the inhabitants and cleaning staff move along the corridors.'[38] The architectural team seemed to expect that residents might *watch* the cleaners and other service workers as they moved along the corridors. The report continues: 'All access to the residential portion of the building will be … continually staffed by a commissionaire … The only loophole is the fire escape … but entrance will be prohibited by a mechanical locking device.'[39]

Ponte's managers and administration were also paranoid about the building's regular cleaning and maintenance. The 'management and administration' section of the report states: 'A high standard of service is maintained at all times. Internal service of flats is provided daily. One cleaner is required to service a typical floor of 13 flats on an efficient basis. All other areas, including lift lobbies, internal access corridors, and garbage areas are swept twice daily and scrubbed twice weekly.'[40] Ponte's management expected a specific apartheid labour model to persist in perpetuity.

Ponte's verticality was associated with both racial and socio-economic hierarchy. Black service workers ('servants') were to dwell in cramped quarters at the base of the inner core, while penthouse apartments enjoyed

1970s shag carpeting and large floor plans, with sweeping vistas. Yet the City of Johannesburg's Department of Development Planning did not approve the initial plan. Wrote planning director J.C. de Villiers in a letter to the City Engineer's Office: 'The Bantu quarters [an apartheid-era term for black residents' quarters] are situated on the same floor level as the caretaker's flat,' a design not in keeping with apartheid-era segregation as the caretaker was presumed to be white.[41] Moreover, City planners were concerned about ratios of black domestic workers and white residents. After much discussion, the City approved an amended plan that required a specific ratio of black 'servants' to white residents; the architects were allowed additional buildable area to design further housing for domestic workers in the building's top three floors, a design more in line with other Johannesburg buildings of the time (see Figure 6.4).[42] Other regulations shaped the building's physical design. Grosskopff notes in a retrospective interview: 'We had some mad by-laws in those days … The sills [of the black domestic workers' apartments] had to be above six foot so that they [the black staff] couldn't look at the white apartments.'[43] Subotzky has examined correspondence with the Department of Native Affairs on Ponte, finding the architects and the Department debating where black South Africans might create the 'least visual nuisance'.[44] The workings of these compromises between the architects and the state speak to apartheid-era rigid racial hierarchy and segregation, reflected in the building's own envisioned vertical hierarchy.

For the white-only residential units, the 1975 Architect's Report proposed a 'Village Concept', denoting a difference in socio-economic status vertically, with the lower floors, primarily bachelor pads and studios, unfurnished, and the upper floors furnished.[45] Starting on the 35th floor, the unit plans changed, and the furnishings were upgraded. Floors 41–6 contained 'luxury flats' and floors 47–50 contained penthouses, described as 'luxury three-bedroomed flats'.[46] But the crown jewel of Ponte was what the architects called the '*Pallazzo-en-Paradiso*' (sic), or 'ultra-luxury four-bedroomed triplex flats'.[47] These apartments came fitted with wine cellars, saunas, patio braai garden areas, en suite roof decks, and private access to an on-site tennis court.[48] Grosskopff notes that there were also economic reasons justifying this vertical hierarchy: the team was able to borrow money at 8 per cent return and calculated that a high number of bachelor flats would provide the best possible return; larger apartments, however, involved

Figure 6.4: While most of the black service workers were housed deep in the building's core, some domestic workers dwelled in cramped quarters at the topmost floors of Ponte. Whether at the bottom or top, black staff were envisioned as invisible in Ponte's vertical socio-economic hierarchy. (Stefan Chavez-Norgaard, 2022)

less turnover and built a more stable, permanent community. Internal calculations projected just over 10 per cent return across the building's 500 envisioned flats.[49]

The material choice to use raw concrete was in keeping with the design team's schooling in modernist and brutalist architecture.[50] The team used a shuttering technique to build the tower floor by floor, complete with cranes and service elevators producing long queues. Although apartheid labour laws permitted only white building-trades workers in oversight roles, Grosskopff reflected on how 'accomplished Black tradesmen' played a key design role and had to make themselves scarce in the event of a government building inspector.[51]

Ponte City was built as a conspicuous 'white whale', aiming to achieve luxury, security and exclusion all at once. Indeed, a 1973 promotional brochure proclaimed: 'It is the ultimate in chic and sophistication. Join us on a guided tour of a building that brings Utopia to life and proves that South Africa has caught up with the world's urban centres ... You get carried away by the exhilarating feeling of immensity. Because the dimensions are huge and, if you are not familiar with the whole layout, you can easily lose your way. But have no fear.'[52]

Ponte's formal structure was designed to exist as an island or sanctuary. Like other high modernist buildings,[53] Ponte was self-contained. It included a base complex 50-shop mall, with cafes, bowling alley and a concert venue,[54] a full on-site security team at entry and exit, sweeping views across the Witwatersrand, and even plans for a ski slope through the brutalist building's columns.[55] Ponte was designed for easy entry and exit by car: 'For ease of management a highly sophisticated parking control has been installed ... Tenants of Ponte are supplied with computerised parking cards ... via the spiral ramp at Hadfield Terrace.'[56]

Yet from the very beginning, Ponte's envisioned representation did not work as intended, with the brutalist design finding itself home to 'uncontrollable spaces' and a 'nexus of illegal activities'.[57] Though the building was 90 per cent pre-let and fully occupied by 1975, and despite the 'battery of watchmen' and paranoid cleaning regimens, the building was host to a number of de facto informal practices, like tenants squatting in the building, seemingly as early as 1978.[58] Ponte, by its own measure, sought to provide an island of predictability and a beacon of security to a privileged few in an unequal society. By that measure it surely failed. Yet the architectural and design team that built Ponte City also built other buildings in Johannesburg and South Africa, and remain active today in 2022. The architectural team led by Hermer were significant cultural critics and interveners in South Africa's built environment. The building is a touchstone that reveals the team's complex motivations and subjectivities.

Hermer & Grosskopff Architects envisioned Ponte as a cutting-edge symbol of a 'modern' apartheid South African society. Yet their vision for a South African utopian project was perhaps contradictory from the start, dramatically mismatched to the changing spatial and political-economic contours of its surrounding neighbourhoods, city and country. Understanding Ponte's architects affords insight into the gaps between Ponte City's speculative premise and its resultant form.

Manfred Hermer was born in 1915 and studied architecture in Johannesburg at the University of the Witwatersrand. He worked alongside Ralph Wesley Green (Green & Hermer) and as part of the Orange Free State Provincial Institute of Architects (OFSPIA), now called the Free State Institute of Architects (FSIA). By the 1960s, Hermer was considered an influential South African architect, particularly in his design and envisioning of major public spaces and theatres, including Johannesburg's Market Theatre and the Civic Theatre Complex.[59] Hermer also constructed buildings in Durban and Cape Town, and worked internationally, designing country clubs, entertainment centres, industrial buildings and private hospitals, including the Ashkelon hospital in Israel.

Starting in 1969, Hermer joined the firm Hermer & Grosskopff Architects as principal. The firm also included Mannie Feldman; Hermer, Grosskopff and Feldman would together constitute the team that designed Ponte City.[60] Hermer & Grosskopff was the foundation for the practice today known as GLH, which is still an active business working in South Africa and globally.[61] Together, the trio constructed projects in Durban, Cape Town, Continental Europe, Tel Aviv and elsewhere. Grosskopff, still alive, continues to give interviews and commentary about Ponte, which was initially seen by critics as a conspicuous brutalist reminder of apartheid ambitions but has recently been reviewed more favourably by historians and architects.[62]

Hermer and his team seemed to hold contradictory views about apartheid and racial hierarchy. They embraced the 'alternative', 'cosmopolitan' Hillbrow neighbourhood as the ideal location for Ponte City. This neighbourhood, then known as the 'Greenwich Village of South Africa', was the most densely populated neighbourhood in Johannesburg and one of the few places where South Africans and new immigrants of different income and racial backgrounds lived with a degree of racial integration in the 1970s and 1980s.[63] Grosskopff, reflecting retrospectively on the team choosing to build Ponte here, said, 'Hillbrow was really the centre of life,' and has since embraced Hillbrow's comparative informality.[64] About the neighbourhood, a Ponte resident from the 2010s and guide with the community organisation Dlala Nje, told me: '[Hillbrow] was the place … in the early '70s. Everyone came through here. The nightlife of Yeoville, Berea, Hillbrow, [it was] super luxury, super vibey. The Telkom tower used to operate at that time as a two-floor revolving restaurant and nightclub. Some of South Africa's biggest businesses nowadays, they actually started in Hillbrow.'[65] This Dlala Nje framing of Ponte, which at the time functioned in its solid, impervious built form as a segregated space *within* Hillbrow, plays on a specific nostalgic appreciation for apartheid-era Ponte as part of the community organisation's efforts to reappropriate the building's meaning and value today.

During this time, Hermer and Grosskopff served as active social critics, weighing in on public debates about apartheid and segregation. Both architects were also authors. Hermer wrote *The Passing of Pageview* in 1978 as a biting critique of the apartheid-era Group Areas Act, which determined the urban areas where different racial groups could reside and conduct business, even while working collaboratively with powerful apartheid officials on construction sites. The Act also provided the legal framework for the forced removal of black residents from urban areas declared 'white' by the state, and for the destruction of 'grey areas', or zones of racial mixing, such as the Johannesburg neighbourhoods of Pageview and Sophiatown.

Mannie Feldman, the second principal architect who designed Ponte, was also a noted socialite. According to Stephen Hobbs, who grew up family friends with Feldman and his wife Anne, the couple had an 'iconic physical presence'.[66] Feldman was very tall and always stood out in a crowd, and both he and Anne, with their expertly coiffed hair and distinctive glasses, were recognisable fixtures of the social and cultural landscape in late 20th-century Johannesburg.[67] The couple's memorable appearance and social elevation gave them notoriety in a distinctively modernist way. Hobbs said: '[Mannie and Anne Feldman] were public figures, or at least socially perceived as such.'[68]

Rodney Grosskopff was the third, junior architect working on Ponte City. Grosskopff's book *Carved in Stone* (2010) presents a 'series of profiles on some of the famous characters who helped develop and mould the history and culture of South Africa ... They have two things in common: They were all Freemasons and members of the same Masonic Lodge, Lodge De Goede Hoop, in Cape Town.'[69] The book includes a profile of Francis William Reitz, a former president of the Free State Republic who tried to prevent the outbreak of the Anglo-Boer War.[70] Grosskopff writes: 'When it was clear that the Boers could not win, Reitz was called on to play his most important role, that of winning the peace. He was tireless in advising, translating and debating the best terms for the Transvaal ... One cannot help wondering if [Reitz] had been stronger and wiser whether he could have achieved his aims without bloodshed and hatred.'[71] Might Grosskopff believe that architecture – buildings, built forms and spatial plans – could 'win the peace' without 'bloodshed and hatred'?

Situating Ponte: Appropriation and Reappropriation in a City in Transition

Ponte's construction took place at the tail end of the architectural and planning era of 'high' or 'grand' apartheid, ill-fit for its moment. Ponte resonates with what Clive Chipkin calls 'Johannesburg Style',[72] Reyner Banham calls 'the New Brutalism',[73] and Bryan Stringer frames as 'chasing late modernism'.[74] Ponte was not designed in isolation. We may understand Ponte in visual conversation with Johannesburg's Trust Bank Building (1970), Carlton Centre (1973) and IBM Tower (1976), among other structures. As Stringer argues, all of these structures, as well as Ponte, were marked by Euro-American aspiration.[75] These architectural drivers fostered and sustained a tower typology that continues to define Johannesburg. According to Stringer: 'The massive concrete, brick and glass structures popping up may not have been beautiful, but the viewer can still feel the weight, and the imposition of the structure.'[76] Denise Lim, citing Chipkin, reveals how these New Brutalist techniques loomed large in architect Mannie Feldman's training and inspiration: '[Feldman was known for] his sense of drama, geometry and monumental scale [which] had been acquired in Ernö Goldfinger's atelier, in London, where he had worked after qualifying at Wits. Like Goldfinger, Feldman saw buildings as giant sculptural forms modelled to promote vigorous expressionism.'[77]

What Chipkin calls 'the great apartheid building boom', marked by such 'vigorous expressionism', was most successful in the 1960s.[78] By as early as 1967, Sandton City was under development,[79] and the metropolitan area's newest sites of elite property speculation were in the Northern suburbs.[80] Areas like Hillbrow, Berea and the Central Business District (CBD), and their New Brutalist buildings, quickly passed their prime. Timothy Hart writes of growing socio-economic differences within South Africa's white population, forming a 'factorial ecology' of Johannesburg separating Northern suburbs from city neighbourhoods.[81] Ponte, while perhaps envisioned in one moment, existed in another. Late 20th-century urban speculation in Johannesburg valorised not modernist monstrosities but peripheral 'edge cities' spiralling outward.[82] Accordingly, despite its iconic presence, Ponte's symbolic and representational meaning jarred with the inhabited, vernacular meaning of its built form.

Brian Larkin examines how 'infrastructures, as technical objects, take on *form* ... both ubiquitously visible yet absent from analytic consideration. Form is thus a relation between humans and technology ... the medium where infrastructure and user meet.'[83] Larkin continues: 'Form leads us to the question of political aesthetics – the way that aesthetics, broadly conceived, establishes a political force enabling and contesting various kinds of authority that circulate in the world.'[84] Ponte City is one such built form that shapes users' subjectivities, about physical power and the rigidity of apartheid. Ponte City was designed to embody largesse and a certain (exclusionary) conception of modernity. Instead, its inhabited meaning as 'concrete fear' embodied a political aesthetic of paranoia. Specific construction and design choices illustrate this embodiment, like the different coloured finishings for each floor, or the 'battery of Watchmen' that surveilled the hollow building 'day and night'.[85] Ponte also embodied a political aesthetic of rigidity, one that would later doom the apartheid state.

Grand apartheid-era spatial interventions with New Brutalist design features often took the form of what James Scott calls 'High Modernism'. Scott examines how knowledge that aims to be scalable, generalising, propositional and 'scientific' fails as it meets inevitably unscalable, organic world systems.[86] Ponte was designed to be orderly and cater to an upwardly mobile sector of the nation's small white elite. Yet while Ponte was among the first places where a space of extreme attempted biopolitical apartheid control imploded, counter-conducts had long before emerged across South Africa. Ponte was not merely constructed by private architects; it was fashioned, embodying specific political rationalities, and stands today as a reminder of those rationalities.[87] As Ponte's promotional brochure states, welcoming residents to the new building in 1973: 'Have no fear, the generous expanse, the serenity and beauty of it all, the smooth functioning of all procedures and processes take a load off your mind, make you feel relaxed and cheerful.'[88]

It is telling that Ponte was built with such extreme rationalities in mind and yet was among the first spaces in which apartheid subjugation broke down. Here, socio-spatial and political-economic logics of the production of space jarred and reappropriation emerged within the cracks of Ponte's vision. Gregory Marinic writes how quickly Ponte went from a container of safety and luxury to a transgressive subversion of apartheid: 'By the late 1970s, Ponte City became an important contributor to the racial integration of Hillbrow … Noticing this shift towards diversity, the minister of Community Development declared [Ponte and its Hillbrow neighbourhood] a "scandal and slum" … [It] embodied the antithesis of Apartheid.'[89] Whether ironic or inevitable, Ponte quickly transformed from a sanctuary of apartheid largesse to a symbol of the regime's impending demise. Reappropriations were at play in Ponte before the building even finished construction.

Ponte quickly transcended its planned residential use. The economic and property-management, development-boosterism and political-aesthetic cases for Ponte were all speculative and in turn unrealised, and the building was never profitable.[90] Flats initially expected to be sold became predominantly renter-occupied and the building's occupants exceeded official capacity limits. Ned Temko cites a 1978 newspaper article which reported that 'hundreds of coloureds and Indians were flooding into the white flatland' and living in 'the luxury Ponte block' under assumed white names.[91] According to Temko: '[Ponte management] said they could not tell the difference between various race groups as many of the coloured people appeared to be Lebanese or Portuguese.'[92] Ponte and Hillbrow were increasingly reappropriated as spaces of latent, implicit miscegenation.

As explained to me by a Dlala Nje guide, himself engaging a contemporary narrative about Ponte that is part of a specific reappropriation project advanced by the organisation and others, the cosmopolitanism of Hillbrow and Berea underpins Ponte's decline:

> These [white] people [of Hillbrow, Yeoville, and Berea] were open-minded. They started falling in love with Indians, Black people. And some of the pubs, restaurants, clubs, ended up allowing mixed races to party together, dine together. But, as soon as the apartheid government heard of it ... they started to barge into people's doors, at around 12 midnight just to check if it was still 'whites' only'.[93]

This was, of course, an impossible exercise. Yet the apartheid government nonetheless made things very complicated for Hillbrow, Berea and Yeoville residents into the late 1980s.

By the late 1980s, South Africa's apartheid state declared the three neighbourhoods surrounding and including Ponte – Hillbrow, Berea and Yeoville – 'grey areas'. The grey-area designation meant that the state effectively stunted new financing and investment in these neighbourhoods.[94] In contrast to redlining in the United States, the apartheid state controlled much of the banking sector during this time.[95] The 'grey area' designation also led to a prohibition on the provision of public services like policing, garbage collection and sanitation; it disincentivised property owners from renovating or keeping up assets.[96] Indeed, there was no financial support for new projects or financing for the sale of existing buildings. According to Morris, who uses the 'grey area' designation and 'redlining' interchangeably: 'Redlining ... led to a serious decline in property prices in Hillbrow[,] encouraging sectional-title landlords to keep maintenance at a minimum and rents as high as possible.'[97] As a Ponte resident and Dlala Nje guide told me:

> [Redlining] pretty much turned life upside down around here. [White residents] couldn't sit here under these circumstances. Slowly but sure, bit

by bit, they left ... These are the neighbourhoods that suffered the most, including the property owners. They have no choice but to just look at their asset, losing value each and every day. They were forced to just block off [their buildings] and start life from scratch.[98]

Redlining mixed with factors like suburban property speculation, racialised fear of crime and high-density living, and late-apartheid white out-migration. Ponte and its surrounding neighbourhoods reached a demographic and political-economic 'tipping point'.[99]

Although initial speculation about Ponte as a luxury apartheid-era project was misplaced, the building quickly began to serve as a container for speculation of another sort: dystopian, racialised fear. In the wake of redlining and South Africa's democratic transition, landlords walked away from Ponte and countless other buildings in surrounding neighbourhoods. Marinic writes: 'Hillbrow morphed into urban legend as the lair of Johannesburg's underworld. Many apartment buildings in the neighbourhood were "high jacked" by gangs who blocked owners from entering and forced tenants to pay them instead.'[100] Ponte's management struggled to collect rents from tenants, let alone monitor apartments. Units quickly and dramatically changed to being predominantly renter-occupied, sublet from afar.[101] Lost revenue led to maintenance delays. In its aesthetics, the building soon became home to visual symbols of disorder. In Owen Crankshaw and Caroline White's longitudinal study of Hillbrow, they find rapid population dislocation and 'inner city decay'.[102] This 1991 case study, commissioned by Johannesburg's City Council, was a survey questionnaire with in-depth interviews. Crankshaw and White reported more and more units overcrowded and without access to reliable water or electricity: 'Landlords, for their part, complained that they were unable to maintain their buildings because their African tenants refused to pay economic rentals, vandalised their buildings, overcrowded the apartments and thereby sent the service costs soaring. One landlord argued that the African township culture of politically-motivated rent boycotts had been applied to the inner city.'[103] Like many of the buildings in neighbouring Hillbrow, Ponte saw its services slide. Property management ultimately left the building altogether.

Urban legend and reality mix to shape the historiography of 'what happened' with Ponte in the early 1990s. As Ponte became increasingly home to immigrants from other parts of Africa, xenophobic myths abounded of trash stacked many storeys high . Stories of suicide and murder were also common about Ponte in the 1990s, as were those of local police attempting to surveil the building by helicopter.[104] Such myths are hard to verify in official statistics and some of them are demonstrably false.[105] Yet Stephen Hobbs, who visited Ponte monthly for seven years to pay his apartment landlord by cheque in the early 1990s, attests to the building's state of disrepair after the P7 parking lifts broke down and he 'happened upon' the building's inner core.[106] Suicides, according to Hobbs, were tragically common.[107] James Mangunza of Dlala Nje writes: 'Ponte was built to house no more than 3 500 people. When it was hijacked, it was estimated over 10 000 people were living within its walls.'[108] Xenophobic attitudes in Johannesburg, culminating in violent pogroms in 2008, found a convenient physical storyline in Ponte.[109] For white residents, the reappropriated Ponte served as a physical manifestation of fears about South Africa's supposedly unruly, sudden democratisation. For certain black residents, the reappropriated Ponte served as a physical reference point for xenophobia justifying violence.

In the late 1990s, developers and South Africa's national government briefly considered Ponte as a site for a vertical prison, before scrapping the idea.[110] The American architect Paul Silver, who had considerable expertise in building and designing prisons, travelled to South Africa and recommended Ponte, saying, 'It's a lousy apartment building, but a perfect prison.'[111] In February 1998, the national government's Minister of Correctional Services held a conference announcing that 'Ponte City would be transformed into a prison in the following year'; renamed the Ponte Justice Centre, it was to be managed by a public–private partnership.[112]

Local civil society and media efforts thwarted Ponte's transformation into a prison facility. Indeed, the myths about Ponte were ultimately made more nuanced thanks to community members and artists doing the unthinkable: entering Ponte, cameras and notepads in hand, and talking to its residents. According to Tom Keenan, media narratives, drawing on 'objective' audio-visual material, make a claim on that material and an argument about the nature of reality.[113] Media present Ponte in different, extreme ways: a site of chaos and informality, an implosion of order, or a 'black hole' of legible, rational, Cartesian knowledge. Policing the building by helicopter, or efforts to repurpose it into a prison, may be reactions to Ponte's elusiveness. Yet media and artists have also presented a more optimistic and humanistic vision of Ponte, one that led to yet another reappropriation of the building.

When the journalist Nickolaus Bauer entered Ponte in 2012 for a work assignment, he decided to rent a penthouse flat. He was soon joined by his friend Michal Luptak, who was then an accountant. The two began to lead tours of the building to interested parties. Shortly thereafter, the artists Mikhael Subotzky and Patrick Waterhouse spent three years in the building completing three artistic projects. One is a visual critique looking outward through every single window of the building onto the social and natural landscape of Johannesburg. A second looks inward at the doors of each apartment. A third examines fragmented spaces of each of the residents' lives – appliances, bathtubs, television sets.[114]

Subotzky and Waterhouse's project, mirroring the built structure of Ponte itself, was regimented and ordered in its precision. Through their relentless, almost mechanical documentation, Subotzky and Waterhouse helped to reappropriate the symbolic meaning of Ponte for Johannesburg residents and internationals alike. Ponte as a building, and its residents, are not 'inherently violent'; rather, as Subotzky put it, 'Ponte is sort of an Ellis Island of sorts of Johannesburg', home to immigrant sub-communities from across the continent.[115] Yet at the same time, as Subotzky notes: 'The spatial planning [hierarchy] inherent to Ponte very much endures and lives on,' reflected for example in rent prices and floor layouts.[116] Their work drew international attention, cast Ponte in new light, and shifted thinking on movement and survival in Johannesburg. It also inspired extensive academic commentary on and artistic production about Ponte.[117]

Throughout the past decade, Ponte has served as a poignant cultural symbol for South African society. Films featuring Ponte City include *District 9*; director Philip Bloom's documentary *Ponte Tower*; Ingrid Martens's docudrama *Africa Shafted: Under One Roof*;[118] the South African film *Dredd* (featuring a fictional skyscraper, 'Peach Trees'); the 2015 movie *Chappie*; and select scenes in Love Supreme's music video for the song 'Lonely Feelings'.[119] The zombie-apocalypse film *Resident Evil: The Final Chapter*

Figure 6.5: The crew for an October 2022 football commercial filmed within Ponte's parking garage. Today, the building regularly hosts media practitioners for films and commercials. (Stefan Chavez-Norgaard, 2022)

was filmed extensively in Ponte's core (see Figure 6.5).

Stephen Hobbs, when visiting Ponte in the 1990s, dropped a camera attached to a parachute from the building's roof, creating an experimental film mirroring a suicide. Hobbs's fascination with the building stemmed from his initial visits to the hollow interior, from which he had vivid memories of the cleaning staff and their brooms: 'To see that kind of inner core negative space, in a brutalist building … [was] profound.'[120] Artists and academics saw Ponte as symbolising modernist dystopia, Johannesburg's rapid shifts and disorder, or South Africa's abrupt and incomplete emergence from racial hierarchy.[121] Media interventions reappropriate Ponte, giving the building larger-than-life meaning, as the building's residential composition remains fluid. Speculation as to the build's meaning and economic value continues.

Contemporary Echoes: South Africa through Ponte

Media representations led to interest in Ponte from community members and international developers alike. The East London-based property landlord the Kempston Group, originally a truck-and-hire company that now has global holdings, saw an investment opportunity. They purchased Ponte in 2001, retaining the company name Vincemus.[122] Ponte's current building manager told me about Kempston's choice to purchase the building, noting: 'When [the Kempston Group] got it, [Ponte] was already hijacked.'[123] With speculative profit in mind, the Kempston Group made significant changes to the building, hiring Elma and Danie Celliers, a husband-and-wife team.[124] They gutted and renovated entire building floors, though they did not alter the building's hierarchy.

Leading up to South Africa's World Cup, property-market speculation boomed. David Selvan and Noor Addine Ayyoub purchased the building from Kempston for some R100 million, and re-envisioned Ponte as an image of its opulent past, complete with media advertisements and remodelling.[125] Selvan and Ayyoub purchased Ponte under the shell company Investagain. According to Bauer, 'They evicted 1,500 residents, gutted floors 11 through 34, and began a complete renovation and reconfiguration of units with fantastical concepts and luxury finishes. Less than a year later [in the 2008 financial crisis], their project ground to a halt and was left unfinished.'[126] The company brought in 'Red Ant' forces, evicting 'unsavoury' tenants.[127]

As a former resident explained to me:

> [The Red Ants] were super super rough guys … They had an ex-cop to come in and oversee all the evictions … it took four to five buses [of Red Ants] just to evict the whole building. They always evicted upward. They would throw stuff out the window. People's tables and chairs, which would smash downstairs into one hundred or one thousand pieces. But, you know, it's super-complicated and a long process. It actually took them a period of three years to have the building cleared out.[128]

Making way for Ponte's new speculative imaginings came at the cost of violent dispossession for the building's actual occupants.

According to Tanya Pampalone, the renovation's timeline was overly ambitious, the team had no financial assets to speak of, and the vision was never ground-tested: '[Following the project], Ponte sits half-empty, a construction zone without construction, mired in would-be lawsuits and promises of what was to be. From unpaid contractors and suppliers to wronged ex-employees and unhappy investors, Ponte is, once again, causing a stir.'[129] Lawsuits revealed that Selvan and Ayyoub never fully purchased the building, and ownership returned to the Kempston Group. A Dlala Nje guide notes that two major events spelled the end of luxurious speculation for Ponte in 2008: South Africa's xenophobic pogroms and the 2008 financial crisis.[130] Yet these serial acquisitions reveal the sustained interest in Ponte as a redeemable, transformable landmark, a building capable of transcending its speculative origin story or perhaps re-enlivening it anew. The project's failures reflect yet another incarnation of overly optimistic attempts to monetise 'concrete fear' as luxury commodity.

Despite the periodical media frenzy, and after multiple false starts and attempts at new, luxury living, Ponte has settled into being a (somewhat) stable home for ordinary low-income residents. It is safe (though now has panoptic security features like biometric-ID entry cards);[131] it is largely occupied (though draconian security measures prevent overcrowding); it is affordable (though locals complain it is overpriced, and culture-bearers continue to see Ponte as a site of potential experimentation, including entrepreneurs of gentrification) (see Figure 6.6). Martin Murray, writing on Johannesburg today, says: 'Ordinary people – those whose marginal existence has been overlooked in the official planning scenarios – have encroached

SPECULATIVE DESIRE AND RESIDENTIAL REAPPROPRIATION

Figure 6.6: Today, Ponte is safe and owned by the Kempton Group. However, security features, like the biometric entry scan above, limit residents' ability to bring guests or subtenants into the building. (Stefan Chavez-Norgaard, 2022)

upon the interstitial spaces of the city, infringed upon regulations governing the proper use of urban space, and intruded into orderly places where they are not wanted.'[132] These 'depleted landscapes of despair' are legacies of mid-century gold booms, segregation and rapid deindustrialisation.

Simultaneously, starting in the 1990s, Johannesburg began attempts to rebrand itself as cosmopolitan, inclusive, market-competitive and investment-worthy.[133] Those efforts initially faltered as white South Africans fled to the suburbs. The city, in marketing boards' imagination, remained unsafe and unstable. In the words of Richard Tomlinson and Robert Beauregard, central Johannesburg was imagined as 'obsolete, so deteriorated as to be beyond redemption, or as taken over by (or left behind for) Africans'.[134] Ponte represents a key node in that nexus: it is home to lower-income people, struggling at the margins of a deeply unequal city. Nonetheless, around 2010, Johannesburg began to see a new wave of intense neighbourhood change. Starting in the university-adjacent district of Braamfontein, then in the former industrial neighbourhoods of Jeppestown and New Doornfontein, investors repurposed buildings and sold them as hip flats and condominiums. Developer Jonathan Liebman's Maboneng Precinct, under Propertuity, included retail, cultural, residential and streetscape interventions, alongside street art and private security.[135] Yet Liebman's precinct and Propertuity's buildings were later liquidated en masse.[136] Despite Propertuity going bust, dispossession of low-income residences is intensifying in central Johannesburg as developers hope to cash in on the city's periodically changing fortunes: The Inner City Federation of the Socio-Economic Rights Institute (SERI) documented 40 looming evictions in May 2021 alone.[137] A 'crown jewel' in Johannesburg's urban regeneration efforts is Hallmark House, designed by David Adjaye.[138] This stylish building stands just off Joe Slovo Drive, the same thoroughfare that Ponte sits on, and just down the street. Indeed, Hallmark House stands in visual conversation with Ponte in this section of post-industrial Johannesburg.

Hallmark House, unlike Ponte, is black, filled with greenery and colour. The building has unique interventions on its giant floors: a hotel, apartments, a jazz bar, a cafe, a rooftop bar. Like Ponte, it aspires to be an island, a sanctuary. This island, however, aims to draw a new, multiracial professional elite from the city's multinational mining, finance and banking industries. Its status and fate are uncertain, seemingly ever-changing. Ponte, nearby, houses a diverse amalgam of lower-income city residents.

Conclusion

The multiple ways in which Ponte City has been reappropriated since the 1970s exceeds its apartheid-era professional planning intentions, and constitutes an alternative logic to the production of space demonstrated on a micro-scale. That logic is transgressive, and indeed it transgressed the neat institutional boundaries of apartheid and democracy. Over the years, reappropriation has given Ponte a second (and third) life, and inspires artistic and cultural fascinations with the building that themselves add layers of meaning over time. Ponte's contemporary viability and beauty can be explained to a significant extent by these tacit spatial logics. Reappropriation exists at a complex and both complementary and contradictory intersection between opportunistic and speculative desire, socio-spatial and financial flux, and residents' repurposing.

Ponte, when designed, reflected and was fashioned to embody grand apartheid desires for regulation and control, material domination, and sheer physical largesse. The building conveyed racialised utopian imaginaries, even though its design was aesthetically and economically out of step with looming social and economic realities. Ponte's utopian imaginaries soon transitioned to dystopian nightmares. It today exists as a concrete container housing varied, contested aspirations. Ponte means different things to different people and represents fractured social and spatial control in the post-apartheid city.[139]

We can learn much from the design, construction, appropriation and reappropriation of Ponte, a symbol of collective memory and the weight of history as it constrains and shapes democratic aspirations. A poignant 'Tower of Babel', Ponte reveals dialectics among architects, planners and designers, and buildings' ultimate users. Ponte was built to serve a distinct, exclusionary purpose. Financial and fictitiously racialised speculation saw that purpose through to implementation and construction. Yet Ponte's inhabitants, at the time the project was completed and today, could not be further from the building's initially imagined clientele. Ponte has transcended meaning as an extreme yet typical modernist spatial intervention: designed to assert 'rational', 'Cartesian', 'ordered' authority in line with apartheid's disciplined, systematic and violent plunder. Today it stands, in durable off-white concrete, as both a testament to that project and in proud defiance of it. Ponte and apartheid have failed, yet their built legacies and projects of subjectivity formation remain ongoing.

Chapter Seven

Political Evolution of a Building Type: Community Centres at the End of Apartheid

Hilton Judin

In the absence of public space and amenities in black townships, few white architects addressed with any urgency the accompanying spatial violence and social neglect of apartheid. Architecture in South Africa was always limited to the bare accommodation of black people in the administration of apartheid – the offices, police stations and beer halls through which order, control and funding were enforced. In the absence of more than the bare minimum of houses, schools and clinics, architects scarcely managed to find a response through resistance and opposition to the immediate social crises. A small number of architects found a way to develop these common shared spaces to indirectly meet demands to put the majority on a path to citizenship proclaimed by civic space. These would be by way of places which surrounding black communities could identify as their own and in which they could find a sense of belonging. From the student uprising in Soweto in June 1976 to the State of Emergency in the mid-1980s – the end of apartheid before the transition to democracy in 1994 – community centres became socially distinctive urban public placeholders.

This chapter examines political meaning beyond architectural form in the development of a building type – the community centre – and how it was shaped by a people and profession under apartheid. In the waning of the apartheid state as a consequence of township insurrection between 1984 and 1989, collective action and empowerment in developing organisational skills and shared aims became as important as actual construction and accommodation in these community centres. White architects had to grapple in the course of this with the question of building and organising for the vast majority of the country, from whom they were segregated and estranged. Solidarity became another element in challenging the apartheid state in working towards a new sense of nationhood. At the same time, communities that were never homogeneous were divided in multiple ways and their interests did not always align. Yet such a collective was reckoned as radical cooperation, a coming together through shared political tasks to overcome differences and unify in opposition. Processes of community destruction, as the sociologist Belinda Bozzoli stressed, long hampered the emergence of working-class communal formations given apartheid's 'extraordinary capacity to remove, destroy and crush budding communities' for which 'time, continuity, the development of internal community solidarity and networks' were essential.[1] Divisions across communities through state-imposed segregation and ethnic enclaves had led to a deepening of cultural boundaries and conflicting interests. Differences had to be overcome and, in the case of architecture, addressed through building by drawing as much upon aspiration and imagination as on pragmatism.

 An examination of this architectural typology follows, not only in terms of formal built structures generated in answer to architectural questions but as a deeper look at social demands and deficits that had left space for it to evolve, the community building finding its way into the lexicon and practice of architecture in the country. With the apartheid state unable to suppress civil unrest or fully address demands around which resistance had coalesced, the urgent provision of civic amenities had been brought to the fore by desperate officials and business leaders in forums such as the Urban Foundation by the mid-1970s. Community had by this late stage of apartheid come to mean primarily black township residents. After another decade of apartheid policies dividing the black population by 'race' classification into African, Coloured and Indian, any idea of a 'public' had been constantly segregated by government into groups living in pre-designated areas. The African population had been further divided since the 1950s by policies of separate development into ethnic Bantustans that were rejected by the liberation movement as political fraud. And attempts to bring Indian and Coloured people into the separate chambers of the 'tricameral' parliament after the whites-only referendum of 1983 sparked further protests and the emergence that year of the National Forum, encompassing a number of affiliate groups including the Azanian People's Organisation (AZAPO), with roots in the Black Consciousness Movement, and the United Democratic Front (UDF), with youth, civic organisations and trade unions working together. Against the backdrop of the apartheid state's reform agenda, even basic administrative facilities in townships would no longer suffice as these minimal urban structures were abandoned, neglected or deliberately burned down in uprisings as symbols of the apartheid regime. By the 1980s township administration boards were deliberately targeted as part of the insurrection, most notably through large-scale rent boycotts. Recognition by the apartheid state of civic administration as central to its control and subjugation of the population left municipal buildings vulnerable and continuously targeted by anger and protests.

Community centres became a matter of collective social processes with engaged professionals as much as they were about the building itself. Community centres had developed specifically in relation to black rural and township residents deprived of civic amenities by a government intent on limiting their right to the city. White residential areas long sported numerous civic amenities, and religious and language affiliation here remained primary. Building in the townships became, for architects, a way of participating as more than professionals, offering them a platform for social practice. Yet for many black residents these projects were often seen as palliatives provided to ameliorate deprivation in their townships rather than transform it – in fact, as thwarting resistance by co-opting and dividing communities. An architect's responsibility in seeking to change society through building would remain constrained and contentious. Could they be a force for social change or were there limits to architecture reliant on the state or compromised in challenging it? Communal identity, if not already well established, came to be seen as forming and evolving during the initiation, design and construction of these new building projects in townships. It was not only a matter of how communities would use and embrace these buildings but what these buildings meant for them collectively over time. With limited means, architects were tackling some of the urgent social tasks facing the country through the development of this particular building type. By the mid-1980s, following the State of Emergency, violence under apartheid was more and more visible across townships and cities. In architecture, community buildings became cultural and social spaces of confrontation with the apartheid government's policies of social degradation and division. These centres could be organised and constructed collectively and in solidarity as actual sites of opposition.

The community work of three leading architects – Roelof Uytenbogaardt, Jo Noero and Carin Smuts – from the mid-1970s through the 1980s at the end of apartheid, is examined in this chapter. It seeks to show a shift through their work from early public monumental through evolving social expression of the process of production of community centres. These centres were central to the early work of each of these architects and, in turn, they proved to be precursors in the development of what was to become an important public building type for architects in the period leading up to and after the first democratic elections in 1994. Community centres provided what the government once denied; that is, respite from relentless oppression as places for people to gather and organise, for celebration and entertainment as well as remembering and recognition. They became in this way both highly visible and subversively symbolic, serving as emblems to themselves and to the government of an established and settled people belonging to a particular place. This chapter draws on archival documentation and discussions with architects over background developments and practices informing these projects. It is important to understand how these buildings challenged the role of architects and their responsibility in a confrontation with apartheid. It looks at what form architecture took in rural and urban areas in addressing a divided society and representing it in coming into being. It asks whether architectural practice was able to take on more direct political action rather than the slow accommodation that followed the building process itself.

Here we are looking at the question of the development of an architectural response in which building form and structure partially tied specific functional relations to a type, one that was called upon despite its context. As the architect Rafael Moneo underlined in his essay 'On Typology': 'To understand the question of type is to understand the nature of the architectural object today ... The architectural object can no longer be considered as a single isolated event because it is bounded by the world that surrounds it as well as by its history. It extends life to other objects by virtue of its specific architectural condition, thereby establishing a chain of related events in which it is possible to find common formal structures.'[2] It is in the community centre that a new collective typology made its appearance to take up the challenge of social deprivation in the absence of public amenities.

'Sense of Presence'

There had to be a way out of the dead end of architecture under apartheid that was more than symbolic but took place in a field of social engagement. Participatory practice increasingly offered the architectural profession a way of undertaking their civic duties in realising their political ambitions. But architectural projects quickly lost legitimacy without active communal involvement. Architecture was at a turning point in not looking solely to the state to address the black population's growing demands for public amenities. The architect's activities had dwindled to speculative development in the private realms, having done little to confront the black housing shortage beyond township sprawl with the 'matchbox' houses. Housing continued to be the task of segregated municipal bodies such as the West Rand Bantu Administration Board and national development agencies such as the strategically named Department of Community Development. Building practices of participation were limited, confronted by political resistance which sought to make the country ungovernable, challenging any modifications to the urban environment that sustained the segregated status of townships. Here the state's ongoing attempts to divide society and sow dissent saw local officials withholding civic amenities and meeting a society's needs in the most substandard and inhumane terms. The question of how architecture could 'solve' or even confront society's problems was constrained by the architect's indifference and sense of helplessness. That community centre and neighbourhood should be conceptualised and planned for in a segregated routine reinforced how few areas architects and their public majority even intersected. Any caring engagement in architecture could only have been imagined within the non-governmental structures of civic, religious and advocacy groups.

POLITICAL EVOLUTION OF A BUILDING TYPE

160

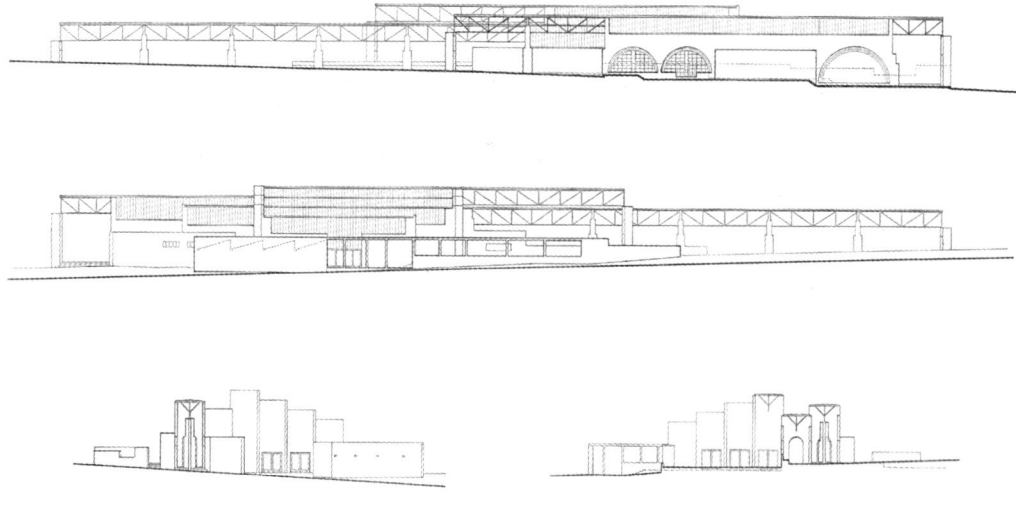

Figures 7.1 & 7.2: Roelof Uytenbogaardt, Steinkopf Community Centre, 1978–80. (Uytenbogaardt Papers at University of Cape Town Libraries Special Collections)

An important early precursor of such emancipatory building practices was the Social Amenity Centre built by the architect Roelof Uytenbogaardt in 1978 for the small town of Steinkopf, originally a missionary station in Namaqualand. Here in 1975 a remote rural community in the northern Cape was presented with a community centre by the loosely formed Urban Problems Research Unit (UPRU) of the University of Cape Town. It looked to help the people of Steinkopf 'in the formulation of their priorities related to the community social needs in order that they might receive assistance from Anglo American Corporation in the resolution of various community problems'.[3] Most of the nearby coastal land south of Port Nolloth had been purchased by De Beers Consolidated Mines, a company partially owned by Anglo American, and was under its tight security control for coastal diamond mining.[4] Steinkopf had been declared a 'Coloured Persons Reserve' in 1961 under the Coloured Persons Communal Reserves Act. The land around Steinkopf was communally owned and families choosing a place where to settle required approval by the town's board. For Uytenbogaardt, apart from the basic programme, the purpose, as it was described at the time, 'was to celebrate the collective and to add something which would enrich the experience of urbanism'.[5] While difficult for the architect to articulate, there was clearly a deeply felt need to go, in his words, 'beyond the programme' to find a communal space sorely lacking in such a barren landscape. The main linear building mass was made up of striking concrete stepped linear barrel vaults that allowed the harsh desert light to softly bathe a bare community hall. Floating steel roof structures glided past simple brick stepped-wall planes in an asymmetrical elongated plan that seemed to plough through the land. One of the roof elements continued on from the building to form a covered widely spaced colonnade linking the road passing from north to south with the surrounding shaded tree area.

The cluster of buildings that together made up the centre surrounded flowing open space, arrangements and forms derived from Uytenbogaardt's study at the University of Pennsylvania under Louis Kahn, remaining true to his teacher's postwar monumentality and modification of vital building typologies. Kahn's Jewish Community Centre (1954–8) in Trenton, New Jersey, demonstrated the integration of space and mass transposing void and solid through room and structure. It was through construction that space would be made manifest, ornament becoming the expression of the construction method. Uytenbogaardt had followed this tactic in his search for an appropriate monumentality, with the main hall shaded and protected by a visibly structured canopy which he had addressed in terms of both stark climate and social deprivation facing this rural community. As he explained, 'The whole expresses a shaded world accommodating some of people's simple needs.'[6] As local men were forced to migrate to cities for jobs, the women were left to cope with families and had need for public facilities to gather, accommodating a local theatre group, brass band, and outdoor and indoor teenager sports. The centre had to become a place for teenagers to hang around as well as for the more organised social functions such as fairs and markets giving it a 'sense of presence'. The architects designed the centre to 'serve – not be served – by the community', a refrain not too far from Kahn's more famous distinction of 'served' and 'servant' spaces. While designing the building to fulfil basic needs, the architects saw the way in which the development 'placed within the overall area and within the immediate surroundings will create opportunities and options in design which must be recognised and made use of, and which will therefore go beyond the strict requirements of the programme'.[7] It was a place that had to have real meaning to the people living there as a whole. The use of local labour, materials and building techniques in construction, such as the concrete blocks produced on site, ensured that the building itself would blend in the landscape and find a place among these rural residents.

Equally important, embedded as it was within a larger urban plan for the area, was Uytenbogaardt's Minor Community Hall designed with Norbert Rozendal in 1984 in the Cape Flats township of Belhar, which had been designated for a 'Coloured' population forcibly removed under apartheid. It was set within pinwheel crossroads of an urban plan by Uytenbogaardt and Rozendal. The central square, in which a 'recreational centre' stood, served to anchor networks of public spaces and streets out of which a neighbourhood was to be carved. For the architects, the 'continuity of the urban fabric' was emphasised in a series of sketches showing 'The Hall within Its Context'. They diagrammed 'the importance of wall as a container', 'the gatehouse announcing the axes and entrance', and 'the continuity of aesthetic of form, materials and colour, all derived from simple masonry construction and decoration'.[8] This multi-purpose hall sat behind an expressive columned loggia and row of service spaces, an unfortunate replication of the Cape

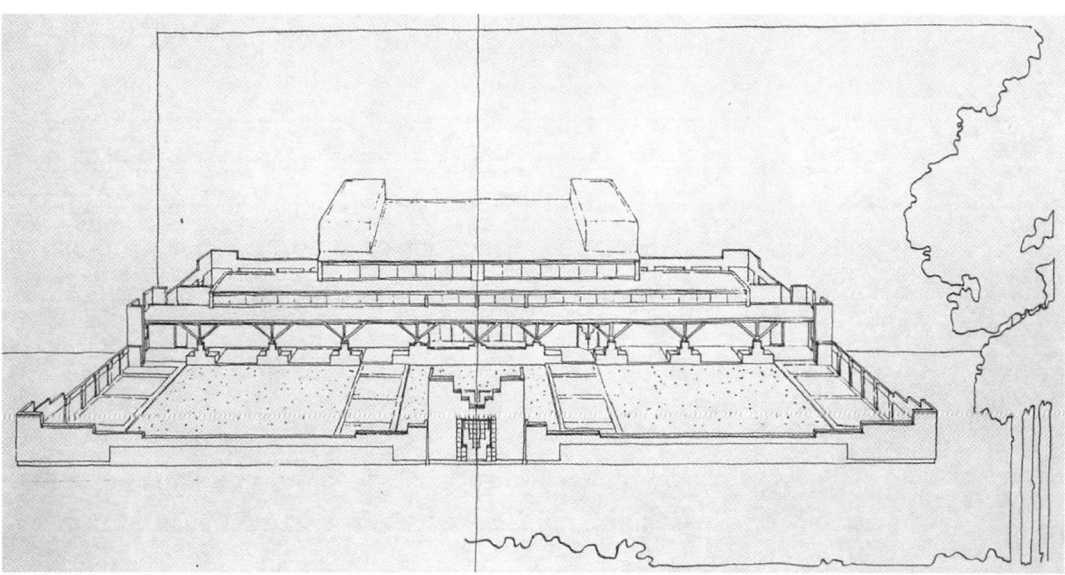

Figures 7.3 & 7.4: Roelof Uytenbogaardt, Belhar Minor Community Hall, 1984. (Uytenbogaardt Papers at University of Cape Town Libraries Special Collections)

Dutch colonial farmhouse stoep (veranda), although the architects saw it serving here as a cross street for (variously) a morning market, soup kitchen or jumble sale. As was the case with Uytenbogaardt's mentor Kahn, classical symmetry, geometry and order were applied monumentally to a simple structure of concrete blocks but, in Uytenbogaardt's case, with incongruous industrial bent corrugated metal roof sheeting. It was erected by Welleman Construction for the Housing Development Section of the Divisional Council of the Cape. The buildings would serve to define and protect the multi-functional tree-covered public space, or 'public realm' of the empty sandy and desolate flatlands, as it was designated under state patronage.

It is not certain how thoroughly the public was able to convey to the architects their needs beyond the programmatic requirements, even with the Belhar Group housing development firmly established early in the process. It is unlikely that the architects were able to translate any of the social pressures and divisions following forced removals. More urgent political demands would have to be met before any viable future could be envisaged. The architects, however, stated that the project had confirmed, for them, 'the importance to a community of an architecture that is obviously "civic" and "public"; by simple means being able to achieve diversity of space and adaptability of use, a many-placedness within the whole; that it is possible to achieve a dimension of radiance in a minimal situation; most importantly, the popular recognition of these qualities by the ordinary people of the community'.[9] Despite consultation with the public and what was seen as model participatory processes at the time over housing, there followed widespread disappointment with the final semi-detached housing units and its construction, and the social violence that continued to escalate over the following decades.[10]

Place for People

In this period of government violence in the 1980s, providing accommodation or social facilities could be seen as counterrevolutionary by many activists in the townships, where repression was leading to widespread resistance and its mitigation to complacency. This posed a dilemma for architects in the 1980s, aiding in a society harmed by apartheid yet challenged by the co-optation and complicity this implied. Opposing the delivery of housing, for example, denied the urgent needs this assistance would provide. Political acts of resistance or outright rejection of construction could have left architects unable to address the immediate remedies that the provision of housing, services and communal facilities offered. Civic structures in townships were still being developed in the 1980s as callous administrative offices and service halls, storerooms and payment counters. Centuries of colonial building and decades of apartheid planning had stripped an entire built environment of living traditions and common civic spaces for the populace. Segregation and racism had reduced public buildings to impositions and antagonisms. Community centres challenged architectural complacency from within a system that they would in turn be propping up in mitigating social and spatial deficiencies. The quotidian of the communal could serve in these instances to disguise an absence of care ordinarily expected within a just urban environment giving hope to people. Under apartheid, the aspirations for belonging and opportunity that such public spaces represented could give little to a black population denied citizenship or a permanent place in the city.

In time, as the country emerged from divisive isolation and social dismemberment with the eventual unbanning of the African National Congress (ANC) and other movements and multi-party constitutional talks beginning in 1990, widely dispersed community centres were the few buildings that architects had found to imagine another place with room for all. Yet it was never clear how buildings could bring together widely dispersed people without a change in power that was more than the symbolic handover of control and governance. While many of the churches played a central role in legitimising apartheid, others became more politicised and involved in organising local groups to confront the regime, channelling funds needed for development and providing a moral force to black residents' right to the city. For architects, this building could serve as a point of reference to the public. Working within society and on the fringes of the state, the church offered architects one of the few channels through which to operate with legitimacy.

Completed in 1984, the St Paul's Anglican Church in Jabavu (White City), Soweto, claimed such a political space for social services and communal life around which church service was organised. Designed by architect Jo Noero around the courtyard of the existing Ipelegeng Community Centre and constructed with funds from the Lutheran Church following the 1976 student uprising, this building was inspired by the family of Hector Pieterson, who were members of the congregation. Pieterson was one of the first casualties of the student uprising in Soweto in June 1976, 12 years old at the time he was killed by the police and photographed by Sam Nzima in an iconic image that was published across the globe. St Paul's was central to black township residents beyond Anglican church members and had become a place for people to meet with the civic leadership of Soweto and among political activist and union members. Circular in plan with a centralised altar, the ecclesiastical space itself was set up to conduct services in three quadrants in three languages. The building was linked through a fourth quadrant to an exterior altar as a communal interface for large services of all kinds, including political rallies for up to three thousand people in the public courtyard.

For Noero, who was commissioned as a young architect to enlarge the original church by the Archdeacon of Soweto, David Nkwe, churches had long served as symbols of hope offering help and guidance, and as such 'the church building itself [was] seen to symbolise the struggle of black people to assert themselves as full citizens of South Africa'.[11] He had met the archdeacon along with the bishop at that time, Desmond Tutu, through Trevor Huddleston when Noero returned to the country in 1980 after his post-architecture degree studies in development theory in England. During his studies, he recalled in an interview, Berthold Lubetkin's Finsbury Clinic (1938) became a notable influence with his approach to addressing social deprivation in society through a progressive and welcoming architecture. Lubetkin described how he achieved this humanising of architecture: 'the curving façade and outstretched arms were intended to introduce a smile into what in fact is a machine'.[12] With its large scale, solid brick bands and singular circular form, St Paul's was a highly visible symbol openly embracing of people across a public square that had become a civic focus to a neighbourhood. While still caught up in remnants of European postmodernism – with decorative brick bands, large round columns and a triangular pediment – the building was able to challenge the fragmented status quo of a surrounding bleak nondescript township landscape as symbolic structure in a place where it was long denied.[13] Noero saw the church as

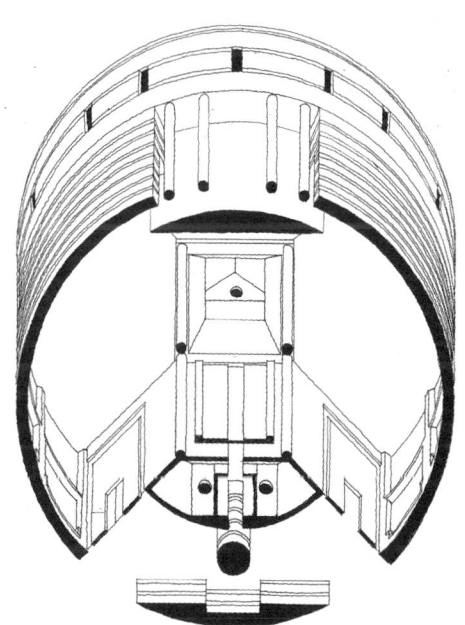

Figures 7.5 & 7.6: Jo Noero, St Paul's Anglican Church and Community Centre, Jabavu, 1984 (Images by Jo Noero)

providing an urban monumental scale to an important intersection in Soweto through the twelve-metre-high drum and four large round columns while at the same time providing social scale to the courtyard on the other side.

Largely built by a local contractor with the priest purchasing materials and architect supervising, the church was a point of pride on account of its self-built construction. Within the church, a large ring-beam topped by square rooflight bound the congregation intimately in facing towards an altar as stage. As much as this space served faith, it would uplift communities as a social centre important to governmental opposition, a case of symbolic typology becoming one with its task. To Noero, it was always more than 'a church site but was a genuine centre for local people to meet and interact' and ultimately 'played a role in being a place where people from different walks of life who were sympathetic to the aims of the ANC could meet and talk about the future'.[14] It was an opportunity for 'active citizenship' of groups such as Architects Against Apartheid and Planact organising at the time.[15] Noero would soon move from the brick and monumental to an additive construction of light steel and corrugated sheeting as an early attempt to integrate the surrounding built landscape of informality and spontaneous building with a new civic sensibility.

Towards an Ideology of Typology

Discussions of architectural typologies in the mid-1980s by theorists of postmodernism postulated it as a method for restoring historical continuity to the city.[16] In architecture, building type is not fixed but undergoes continuous transformation just as social and cultural environments do. Type is one of the principles of architecture exemplified by differences from a model described by the French architectural theorist Quatremère de Quincy as 'less the image of a thing to copy or imitate completely than the idea of an element which ought itself to serve as a rule for the model'[17] – the 'precise' model in this case repeated as it is. The 'more or less vague' type conceived in each case without resemblance to the antecedent is of no fixed use. It is thus able to evolve over time to be readily displaced. In debates about typology from the 1960s relating building type to urban morphology, the art historian Giulio Carlo Argan examined interactions between architects' working processes and their historical conditions. 'The birth of a "type" is therefore dependent on the existence of a series of buildings having between them an obvious formal and functional analogy,' as he wrote in 'On the Typology of Architecture'. 'In other words, when a "type" is determined in the practice or theory of architecture, it already has an existence as an answer to a complex of ideological, religious or practical demands which arise in a given historical condition of whatever culture.'[18] In this manner, a hall that historically developed for meetings of all kinds, from church to concert to education, had in time only the surrounding envelope and internal structure to distinguish it. Its scale and position within a complex of rooms or surrounding buildings was over time used to bring specific functional and, in some cases, symbolic clarity to what could be an empty container or stage.

For the architectural historian Anthony Vidler in 'The Third Typology', a 'concept of the city as the site of a new typology is evidently born of a desire to stress the continuity of form and history against the fragmentation produced by the elemental, institutional, and mechanistic typologies of the recent past'. Vidler writes of a typology 'not built up out of separate elements, nor assembled out of objects classified according to use, social ideology, or technical characteristics: it stands complete and ready to be de-composed into fragments'.[19] This 'ontology of the city' denies for him all social utopian or positivist definitions of architecture, released as it is into its own autonomous domain, a realm that does not need to relate to a hypothesised society in order to be conceived. Nor does it have to be particularised as a specific social condition in a specific time or place in order to write history. Architects are able to invent objects and environments that do not have to include statements of fit between form and use. 'Here it is in the adoption of the *city* as the site for the identification of the architectural that typology becomes crucial,' as Vidler goes on to describe the process. 'In the accumulated experience of the city, its public spaces and institutional forms, a typology can be understood that defies a one-to-one reading of function, but which, at the same time, ensures a relation at another level to a continuing tradition of city life.'[20] Here the precise demands of the present were addressed by giving a critical role to the public nature of architecture.

Within Modern Movement architectural history, a community typology stretched back to the Russian 'people's houses' that evolved into workers' clubs and 'social condensers' in the constructivist architecture of the Soviet Union in the 1920s. These venues of acculturation with auditorium, canteen, gymnasium and library embedded were bold, expressive and innovative in form. The building itself came to serve as monumental propaganda, the most famous example being the Rusakov Workers Club (1927–9) in Moscow of Konstantin Melnikov with its massive projecting auditoriums (criticised by some for being overtly theatrical). Another building typology, the 'communal house', was a residential complex with small living units and shared integrated service 'streets' of eating, sports and nursery that figured prominently in Moisei Ginzburg's Narkomfin Communal House (1928–30), which imagined transforming Soviet citizens through new forms of social revolutionary life.[21] The Narkomfin 'social condenser' was perceived, following Stalinism and growing Social Realism, as one of the failures of the socialist utopian vision. These residences with services were descendants of the Phalanstère – developed by one of the founders of utopian socialism, Charles Fourier, in the early 19th century – a building type designed for a self-contained utopian community of people working together and holding property in common for mutual benefit. Integrating urban and rural features, the phalanstery was made up of parts for quiet activities such as dining, meeting and study and for noisy activities such as carpentry, child care, dancing and demonstrations for visitors, not unlike the monastery or ship, which serve as a typological forebear. This legacy was to become more than a building type, inspiring social movements across the globe striving to bring together a social integrated community. Communal buildings developed beyond physical structures, becoming radical enough to encompass social activism required to tackle lack of public space in environments where planning had been used as a means of underdevelopment.

For the architectural historian Manfredo Tafuri, as he writes in *Architecture and Utopia*, the decline of the architect's professional status and loss of an ideological role by the 1970s had made such political action inevitable: 'Architects, after having ideologically anticipated the iron-clad law of the plan, are now incapable of understanding historically the road travelled; and thus they rebel at the extreme consequences of the processes they helped set in motion. What is worse, they attempt pathetic "ethical" relaunching of modern architecture, assigning to it political tasks adapted solely to temporarily placating preoccupations as abstract as they are unjustifiable.'[22] Never able to settle questions of whether it was at all possible to support resistance through architectural design, community projects came to represent the next best hope of immediately ameliorating depleted living conditions while preparing spaces for organisation and activism in politically stressed environments in Europe in this period. Architects needed to engage and empower future users through participatory design processes with workshops, protests and performances incorporating in design flexible layouts and models adapted to users' needs and through 'self-build' opportunities in construction for impoverished communities.

Clearly there was not always a single cohesive community without competing interests driving factions apart. This was apparent across the globe in any number of communities that would require continuous engagement and resolution through cooperation and often compromise.[23] Early examples of participatory processes in the postwar architecture of the 1970s can be found in the practices in Europe of Lucien Kroll in Belgium, Ralph Erskine in England, and Giancarlo De Carlo in Italy. Kroll's Mémé Medical School student dormitories (1970–6) for the Catholic University of Leuven, Woluwe-Saint-Lambert, had come about through intense consultation with students who had initially approached the architect. It employed a fragmented collection of different materials, colours and varying proportions applied to buildings but resulted in an eclectic and diverse mix of living units that each group of tenants had designed for themselves. Erskine in Byker Wall (1968–74) in Newcastle upon Tyne explored a radical process of living on site and engaging daily with an existing community slowly being rehoused over several years. In the end, a deep and penetrating collaboration brought about a reorganisation of the community itself.[24] For Giancarlo De Carlo, engagement with a worker organisation of the steelworks in Terni as future inhabitants of the restructured Matteotti Quarter (1969–74) stemmed from his research and search for a method not caught up in what he regarded as the mythology of participation. A continuous exchange with workers saw typological variation of five basic housing types being developed with a range of layouts that resulted in a great number of different building forms within a three-dimensional grid proffered by the architect.[25] This urban cluster of private terraces and public walkways was in part compromised by the choice of a national rather than local contractor and the eventual demise of a socialist government. It is notable that both De Carlo and Erskine presented papers at the important Housing Conference in Johannesburg in 1975 arranged by the Institute of South African Architects (ISAA).[26]

Other global housing schemes known to architects at the time that were notable for public participation include the work of Balkrishna Doshi in India. While not employing full participatory practice, Aranya housing scheme (1982–9) in Indore managed to draw on local building traditions, materials and relationships to bring in communities, leaving the architect as urban designer of living patterns and spatial advisor to participants. Using a high degree of choice and flexibility in the design and construction of the housing, owner-builders were able to modify, decorate and extend their units within their economic means, needs, skills and individual preferences following an urban framework set out by the architect. Valuable lessons could also be learned closer at hand from the work of architect Iain Low with the Training for Self-Reliance Project undertaken by the government of Lesotho, involving the upgrading of schools. The architecture unit of the Project embarked on a phase of 'built experimentation' in the early 1980s for building prototypical schools as test cases based on shared knowledge of materials, siting and local customs. In devising a building system able to respond to various conditions, the architects were constantly able to improve on their designs and gradually entrust younger members of the team, empower contractors and share skills.[27] In terms of early models in South Africa, the architect Julian Beinart documented extensively in the early 1960s the decoration and alterations practised by residents of Western Native Township in Johannesburg. He surveyed with his students hundreds of 'matchbox' houses as manifestations of distinction, pride and resistance in the face of apartheid planners. Although white architects had been looking at vernacular architecture such as Ndebele villages and Nguni homesteads from the 1950s – primarily in terms of ethnic settlements and decorative patterns through the work of James Walton – they were for the most part uninfluenced by more expansive indigenous models of communal living and traditions of collective production that could have served as precedents for an expanded idea of practice.[28]

Offering both space for cultural activities and civic organisation, community centres, by the time they had developed in the late 1970s, were overwhelmed by the spatial demands placed on them. A basic community hall had come to stand for more extensive needs, as local organisations had few resources and the government had relinquished any role in the civic. Community centres were offered as multi-purpose halls for everything from meetings and workshops to performances and hearings, available for social functions, weddings and funerals. As such, their precedents were primarily churches, town halls and school facilities which had multiple purposes. They were frequently bare brick warehouse structures with steel or concrete framework, steel windows and sheet metal roofing. Community centres had by default developed as an architectural type with a rather ill-defined tectonic form standing in for more specific typologies, functional as opposed to formal, opportunistic as opposed to responsive. Most architects resorted to generic building in response to a programme of activities that were undifferentiated, with no clearly discernible activities that could be realised through any kind of conventional typological response. Without definitive purpose, position or tenure, such a building had to find form through innovative spatial practice to address and support the people living in its shadow who had yet to find their place.

Emancipatory Spatial Practice

Bringing together and maintaining community in the face of apartheid divisions and sustained political attack was an ongoing everyday battle. It was not always certain whether the building of a community centre or maintenance of the building could serve to ameliorate or repel these threats. It remained an important debate whether a building typology such as community centre would ever be able to fully address the civic burden placed on it by architects. Just as buildings buckled under overwhelming and opposing strain, so the demands on an architect having to bring about social cohesion in constrained environments often proved to be a step too far. Such disparate prospects led to conflicting or abandoned amenities unable to thrive or meet the challenge of overburdened buildings, and architects destined to fail, caught as they were between rescue and revolution.

For the architect Carin Smuts, such challenges remained central to her early architectural practice where processes of developing a community centre coalesced as much around construction as they did around social development for communities themselves to grow. Through participatory

POLITICAL EVOLUTION OF A BUILDING TYPE

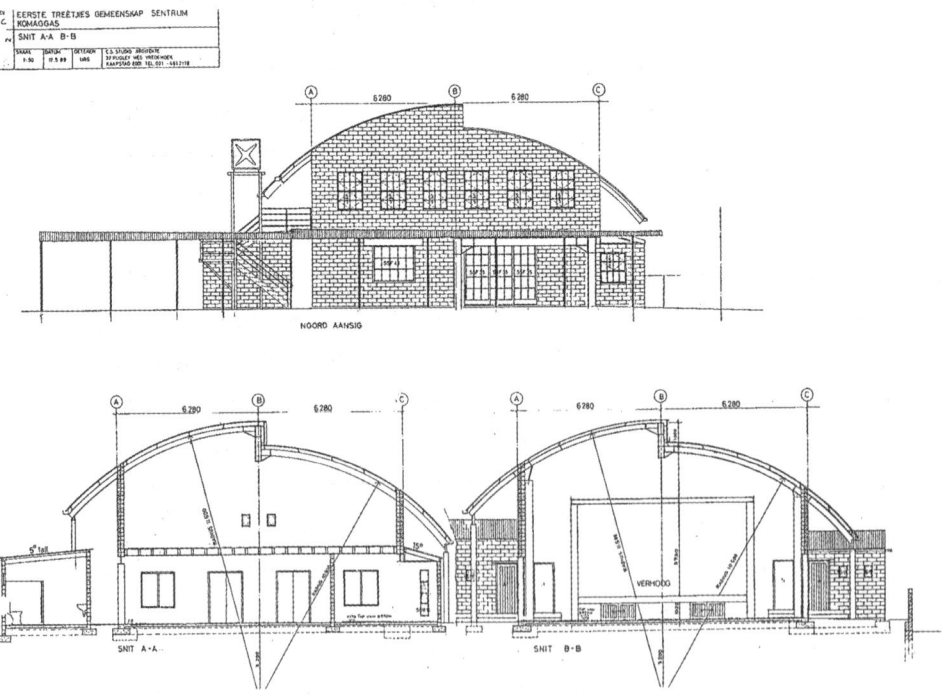

Figures 7.7 & 7.8: Carin Smuts, Eerste Treetjies Community Centre, Komaggas, 1986–90. (Images by Carin Smuts)

processes, she sought to expand a sense of empowerment and deeper sustainability through which such projects would need to survive. Her practice, CS Studio, explained that each project demanded its own activities. 'Interactive processes are a powerful tool in any design phase as it allows everyone to have a say and often leads to much better spatial solutions,' they proposed in their online statement, 'Our Philosophy'. 'By listening to people, the architect is provided with a wealth of information to feed into the design process. In the process of participation, role players are empowered, and they take ownership of their design decisions. However, participation is generally seen only as a social process. This is when it fails. It needs to be underscored by making.'[29]

In a project such as Eerste Treetjies (First Steps) Community Centre in the rural settlement of Komaggas, one of six so-called 'Coloured' reserves in Namaqualand, a lengthy series of negotiations with delegates from the local church and community and an adherence to interpretations of a local vernacular allowed architects to cultivate this building over the period 1986–90 in a much wider regional context. The name Komaggas can be translated as the 'place of many wild olive trees'. The project had been initiated by the Social Change Assistance Trust (SCAT) under Barry Streek and Diana Oliver with funding from the Church of Norway. SCAT saw their mission as empowering local communities, strengthening civil society and promoting social change as 'community-driven responses to social justice'.[30] Local community leaders from the school, crèche and church brought together residents and local builders to enable the building to be negotiated, designed and constructed on the chosen site within a year. Combining the making of building blocks on site with trusses by woodwork teachers from the local school meant that building processes were able to bring together members of this dispersed rural community in a collective effort for which they would feel and retain a deep sense of ownership. Future users such as spinners and weavers who would operate in the multi-functional space took part in defining programmes and spaces. Above all, what would be achieved was a collective space in which people felt 'safe' in a society where apartheid had made such feelings tenuous in public.

CS Studio describes the importance of vernacular architecture and urban informal settlements to their practice: 'A traditional village is made up of a number of structures which are spaced apart, with most of the social interactive spaces being outside. The structures are also placed with the doors facing east to bring in the morning sunlight. Roofs hang over the mud walls to protect them from rain while also shading them. It is a perfect system of natural materials, natural use of light, and it is thermally appropriate.' The people of Komaggas were of Nama (Khoi) and Baster heritage who originally practised a mixture of pastoralism and agriculture until, first, the copper rush in the 19th century and subsequent diamond operations in Kleinzee, which became the biggest employer in the area. The apartheid state under the Population Registration Act of 1950 regarded them as 'Coloured'. A sense of community developed, however, through the retention by the people of their land as common property and a common identity with those who shared these rights, using the past to speak to the present in different ways.[31] The church leaders from the Rhenish Missionary Society had brought to the attention of the architect a local *matjieshuis* (mat house) vernacular of nomadic goat and sheep herders, who had long made up the local population. It became one of the ways that building traditions and construction methods could in fact anchor, protect and sustain a social collective such as this, long alienated by 'Coloured' policies of apartheid. The Komaggas community, represented by the local land committee, has long engaged in trying to recover much of the land it claims historically belonged to it and was used over extended periods of time by their ancestors before it was lost to the state and De Beers Consolidated Mines.[32]

Materials often regarded as degraded or basic were worked carefully by the architects into the scheme of things.[33] Fragments of all kinds – stairs, walls, windows, corrugated roofs and steel frame structure – were distinguished components, exposing and highlighting new paths, entries and cavities for light, people and movement.[34] Seemingly banal everyday objects and materials – *objet trouvé* in brick and corrugation – were placed in the forefront as much more than scenic backdrop or prop to what came to be seen as 'social theatre'. Unlike the *art brut* of the 1960s, which drew on a brutalism of the archaic and primitive, material was transformed by the architects and constructors in a utilitarian manner as conditions and conventions of an evolving public life. As CS Studio explained: 'The way in which the buildings are ordered and placed in the landscape also provides valuable information regarding social and cultural structures.'[35] In this architectural propagation of empowerment, the community becomes aware of who built it and who uses it. In fact, uses of these intermediate social spaces – switching between preschool crèche, wedding venue, library, ballroom dancing venue – would remain central to the construction of public spaces and the usefulness of in-between spaces derived from juxtapositions of smaller programmatic units – an informal display of a social typology, in the end, for the charm and benefit of the community.[36] Within this *bricolage*, functionality was dissected and re-examined, allowing individual architectural elements and features of an ordinary hall to take on – through organisation, construction and operation – the rich expressiveness of its manifold activities and social arrangements: the architect was not immune to the constructivist poetics undergoing a revival at the time. Growing assertion of indigenous as opposed to 'Coloured' identity continued to be developed collectively through debate over tradition and contemporary life in what it meant to be Nama.[37] The political life of the building had evolved over time to address more than the community's original intentions by gathering people, sponsoring civic action and progressively transferring agency, offering some hope despite enduring impoverishment through mining retrenchment, dispossession, and a lack of resolution in respect of the issue of land distribution.

In detailed studies of the three-way relationship between participation, empowerment and sustainability in a number of development projects including CS Studio, Carin Smuts along with Michael Lyons and Anthea Stephens found that outcomes depend on local politics and community structures (even with an emphasis on capacity building and skills training). But as they make clear in their report 'Participation, Empowerment and Sustainability': 'Where local-political structures are not transparent and accountable, and where there is little social mobility possible within the community, intervention at the organisational level is likely to entrench existing power structures.'[38] Even with a clear link between the nature and extent of participation and the sustainability of development, the actual sustained use of buildings can be reduced and opportunities for further development lost to the community. Fully empowered communities can, however, contribute towards the sustainability of projects with the creation of employment opportunities in the construction, maintenance and operation of the building and its embedded programmes. A feeding scheme continues operating the kitchen in Eerste Treetjies as part of a post-apartheid governmental nutritional programme, and the ongoing community crèche and social calendar ensure that there is a place for children and weddings of the next generation.[39] These sustained social engagements and the everyday economic spin-offs of spinning and weaving mean architecture had become a force of social change.

Typologies of Dissonance

A few of the white architects studied in this chapter became social activists, with their work standing in for government's failures in the civic realm. They had sought to establish civic spaces in black townships, segregated areas and buffer zones left abandoned after decades of government control and neglect. Few of the buildings within these places fully represented the communities living within them. These were not social utopias delayed nor great bastions of resistance. Instead, in the midst of strife and division, community buildings found a way to give communities a shared site of resistance through meeting halls, memorial spaces, organisational rooms and an open public space. At the time in the mid-1980s, lack of social amenities together with overcrowding, labour restrictions, influx control and unequal access to the city helped fuel the township revolt. Community centres were social amenities drawn from the belief in public being equally a place, process and people that could be forged. In this development from the monumental typology of Uytenbogaardt to the symbolic of Noero and the social participatory of CS Studio, buildings evolved over this period in response to a changing sense of 'public' and a transforming notion of 'practice'. For, in some way, all the centres analysed in this chapter were resonant with communal identity fostered through public participation in search of a more certain (established) architectural form. Needs and grievances had coalesced in urban areas around public space and amenities and, in part, were to drive the establishment of organisation and activism in these communities and places. In the shift of emphasis in building from government agencies and contractors (with Uytenbogaardt) to greater reliance on self-build and community participation (with Carin Smuts), new roles opened up as the needs of building and society became further entangled in a burst of civic organisation at the time of apartheid's demise.

More homogeneous rural communities were better able to develop and sustain a sense of ownership over generations than many communities in townships were. Historical forms and fragments first brought back into architectural practice during this shift from modernism to postmodernism in the 1980s were led by a re-examination of inherited building typologies. At the same time, rather than being able to resort to monumentality in civic building, architects were forced to reckon with vacant spaces, constrained budgets, indifferent government officials and threatened communities. A typology of dissonance ensued, reflective of schisms between good intentions and sharply contested realities, and collaboration and resistance were often intertwined, split between compounding social factions and emboldening political confrontations. It tracked the difficult and often irreconcilable demands of belonging and building. Community buildings embodied an alternative social practice that would come to the fore in the decade following the transition to democracy as it was incorporated into urban practices of non-governmental organisations such as Actstop and Planact in Johannesburg, the Built Environment Support Group in Durban, and the Development Action Group in Cape Town. Such an evolving typology had to bring a sense of identity as a public building to fractured communities; a feeling of belonging to a larger social body as much as a symbol of political reckoning to a nation. In one moment it was confined to a local neighbourhood and in another anticipating a future bringing about urban citizenship and a place in the city that the black majority were long denied.

As buildings evolved, they did in part bring with them a recognition of the limits of a cultural capacity to fully comprehend forms needed to take up a shared civic consciousness. But there is little doubt as to what even limited public participation had brought about to the social landscape of a country in conflagration, redeeming by formal invention and political action the aspiration embedded in such architecture. Nor yet in the 1980s was it obvious how – in a society divided and without intimate social confrontations – there would yet be common cause as a public architecture. What was never absolutely clear was whether architecture could be found in social shared purpose, one that would be reflective of the collective ambition and desire of a community in collaboration with the architect, no matter how estranged. In the end, it was neither buildings nor the architect's imagined communal gestures that would see this challenge as more than gesture in the long struggle against apartheid. Yet some of the ambition and symbolism of public emancipation were embedded in everyday tasks such as community building. In South Africa, shared civic buildings and public spaces would not come about as expected or imagined. For civic buildings remain largely unbuilt in black townships, and architecture struggles to address a public with sufficient attention to leave those a generation after apartheid with a greater sense of belonging in making their environments.

Chapter Eight

The Rescripting of the Johannesburg West Dutch Reformed Church

Brendan Hart

The (former) Johannesburg West Dutch Reformed Church (in Afrikaans, the Nederduits Gereformeerde Kerk, or NGK) feels very familiar. It looks (not by accident) like hundreds of other Dutch Reformed churches across South Africa, familiar landmarks in small towns and early 20th-century suburbia. Located in Mayfair West, a formerly white[1] and predominantly Afrikaans suburb located to the west of the Johannesburg city centre, the Johannesburg West NGK is not what it initially appears to be, having functioned as a progressive mosque for the area's growing (and increasingly diverse) Muslim community since the late 1990s. This is not unique to this building or community but is rather a sign of the social and physical changes experienced in post-apartheid, postcolonial South African cities. The suburb of Mayfair West was (like all apartheid South Africa's cities) formerly a culturally static and artificially controlled community and built environment, ruled by the legislated racial segregation policies of the state. The evolution of the church building offers an opportunity to examine and understand the changes and responses that have occurred in the city over the past thirty years.

The study of the adaptation of religious buildings for different purposes is well established in the field of architectural history, with examples in South Africa having been examined by scholars such as Schalk Le Roux.[2] What makes the adaptation of the NGK building significant is that it was once seen as a potent symbol of colonial and apartheid power and prejudice. It is a vestige of the colonial and apartheid landscape that, possibly through its ubiquity, has remained unconfronted. The conversion of the building into a mosque therefore becomes a far more powerful symbol. This study looks at the building's conversion both by considering the social, political and architectural history of the NGK and Islam in South Africa and also by asking questions about the meaning of the building both for those communities who once used it and for those who do so now. Can a building's meaning be rescripted in the postcolonial, post-apartheid context and become more than just the accumulation of its own history?

Early Origins of NGK Architecture in South Africa

This familiar architecture of the NGK was not accidentally or benignly conceived. It was, at least initially, specifically developed as part of the construction of Afrikaner identity in the early 20th century. The history of the NGK is closely linked to the rise of Afrikaner nationalism and the apartheid state.

The NGK arrived in South Africa with the first Dutch settlers at the Cape in 1652. The church (the NGK) and the authorities (the Vereenigde Oost-Indische Compagnie)[3] were inseparable, early ministers being Company employees. The Reformed Calvinist faith of the NGK was the only permissible religion at the Cape for over a hundred years and greater freedom of religion was only introduced in 1795 with the first British occupation of the Cape (1795–1803).[4] The combination of 'capitalism and Calvinism'[5] that the NGK represented was very influential, and the church influenced all aspects of life in the early colony, from education to politics. Being Christian (and therefore a member of the NGK) equated to 'being civilised' and was often used to justify a sense of entitlement and domination.[6] Even after the Cape fell under British control, the NGK was still financially supported by the state, an astute decision as many ministers now 'felt obliged to defend the government' when faced by criticism within their congregations.[7]

A pattern emerged in the NGK from early on in which different racial and ethnic groups worshipped separately.[8] Later, measures were taken to make it church policy that different racial groups attended separate services. This was justified as a concession made 'for the sake of the weakness of some' members, a comment on the part of the church that apparently acknowledged that there was no theological justification for segregation. The evolution of this practice made the NGK one of the first social institutions to practise a form of apartheid long before it became national policy.[9]

The Rise of Afrikaner Nationalism

The late 1800s and early 1900s saw the emergence of a large, poor, newly urbanised Afrikaner community in both Pretoria and Johannesburg. Coming to the cities in search of work, Afrikaners sought to escape rural poverty and landlessness that intensified in the wake of the Anglo-Boer War (1899–1902). Their rapid urbanisation has been described as a 'natural and inevitable process'.[10]

Urbanisation was often traumatic. Hendrik Hoffman, who arrived in Johannesburg in 1933, described it as follows: 'Man, I felt like a rabbit thrown into a cage full of dogs. You don't know which side to run to. Wherever you look, there are people ... I wasn't used to so many people ... It was a frightening discovery to walk in the streets ... I was far removed from the open plains of the Free State, and to be in Johannesburg was a terrible thing.'[11]

This situation deeply concerned the NGK as well as the government. It was feared that impoverished people of all races would start living in close proximity, leading to 'social intimacy' and eventually the elimination of 'race consciousness'.[12] Coupled with the post-war British government's 'vigorous policy of Anglicisation'[13] and the dominance of English speakers in the towns and cities, this was seen as a threat to Afrikaner identity and culture. 'Being Christian and speaking Afrikaans was central to Boer [Afrikaans] identity.'[14]

The NGK was central to the rise of nationalism, for the church feared that loss of language would lead to a decline in faith.[15] 'The church became their fortress against what they experienced as a total onslaught on their identity', to the extent that 'it became increasingly difficult to distinguish between the NGK and the Afrikaner nation'.[16] Strong nationalist and religious themes were explored in the works of Afrikaner writers and thinkers of this period, including the idea of Afrikaners as 'God's chosen people', which gave rise to a religious interpretation of their history.

The NGK was a powerful force and many future National Party[17] leaders came from its ranks. It is perhaps not surprising that in a 1929 speech by the NGK minister the Rev. J.C. du Plessis, the term 'apartheid' was first used;[18] he argued that 'it was in accordance with God's will that different races and *volke* [cultural groups] exist'[19] and justified this through a 'pro-apartheid reading' of the Bible.[20] While the NGK was careful not to condone blatant racism, its own policy of apartheid – with separate churches for different racial and ethnic groups – showed the way for nationalist politicians and academics.[21]

After 1948, with the increasing power of the apartheid state, the views of the church were 'kept' in line with those of the state as an act of self-preservation. It was only in the 1980s that more direct challenges were made to the racial order and faith became the only criterion for membership of the church.[22] In 1990 (with the unbanning of political parties and the release of political prisoners) the NGK 'confessed', accepting responsibility for the injustices and suffering under apartheid and acknowledging that it had been mistaken in its biblical justification of apartheid and its active participation in the apartheid regime.[23]

The Architecture of the NGK

Most early NGK buildings in South Africa were locally designed and constructed without any overriding architectural concept. The result is a group of buildings of varied architectural styles and forms. After the second British occupation of the Cape in 1806, NGK buildings tended to follow the neo-Gothic style prominent among churches of other denominations.[24]

With the rise of Afrikaner nationalist consciousness in the late 19th and early 20th century, it was felt that a more specific 'Afrikaans' architectural style was needed for church buildings (*ons eie kerkboustyl*).[25] This call was led by the architects Gerard Moerdijk (1890–1958) and Wynand Louw

(1883–1967).[26] Their reference to an 'Afrikaans' architecture has also been interpreted to mean an African architecture distinct and different from the colonial Cape Dutch and colonial British building styles (which came with their own social and political baggage) and drawing more direct inspiration from place, specifically the Highveld.[27]

Between the 1930s and 1960s the debate on what was an appropriate church architecture was played out in public: various proponents published articles and made their views clear in the popular and church press.[28] In 1935 Moerdijk stated that 'no matter how poor, how humble his home is, the Afrikaner always gives generously to the building of his church. This is one of the most worthy character traits that distinguishes our people. The church and religion are still at the centre of Afrikaner society, despite all modern trends, a fact which bears testimony to the value of tradition and history.'[29] It was Moerdijk's design principles (applied to his own architecture and adapted by his followers and protégés) that became dominant in Afrikaner church architecture. In his 1935 article 'Kerkgeboue vir Suid-Afrika'[30] he laid down that the building should make use of locally available materials, must 'grow' out of its site, must have 'life' and atmosphere, and should be designed in a building style that was *volkseie* (a nation's own).[31]

The last point, as Irma Vermeulen has noted,[32] was the most important for Moerdijk, who used this as a motivation for moving away from the neo-Gothic architectural style (associated with Catholic or Anglican churches) towards a Romanesque and, later, neo-Byzantine style of architecture. Moerdijk was very convincing in his arguments and many communities chose to demolish their older 'unsuitable' churches and replace them with new buildings often designed by him.[33]

Modernist and functionalist architectural thinking similarly influenced the design of NGK buildings. Moerdijk, on functional grounds, argued for the plans of NGK buildings to be based on a Greek rather than a Latin cross, a form that he felt had fewer acoustic problems and, with a theatre seating format, drew the focus towards the preacher, thereby creating what he called a 'Byzantine' spatial arrangement.[34] Moerdijk's 'neo-Byzantine' style of architecture embraced Art Deco and, later, modernist architectural languages. The dominant use of exposed brickwork sat 'comfortably with protestant conscience'[35] with its 'honesty' as well as with modernist functionalism and Moerdijk's desire to use locally available materials. Moerdijk's style of NGK architecture was the dominant language for the church's buildings until the Pretoria-based architect Johan de Ridder's 'tent kerk' designs from the 1960s and 1970s.[36] These cost-effective and functional buildings were stripped of all decoration with the result that 'the building becomes a diagram, a story in concrete materials of what happens inside and of what it stands for'.[37]

The Origins of Islam in South Africa

The arrival of the Dutch settlers (and the NGK) in the Cape in 1652 also brought about the arrival of Islam in South Africa. The first Muslims in South Africa were slaves owned by the VOC, brought from what they referred to as their 'Indian Empire'.[38] While they came from diverse origins (the coastlands of India and Ceylon (now Sri Lanka), the Malaysian–Indonesian archipelago, Madagascar and the coastlands of Africa), their shared religion led them to form the core of the Cape Muslim community.[39] In addition to the slaves, high-ranking Muslim political prisoners, who included educated princes and imams, were brought as prisoners by the Dutch to the Cape and, after their release, they settled into the Cape Muslim society.[40]

As the NGK was the only permitted form of religion in the colony, Islam was initially practised in private. With greater religious freedom after 1795 the practice of Islam was more openly tolerated. It was only in 1804, when the Cape was returned to the Dutch by the British, that religious tolerance became official policy and Islam was allowed to be openly practised.[41]

As the Cape Muslim community was composed of a geographically and culturally diverse group of people, Afrikaans was adopted as their common language. Some writers, such as the historian Achmat Davids, argue that Afrikaans was actually created by the community, adapting the Dutch spoken by their masters and adding words from their own individual cultures and languages.[42] The language was used for religious instruction by the community and the first text of written Afrikaans was produced at the Cape in 1856 using Arabic script.[43]

The Second Wave of Muslim Immigration

The second wave of Muslim immigration to South Africa started in 1860. These immigrants consisted largely of indentured labourers from India brought the British Natal colony to work on the sugar plantations. Most of these indentured immigrants chose to stay in South Africa rather than return to India.[44] Later (from the 1870s onwards) Indian Muslim traders (so-called passenger Indians) moved to South Africa in search of business opportunities. While many of the indentured immigrants were Hindu, the traders were predominantly Muslim. With their financial backing, new mosques and madrassas were soon constructed.[45]

Muslim traders soon started migrating inland to the Boer Republics, establishing shops and business in most small towns. This migration increased after the discovery of gold and the establishment of Johannesburg in 1886, creating the nucleus of the future Transvaal Muslim community.[46] Immigration to the Boer republics was difficult both because of the distance and the discriminatory laws. Trade was often the only occupation available to the community given that land rights were limited and restrictions were placed on participation in mining.[47]

After the Anglo-Boer War, Muslim immigration to South Africa virtually stopped. The small, economically independent Muslim communities in both the Transvaal and Natal established their own mosques, madrassas and schools in relative independence from external influences.[48] This isolation was further deepened under apartheid when discriminatory legislation reinforced the social and religious identity of the predominantly Indian Muslim community. The Group Areas Act physically consolidated the community and removed them to outlying segregated townships (such as Lenasia in Johannesburg) while policies such as Christian National Education continued to undermine their identity.[49]

It is not surprising that the South African Muslim community should always have been active in resisting oppression, be it early religious restrictions or apartheid policies. The mosque, the centre of Muslim religious life, was often also the site for acts of resistance. The Hamidia Mosque in Newtown, Johannesburg, was, in 1908, the site of Gandhi's first passive resistance campaign involving the burning of passes prescribed as part of the Asiatic Law Amendment Act.[50]

The decline and eventual end of the apartheid state from the 1980s onwards led to a third wave of Muslim immigration. The new immigrants have more in common with South Africa's original Muslim community, coming from diverse backgrounds (in Africa, Somalia, Malawi, Morocco, Tunisia, Egypt, Nigeria and Ghana; and in Asia, India, Pakistan and Bangladesh), bound only by their shared religious identity. Many come as political and economic refugees, adding to an increasingly vibrant multicultural Muslim community.[51]

Islamic Architecture in South Africa

While there is a long tradition of Islamic architecture in Africa, the South African variant developed in isolation from established architectural traditions in the Muslim world. South Africa's first mosque, the Auwal, located in Upper Dorp Street in Cape Town, dates from the late 18th century and was adapted from an existing warehouse.[52] Early purpose-built Cape mosques differ little from contemporary churches, being largely in the contemporary Gothic Revival style, which was also predominant for NGK churches of this period. With Cape Muslims being both diverse and removed from their cultural origins, there was no other precedent for them to follow. The Natal and Transvaal Muslim community had, by contrast, strong connections with their home cultures and architectural traditions.[53]

In his study and documentation of the Transvaal mosque, Le Roux[54] observes that there is little documentary evidence for the architectural origins of local mosque architecture. Traditional Indian Muslim architecture does not provide possible architectural precedents. While early Indian mosques in South Africa followed the pattern of mosque planning that originated in the Middle East and North Africa, new spatial arrangements and architectural expressions emerged over time. Local architectural traditions and building techniques influenced the form and appearance of the buildings, resulting in a style described as 'the least Islamic of the great Muslim architectural styles'.[55]

The first permanent Transvaal mosques, it has been argued, were designed with the image of the Indian mosque in mind. While the designers of these early mosques are unknown, it is thought that they were indirectly designed by their communities, by instructing a builder or draughtsman.[56]

Figure 8.1: The former Johannesburg West NGK / Masjid-ul-Islam. (Photograph by Brendan Hart)

They were free-standing structures, simple in form and built out of locally available materials (clay brick, corrugated iron and precast concrete) and painted white as were their Indian progenitors. Their corrugated iron roof is often hidden behind a decorated parapet (often using readily available precast concrete elements). Minarets were not often used or, when they do appear, were greatly reduced in size and purely decorative (such as in the old Juma Masjid, or Friday Mosque, in Johannesburg). Le Roux describes these buildings as being '*maquettes* of the original', 'tempered by the economic reality' of the immigrant community in the Transvaal.[57]

The 1989 demolition of the original 1918 Johannesburg Juma Masjid marked the beginning of a new period of mosque architecture in the city. With a growing sense of confidence, the Johannesburg Muslim community proposed a larger mosque in a more international 'pan-Islamic' style of architecture, thereby reasserting the identity of formerly isolated communities as part of the broader Muslim world.

The Masjid-ul-Islam

Built in 1940, the Mayfair West Dutch Reformed Church was part of a collection of new NGK buildings developed to serve the rapidly growing Afrikaner population in the western part of Johannesburg. The formerly 'rural' church and its congregations were fast becoming urbanised as members moved to the city, a process that the church authorities themselves still saw as essentially regressive and associated directly with moral decline. The church's response was to establish many smaller congregations to attract people to the faith and better serve these 'strangers' in the city.[58] With individual churches having congregations of around 300 to 400 people, the concentrated Afrikaner population in Johannesburg's western inner-city suburbs gave rise to a large number of small NGK congregations (and those of other Reformed churches) developing in close proximity to one another.

The 1940 Johannesburg West NGK was established six blocks away from the original church building. The prolific architectural firm of Geers and Geers was commissioned to design the building, one of many NGK churches the practice would design for a period of over a decade from the mid-1930s.[59] The practice was a partnership between father Leendert Marinus

Geers (1877–1957) and son Geurt Marinus Jacobus Geers (1909–45). The younger Geers had been apprenticed in Gerhard Moerdijk's architectural practice and the latter's influence can be clearly seen in the Geers' work,[60] as their buildings are a variant of Moerdijk's preferred 'neo-Byzantine' style with some Art Deco and even early modernist architectural overtones.

The plan of the building is based on Moerdijk's Greek cross. As it is located on a small suburban site, the southern leg of the cross had to be 'amputated'. Internally the building had raked amphitheatre-style seating focusing on the pulpit which was located on the southern wall. Finishes in the building were kept very simple: the materials were often left in their natural state; a face-brick dado (using the same finish as the outside of the building) was paired with plastered and painted walls above; and there were simple geometric stained-glass windows.

Social Change

An acute housing shortage from the 1970s onwards forced a number of upper-middle-class Indian and Coloured families to move into the greater Mayfair area, which was then still by law a 'white' suburb. This process of breaking the apartheid state's segregation laws (for largely economic rather than ideological reasons) was termed 'greying'.[61] While it was illegal for non-white families to move into the area, the white residents responded with few complaints. A contemporary publication by the South African Institute of Race Relations suggests that this was because the new upper-middle-class Indian residents had 'well-paying jobs' and were of 'sober habits', and were possibly preferred by the existing white residents and particularly by landlords to low-income white tenants.[62] Government resistance was ineffective, leading to the effective (if not legal) desegregation of the area.

The end of apartheid and the repeal of the Group Areas Act in the 1990s allowed for the already established Indian community to expand. This expansion corresponded with the decline of the original Afrikaner community. While this could be seen as a reaction to social changes, it seems that it was at least equally driven by economics as properties in the area began fetching far higher values than before.[63] It thus became profitable to move.

The shrinking Afrikaner community meant that it became difficult for

Figure 8.2: Signs of change in Mayfair West: The former church hall of the Johannesburg West NGK converted into a mosque. (Photograph by Brendan Hart)

so many small congregations to continue as before. Existing congregations began to merge (a reversal of the expansion of the 1930s and 1940s). With more buildings than were needed to serve the western suburbs of Johannesburg, the congregation decided to sell the Johannesburg West NGK building. In 1995 the building and church hall were sold. Eventually the Brixton, Cottesloe, Crosby West, Langlaagte and Johannesburg West NGK congregations all merged, and their redundant buildings were sold.

The Johannesburg West NGK building was purchased by Mr Akhtar Thokan, who had been looking for premises for the establishment of a mosque in the area. He noted that the sale was 'about economics, not religion' although the minister of the church added that the congregation's preference was that the building should continue to be used for religious purposes. Other congregations did not necessarily share these sentiments, and the local Gereformeerde (or Dopper) congregation chose to sell their building for conversion into a private home.

The emergence of mosques in formerly white areas has followed a general pattern, starting with the establishment of a *jamaat khana* (prayer facility) by the community to fulfil their immediate needs. As the local community grows and funds are raised, a mosque is built. With time this is often followed by a madrassa and, if the mosque is big enough, even a hall.[64] For the Masjid-ul-Islam, the process was different: the building was purchased with the intention of creating a progressive mosque without the preceding smaller prayer facilities.

The conversion of the former church into a mosque was surprisingly simple. Initially only minimal functional changes were made. Pews were removed and, in order for the building to be oriented towards Mecca, the internal spatial orientation of the building was rotated by 180 degrees. While initially prayers happened 'uphill' on the original raked floor, early renovations corrected this and added facilities for the required ritual ablutions. Being a progressive mosque, women participate fully in the life of the mosque and the main prayer space has designated (but equal) facilities for both sexes. Externally no changes were initially made though there were later some minor functional additions. All original finishes remained and the former steeple is now referred to as the minaret. The founding mosque committee decided that 'simplicity be used as a benchmark for all decisions', and money should be spent on the development of people rather than buildings,[65] in

Figures 8.3 & 8.4: The former Brixton Hervormde Church building (left) converted into a Hindu temple and the former Brixton Gereformeerde Church building turned into a house. (Photographs by Brendan Hart)

accordance with the hadith (or saying of the Prophet) that 'all the world is a masjid', and that any temple built by a previous faith can be repurposed as a mosque because 'there is no other god but Allah'.[66] This builds on the long tradition of mosque architecture adapting and developing from local architectural traditions and thereby creating local Islamic architectural styles that respond to their own individual culture and context.

It is popularly thought that the community response to the conversion of a former church into a mosque always involves cultural and religious conflict, arising from the displacement of one cultural or religious group by another. Evidence for such a view could be found in the Johannesburg daily newspaper *The Star*, which in 2012 published the headline 'Holy War for One of City's Oldest Churches'.[67] This article, as well as others in other newspapers, and discussions on local talk radio, described how the Langlaagte NGK (one of the oldest in the city) had become a 'casualty' of the progressive emigration of Afrikaners from Johannesburg's inner-city suburbs. The NGK was 'lambasted' by an independent bishop (who had been renting the building) for selling it to a 'foreign religion'[68] for use as an educational institution.[69] These comments reflected the tensions felt as a result of changes to the fixed identity and demographics of the apartheid city.

In this light, the response of the remaining members of the former church congregation is surprising, and is possibly a more realistic representation of their sentiments without the sensationalism or rhetoric of the press. The mosque committee, when pressed for comment on what the former congregants might feel towards them, had expressed a certain reticence. Those spoken to were circumspect as to how they would respond, perhaps aware of past prejudices while projecting a degree of uncertainty as to how the building's 'conversion' would be received outside the Muslim community. While the dominee (minister) of the church did receive threats when the sale of the building was proposed, he felt that these threats came from outside the community.[70] They were more an expression of fear of loss of identity or simply a matter of prejudice and ignorance.

In general, congregants who were interviewed spoke of the church as 'just a building', reflecting the common Christian attitude towards deconsecrated churches. At an individual level, where there was possibly even a greater sense of attachment and of the building having personal significance, the feeling of loss or regret was far less than might have been expected.

Part of this acceptance of change and of the rescripting of the building may be due to its visual continuity. The former dominee explains that when looking at the building, 'I am able to recall my fond memories'; 'I appreciate it that the building has not been changed', explaining that he is unsure what he would feel if the appearance of the building had been dramatically altered. He muses that the attachment that a person has to a building is much like that to a piece of art or design. It is something very personal and can have a profound effect on you. Although the change of use of the building can be seen to represent a loss, the building has become a very 'powerful symbol'. It represents both the changes in area and, perhaps more importantly, 'the interactions of us as people'.

The congregation show a similar mix of sentiments. For some, the former church building 'reminds you of who you are and where you come from', but they express sadness that 'the style of the suburb [the built environment] has to change', explaining that 'it is important to keep the old character of the suburb. I get a bit heartsore about the visual changes.' Perhaps this is an expression of sorrow over the loss of the community rather than of the building itself. Others, while nostalgically recalling their association with the building, feel more sympathetic towards the new community. 'When the Indian people moved into the area, they had to travel far to go to mosque. This was not fair … Muslim or not, they become your community … The fact that it is now a mosque is not important to the memories … You still "own" a part of the building.'

How the congregation chose to dispose of the church building is perhaps the clearest expression of its value to them. While a church building is deemed no longer to have value after deconsecration, the congregation preferred (in the dominee's words, were 'happy') to sell the building knowing it would continue to be used for religious purposes. There is a 'general truth of God in all religions', the dominee explains, a shared history and spiritual continuity that can be used as a means for unifying the greater community.

A Hybrid Architecture?

How do you go about understanding the development of the Masjid-ul-Islam in the context of post-apartheid, postcolonial Johannesburg? One could look at it simply as a form of neo-conservative postmodernism, with one dominant social group with its own set of values replacing another. This is, however, very likely an oversimplification of the social complexities of both the building and the post-apartheid city. The rescripting of the building is also not simply the replacing of one set of meanings, values and associations with another, as both seem to continue to (co)exist. Is this, then, the archetypal postcolonial hybrid, expressed as part of postcolonial thinking – the emergence of a new state of being that is made up of both historical pasts but remade (unintentionally and not necessarily by choice) into something new? In postcolonial thought the tension that exists between the colonial and postcolonial (apartheid and post-apartheid) is often used in reference to the power relations that exist within issues of 'cultural diversity, ethnic, racial and cultural difference'.[71] One potential outcome of this tension is 'hybridisation'. Does this mean that the rescripted form of the Mayfair West NGK (the Masjid-ul-Islam) is an emergent postcolonial, post-apartheid hybrid?

Given that precolonial 'purity' can never be completely recovered, the postcolonial person, environment, discourse and identity will all be affected and altered.[72] Hybridity, a term originating from the biological sciences, is an expression of this. The hybrid is a 'cross-fertilisation'[73] between two different sources, resulting in the creation of something new.

Homi K. Bhabha's concept of hybridity emerges out of an understanding of the differences between 'cultural diversity' and 'cultural difference'. In his understanding, cultural diversity speaks of many different cultures, each with its own nature and 'pre-given state', living side by side but not affecting or interacting with one another. Cultural difference, on the other hand, is seen as a statement on or of culture.[74] Cultural diversity implies the possibility of simultaneous coexistence between various cultures. Cultural difference, for its part, does not have the same implication of the possibility of unaffected coexistence.[75] It is from this difference, this inability to coexist in their 'pre-given state' without some sort of interaction, that hybridity emerges. The apartheid state relied on the idea of cultures being able to coexist separately (even if forced to do so through state oppression) while denying (and actively fighting against) the potential or risk of hybridity.

The tension between two cultures that are forced to interact creates a boundary or 'third space' where 'meanings and values are (mis)read or signs misappropriated'.[76] It is in this 'third space' between the tensions that the hybrid emerges. For Bhabha, the hybrid is not a simple mixing of the two cultures and does not resolve the tension. It emerges as something new and separate from its conflicting cultural origins.[77] The hybrid takes aspects of both of its 'parent' cultures, both the oppressed and oppressor culture.[78] The hybrid belongs to both, but at the same time to neither, of its parent cultures. While a hybrid's difference may be seen as threatening, it allows the hybrid to 'challenge both the hegemony of the norm and the power of the dominant majority'.[79]

The architecture of the NGK forms part of the constructed identity of the Afrikaner people. It is part of an attempt, as Bill Ashcroft and colleagues argue,[80] to deal with the 'sense of place and placelessness' felt by settler societies located between the colonial centre and the colonised. The culture of the colonial Muslim immigrant is similarly complex, being 'both plural and partial', part of two countries but not belonging to either.[81] While the architecture of the NGK can be said to be intentionally constructed, that of the Transvaal mosque is best interpreted as hybridised, emerging out of the cultural clashes (and clashes in building traditions) felt by the early Muslim community.

The Masjid-ul-Islam and other similarly converted NGK buildings can also be seen as examples of potentially hybrid space, spaces that emerge at the boundary or overlap between two different cultures that are forced into some sort of interaction. Bhabha's concept of hybridity, of the 'third space' that allows for the emergence of the hybrid, is to an extent spatialised even if it was developed metaphorically. The post-apartheid city, particularly in areas where there has been rapid social change, is that third space. Newly integrated communities have created opportunities for the cultural conflict necessary for the emergence of hybridity.

What a rescripted building such as the Masjid-ul-Islam does is to allow for a degree of simultaneity out of which the hybrid emerges. It allows for both continuity and discontinuity in the urban fabric and, psychologically, for the former congregants. These types of artefacts can be referred to as fossils.[82] Fossils are colonial relics that have been left behind and, lacking their original communities, have lost much of their original power and significance. Fossils have great potential, the potential to be reimagined and layered with new significance. The potential of the fossil parallels the nature of the hybrid. The creative reuse of these fossils is more that the simple mixing of two different cultures or architectures.

The old church in Mayfair West has gained a new life. As a mosque, it leaves behind and moves beyond its former church congregants. While it may be an anchor for their memories, an object of nostalgic reflection, it is in itself no longer representative of them. In the early stages of this hybridisation of space and place, it is easy to see the physical and social remnants and layers of the past and maintain a sense of connection and identity. The building and community are, however, not static. They are both constantly changing and evolving because of the 'third space' in which they find themselves. Will the passage of time and the passing of the original church community change this? Will new congregants and Muslim immigrants, who only identify with the building as a mosque, perpetuate its hybrid identity? Similarly, will the proposed (but as yet unrealised) more substantial external changes to the building, to make it more visually identifiable as a mosque by playing on Islamic architectural references, build upon or negate its potentially transient hybrid identity?

The emergence of new hybrid spaces and identities in the postcolonial, post-apartheid city offers an opportunity to look at and understand how people and communities deal with the complex social and physical realities of post-apartheid Johannesburg. The former Johannesburg West NGK/Masjid-ul-Islam provides us with a successful and living hybrid response to this. While it may be viewed as a possible prototype for a postcolonial, post-apartheid mosque, it is perhaps better seen as a prototype for the layered process and engagement involved in the emergence of the building and community. As an architectural hybrid, it may be an isolated example, the product of a particular set of values of its particular congregation, rather than the emergence of a new typology. But it embraces its diversity and difference as its strength. Its rescripting has created the space, both physical and psychological, for the emergence of a new (hybrid) postcolonial, post-apartheid identity for its community, both the new and the old one – an identity that can navigate and comfortably exist in the tension between seemingly different worlds and cultures of the post-apartheid city.

Chapter Nine
Tropical Bungalow

Roland Gunst and Esther Severi

During the Belgian colonisation of the Democratic Republic of Congo, the entire Congolese territory and population were marked by squares, circles, lines, hooks, boundaries, walls, zones ... Congo was fragmented and scarred by spatial and social categories. Call it 'zoning'.

Spatial architecture was an instrument of oppression to mould a social architecture, assigning to blacks and whites specific roles, privileges, prohibitions and controlled access to zones. An ideology of oppression made black bodies the servants of white masters.

One of the most noticeable remains of colonial urbanism in Boma is the Tropical Bungalow. Some are more than a hundred years old, but are still used as governmental offices, homes or businesses or combine professional and private spheres.

TROPICAL BUNGALOW

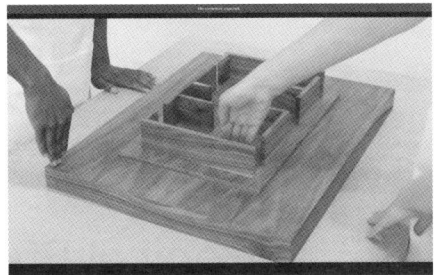

The bungalow was made of walls of clay bricks, concrete or wood, the roof of straw or corrugated iron. Some used a prefab iron structure. The Tropical Bungalow was the first building typology to be constructed by Belgian colonials in the Belgian Congo. The late-19th-century prefabricated metal structures were produced by Belgian firms.

These prefab iron structures were once presented as a sophisticated means of hastening the process of colonial expansion, extraction and control. Iron and technology placed a line between the scientifically evolved coloniser and inferior colonial subjects.

The sole function of the bungalow was to keep the coloniser mentally and physically sane and to guarantee maximal exploitation of Congo, the men-devouring iron machine.

The iron framework, elevated above the ground, staged the daily colonial theatre of life for a Congolese audience. The exhibition of the interior life through many open doors and of the exterior life on the veranda around the house and a large garden delineated the binary between the inside and the outside world. This colonial exhibitionism exposed the privileges of the coloniser and the endless labour of Congolese 'boys' navigating the house. The iron frame functioned as a monument performing the social architecture.

In the bungalow, interracial interactions were regulated to prevent

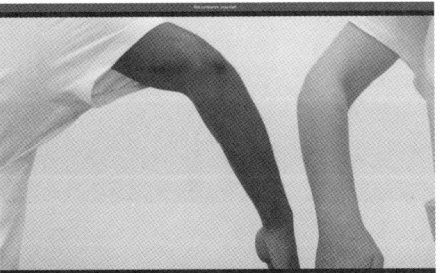
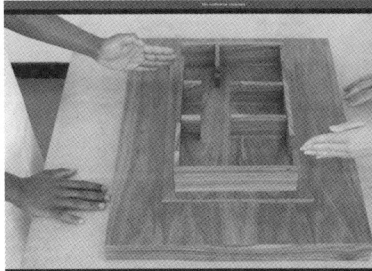

mental, physical and sexual degeneration of white bodies through Congolese influences. This meant a separation of the life and movements of the white coloniser or masters from the 'boys', the black male domestic servants. The servants became submissive because of their specific role, their assigned 'place' within the colonial system and their regulated movement patterns in their daily living environment.

Colonial infrastructures maintained the Congolese in a more or less permanent state of trance. The colonised was constrained by a series of rituals of submission. He might be commanded to shake, cry and tremble, to prostrate himself while shivering in the dirt, to go from place to place singing, dancing.

The 19th-century design of the Tropical Bungalow evolved from bungalow models made for single white males to villa models adapted for European

 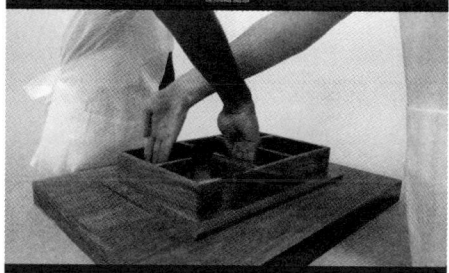 

couples. The presence of European women prompted the progressive disappearance of the veranda with many doors and the creation of an inward-oriented and protective existence. The design redefined the circulation, interaction and access of black bodies to white bodies. The 'boys' would minimise the amount of time spent inside the bungalow, the white space. Cooking and other lengthy activities happened behind the bungalow in a neutral zone.

This type of 'trance' architecture generated structural micro-aggressions, causing trauma and post-traumatic stress disorder (PTSD) for black bodies. Trauma creates dissociation between the body and the mind, memory loss; it affects self-esteem and (bodily) identity. Trauma influenced the way Congolese talked, walked, thought, saw ...

Today many Congolese who experienced colonisation and who live surrounded by colonial architecture long for the colonial era.

Are oppressed bodies today still under a spell, a trance, to the point where they forget the dark side of the colonial experience?

Victims of oppression and prosecution adopt different strategies for dealing with trauma. For example, the collective memory of Angolan refugees in Zambia did not focus on the violence of the civil war they fled, but on fish: they fondly remember how they caught, prepared and ate fish in Angola. It indicates that they have repressed those memories, into the ground, into unofficial consciousness. For some reason, they cannot articulate their memories of the violence. The collective memory does not collect facts but constructs a story.

The Congolese remember the best aspects of Belgian colonisation and forget the worst.

The absence of a canonised historiography leaves much room for a fragmented collective memory, which in turn is symptomatic of the disintegration of the social fabric in Congolese society and its failing state.

Communities creatively select, organise and interpret events that promote community spirit and forget internal contradictions so as to emphasise what they have in common.

Reminiscing is pre-eminently a social event. Every person has only one past but tells or writes about it in different ways, depending on the context in which he or she finds himself and the person(s) with whom he or she communicates.

Even absolute systems and constructions are always inhabited by spaces of negotiation: blind spots where squares, circles, lines, hooks, boundaries, walls or zones can be discussed, where ideologies can be countered. Domestic servants made arrangements with their white bosses to facilitate their cohabitation.

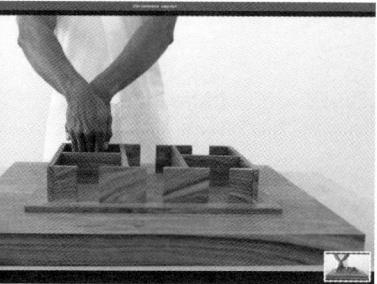 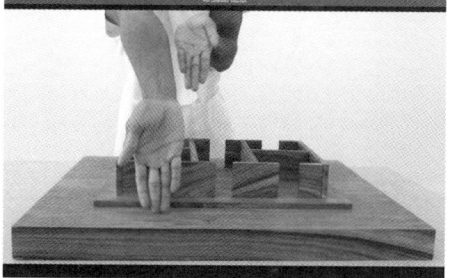 

Congolese labourers used urban tactics, for example by hijacking a bridge in the city of Matadi on 26 November 1945 and organising a strike on that vital point of access to and from the European city and the port to obtain better working conditions and better wages. Even though the strike was short-lived, as it was crushed with the use of major force causing several deaths, this particular episode revealed the fragility of the colonial authorities' spatial strategy of racial segregation.

The colonised had their own understanding of colonial space to define symbolic spaces for use as spaces of resistance.

Research on the current situation of colonial (infra)structures like hotels and governmental buildings in DRC reveals more spaces of negotiations. The colonial structures are now firmly occupied by various forms of life. Different kinds of people, enterprises and materials mingle with colonial remainders. Ingenious survival tactics are at play. A dual process of identity construction continues to develop. These structures can have a hybrid identity, simultaneously representing different things.

Colonial remainders blur the line between zones and identities, between the foreign and the indigenous, the inside and the outside. They explicitly embody an in-between state of constantly renegotiated space.

As opposed to trance architecture, anti-trance architecture is the hijacking of space or the encoding of strategies of rehabilitation in the existing spatial architecture. Infrastructures are multi-layered and alterable when one finds new readings and encodes new meanings in the spaces. Organic street revolutions and hybrid designs are just a few examples of what anti-trance architecture can be.

The absence of a Congolese collective memory of the colonial era linked to the remaining architectures of oppression is problematic for identity building.

TROPICAL BUNGALOW

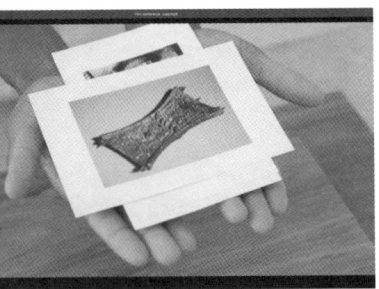  

How should the Congolese people deal with that colonial patrimony? What other readings and strategies of rehabilitation can be activated in colonial spaces? Research indicates that a combination of psychological and movement therapy is the best strategy for healing from trauma.

To arrive at a radical proposition for a new strategy to renegotiate history and to access trauma, we must compare the Tropical Bungalow with a Congolese memory board.

A memory board is an mnemonic device used by Luba court historians to recall memory during a performance called Milandu. A memory board can be a body, an object, a space.

Milandu is a verbal and performative practice in which different parties negotiate around one historical event in an attempt to solve an ongoing dispute. Around this one specific event each party adapts its own critical narrative according to social, political and economic motivations and to the audience present. The chosen performed narrative defines, imposes and declares the social and political identity of a speaker or a community. Generally Milandu could be applied to any trauma. You just need one common event around which the dialogue is built.

The memory board divides a space into zones in which memory events are encoded. The narrator navigates the memory board and performs in a specific zone so as to provoke memory reproduction.

To critically reconstruct history, facing the past and confronting the mechanism of oppression that caused certain forms of amnesia could act as a psychological and kinetic therapy to heal the trauma of an individual or a community.

Might the Tropical Bungalow become a space of negotiation and rehabilitation where collective memory and (body) identity can be (re)constructed through a polyvocal performative ritual inspired by Milandu?

A radical approach demands a fluid architecture, where architecture is at the intersection of many identities and histories in a fluid state, a permanent state of evolution and change.

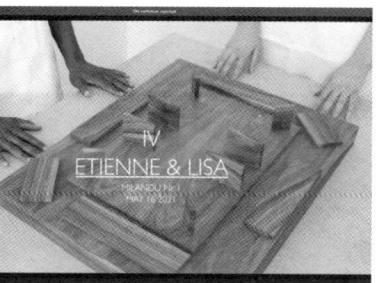

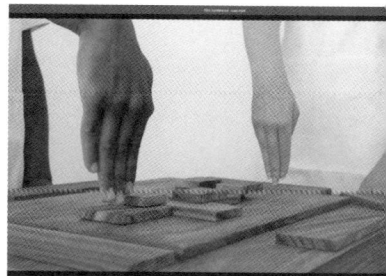

The colonial bungalow must be fully deconstructed to dismantle its original function.

A modular version of the Tropical Bungalow, used as a memory board, becomes a public space and functions as a stage.

The roof must be removed and the walls replaced by a modular system made of locally produced, light, organic, environmentally friendly materials like wood. The walls are multifunctional and can be moved around to create a new interior visible to the outside.

This wooden modular system is the answer to the European iron prefab strategy of oppression.

MILANDU TAKES PLACE IN AN *open space and in dialogue with speakers, victims, perpetrators, witnesses, any related party, and a surrounding*

TROPICAL BUNGALOW

 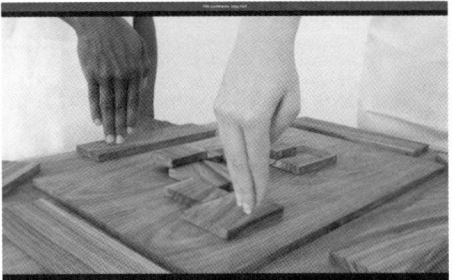

audience.

The bungalow opens up and reconnects with the external environment and engages with the reality of daily life surrounding that space. The boundary between the inside and the outside disappears to become a fluid space, a trans space where architecture is never static but fluid and in constant movement – as life is.

Walls become benches and zones on the floor to which memory events are assigned. Each speaker creates a unique constellation of zones, a fluid architecture. Each speaker adapts a critical reading of the space according to his motivations and the audience present. The memory board stays open for change. During the Milandu, the architecture changes to serve the narrative of every speaker.

Etienne and Lisa engage in a Milandu over an event that happened on 1 July 1946.

Etienne enters the first zone. It is the garden at the back of the bungalow. Etienne is 25 years old. He stands in front of his boss and hears complaints about his work ethic. Etienne bows his head and listens.

Lisa enters the third zone. It is the master bedroom …

To watch the video, please scan the QR code below:

Part Three

Residual Places

Chapter Ten

Notes for a Visual Essay on the Experience of Art Deco in South Africa

Pamila Gupta

Introduction

> 'We sucked our smoothies – mine had a protein supplement – sitting on a wall by the beach, and I made notes for an essay on Art Deco.'[1]

For this chapter, I am interested in thinking through the experience of Art Deco and locating it in South Africa. I take British writer Geoff Dyer's inspiring and insipid (equally, at different turns) piece entitled 'The Despair of Art Deco'[2] with its focus on Art Deco in Miami, Florida,[3] as the impetus for developing my own visual ethnography of the Art Deco movement in South Africa and its urban specificities. I meditate on certain features of Art Deco that I witnessed and photographed on three separate architectural tours of three cities (Springs, Johannesburg and Durban) during the second half of 2018. That I was accompanied alternately by a motley group of urban planners, artists and writers no doubt influenced the way I perceived these architectural sites with their layered histories of renovation,[4] and proceeded to develop my own essay. That I experienced

Art Deco by alternately driving (two locations), walking (one location) and photographing (all three locations) in these places becomes my research methodology for approaching African cityness and its built environment.

I provide a general overview of the Art Deco movement in South Africa before detailing my own experiences by way of a set of anthropological musings, which are threefold: (1) I look at the façade of Art Deco, and what perhaps lies behind, below, above and alongside these buildings; (2) I contemplate the typologies of Art Deco buildings in the three cities that I saw and photographed (which include public offices, hotels, and private residences and flats) and offer a template of Art Deco styles; (3) I address certain Art Deco ornamental features that caught my eye for the South African case – specifically, light fixtures, fonts/lettering and paint colours, that they are simultaneously forms of infrastructure and affect in South Africa also attests to their enduring role in city life.[5] As well, the series of photographs that accompany my essay reflect these same musings, a fine-tuning of the aesthetics and politics of ornamentation.[6] Lastly, I conclude on a less despairing note than Dyer to ponder the role of the Art Deco enthusiast instead, and the way in which the incompleteness of Art Deco in South Africa compels a response of 'conviviality' (following Francis Nyamnjoh)[7] from its 'frontier African' urban residents and from viewers alike.

The Art Deco Movement in South Africa

> 'Art Deco buildings are inhabited, of course, but whereas, from the outside, they look extraordinary, inside, the experience is fairly ordinary. But this is why the Art Deco style is so alluring.'[8]

Historically, the Art Deco decorative movement in the South African case was directly tied to the unfolding of industrial and racial capitalism across the wide swathe of the country.[9] As camps and small towns cropped up and took shape in the aftermath of the discovery of gold on the Witwatersrand, and the making of Johannesburg as a city in 1886, a set of new immigrants arrived alongside, seeking their fortunes largely in service of the mining industry. These small towns slowly made way for metropolitan centres with downtowns, paved boulevards and high-rise buildings in the period after the

Figure 10.1: Durban Arcades. (Photograph by Pamila Gupta)

turn of the century, and in relation to an increasing demand for places to work and live: this process reflected South Africa's coming into being as an empire, country and nation-state.

The three cities that I will focus on here – Springs, Joburg and Durban – much like other Global South (colonial) cities during this time frame, increasingly became sites to fulfil the modernist aspirations of the Art Deco movement,[10] streamlined technology alongside industrial and nautical motifs inserted into crevices and corners as a sign of South Africa's self-assured worldliness (as a centre of both mining and trade) in the period between the 1920s and 1950s. Concurrently, architects and urban planners were sought out both locally and overseas to help envision these places of grandeur, big and small, across the country. They, in turn, employed certain 'geographies of affluence' like Art Deco to help define their city sense of selves.[11] The architectural historian Federico Freschi writes:

> In the context of a city and a country in the throes of dramatic urbanization and modernization, the binary tropes of primitivism and progress set up in this decorative program [Art Deco] become emblematic of the emerging construct of the twentieth-century white South African, emphatically urban rather than rural, and standing on the brink of a fully mechanized future. While the scenes of unspoiled nature serve as a reminder of the wildness of the African context in which this imaginary is rooted, they are contained and neutralized within the streamlined envelope of the overall form. In the final analysis, modernity is victorious, the billowing pollution a proud testament of the triumph of culture over nature.[12]

This decorative movement was also used as a form of public expression, through large-scale architectural projects, of enduring political and economic times, that of imperial and nationalist white South Africanness.[13] The urban historian Keith Beavon writes that after 1932 Johannesburg was a city 'where there was plenty of money for projects, buildings, and public works that caught the imagination of the Council, companies, and private investors'.[14] Equally, it was about conveying 'optimism' by way of the 'fortunes' and 'fashions' in smaller towns, as Arianna Lissoni and Roshan Dadoo argue for the case of the new Jubilee House building constructed in 1940 by Indian businessman and entrepreneur M.M. Dadoo in Krugersdorp. They write: 'Jubilee House's modernity, glamour, sophistication and celebration of exuberant capitalism reflect[ed] the Art Deco spirit of the age.'[15] The architectural historian Clive Chipkin, in his monumental book entitled *Johannesburg Style*, dedicates a whole chapter to Art Deco Johannesburg, describing the residential buildings in my own neighbourhood of Killarney, specifically the buildings named Whitehall Court (1920s) and Mentone Court (1935), as capturing the 'essential period-feel of the times'.[16] As well, Art Deco's flourishing appeal was also helped by the fact that changes in technology and construction throughout this same time frame allowed for these relatively inexpensive embellishments to be incorporated with ease, particularly as buildings moved away from high design and specialised craft to absorb rising economic and labour costs in the face of looming apartheid.[17]

It is now some eighty years after this 'spirited' age and 'period-feel' in South Africa; while a large number of these buildings still exist and have been actively preserved, many others have been destroyed or demolished, rebuilt or renovated, neglected or abandoned in the interim. My interest in this chapter is less a focus on the *how* and *why* of Art Deco 'loss' in the midst of its tumultuous apartheid past and post-apartheid present, than a visual study of that which actively remains and endures in the here and now of South Africa,[18] including the politics of redress and recuperation, for a book that is very much focused on confronting the infrastructural vestiges of colonialism and their positionality today. In some sense it is the irrelevance of 'in whose place' these Art Deco buildings and spaces are regarded now. Moreover, it is these general traits of this decorative movement detailed here that serve as a necessary backdrop for later sections of the chapter, which take up the urban specificities of Art Deco in my three case studies: Springs, Joburg and Durban.

Experiencing Art Deco, the Driving vs Walking *Flâneur*

> 'As soon as we had moved our stuff into [room number] 6 we went for a walk … to experience the Art Deco experience for ourselves.'[19]

We began our Art Deco experience of Springs on a crisp sunny September day in 2018, only, instead of walking as Geoff Dyer did in Miami, we went for a drive in South Africa[20] to Springs, one of the most preserved Art Deco

Figure 10.2: Springs Fire Station. (Photograph by Pamila Gupta)

heritage sites in the country. Interestingly, it is second only to Miami in terms of the number of Art Deco buildings, which perhaps compelled me in the first place to think relationally about Miami and Springs.[21] The town is less than 40 kilometres from Joburg, so we had planned for a half-day outing in which we would take in the sights and go for lunch before returning home. It was in the car, after our first stop at the Springs Fire Station in its full Art Deco regalia, that we started chatting about our individual interests in Art Deco and why we willingly signed up for this driving tour together. We contemplated what it means to move beyond an academic interest in the history of this decorative movement, and dwell inside Art Deco today. It was Ivan Vladislavić, ever the reader and writer, who in a passing moment mentioned the essay by Geoff Dyer on Art Deco (included in a book with the intriguing title of *Yoga for People Who Can't Be Bothered to Do It*), which in some sense prompted this chapter,[22] and helped me navigate a way forward, using his meditation on Art Deco in Miami for my own in a very different place located in the Global South. In other words, I set up Dyer's carefully crafted text as a productive counterpoint to my own essay, by way of three features: (1) My focus is on South Africa in contrast to his writings on the US, and, specifically, on Springs; (2) My experience of Art Deco is largely through the acts of driving and photography as compared to that of walking for Dyer; (3) I want to counter his despair when confronting Art Deco with my enthusiasm instead, and as a form of Global South politics.

Our driving tour of Springs was followed by a walking tour of Joburg's Art Deco built environment a month later in October 2018.[23] This time round, the conversation focused on the differing styles and motifs of Art Deco interiors and exteriors we had just witnessed in the face of stark impoverishment lingering outside these same buildings. Our discussion continued over drinks and snacks at Ruth Sacks's small dining table in her Art Deco-styled flat located inside Anstey's Building (1937), before we climbed up to her rooftop for the majestic views it afforded onto inner-city Joburg. My third Art Deco experience took place in November 2018; two of us[24] were the last of the Art Deco enthusiasts to go on a driving tour of Durban, an Indian Ocean port city with a thriving business in Art Deco heritage. We passed through pastel-coloured neighbourhoods, meandered around the port itself with its nautical details (of shells and snails) on fences and boards, and drove through an inner city littered equally with Art Deco façades and rubbish. All three tours, as well as my enduring interest perhaps in all things that reflect this decorative style, are also shaped by my own everyday experience of living and thinking with historic Art Deco in my Joburg neighbourhood of Killarney.[25]

My alternation between driving (for Springs and Durban), walking (for Joburg) and photographing (from both vantage points) becomes my methodology for approaching African cityness and its Art Deco built environment in the 21st century, as a driving, walking and photographing *flâneur* in some sense. Here I want to briefly introduce driving as a different modality from walking for viewing cities more generally; this is a topic I have written about previously with regard to Johannesburg's Southern Suburbs and its Portuguese Madeiran community.[26] I point to the fact that driving (vs walking) changes one's viewpoint and framing for entering urban settings; it is also very much tied to the inequalities (of both race and class) of South African city life, and who has access to a car vs who does not. I ask how one's privileged view of a city is both restricted and opened up from the perspective of a car window, as a passenger or driver – in themselves two distinct viewpoints. Does it allow for a different vantage point, where the window becomes a protective text or screen between inside and outside? Does the city become subject to alternate ways of looking (up, down and sideways) than when walking a city at eye level? How does driving spatially orient you in a way that walking does or does not, where the sounds, smells and sensorium of city living are purposely kept at a distance? As well, can we think about photographing from both these vantage points, driving and walking, and the kind of analytic work visuality takes on? Finally, can we ponder the 'socio-nature' of city landscapes, following Jeremy Foster, who describes South Africa as 'washed with sun' in which aspects of natural beauty and political turmoil are always manifest, in its buildings as well,[27] or, following Peter Merriman,[28] who describes its routes as having 'pleats and folds' that we seam together as driving, walking and photographing *flâneurs*. These were my points of reflection as I alternated between my Art Deco experiences in Springs, Durban and Johannesburg.

Figure 10.3: Delta Park, Johannesburg. (Photograph by Pamila Gupta)

Art Deco Musings in South Africa

> 'Art Deco, after all, means nice looking, or more exactly, not as nice as it looks.'[29]

Walter Benjamin's Arcades Project[30] was an experimental work, a form of montage that juxtaposed photography with reflections on materialities as an alternate format for writing in and from Paris. In this section, I bring his musings on city life to bear on South Africa. Benjamin finds 'the lost time, of the times embedded in the spaces of things' by following 'kaleidoscopic distractions' to write about placeness.[31] I am interested in a similar pursuit; it was certain 'kaleidoscopic' impressions of Art Deco as well as their ability to provide a sense of 'placeness' for South Africa's built environment that captured my attention on our driving and walking tours, and that compelled me to write about and visualise it through an exploration of infrastructure and affect. Following Benjamin, I wanted to 'wander' through and 'wonder' about South Africa's history of Art Deco as a manner for understanding its present built environment. I decided to start collecting Art Deco ideas and features and put them together (just as Benjamin was prompted to do with his Arcades Project set in Paris, and Dyer with his writings set in Miami) in the form of a visual essay. I was also very much prompted by Ivan Vladislavić's writings on South African city life, set in Johannesburg. He writes:

> In Johannesburg ... the backdrop is always man-made. We have planted the forest the birds endorse. For hills we have mine dumps covered with grass. We do not wait for time and elements to weather us, we change the scenery ourselves, to suit our moods. Nature is for other people, in other places.[32]

Mindful of these distractions, I wanted to gather up my musings on Art Deco by way of three themes based on curious details I collected from my driving, photography and walking experiences of Art Deco in three different South African settings.

The Façade of Art Deco, or the Art of Display

'It is not accurate, I wrote, to say that a shabbiness lurks behind the façade of Art Deco: Art Deco is the façade. Art Deco is the most visible of architectural styles, arranged entirely for the eye – it's in colour! – rather than to be inhabited.'[33]

It struck me on my Art Deco tours in South Africa that this architectural movement, following along the lines of Geoff Dyer's reflections, was realistically about ostentatious display – of wealth, power, industry, of moneyed might and muscle. It very much functioned as a facade, one that Ming Wei describes as 'the face or front of the building towards a public space ... [and] a form of architecturing of the exterior [that] sets an order of visibility'.[34] Art Deco was a form of display that I both indulged in with my photographs and wanted to puncture from within the façade. I started to notice small things as I zoomed in with my camera lens on certain South African Art Deco details. I began to think about the inside vs the outside of these Art Deco fronts. I noticed the majestic views that Art Deco rooftops afforded of cityness more generally, just as the grand entrances below were heavily decorated with a range of Art Deco features – tilework, statues, trimmings, etc. What happens to the floors between the heavily decorated bottoms and tops of buildings? Who occupies those spaces? Are they empty zones or living, breathing, working spaces?

One Art Deco building in inner-city Durban that Jonathan Cane and I wandered into had been partitioned off into thriving small businesses of tailors and hair salons inside, an important detail I would not have noticed had I not ventured inside the building, a reminder once again of the enduring power of the façade of Art Deco in that city residents (like myself) rarely enter inside (unless for a specific purpose), compelled as they are by the polished finished outside. It is a point that requires further elaboration through careful historical and ethnographic study, specific to South Africa's built environment and its multiple inner-city Art Deco-lined streets. We chatted with one friendly hairdresser, and I took a photo of his self-designed, appropriately matched Art Deco signage. My encounter with this entrepreneurial hairdresser, as well as my witnessing (and photographing) of a plethora of hair salon signs plastered outside many an Art Deco building (in both Durban and Johannesburg), made me ponder the enduring commercial value of this architectural style throughout South Africa, a topic that requires more in-depth site-based research. As well, it made me think more carefully about the relationality of outside and inside, a shared pull perhaps towards aesthetics that drew this particular hairdresser, and many others like him engaged in the business of beauty, to seek out such decorative types of buildings, and rent spaces inside for discerning clients.[35] I still remember one particularly enterprising young man who asked us if we wanted to buy the valued building we had just entered; he called out that he could offer a good price as we grabbed hold of its Art Deco-styled banister and descended the staircase.

I also thought about the relational quality of Art Deco buildings to one another. Is there a tempo or rhythm that gets established between and among Art Deco buildings on the same street, like the row after row of them that we saw in downtown Springs from the car window? And what happens to those buildings not invited to join in the Art Deco dance of sorts? In Durban, Jonathan and I had a compelling conversation about what happens to non-Art Deco buildings that are located next to Art Deco ones. Do their old or new owners start to feel the need to dress them up, to imitate or copy Art Deco (by way of a fake version, or a few casual elements thrown into the mix), or pull them in another completely different architectural direction so as not to compete with their stylised neighbour who may have reigned in the past. Peering up, down and sideways at these buildings from inside and out made me ponder how one goes about seeing the back of an Art Deco building – is it even possible? In a phone conversation with the late Bill Freund (February 2019), a historian of South Africa and an Art Deco aficionado, he pointed out that the seven-storey heritage Art Deco building that he lived in (Surrey Mansions, built in 1935) in Durban's residential suburbs has only two good 'fixed-up' sides, on Currey and Crosby roads respectively, the ones that face the more visible streets, functioning as eye candy for the passerby, which, in turn, returns us to the power of the façade of Art Deco.

Typologies of Art Deco Buildings

'Effectively, the Art Deco experience is the hotel experience.'[36]

Here I disagree with Dyer, but then his experience is based on Miami, where it is largely a tourist hotel experience. Instead, I suggest the value of thinking of Art Deco in relation to the historical specificity of a city as opposed to viewing it as a worldly architectural design that more or less presented itself the same everywhere during a particular epoch. As well, it is worth looking at the layered processes of renovation that buildings have undergone in certain places (I have looked at this more carefully in relation to the city of Beira in Mozambique),[37] which tells us something about a city's built environment, its past and present sense of placeness. I noticed that the Art Deco experience in the South African case is littered with a range of building types and motifs – municipal buildings, office buildings, arcades, private homes, inner-city flats and suburban apartment buildings full of refurbished flats.

In Springs, we were given a grand tour of the perfectly (almost obsessively) restored Art Deco fire station by the manager, who took pride in detailing all its finer fixtures and features at the same time that he kept busy flirting with Noeleen.[38] We quickly took photos of several historic Art Deco arcades we spotted during our driving tour of downtown Springs, places that felt busy, lively and full of inner-city residents toing and froing as they went about their daily routines, entering and exiting small shops located inside arcade ambulatory inner hallways that also provided passageways between crowded main streets. We walked on Art Deco-styled alternating green and white tiles inside the majestic Johannesburg City Library, and quickly took photos from the second floor before we were told to stop by the security guard on duty.[39] We first drove by the beautifully restored Customs and Excise building located at the Durban port before turning inland to find a suburban sea of pastel blue, green and salmon pink Art Deco apartment buildings on Musgrave Road in Berea, Durban. Jonathan and I smiled as we chanced upon a miniaturised Art Deco-styled Protea Hotel Edward in Durban's beachside Mini-Town, which we visited on our last day there, its existence proof once again of Art Deco's iconicity in Durban.[40]

After three tours together, Jonathan and I began cataloguing two opposing Art Deco styles we were witness to in these three specific urban sites, each with its own distinct histories of architecture. We named it 'muscular' style in places like Springs and Johannesburg, cities that not coincidentally were mining centres, and linked the label directly to themes of ostentatious colonial display, work, capitalism and industry, masculinity, apartheid racial inequalities, land, silver and chrome. It is Joburg's cosmopolitanism,[41] including both its enduring 'elusiveness'[42] and 'evasiveness'[43] as a city, that its Art Deco features very much encapsulate, even embody. We named it 'cake' style for Durban, an Indian Ocean port city that also has a long history of seaside tourism (and that was included as a stopover by the Union-Castle cruise liners in the 20th century),[44] and we linked the term to themes of (white) settler-colonial leisure, the oceanic and nautical, the decorative, the tropical, femininity, frills and pastel colours. Perhaps the naming of these alternating styles (of 'muscular' vs 'cake') made sense only to the two of us, but it did make me return to Dyer as a springboard for what I witnessed in the different place of South Africa. His description of Miami was very dissimilar to what we experienced in Springs and Johannesburg (and perhaps more akin to Art Deco in New York), but not so far off from the tourist tropical oceanic dream space of Durban.

Art Deco Features, or Art Deco as Infrastructure and Affect

> 'An Art Deco lampshade bathed the Art Deco sheets in an amber of Art Deco glow. When we drew back the curtains the Art Deco spell was broken.'[45]

In this third section, I want to briefly contemplate certain decorative features of Art Deco that I saw on my South African tour. I am less interested in their ability to disappoint (as was the case for Dyer in Miami) than in their continued capacity as part of city living. My response to Dyer would also be that Art Deco has simultaneously endured as a form of infrastructure and affect in the South African case. In other words, I became curious about and focused my camera lens on certain Art Deco features that held an affective register for me. Here I follow Stephen Graham and Simon Marvin[46] in their proposal to rethink why we study certain infrastructures in certain places as a form of suggesting something about placeness. In other words, what can these features of ornamentation possibly say about South African city life? Here I am reminded of Italo Calvino's focus on certain detailings such as corners, window gratings and banisters[47] during his strolls through European city life; whereas my comparable focus was on light fixtures, fonts/lettering, and paint colours for the cities of Springs, Joburg and Durban. I peered up at a functioning Art Deco wall lamp inside the Springs Fire House, and noticed Art Deco-styled wooden reading carrels in full use in the Johannesburg City Library. I saw from the passenger seat of our car an Art Deco placard advertising an arcade in downtown Springs, and a freshly painted Art Deco-styled font featuring 'Loading Zone' on the street in front of Durban's Excise and Customs house. I zoomed my camera lens onto small perfectly gold-painted seashells and snails that I saw on blue-painted fence posts with nautical Art Deco features at the Durban port. My phone conversation with Durban Art Deco resident and aficionado Bill Freund also included a discussion of the pastel paint colour palette offered by the trustees of Surrey Mansions for its biannual repainting.

I would also add that my textual and visual focus here is on those original Art Deco features that have been retained in South Africa's built environment. Put another way, it is a form of reckoning with the incompleteness of the Art Deco built environment we face today, by responding with a disposition of 'conviviality'[48] instead, one that allows for recognition of the here and now rather than denigration of what was once in relation to what it has become. Thus, I would rather say that I saw light fixtures, fonts/lettering and paint colours as signs of Art Deco put to creative service, of thoughtful care being taken, of pride in past workmanship and of their continued value in a very different time. Certain Art Deco infrastructures are still very much put to practical use in day-to-day urban living by a racially diverse set of South Africans for whom these buildings retain a sense of home or work as well as belonging. It is a way of making do by urban residents through acts of 'improvisation' (following AbdouMaliq Simone),[49] as one of many practices for living with instability and marginalisation. I also follow Bettina Malcomess and Dorothy Kreutzfeldt[50] in their suggestion that since the early 2000s major rebuilding in Johannesburg has not been possible (both from a built environment and financial perspective); instead, there has been a specific focus on renovating what is already there. It is small hopeful acts of 'repair' (following Steven Jackson)[51] that take place instead to maintain steadiness; for this case of three South African cities, I witnessed and photographed the continued use of Art Deco lamps and chandeliers, a functioning fire station, fonts on buildings and street signs, and carefully chosen paint colours for trims of buildings. It is a politics of ornamentation that is at work here. These features say something, then, about Springs, Joburg and Durban as distinct places with enduring senses of self, and are very much part of their respective infrastructural and affective cityness today.

By Way of a Conclusion, or Art Deco Enthusiasm (as Opposed to Despair)

'Perhaps Art Deco generates a Kind of Despair.'[52]

In this last section, I want to write against Dyer's despairing and disparaging of Art Deco in Miami, with an enthusiasm for Art Deco in the South African case. Perhaps Dyer had Art Deco in New York in mind when he wrote negatively about his Art Deco experience in Miami. In some sense, though, and here I follow in Dyer's footsteps, Art Deco touring the world over is always a relational experience. I myself felt compelled to counter Dyer's comments (again, both insipid and insightful) on Miami with a focus on Springs (second to Miami in Art Deco features) and my own visual essay. I also constantly compared Springs with Johannesburg and Durban, weighing up my Art Deco experiences in each and in relation to one another. Along with enthusiasm come Art Deco enthusiasts like myself, Jonathan Cane and the motley crew of writers and urban planners who joined us on our Art Deco walks and drives. It also includes the entrepreneurial Durban inner-city resident who recognised the value of a particular Art Deco building and saw Jonathan and me as potential buyers interested in ownership because of its heritage design. As well, we could consider the late Bill Freund as very much an Art Deco enthusiast; it is his insightful comments that are woven throughout and it is he to whom I dedicate this visual essay.

It was Bill who briefly explained to me both the pleasures and difficulties of living inside an Art Deco apartment building. In our phone conversation,

Figure 10.4: Durban Port. (Photograph by Pamila Gupta)

Bill told me that Art Deco has allowed for generous proportions, beautiful views on three sides (except south-facing in his case), polished wooden floors and elaborate glass tilework. He pointed out that the lighting in his flat was 'nice but Art Deco is not really about lighting (in the way that architecture is today)', he said. He described his windows as 'rather high and narrow'. Surrey Mansions also has continued infrastructural problems with an outdated steel lift that is too expensive to replace, and constant plumbing problems that the body corporate has to deal with – costing 'an arm and a leg', according to Bill, to repair. There is an Art Deco phone booth in the lobby that had undergone a recent renovation, he told me, even as it was awkwardly positioned there and had no use value beyond being a heritage reminder of a past time and place. We ended our phone conversation with his telling me how he took care and pride in living in Surrey Mansions amidst a racially diverse group of residents who had chosen it for its Art Deco features.[53] In other words, I would like to suggest that Art Deco endures as a form of South African infrastructure that a range of urban residents, including myself here, experience on a daily basis in the cities of Springs, Johannesburg and Durban. As 'frontier Africans',[54] we encounter, innovate, improvise,[55] and dwell *inside* Art Deco as much as we speculate from *outside* Art Deco with commercial, financial, aesthetic and civic purposefulness.

Moreover, I believe architectural movements such as Art Deco compel us to respond affectively to it, to make it resonate with us in a way that reconciles its colonial and apartheid past with its democratic future. It reminds me again of Bill Freund and a comment he made in passing, that when he first moved into Surrey Mansions, he tried to match the Art Deco outside with an Art Deco inside, in the form of stylised bookcases. He felt compelled to do so, even as his preference was for another era, a different imaginary, he told me. In the end, he took down the Art Deco bookcases, and replaced them with what he desired. In the same manner, I felt compelled to experience Art Deco in South Africa but distilled by way of my own set of anthropological interests: as a driving and walking *flâneur* writing about and photographing distinct built environments (Springs, Johannesburg and Durban), I combine text and image to think about architectural features as simultaneously infrastructure and affect.

It is a form of meditation or musings (in a Benjamin sense) alongside a series of ethnographic notes in the form of a visual essay (following Dyer) to think about African cityness by way of placeness, affect and its history of Art Deco design and construction. Finally, it is also about confronting the lingering past of Art Deco as a geography and property value of affluence, class and whiteness (specifically, white settler colonialism) across South Africa's urban landscape in order for interrogation, redress and recuperation to take place in a post-apartheid African present.

Figure 10.5: Bretton Woods Building in Killarney, Johannesburg. (Photograph by Pamila Gupta)

Chapter Eleven

Garden of Ruins: The Urban Production of Colonial Bissau and the History of a Dilapidated Present

Rui Aristides Lebre

Whose Ruins?

When John Soane presented the drawing of the ruins of the new Bank of England, which he had designed, to the Royal Academy two centuries ago, he was not just claiming that architecture would stand the test of time, even in a ruinous state. He was also claiming that the British Empire, represented in what was then the novel institution of a central bank, would belong to the history of civilisations, just like the Acropolis, the Pantheon and other greatly admired ruins from antiquity. Colonial architectural ruins in former African colonies can be understood in a similar light. Like Soane's ruined bank, these present claims of continuity over history, place and culture by former settlers, colonial agents, academics and professional cultures.[1] Architectural historiography has often read late-colonial architecture in former European colonies in Africa as sources of modernist reinvention and, after decolonisation, as the ruins of a modernity that could have been.[2] The underbelly of this argument presupposes the overall failure of modernity in Africa, positing modernity as an imposed external phenomenon and neglecting African agency. This obscures the complex history of producing modernity in many African countries and the various meanings modern architectural ruins have come to acquire.[3]

This chapter is the product of a preliminary attempt at deconstructing the image of African urban ruins as a synonym for underdevelopment or the grand failure of Western-led modernisation in the Global South, which still permeates architectural scholarship on late-colonial Africa.[4] The urban study presented here confronts this scholarship by addressing in particular recent Portuguese studies of modern colonial architecture, which often adopt hagiographic and celebratory discourses of colonial modernism.[5] Learning from what André Frank and others identified as the structural relationship between development and underdevelopment in capitalist modernity, this chapter elaborates on the idea that African ruins structurally emanate from European ruins and vice versa, in a to-and-fro movement of influence and contamination.[6] The chapter seeks to move beyond the asymmetrical duality between European and African agencies inherent in the idea of modernising development. Ruins and ruination serve here as a way to approach an ongoing process of unexpected tension and transformation and, ultimately, to inform overlooked aspects of late-colonial architectural history and how these can reframe our understanding of a decolonial present.

Figure 11.1: Aerial cutaway view of John Soane's plan for the Bank of England, by Joseph M. Gandy, 1830. (Wikimedia Commons)

This chapter will focus on the small capital city of Bissau, in Guinea-Bissau, developing a brief historical interpretation of the city's emergence as colonial capital in the mid-20th century until the country's independence from Portugal in 1974. Bissau was selected as a means to approach the larger debate of architectural ruins and ruination as creative processes because of the conflictual dialogue between capital, power and life offered by its colonial past.[7] The tensions arising from this dialogue in Bissau lent themselves to an exploration of the idea of ruination as offering the potential for insurgent presents beyond normative prescriptions, namely those laid down by late-colonial history and spatial practices. Observation of tensions between capital, power and life has grounded the experiment in urban history which writing this chapter aims to be, particularly of late-colonial architecture and urban planning. It foregrounds failure, corruption and incompletion as categories of critical historical interpretation.

The chapter is divided into five parts. Firstly, we start by briefly presenting how architectural ruins and ruination are understood here, placing this study within the growing field of critical urban theory on sub-Saharan Africa. Moving into the case study, the chapter then contextualises Guinea-Bissau within 20th-century Portuguese imperial claims and colonial discourses. Bissau is here presented as a node of several colonial anxieties and dreams, which makes its urban production and government a particularly rich case of an attempt to implement modernity in the defence of a waning empire. In the third part, the chapter deals with the actual attempts by colonial bureaucrats and technicians to plan and rule Bissau. In the fourth part we address the ways in which housing policies and architectures, in particular wartime resettlement schemes, aiming to create a modern Portuguese Guinea-Bissau, ultimately failed to restrict Guinean agency, leading to the country's independence. Lastly, the chapter finishes by asking how this exploration of urban ruination may open debates on the challenges of working for more egalitarian futures amidst ruins.

Developing Ruination: A Contribution to Our Understanding of Urban Modernity?

As Ann Stoler has argued, colonial ruins are 'unfinished histories', symbolic places of both colonial hubris and postcolonial possibility.[8] We can add that colonial ruins are also spatial processes harnessing a variety of agents in contested histories, and that ruination is not an exclusively social and cultural phenomenon, since it emerges from everyday ecologies. We can understand ruination as a bio-social process that signifies the corruption of a past and an ongoing present, whose study is concerned with the creative disjuncture of spatial configurations. Reading modern architectural ruins mainly as symbols of a modernity that could have been fails to grasp the creative power of ruination while identifying modernity with colonialism, when in fact these should not be read as the same.[9] In this chapter we are interested in seeing ruins as a creative ongoing present that tries to move beyond given structures of power and their hegemonic histories. Focusing on architecture and urban spatial practices, we address two main questions: What can architectural ruins teach us about the process of modernity in highly unequal societies? And what can we learn from colonial ruins for a supposedly decolonial present?

This exploration of architecture as ruin, and of ruin as a process of creating a non-aligned present, draws inspiration from Edgar Pieterse's notion of the 'relational city' and a search for urban sense in the 'plurality of action spaces'.[10] The aim of developing more inclusive and nuanced views of what constitutes experiences of urban modernity in Africa grounds this study in the growing body of critical urban theories and practices addressing African urbanity, to which this chapter sets out to be a small contribution.[11] In this respect, the chapter draws on Stoler's notion of differential futures to address how everyday resistance to colonial order performed other collective possibilities.[12] In order not to confine this discussion to the cultural and technical dimensions of urban rule and production, the chapter also draws on Alfred Crosby's work on biological imperialism, understanding it as an invitation to read buildings and cities as historical bio-geographical bundles.[13] Hence, while the urban study here presented forms part of late-colonial historiography and debates on colonial urban planning, it also engages with attempts at expanding architecture's environmental dialogues. To this end, it focuses on dialogues between disciplining machines, such as urban plans, and bio-social processes, such as the effects of monsoon rains on labour rhythms.

This study is grounded in original archival and field research, collected during two short-term research stays in Guinea-Bissau in 2019 and 2022, which included an extended visit to its national archives and interviews with several informants in Bissau.[14] Colonial reports, plans, letters and other documents collected in Bissau and Lisbon are treated as situated practices whose agency is concrete, imagined and reactive. Images of archival documents are thus presented here unmediated and as representing objects in themselves. Indeed, this chapter attempts to read the archive against the grain, showing how documents are as informative in what they conceal as in what they reveal.[15] For this purpose, field research in Bissau involved extended walks or drives with the express aim of identifying patterns and situations of everyday appropriation that could critically reframe archival evidence. During the same field trips several interviews were conducted with residents of former colonial housing plans in Bissau and inhabitants of former wartime villages in the regions of Bafatá, Tombali and Quínara.[16] This conjunction of methods attempted to redress the neglect of African agency, which is not uncommon in architectural scholarship, by confronting the archive with actual livelihoods and oral histories. Yet the chapter is at best a preliminary exploration in this direction, since much of its discussion relies on archival materials.

The Promised Colonial 'Garden': Introducing Bissau as Colonial Capital

Guinea-Bissau is a small country on the coast of West Africa, bordering Senegal to the north and Guinea to the south. Its modern borders result from the European scramble for Africa in the mid-1880s. Its rich history has unfolded in the region between the Gulf of Guinea and the southern limit of the Sahel; this can be divided into an ecologically rich coastal area and a semi-arid inland one. Its monsoon tropical climate has given rise to an abundance of flora, fauna and viruses, which defeated most European armies until the late 19th century.[17] The country's western half is almost one vast floodplain, marked by great saltwater ways and basins, seasonally flooded by the Atlantic, while the eastern half consists of arid savannah. Even though full of water, freshwater is scarce given the porosity of the land and its continuous contact with the sea. Similarly porous, Guinea's population is made up of a great variety of communities with long and multiple social histories that stretch throughout the whole region of the

Figure 11.2: Map of Guinea-Bissau. (Perry-Castañeda Library Map Collection, Wikimedia Commons)

Gulf and the semi-arid regions south of the Sahel. At different points of its history, sections of its current territory, namely its semi-arid zones, were part of different African empires, such as the Mali (13th–16th centuries), Gabu (16th–19th centuries) and the Fouta Djallon (18th–19th centuries). However, no empire or state ever fully controlled and ruled over Guinea-Bissau, and this includes the Portuguese Empire.[18]

For most of its history with Guinea, Portugal's presence was concentrated in a few fortified outposts situated on the coast, namely Bolama, Cacheu and Bissau, key ports in the Atlantic trade involving enslaved people. Only in the context of growing European competition for colonial dominion in the 19th century did Portugal undertake military campaigns of occupation. For Angola and Mozambique these took place around the time of the Berlin Conference (1884–5), while in Guinea the Portuguese state had been militarily engaged in trying to keep its foothold there since 1840. The end of the First World War ushered in a period of relative peace, with most military campaigns ending in the 1920s. Thus, Portugal's peacetime 'dominion' over Guinea was very short-lived, only lasting from the 1920s to 1963, as well as very thinly spread in its presence. After the occupation wars, the Portuguese mainly extended their existing fortified outposts on the coast and established a few medium-sized towns and outposts (São Domingos, Teixeira Pinto, Bafatá, Nova Lamego, Buba, Cátio and Buba). In contrast with Angola and Mozambique, where the occupation wars were intended to achieve the military conquest and settler occupation of most of the territory, in Guinea they involved winning over key societies for the colonial cause, such as the Mandinga and Manjaco, who had had commercial relationships with the Portuguese since the 18th century, and the Fula, who constituted a majority amenable to Portuguese interests by the late 19th century.[19] At the same time, Guinea's social and ecological diversity meant resistance to colonisation every step of the way, namely from the Papel, Nalu and Balanta societies.

By the early 20th century Guinea was known to Portuguese colonial agents for three things: rice, enslaved people and as a dangerous 'virgin' landscape. Cacheu had been one of the first points of contact for Europeans with West Africa back in the 15th century, as well as one of the first Atlantic markets for enslaved people. The abundance of rice on these shores seems to have impressed Portuguese seafarers, who named the Gulf of Guinea the 'Rice Coast'.[20] As for the idea of a perilous 'natural' landscape for the Portuguese, this was best expressed by the 16th-century traveller João de Barros: 'in all the entrances of this great Ethiopia that we navigate along, He [God] has placed a striking angel with a flaming sword of deadly fevers, who prevents us from penetrating into the interior to the springs of this garden'.[21] The image of Guinea as a 'garden' was elaborated by Portuguese colonial agents very early on, encapsulating a male anxiety about 'penetrating' this landscape, as well as constant frustration in achieving this. Four centuries later, modernising colonial bureaucrats and propagandists were still caught up in this imaginary. By the 1930s the Portuguese identified rice as Guinea's main staple alongside palm oil and tropical nuts. While rice production was abundant, it also required heavy labour, using a combination of productive systems, such as *bolanha seca*, *sequeiro* and *bolanha salgada*. The last was the most productive and best performed by those societies resistant to Portuguese rule, such as the Balanta.[22] Portuguese rulers and colonial bureaucrats complained that Guineans were 'stuck in their ways', resisting integration in the metropolitan market.

Beginning in the early 20th century, agricultural 'development' plans came and went. By 1934, the agricultural officer of Guinea, António J.M. Filipe, repeated what was already an established mantra that 'it is in rationally conducted agribusiness that the prosperity, civilisation and richness of its [Guinea's] people must be based'.[23] This was wishful thinking, presented in the propaganda-ridden and celebratory context of the First Portuguese Colonial Exhibition held in Porto in 1934. The Portuguese imperial dictatorship ruled by Oliveira Salazar had just formalised itself by way of the political constitution of 1933, and consequently the 1934 colonial exhibition became a show of force, while presenting opportunities for the remaking of colonial agendas. At this occasion of colonial reorganisation, the watchword among the colonial elite was 'Guinea is in crisis'.[24] The 'garden' was still forbidden and dangerous.

In the fragile state of peace or truce after the occupation wars, the 1934 colonial exhibition marked a watershed moment, introducing a supposedly new period of colonial expansion. While Angola and Mozambique had large hinterland economies that existed in close relationship with the economy of South Africa, around which the two colonies formed a cordon sanitaire until the 1970s, Guinea-Bissau was peripheral at best and resistant almost by default to the colonial expansionism which the Portuguese dictatorship wanted to impress on its European peers. For the empire, the role of Guinea, with its handful of fortified towns, seemed to be of a more symbolic nature, given that Guinea-Bissau and the Cape Verde islands were detrimental to Portugal's continued presence in the Gulf of Guinea after the Berlin Conference. One would think that this would have made colonial entrepreneurs look to other shores. Yet political ambition, European competition and self-preservation made Guinea an essential part of Portugal's African empire in the mid- and late 20th century. In order to consolidate Portuguese colonial power and interests, the 'garden' needed to be disciplined, and a city, a colonial capital, was the means for this task. This is the origin of Bissau as capital, brought into existence by the 1919 urban plan of the engineer José Quinhones, though it only reached fruition after the Second World War.[25]

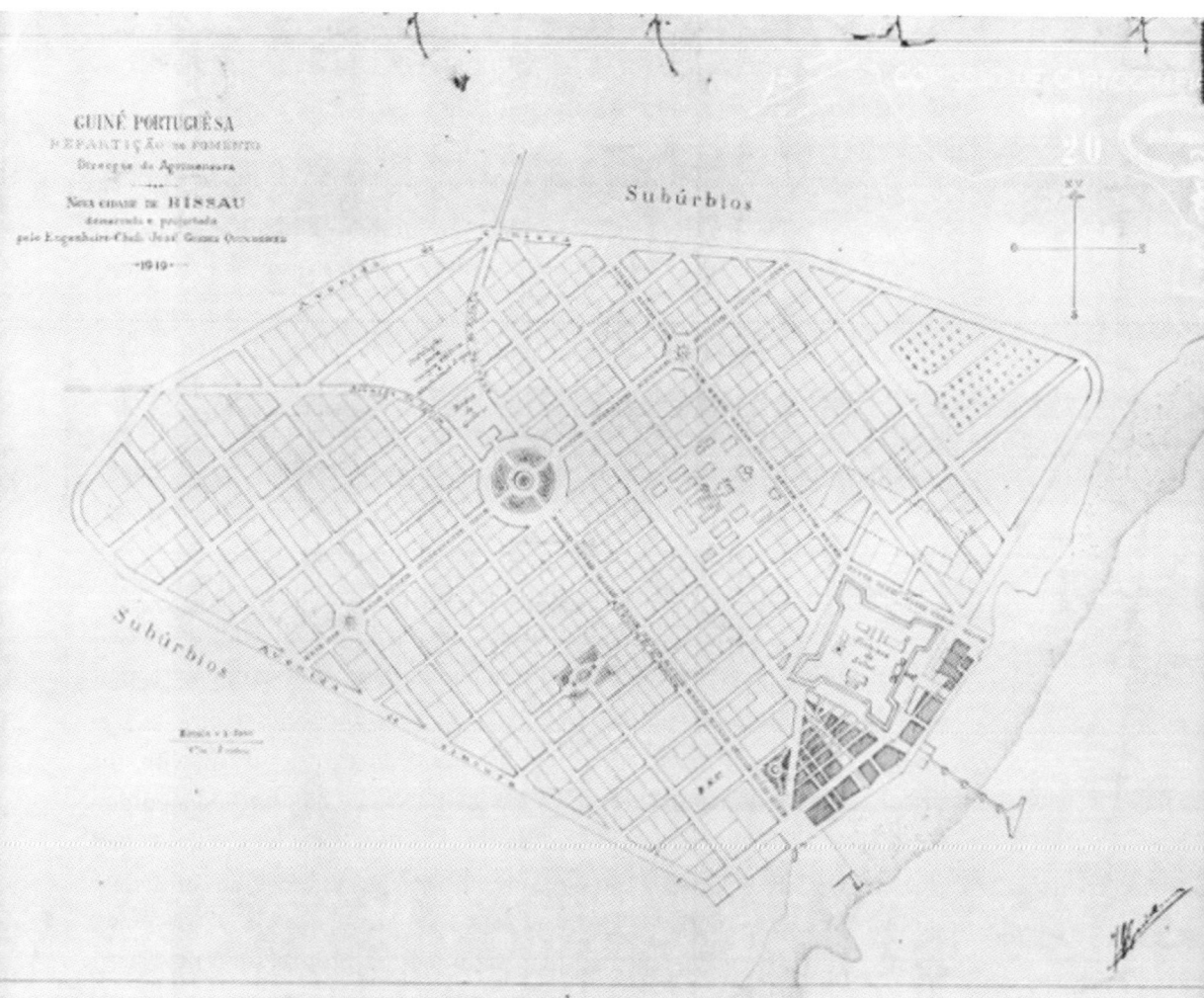

Figure 11.3: 'Nova Cidade de Bissau', by José Guedes Quinhones, 1919. (Arquivo Histórico Ultramarino, Portugal, PT-AHU)

Conceived as a regular grid starting from the old fort in the port, Quinhones's urban plan created a city from scratch, removing any Guinean in its path and defining a new urban perimeter. The plan's main avenue linked the new governor's residence with the old colonial fort, and along it were placed the more prominent embodiments of colonial power behind modern architectural façades that are now crumbling. The main avenue was surrounded by small plots of low-density housing; this, together with the design of green public spaces and its place in time, has led architectural historians to read the town as a 'garden city'.[26] Buildings followed a sort of Portuguese-inspired vernacular of white walls, wooden shutters and clay roofs, combined according to taste with more or less modernist elements. This was an architectural design pattern that had been slowly developing since the early 20th century as a search for national roots, and that came to articulate the dictatorship's representations of Portugueseness.[27] For all intents and purposes, however, the plan's domestic architecture followed the international logic of the colonial bungalow with its veranda and front porch.[28] Beyond the perimeter of 'New Bissau' was an invisible city that Quinhones called the 'suburbs' and that was left empty in the plans. This was where native Guineans were supposed to live (see Figure 11.3).

This new capital took a long time to be realised. After 1933 and the reorganisation of colonial development in terms of the dictatorship's fascist agenda, its construction moved faster. However, only after the Second World War did Bissau's new main avenue and public buildings, street grid and urban perimeter become clear. Coincidentally, the new Bissau, both in its urban vision and process, may have been confused with an actual garden, given its long-lasting incomplete state. In this sense, it tapped directly into the imperial imagination of the forbidden colonial Eden. As we have seen, the mythology of the 'garden' was present from very early on in Portuguese colonial discourse. By the 19th and 20th centuries, however, it helped articulate government discourses through a clear bio-medical approach to colonial dominion and discipline.[29] Beyond that, it also helped express a sense of colonial promise and success. The 'garden' that was being opened with Bissau's new urban plan signified the promise of a new start, with the possibility of unlimited capitalist appropriation for colonial agents and settlers. The entrepreneurial colonial governor between 1945 and 1948, Manuel Sarmento Rodrigues, conveyed this sentiment in 1947: 'Who

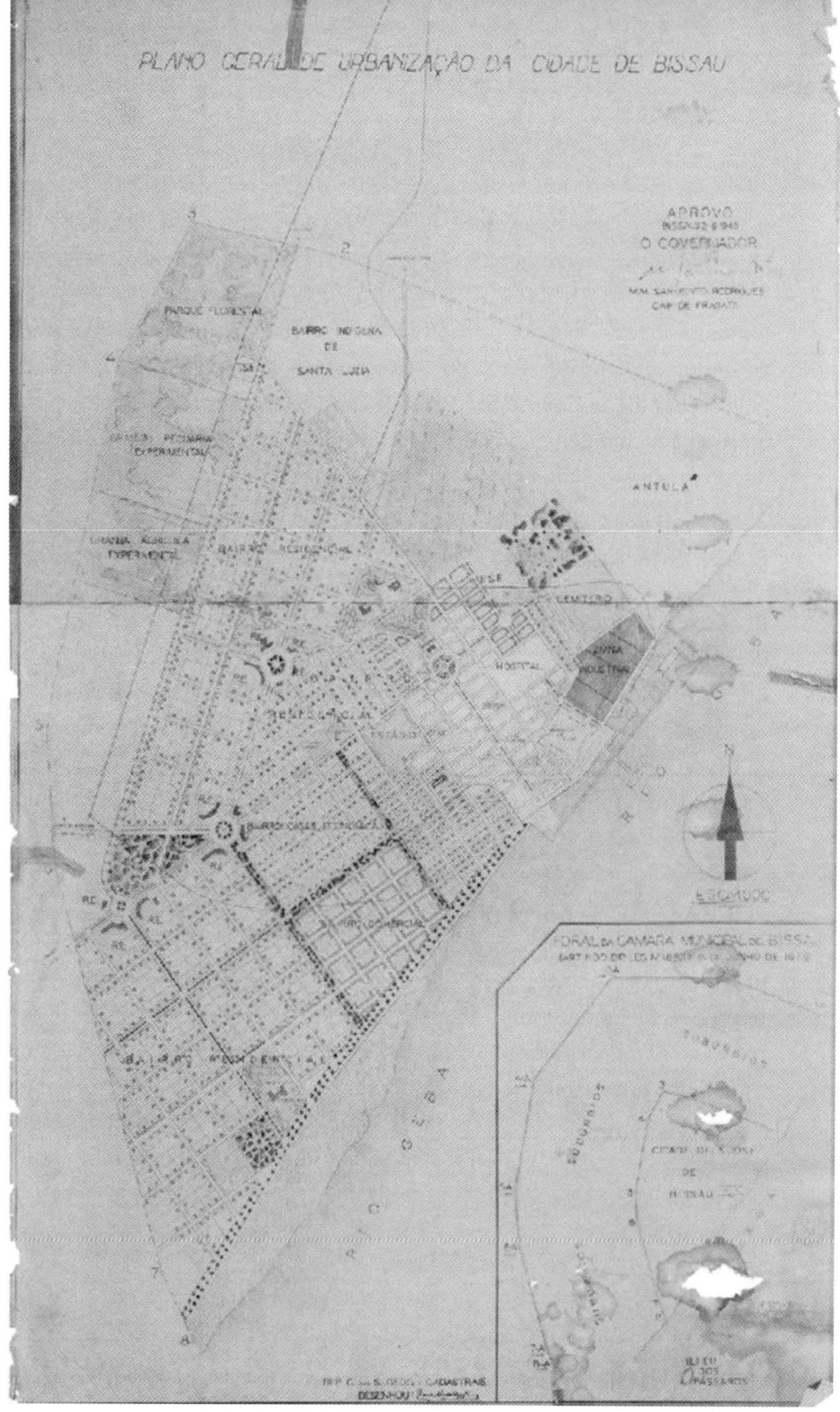

Figure 11.4: 'Urbanisation plan for the city of Bissau, 1948. (Courtesy of PT-AHU)

could say to those troubled settlers earlier in this century that that Bissau surrounded by palisades would, in so little time, be the welcoming city of today? That the very disquieted Guinea would become this pleasant garden [*jardim aprazível*], where one lives peacefully in the fraternity of work and mutual respect?'[30] For a Guinea that was 'in crisis', Quinhones's plan with its garden city apparel made the colony appear once again as a promised land. What the optimistic speech of Rodrigues did not reveal was that the creation and maintenance of this 'pleasant garden' required a lot of policing, discipline and work, none of which was usually successful.

Discipline and Rain

In *Discipline and Punish*, Michel Foucault famously argued that the power of modern states resides in their exhaustive capacity to surveil and discipline life.[31] European colonial apparatuses are perhaps some of the most thorough experiments in this power. In a meeting of Portuguese colonial administrators in Bissau two months before his optimistic speech, Rodrigues and his staff specified a number of measures to bring that 'fraternity of work and mutual respect' into existence.[32] These measures ranged from the prohibition of settlers trading directly with Guineans in 'eggs, milk, animals, rice, among other products', which was supposed to occur only in the municipal market. It was 'explicitly' forbidden to 'transport water from local fountains by use of natives', or, as they put it, 'native girls'. The 'cleanliness of indigenous houses' also held the administration's attention: inhabitants of 'houses by the road' had to refurbish them in order to improve their appearance, by redoing roofs and whitewashing walls. Furthermore, it was necessary, they claimed, to 'stop the reprehensible appearance of insufficiently dressed men, at least near centres of civilisation'. Insufficiently dressed women apparently were not a problem. And many other norms and regulations were specified and enforced by the police. They were meant to apply to the whole colony and to Bissau in particular as the main 'centre of civilisation'.[33] The ideal 'garden' required fines and punishment, ranging from suspension to imprisonment, specifically directed at Guineans. For example, a Guinean driver sometime in the 1960s was suspended for three days because of arriving late at an appointment. The judgment reported as an aggravating factor that the driver had lied about his time of arrival.[34]

In contrast with Foucault's argument and despite the example just given of judicial rigour, this experiment in discipline was a series of failures and resistances. Rodrigues tried to uphold the promise of 'New Bissau' as a shining example of Portuguese colonial modernity for specific reasons. Beyond personal advancement – Rodrigues would be promoted to Minister of the Colonies in 1950 – Guinea-Bissau, as well as the other Portuguese colonies in Africa, was a matter of great concern for the dictatorship in the post-war world amid the pressures for decolonisation. Besides reorganising colonial administration, promoting agricultural and health surveys, and ensuring housing provision, Rodrigues managed to secure Bissau as the venue for the second Conférence Internationale des Africanistes Occidentaux (CIAO, or International Conference of Western Africanists).

Founded in January 1945, this conference was a response by European colonisers to growing pressure from the US and the UN for the self-determination of colonial dominions.[35] It was a biannual political-scientific affair established on the initiative of France's Institute Français d'Afrique Noir (IFAN) and sought to share knowledge on development schemes across various African colonies. In 1950 it set up the Commission for Technical Cooperation in Africa South of the Sahara (CCTA). According to a report on the preparation of the second CIAO conference, the first conference of West Africanists was held in Dakar in January 1945, which gathered together ethnologists, botanists, geographers and physicians, among other colonial experts, from Spain, Portugal, France and England. In the first conference, the permanent committee for CIAO consisted of the Spanish archaeologist José Martinez, Professor Théodore Monod from IFAN, Paul Rivet from the Musée de l'Homme in Paris, C. Daryll Forde from the London-based International African Institute, and the Portuguese anthropologist António Mendes Correia, director of the Colonial Superior School in Lisbon.[36] In 1947 and 1948, the 'pleasant garden' of Bissau thus also served to secure Portugal's place in discussions of Europe's continued colonial dominion over Africa.

Notwithstanding all this effort in positioning Guinea-Bissau internationally, the colony and its new capital were far from being the shining land of opportunities that Portugal so desired. If the state of buildings is any indication, the truth was quite different. Six years before, in 1941, in a municipal report listing the colonial government's accomplishments, the chief engineer of Bissau's public works gives us a concrete idea of the actual condition of the city and the colonial state's ability to build and maintain it.[37] The main issue of the report was the lack of technical personnel in the colonial administration, but it ended up specifying the administration's continuous failures. Concerning bridge building, for instance: 'General Carmona Bridge, after costing the state many thousands of *contos*, collapsed, barely two years old.'[38] This was not an isolated case, as the engineer listed another three bridges in similar conditions, then moved to equally distraught depictions of harbours, roads, wells and the general cleanliness of cities. On the last topic: 'nothing is done or studied regarding this. Mosquitoes freely swarm in Bissau, reproducing at ease and spreading malaria everywhere.'[39] Regarding roads, for instance, he reported: 'everything remains to be done regarding their rational organisation and construction.'[40] Roads were badly laid down, poorly constructed and easily degraded, as described in the report. As far as government buildings were concerned: 'the majority [were] in a state of thorough ruin', while colonial state employees' houses were 'expensive ... and their condition and appearance are not dignified for those who dwell in them'.[41]

With growing international pressure after the Second World War to 'develop' or decolonise the colonial dominions, the Portuguese dictatorship tried to correct course. Rodrigues's governorship was the start of this period of colonial modernisation. By then, public buildings were being repainted, and the harbour and roads repaired, in an effort to embellish the 'garden'. Yet, the problem – the continuous state of ruin affecting everything the colonial state did – persisted. Report after report sounded complaints about the poor state of the same things throughout the 1960s and 1970s. Municipal reports from Bissau's public works services are particularly detailed in their attention to expenses and budget allocation. Several reports focused on road construction and maintenance, which was apparently a major problem throughout the last phase of Portuguese colonialism. For instance, as late as November 1971, considerable stretches of the road network of Quinhones's plan were still to be completed (see Figure 11.5).[42] Many words in official reports were devoted to the poor state of the sewerage and the need to increase efforts in that regard. By the late 1970s, however, most sewerage plans involved septic tanks and the indirect recognition that a centralised sewerage network and treatment system were impossible to achieve. Garbage was another burning topic. A clear distinction was drawn and maintained between the 'white' city and the 'suburbs', where most Guineans were forced to live. Bissau's administration, recognising the health hazard posed by the absence of a garbage removal system, promoted a series of 'cleaning operations' with the support of the Portuguese military. This never solved the problem. By then, Guinea-Bissau, like Angola and Mozambique, was overwhelmed with Portuguese soldiers and the colonial state underwent a process of militarisation to tackle the liberation wars that had started back in 1961 in Angola and in 1963 in Guinea. Garbage removal by the military's 'cleaning operations' also served as social cleansing operations directed at supporters of the liberation movement, as will become clear later in the chapter.[43]

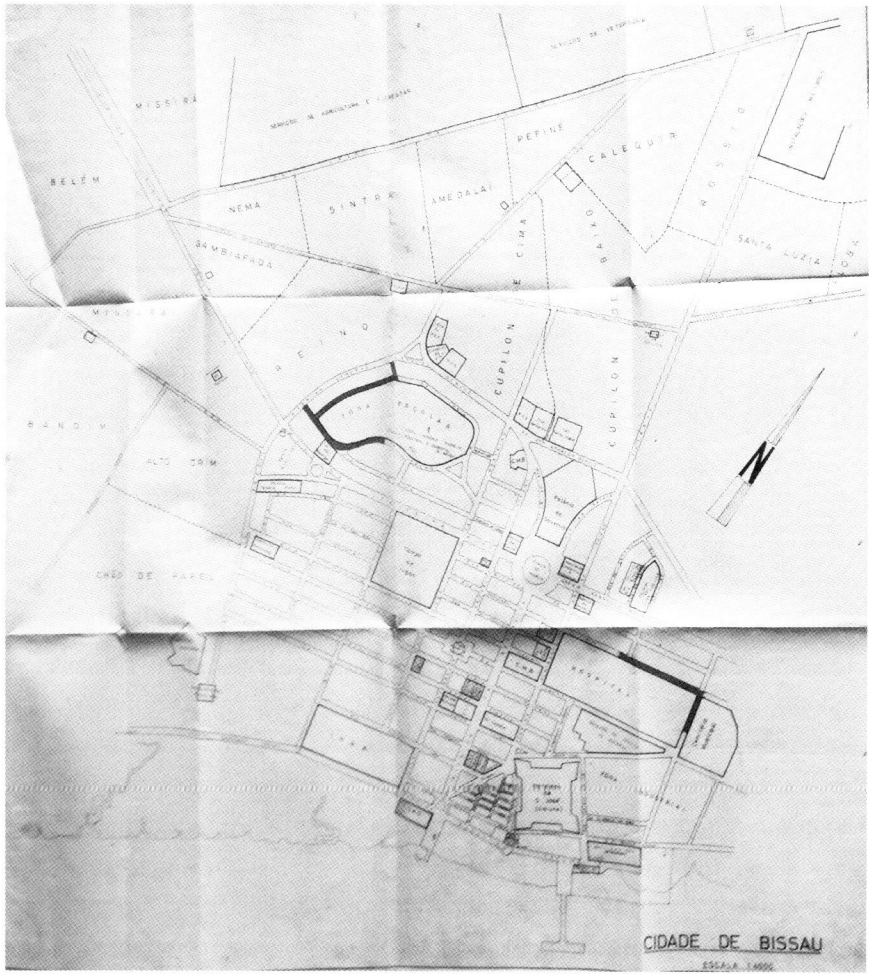

Figure 11.5: Plan of roadworks for 1971, drawn up by Bissau's colonial government. (Instituto Nacional de Estudos e Pesquisa, Guiné-Bissau, INEP)

By 1948 Bissau, the supposed shining example of Portuguese colonial modernity, was terribly unfinished and riddled with problems. This was well expressed in municipal budgets. For instance, the budget for 1974, when Guinea had already been declared independent by Guineans but was still considered a Portuguese colony or 'province', allocated the greatest share of its expenditure to long-delayed road, sewerage, electricity and maintenance works.[44] It was not just that the city was continuously unfinished in respect of its ideal modern image, but also that it seemed to be in a perpetual state of decay. Comparing the municipal budget of 1974 with others from previous years, one is surprised to find how much of the expenditure was allocated to the maintenance and cleaning of public buildings and spaces.[45]

Colonial technicians and administrators blamed lack of able personnel and lack of budget as the main culprits for this situation. This was repeated from the time of the 1941 report by Bissau's head engineer onwards. For instance, the implementation study for the third development plan of 1968 openly acknowledged that its implementation was impossible given the 'present executive organisation', shifting the blame from lack of personnel and budget to Guinea itself, which was 'merely in an embryonic stage of development'.[46] The architect Miguel Veloso, sent to Bissau in 1971 in the service of Lisbon's Colonial Planning Bureau, found that just one architect was responsible for all planning works in Guinea, and in addition worked as a liaison officer with the military for the vast forced villagisation programme conducted by the army. The lack of personnel no doubt had an impact on the colonial state's ability to discipline the 'garden'. The singular focus on this issue, as if all that was needed for the 'pleasant garden' to emerge was more qualified people, hides the fact that these reports, by their very 'inside' nature, neglected specific points of resistance and agents of colonial ruination. Among the many agents of ruin we can identify, rain was perhaps one of the most active.

Guinea-Bissau has a monsoon rain season lasting from May to November, and its dominion over the everyday is thus hegemonic during a considerable part of the year. In effect, the colonial administration and military were almost exclusively organised to be operational and effective during the dry season, compressed from December to March, during which time most public works programmes and military operations were conducted. Hence, the rain reduced the space-time of Portuguese colonial

Figure 11.6: A road in the old colonial city of Bissau. (Photograph by Rui A. Lebre, October 2019)

agency while, simultaneously, it repeatedly caused the deterioration of those works that had been hastily finished through December to March. Roofs, walls, roads and sewerage fell particular victim to the powerful gravitational agency of water. Portuguese colonial architecture's whitewashed walls, clay tile roofs and concrete structures came undone, some within a year, others taking longer. Year after year, repainting and refurbishing had to be carried out to maintain the image of the 'pleasant garden'. Roads in particular were no match for the rain. Each season opened new holes in the finished roads of Quinhones's plan, while the unfinished and those yet to be started found their ground moving beneath them. Hence the intense preoccupation with finishing and repairing roads, among other technologies, to discipline the 'garden' and ensure its path to capitalist progress. But the colonial technicians in all their reports forgot to mention the rain.

Myth and Housing

The lack of properly trained Portuguese engineers and architects, among other technicians, took its toll on the creation of the 'pleasant garden'. This brings us to a key dynamic in the colonial endeavour to create ideal Europes: in this case, an ideal Portugal.[47] There was an immense distance between the disciplinary and technological machinery organised to produce modernity and the actual multiplicity of existences that suffered, resisted and tensioned these devices to the point of failure. In this respect, colonial design as specific architectures for governing particular forms of colonial citizenry can be considered ruinous from the start or else a ruin-creating activity. Nowhere is this more evident than in the colonial plans for housing Guineans.

The first housing scheme for Guineans emerged during Rodrigues's governorship between 1946 and 1948. The Santa Luzia neighbourhood was targeted at 'assimilated' Guineans, most of whom worked directly under the colonial state. This represented a rare first attempt by the colonial state to plan the 'suburbs'. The housing scheme involved an urbanisation plan extending the perimeter of central Bissau through a regular grid of single-family houses, built in a bungalow-like architecture of vernacular inspiration (see Figure 11.7). Following the Portuguese 'Indigenous Statute' of 1933, which regulated the asymmetrical citizenship between Portuguese and Guineans, the neighbourhood's dwellers had to prove their European habits: monogamy, proper eating rituals, speaking fluent Portuguese, etc.[48] The housing scheme used architecture and urban shape to articulate the colonial strategy of civilising by means of influence. For this, architectural form assumed the role of projecting a Portuguese Africanness based on an interpretation of Guinean housing forms. This constituted a process of inventing tradition grounded in the scientific colonialism of 'indigenous surveys' (see Figure 11.8), such as that led by Lieutenant Avelino Teixeira da Mota concerning Guinean 'native dwellings' between 1946 and 1948.[49] Whereas the traditional-inspired colonial architecture would positively influence Guineans to achieve the legal and social standards of 'assimilation', these in turn were supposed to positively influence non-assimilated Guineans.[50]

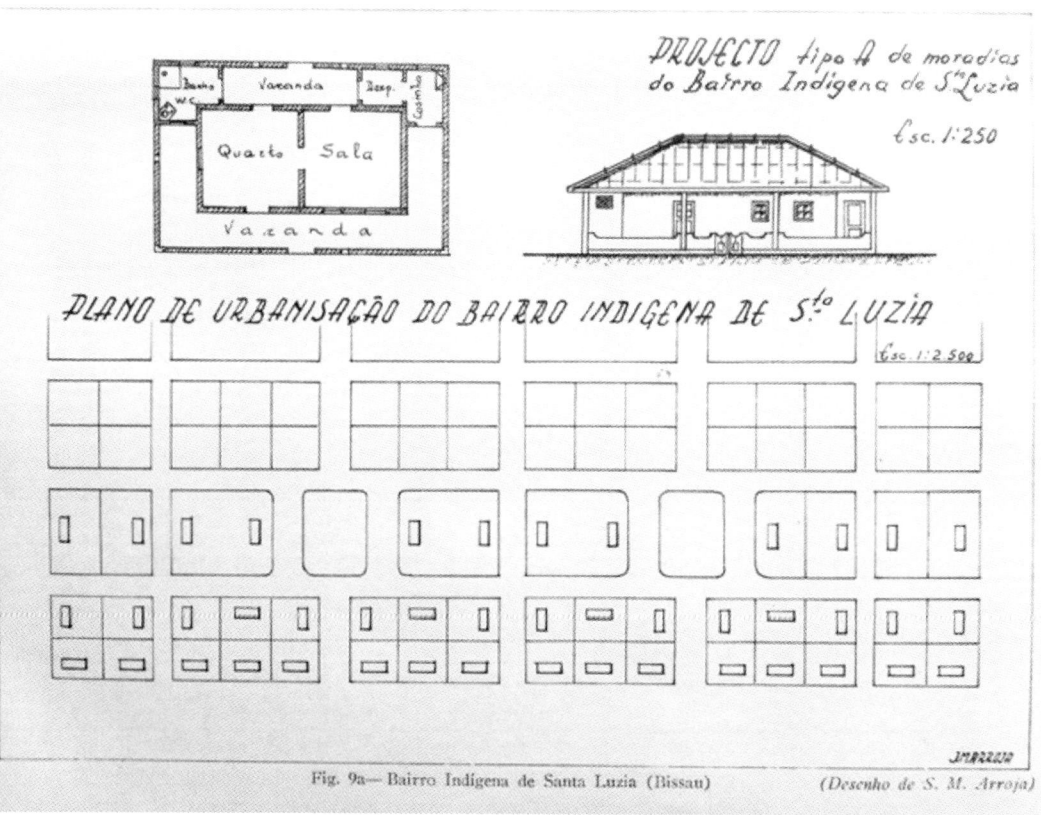

Figure 11.7: *Plan of the Santa Luzia neighbourhood (Mota, Habitação indígena na Guiné portuguesa, Bissau, Centro de Estudos da Guiné Portuguesa, 1948)*

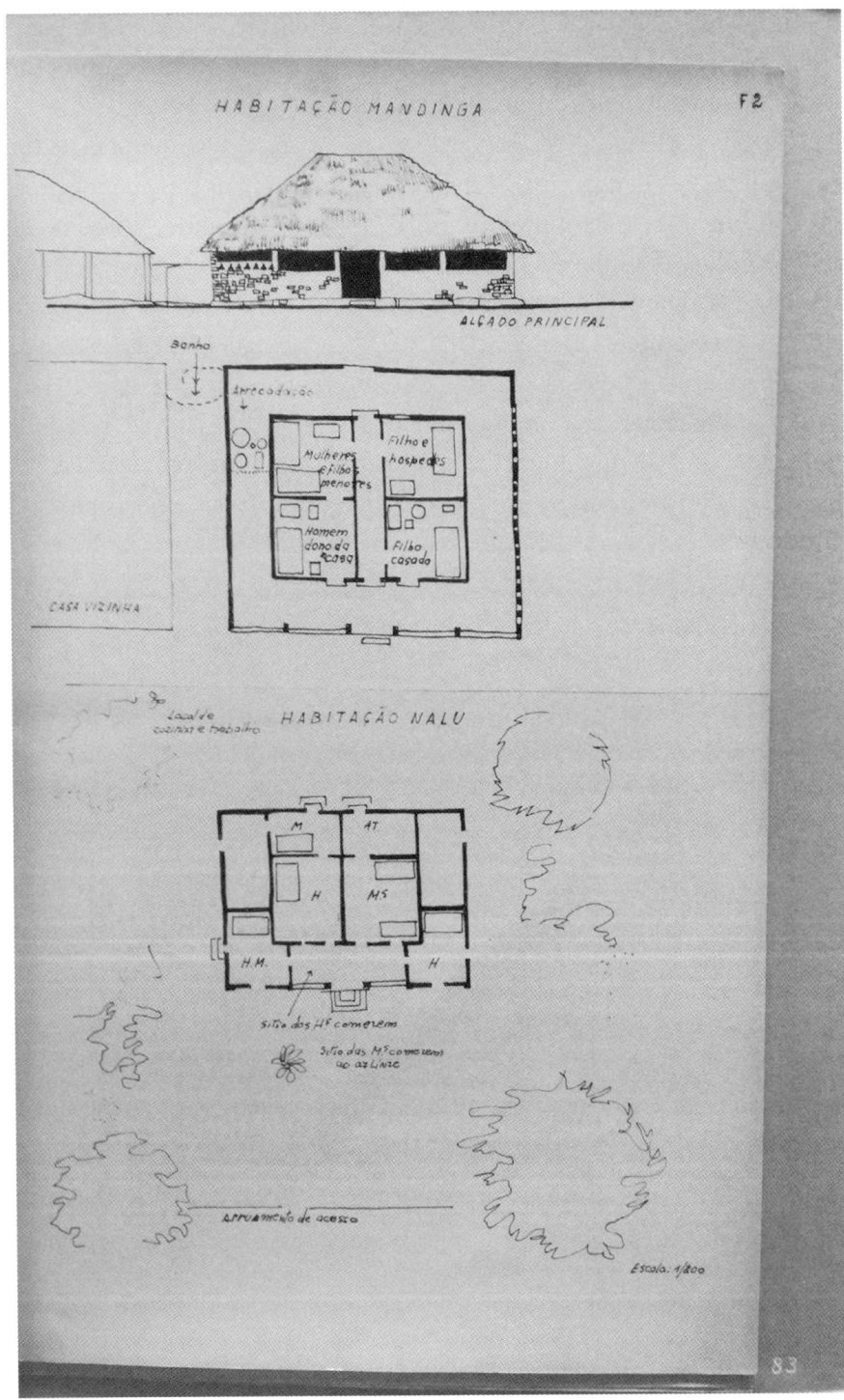

Figure 11.8: *Survey of a 'typical' Mandinga house, in a municipal study entitled 'Study of Bissau's Habitat', 1968. (PT-AHU)*

Santa Luzia's housing plan was never fully realised. Visiting Bissau today, little more than the first two lines of plots can be seen, although the plan involved a wide urban space between the city centre and the military barracks further down the present Pansau Na Isna avenue. Furthermore, later reports collected by Portuguese architects suggested that as soon as the first residents settled in, their houses started to be transformed.[51] Given that the architectural typology was a non-modifiable shape, the small and not so small changes to the houses soon involved a subversion of the architectural form and idea. By 1962, the colonial architect Mário de Oliveira deemed Santa Luzia a failed experiment, making it necessary to place 'more evolved' Europeans, with a 'more valid culture', people capable of 'civilising ... natives and non-natives' living in Santa Luzia.[52] Guineans were not the only ones having problems with living in the 'pleasant garden' and its Luso-tropical dream. Reports such as these unintentionally indicated that colonial public housing made for subjectivities that did not at all fit the colonial imaginary of a Luso-tropical citizen.

Figure 11.9: One of Santa Luzia's original houses today. (Photograph by Rui A. Lebre, October 2019)

The biggest issue around housing for the colonial administration, however, was not the Luso-tropical discourse, nor the very few housing schemes promoted by the colonial state.[53] It was instead the 'suburbs', more specifically how to surveil and discipline this urban landscape where most Guineans lived. The regime's approach since Quinhones's time for this part of the city was one of neglect. With no urban plan and apparent oversight, an urban landscape grew with rules and spaces that made state discipline impossible. Plot arrangement and appropriation followed the web of family and community solidarities and enlarged social networks. Houses were built with the means and shapes shared by many Guineans, which involved mud brick, thatch roofs and also imported concrete, clay tiles and different forms of metal, such as the ever-present zinc sheet. This landscape was not only difficult to discipline by way of the social categories of the Portuguese colonial government, but also morphologically impenetrable, as colonial inspectors and technicians found it impossible to establish any kind of orderly land survey. And this situation was not confined to the 'suburbs'. Houses built by more affluent Guineans closer to the centre of town with municipal approval were just as easily converted into residential compounds, with a string of backyard constructions that were rented out and eventually deemed illegal by the authorities. The city was never what it seemed, especially on paper.

The asymmetry in urban government and its duality of colonial city and indigenous city have clear ramifications today. The *toca-toca* private system of transport, a bus network operated with old Mercedes vehicles, was recently kept from entering the former colonial city planned by Quinhones, for reasons yet unknown, but the effect was an eerie seepage of colonial ambiences into the present. Until the 1960s, this dual city did not disturb colonial authorities much, besides the occasional report by a colonial architect complaining of the lack of proper planning. This is not to say that attention and frustration were not directed at the 'suburbs'. The Santa Luzia neighbourhood was precisely an attempt to start addressing this part of town. The main issue, however, was that until the start of the liberation war in 1963, the colonial state could not be bothered with the living conditions of its cheap local workforce. After the Pidjiguiti massacre of 1959, involving the killing of dozens of stevedores in Bissau by the political police, how to surveil, regulate and somehow order the 'suburbs' became a priority. Municipal and state reports coalesced around 'clandestine' housing and what in the late 1960s became Bissau's 'demographic problem'.

In 1971 the Institute of Work, Welfare and Social Action (ITPAS, or Instituto do Trabalho, Previdência e Acção Social) set out the 'very urgent' task of surveilling Bissau's Guinean population, which implied surveilling the 'suburbs'. The main goal was to identify those 'elements' that might form part of the city's population of delinquents or 'subversive elements, helping the liberation movement'.[54] It was equally an attempt to come to grips with the rural exodus produced by the war and by the vast ecological destruction, especially of rice paddies, by Portuguese napalm. Ultimately ITPAS hoped to conduct a campaign of work allocation directed to rural areas, so as to divert migrants and young 'idle' people from the city. Building on these concerns, the colonial administration created the Commission for the Study of Bissau's Demographic Problem, which, in a confidential report a few days before the ITPAS document, highlighted the 'beneficial effect of decongesting [Bissau] to solve the complex problem of clandestine houses'.[55] Apparently, the colonial administration was seriously considering the forcible removal of Guineans to the countryside – a possibility created by the Portuguese army's strategy of forced villagisation.

This was a 'hearts and minds' approach to the war informed by similar practices by the British in Malaysia and Kenya (1950s), by France in Algeria (1957–62) and by the US in Vietnam (1961–3). It proposed forcing Guinean peasants into 'new villages' in rural areas, at the same time enticing them with better living conditions. This military scheme involved forcibly displacing communities through the various moving war fronts into contained and surveilled village camps, thereby depriving the liberation movement of personnel and supply lines. The village camps followed a standardised plan and typology whose authorship is still unknown, but whose construction was forced on the residents themselves. The programme started as early as 1961 in Angola, and then was applied in the mid-1960s in Mozambique and Guinea. Towards the end of the war, the programme involved up to two million African peasants in the three countries and at least ninety thousand people in Guinea. It effectively constituted the backbone of the Portuguese war strategy, militarising vast stretches of the hinterlands of Guinea, Angola and Mozambique, and complementing violence with development measures and promises of modernisation.[56]

Figure 11.10: Unknown 'new village', Guinea-Bissau, n.d. (Museu Militar do Porto, Portugal (MMP): MMP013CE670)

With this militarisation of the landscape, the municipal approach to Bissau's 'suburbs' involved collaboration between the district administration, state police and the military acting as stewards of the city. This assemblage of different forms of colonial power was what accomplished the various 'cleaning' campaigns directed at clandestine houses. The 'suburbs' with their unsurveyable architecture had become a site for what the Portuguese called 'terrorists'. A middle-aged Bissau urbanite, interviewed in 2019, who shall be named António for reasons of anonymity, a descendant of one of Santa Luzia's first residents, told how clandestine houses were detected. During the late 1960s and 1970s, raids by Portuguese state police, usually with the help of the military, occurred throughout the city but not in Santa Luzia, which, according to António, was considered 'reputable'. Raids occasionally passing through Santa Luzia were directed at an unplanned neighbourhood behind it, mostly built by a Papel community that had been displaced by Quinhones's plan earlier in the century. The Portuguese police and military crossed Santa Luzia, using it as a base from which to launch the raid. According to António, they never found any weapons or 'terrorists' while in Santa Luzia, which they had to pass through to reach the Papel neighbourhood, his father had a radio transmitter for the liberation movement in the attic, and his neighbours stored weapons for the movement. Apparently, these were never found by the Portuguese authorities.

The fact that the means for the liberation of Guinea were located in Santa Luzia and its promise of a Luso-tropical citizenship, and not in the 'clandestine' Papel neighbourhood, is almost too perfect a metaphor for the problem concerning this chapter. It neatly encapsulates Portuguese colonialism's failed attempts at creating a 'pleasant garden' and how these backfired. More importantly, it illustrates the disjunction between modernity produced through colonial discipline and its actual effects. This was a disjunction continuous enough to produce such a distance between the myth of a Luso-tropical situation and its actual reality that it generated a whole other 'everyday' by itself. Organising housing in Bissau, both through design and neglect, revealed itself as part of the ruin of the colony, in both senses, as something that causes downfall and as something that remains incomplete through time.

Questions about Architectural Ruins and How They May Clear a Path to Decolonial Histories

As is well known, European colonial utopias were continuously riddled with failings, unresolvable tensions and the unrestrained violence of war, with hubris being the unavoidable result. This chapter's main conclusion is that colonial Bissau was a ruin to start with. Not only because the ideal of modernity, as well as its disciplining apparatuses, was contradictory and misplaced. But also because the efforts in disciplining a 'New Bissau', and by implication enforcing a Luso-tropical Guinea, created the ruins which made their reality untenable. Portuguese colonial governors and their technicians never managed to discipline the rain, or the 'suburbs'. Neither did the vast military investment in forced villagisation manage to win the population and ensure the continuity of Portuguese rule. The hopes in 1934 of making Bissau the centre of a productive colonial agribusiness died in the war-torn *bolanhas* (rice paddies), and not because of the lack of qualified personnel or money, although this played a role. Just as with the attempts to forcibly move Guinean urban dwellers to the countryside in the late 1960s, colonial power was unaware of and unprepared to deal with the consequences of its power of displacement. It could not deal with the differential futures it was creating and instead, guided by a techno-scientific horizon, it promoted plan after plan, produced layers of reports and documents, trying to force a 'pleasant garden' into existence. In this way it perfectly illustrated James Scott's arguments about the failures of high modernism.[57] But the ruin of 'New Bissau' is not just the symbol of the failure of its high modernist aspirations to improve the life of the Portuguese and, to a lesser degree, Guineans. What is more important than declaring the failure of this urban vision, which presupposes that it is something that was achieved and that belongs to the past, is recognising that it endures as a history of the present: its ruins are not something to be looked at from afar, but the ground we live on or, in this case, the place where most Guineans currently negotiate a modern life.

Santa Luzia brings this idea home. It was intended to produce an 'assimilated' colonial citizenry, aiming to tame the 'uncivilised' growth of the 'suburbs' and standing as a metaphor for the whole of Guinea beyond the Portuguese colonial city. As soon as it was built, it became something else. From this ruin of an idea, lives emerged that circulated in and out of colonial discipline but were neither in nor out. What was António's father: pro-Portuguese or a revolutionary? What we may perceive today as a ruinous urban plan, when walking through Santa Luzia, is in fact the history of how tactically moving within, while simultaneously moving against, the colonial development grid brought about a whole other set of living possibilities. The ruins of modern colonial architecture and its landscape-creating power should not be read as the end of a period. Nor, as with Soane's bank, as a connection to eternity and the artificial permanence of civilisations. Neither should they be read as the left-over spaces in a make-do culture of the present. Ruination can be better understood not as demise, and all that comes with that, but instead as a process whose rule is creative incompleteness.

As I have tried to argue through the making and unmaking of Bissau as a 'pleasant garden', modern colonial architecture was a ruin-creating process from its inception. It emerged from a dialogue with a 'Guinea in crisis', as claimed during the 1934 Colonial Exhibition in Porto – crisis being an impending threat of ruination, in this case of the Portuguese Empire. At the same time, this impending ruination sparked modernising plans and disciplining apparatuses, as well as new possibilities and, ultimately, freedom from colonial dominion for Guineans. To overcome the 'crisis', Portuguese colonial agents produced an architecture that sought to bring a Luso-tropical empire into existence. This process created its own states of incompletion, such as the appropriation and lively quality of Santa Luzia, which, during the 1950s and later, was a racially and class-mixed neighbourhood. Ruination and ruins, more than past defeats, represent the opening up of unintended possibilities that emerge from the gap between techno-scientific power and actual life in its myriad ecologies. Colonial technicians at the time understood the multiracial Santa Luzia of the 1950s as a 'failure': this shows that the unintended states of architectural ruins are as present as they are misunderstood.[58]

In conclusion, this chapter tried to explore the interpretative possibilities of writing urban and spatial history from its supposed failures, looking at ruins as processes.[59] As Ayala Levin has proposed, ruins have a 'present(s) and future(s)' and, specifically in the context of postcolonial nations, understanding ruins in this way may help overcome their connection to a 'teleology of crisis'.[60] Building on this, the chapter's main argument is that ruins and ruination have a present and a future as potential for other, non-aligned living situations because of their creation of incomplete states. Ruination supposedly makes something that was at some point whole no longer so. But if we consider the colonial plans, designs and visions we have been addressing to have been incomplete from the start, ruins at their inception, then we can reframe the question. Instead of just asking what are the ruins of our present, from which pasts, we should also ask what sort of ruins we are making and working through, for it seems we are always amidst ruins. This requires reading architectural conceptions and effects beyond the realm of the technological and cultural, and into the environmental and bio-social. So a key point about this brief urban history of colonial Bissau is not only that Portuguese colonial architecture was the creator of a plenitude of ruins, but also that while solving a 'crisis' we are inevitably creating some ruins or unintentionally opening up differential futures, other worlds. As a result, a concluding question could be: how can we learn to see the ruins in our process of creation and perhaps even build from their admirable incompleteness and imperfection, for they may hold a better world than the one we are currently projecting?

Chapter Twelve

Reclaiming South African Railway Spaces: Ruination and Remembrance in De Aar and Usakos

Giorgio Miescher and Raffaele Perniola

The photographic view of the railway station from a bridge in De Aar provides a sense of the dramatic decline of railway transport in South Africa during recent decades. With no train in sight, the many tracks, power lines and platforms that dominate the picture have seemingly lost their purpose, and the railway infrastructure, overgrown by shrubs, bears no perceivable meaning anymore. The photograph evokes nostalgia, highlighting present abandonment while implying past grandeur. As such, the image encapsulates the contradiction of South African Railways' history.

This chapter examines a specific period of South African railway history, from the Union of South Africa's founding in 1910 to the collapse of apartheid in the early 1990s and its repercussions. During this time, South African Railways played a pivotal role in shaping white South Africa's nation-building, unlike the late 19th-century colonial phase focused on facilitating mineral transport. The chapter challenges traditional South African railway history, by committing to the school of thought that views post-1910 history in the context of imperial formation rather than as a purely national endeavour.[1] Following a brief overview of the role of the railways in this period, we

*Figure 12.1: Overlooking De Aar railway station.
(Paul Grendon, 2018; Courtesy of Tina Smith)*

focus on the active creation by the apartheid regime and settler society of romanticised narratives of an imperial railway through memorialisation, especially on the peripheries of the envisioned imperial sphere. We then move to our case studies of De Aar, situated in South Africa, and Usakos, situated in Namibia, by highlighting the parallel histories of these towns in the context of railway expansion and, later, decline to examine, first, the repercussions of infrastructural ruination and, second, the engagement of inhabitants and administrations with inherited ruins, empty spaces and deep-seated narratives of prosperity through infrastructural development. In sum, the chapter explores the impact of railway imperialism in former settler colonies overall but uses case studies to discuss the specificity of apartheid South Africa's peripheries while underscoring strategies and challenges relevant to small towns in settler-colonial regions overall.

The South African Railways: From Imperial Ambition to Ruination

Like a matrix cast in iron, the South African railway network defined the movement of goods and people through space for most of the 20th century. Iron tracks, train rhythms and station locations boosted economic growth in some areas, leaving others marginalised. The South African Railways and Harbours (SAR&H), founded by the government in 1916, was an integral part of the establishment of the Union of South Africa,[2] being a central instrument in enabling and ensuring the country's economic development.[3] Transport developed to service the needs of the settler society in a racially defined 'white man's land'.[4] SAR facilitated both transport and logistics, and built secondary infrastructure, for example by expanding into agricultural support by building farm infrastructure. It offered services to its white workforce and was a dominant employer.[5] This made it a 'state within the state',[6] which monopolised transport by means of a privileged legal position[7] as well as by expanding early on into competing transport infrastructure such as motor transport and aviation.[8] Through its support of white workers and agriculture, SAR also grew later into a central vote-garnering tool for the ruling party and, through its effective commercial propaganda, helped shape the vision of settler South Africa.

SAR expanded South Africa's territorial influence, incorporating railways from German South West Africa, today Namibia, in its network immediately after South Africa occupied that territory in 1915.[9] Despite continental aspirations of a Greater South Africa dissipating in the early 1920s,[10] SAR came to control a vast subcontinental transport system that extended into neighbouring territories.[11] Unless one preferred to walk or owned a private car, SAR was the only means of transportation for generations of travellers, who therefore shared common experiences of railway mobility – experiences which varied dramatically, due to racial segregation on the railway system.[12] For the scope of this chapter, we do not dwell on railway travel itself in its many facets (goods transport, tourism, commuter traffic, migration and so on) but rather on the hubs emerging on the nodes of this vast network; railway towns, owing their existence and prosperity to the railways, whose inhabitants were among those most affected by SAR, despite often not being travellers themselves.

The end of SAR's large-scale societal impact started in the mid-1970s, when SAR lost its transport monopoly and faced competition from private road transport,[13] which, coupled with its negative reputation among black passengers, caused SAR's rapid erosion. Many railway lines closed and long-distance passenger traffic largely collapsed in the 1990s. This resulted in infrastructural decay: feeder lines closed, tracks became overgrown with vegetation and stations deteriorated. Once a proud railway giant, SAR often became a matter of remnants scattered across the landscape, especially in former railway towns. This chapter examines how colonial and postcolonial societies have handled South Africa's railway heritage, focusing on two railway towns: De Aar and Usakos, whose vast amounts of decaying physical remnants of railways – stations, workshops, locomotives and wagons as well as whole tracts of unused land – we define as railway spaces.

Both towns were vital junctions for SAR, enabling a cross-border comparison beyond the framework of the nation-state.[14] The chapter contends that the significance of the apartheid-era railways, and the culture of railway monumentalisation that emerged from it, have influenced perceptions of the railways to this day. Postcolonial approaches thus inevitably grapple with the legacy of railway imperialism, particularly in these once central locations that are now left with infrastructural ruins.

Railway Memorialisation

Material ruination does not account for the full story of SAR. Railways remain at the heart of tangible and intangible heritage; and the promise of prosperity, the wonders of modernity and the fantasy of racial superiority continue to cluster around SAR and its history. The promise of modernity was programmatic for the railway's inauguration and expansion, and for its symbolic charisma, and it was thus strategically produced and mediated through texts and photographs.[15] Photographs adorn numerous railway-themed museums along SAR's former network today, showcasing the lasting influence of SAR and its ongoing grip on the land and on historical imagination, especially among those who benefited from its omnipresence.[16] These museums often originated from grassroots efforts by white settlers, especially in Namibia, with its long tradition of settler museums supported by members of the German-speaking settler community, claiming dominance in the domain of public history so as to contest South Africa's controlling mandate in Namibia.[17] In the 1980s, these institutions shifted their programmatic orientation towards non-partisan integration and a consolidated whiteness in opposition to decolonisation and majority rule.[18] Most institutions of this kind today preserve exhibits related to transport, particularly ox wagon and railway transport to emphasise the alleged 'positive' aspects of colonialism, such as prosperity through European investment in infrastructure and commerce.[19]

This push to memorialise white transport history in a specifically modernist framing was not only the work of private settler museums. While the role of the ox wagon in Afrikaner nationalist and official memorials such as the Voortrekker Monument is well known, the apartheid state also promoted railway memorialisation. Here it is especially important to look at empire from its periphery, since monumentalising the railway was central to the cultural politics of South West Africa's occupation by South Africa.

Founded in 1949 in Windhoek,[20] the Historical Monuments Commission of South West Africa embarked on identifying sites and objects of interest for declaration as national monuments in accordance with the remit of the Union Historical Monuments Commission, of which it was part. The commission's ultimate *raison d'être*, we argue, was to find symbols of white unification that would help transcend inner-white division and ethnic nationalism in South West Africa.[21] It is in this context that the commission campaigned for the preservation of railway objects and buildings, especially in the 1970s, when railway monuments secured a privileged position as prospective national monuments in South West Africa.[22] In view of a major technical transformation of SAR then under way – the transition from steam to diesel and the dismantling of narrow-gauge lines in Namibia – the commission produced and nurtured railway nostalgia. Narrow gauge was a relic from the German colonial period and was replaced in the 1960s. It embodied the German contribution to the colony's development, but it also symbolised a concern with infrastructure shared by both colonial governments. Even though South Africa's war of conquest against Germany had been fought along the railway lines, in the course of which much of the German colonial infrastructure was dismantled,[23] narratives of railway modernity were later seen as potentially unifying. South West African 'whites', be they German, English or Afrikaner settlers, would ultimately identify with the railway's role in modernising and boosting the economy, and in consolidating 'white settlement' in the territory.

Railway monumentalising was not an uncontested process, however, even within the state. In Namibia, SAR and the local Monuments Commission were often at odds, given that the railways pursued a policy of renovation and modernisation and repeatedly found ways to successfully oppose the commission's attempts to list infrastructure and buildings for preservation.[24] SAR's status as a state within the state exposed the occasional tension between racial ideology and orthodoxy, on the one hand, and capitalist interests, on the other hand. Ultimately, however, the company was conscientious and willing to put itself in the service of an overall concern for the material and symbolic production of apartheid's territorial hegemony.

In recent years, there have been attempts to counter the monumentalisation of SAR within the framework of settler-colonial historical narratives as they persist in many local museums across South Africa's imperial ambit. For instance, the new railway museum in Maputo, inaugurated in 2015 and housed in the beautifully restored Central Station built one hundred years ago, understands itself as a tribute to the railway company's history and a 'homage to generations of rail and port workers who made CFM [Caminhos de Ferro de Moçambique, the Mozambican railway company] possible'.[25] In South Africa, railway history is still almost exclusively approached from an institutional, architectural and infrastructural angle, and is nurtured by many railway enthusiasts in and outside the country.[26] However, there are exceptions, among them an important initiative at the Transnet Heritage Library, the successor organisation of SAR's own heritage centre located at the railway headquarters in Johannesburg. Here, there is a serious concern with making the huge archival collection accessible to the public and encouraging fresh historical interpretation that can help undo the tenacious narrative of colonial capitalist modernity and its biased solidification in monuments, museums and an extensive visual economy.[27] Clearly, a change of perspectives is required. Workers' histories or the histories of communities affected by infrastructural transformation are usually absent from institutions such as railway museums.[28] In what follows, we turn to two contexts in which there are attempts at transforming colonial notions of the SAR and reclaiming infrastructural heritage. Our case studies are De Aar and Usakos, both peripheral rural towns that were once nodal points in SAR's railway network. Today, they are left with substantial railway infrastructure in a state of dilapidation and decay. The rationale for choosing the two towns is, as already mentioned, their specific location within the railway network and a deliberate attempt to think beyond national historiographies.

The Rise and Fall of Railway Towns: De Aar and Usakos

De Aar and Usakos owe their existence, growth and prosperity to the railways, which shaped their urban landscapes. As crucial railway junctions in SAR's network, the railways' dramatic decline resulted in their economic downturn and an erosion of communal identity. Their histories echo the rise and fall seen in many southern African railway towns, akin to other locations reliant on a single industry like mining towns. Yet De Aar and Usakos differ upon closer examination. Both began as railway station sites owing to geography and water access, but their unique specifics highlight a degree of historical variation after infrastructural consolidation at the local level.

The first train arrived in De Aar in 1884 and the station soon became one of the most important railway junctions in South Africa.[29] 'You can't go far on the S.A.R. without passing through De Aar'[30] – the popular rhyme captured the town's central meaning in SAR's railway network. Here, four trunk lines met: the lines from Cape Town, Port Elizabeth, Kimberley (and thus, by extension, Rhodesia and the Rand) and Prieska, the last-mentioned extending from 1915 into South West Africa/Namibia. The settlement gained the status of a town in 1902, when private investors, the Friedlander brothers, bought the land, surveyed the entire town and established streets, squares and hundreds of standardised private plots, which they sold to individual buyers.[31] Under supervision of municipal regulation, urban development was based on strict segregation, and bigger plots reserved for white buyers were separated by railway buildings and infrastructure from smaller plots for black buyers.[32] However, railway infrastructure and accommodation for railway workers remained beyond municipal control until 1940. Even after that, the cluster of railway buildings and adjoining premises remained a fenced-off domain in the centre of town under the direct control of the railway company. This spatial assemblage henceforth divided the city into two separate areas – one for whites and one for blacks – connected only by a bridge and a subway. This structural urban layout persists until today. De Aar's prosperity went hand in hand with the growing importance of the railways, which peaked in the 1960s and 1970s. By then the town's population had grown from a few thousand at the beginning of the century to twenty thousand 60 years later.[33] In other words, population growth was substantial but never exponential, given that railway jobs were limited and there was no other local industry of note.

The beginnings of Usakos, on the other hand, are linked to the Otavi Mines and Railway Company (OMEG), a private venture which in 1906 opened a railway line between Swakopmund on the Atlantic coast and the copper and iron-ore mining centres in the Namibian highlands.[34] Usakos was situated on the edge of the Namib Desert, but its railway station occupied a strategic position at the crossing of the two main lines to the coast. The town's importance grew once it came to house OMEG's headquarters and its main workshop. Changing ownership of the railways – from OMEG to the German state's railway utility and, after 1915, to SAR – did not detract from Usakos's importance for the Namibian network. On the contrary, amalgamation into SAR's expansive, transnational network boosted the town's significance, even if it involved a significant technical adjustment from narrow-gauge to Cape-gauge rails with local transhipping facilities. In terms of municipal administration, Usakos remained less regulated than De Aar throughout its early period, although population numbers grew and the economy flourished, with effects on urban development. Alongside a huge railway yard owned and controlled by SAR, there were two distinct types of neighbourhoods, namely a small block of streets serving as a predominantly white residential and business area, and several non-regulated locations mainly for African residents. Usakos became a municipality in 1927,[35] and in the following three decades the town was developed more consistently along racial lines. All African residents were forced to live in a consolidated municipal location with a minimum of services provided by the town. The remaining part of Usakos was subsequently transformed into a 'proper' white town where residents enjoyed full access to services and amenities.

As in De Aar, the railway yard continued to form the centre of the town, but at Usakos the economy entirely depended on the railway. Employment was thus even more limited, as was the prospect of population growth, which reached a peak of around five thousand in 1960. The hegemony of SAR was both a blessing and curse for the town. In 1960 the railway line to Tsumeb was broadened and Usakos thus lost its function as transhipping station and maintenance centre for small-gauge locomotives and rolling stock. Three years later, diesel locomotives replaced steam engines, and SAR moved its main repair and maintenance facilities to Windhoek, abandoning the infrastructure in Usakos. The town lost its economic foundation and experienced an exodus of residents, who moved on to more promising urban locations on the coast or in central Namibia. SAR's overwhelming presence became a matter of memories and ghosts, and the company reduced its activities in Usakos to basic maintenance and low-scale operations until Namibia's independence in 1990.

Inheriting Infrastructure

The decline of the railways hit De Aar much later than Usakos. In the early 1990s, the railway company fired many employees or sent them into early retirement, and by 2001 the railways had ceased operations almost completely.[36] De Aar is no longer the prosperous railway town it used to be for almost a century. However, thanks to being an administrative centre in the region, the town's role shifted, albeit to a less lucrative function.[37] Population numbers continued to grow, reaching over thirty thousand people.[38] At present, there are practically no more trains and nobody works at De Aar's railway operating centre. Nevertheless, SAR, today known as Transnet, continues to shape De Aar's urban landscape. As in the past, the huge railway yard defines the spatial layout of the town and separates the generously designed former white part from the poorer neighbourhoods on the other side of the railway line. Despite its enormous size the railway yard – once the beating heart of the town's economy – has figuratively moved to the edge. Most activities happen along Voortrekker Road, which runs parallel to the railway lines. The most important government institutions and offices, banks, shops and restaurants are here, and they are easily accessible by car. Neither visitors nor residents of the former white township ever venture close to the railway yard. For them, the railway remains literally out of sight.

The situation is different for residents who live in the former black area of De Aar. They have to cross the huge railway yard if they wish to go to the central areas of town, where all services are provided and most formal employment takes place. Few have access to motorised transport (or bicycles), and many use the pedestrian bridge that takes them over the railway yard. It is the bridge from which the photograph at the beginning of this chapter was taken. For them, the railway yard remains a physical barrier that separates their residential areas from the economic centre of town. At night, especially for women who walk alone, crossing the bridge can be dangerous, given that footpaths through the wasteland are not secure and it is hard to avoid threats encountered on the bridge.[39] The railway yard itself remains inaccessible and fenced off. Here and there the fence is broken and shows signs of neglect and decay. There seems to be no impetus to retake this unused tract of land, on the part of the inhabitants, the municipality or activists.

The huge railway infrastructure, though mainly dysfunctional and deserted, continues to mark the urban space of De Aar, its presence perpetuating the practice of a spatially segregated town even after apartheid. To be clear, De Aar is no longer a racially segregated town. Some of the former railway houses, for instance, now offer affordable accommodation to black people in the previously white section of town. But while people can and do move to neighbourhoods on the other side of the tracks, the central railway infrastructure makes it impossible for the different neighbourhoods to grow together. The legacy of an existing dysfunctional infrastructure for the development of a town is not specific to De Aar, but the sheer size and prominence of this infrastructure in the town's layout is certainly exceptional. SAR's presence and hints of its past grandeur show in other places around De Aar. Former railway houses are scattered at certain points across the town and materially delineate shifting standards in housing provided to white railway workers between the 1930s and 1960s. They are now mostly privately owned and appear in good shape.

*Figure 12.2: Bridge Crossing De Aar railway yard.
(Paul Grendon, 2018; Courtesy of Tina Smith)*

The recreational Excelsior Park, situated in the middle of the former white town, shows signs of neglect but remains functional. Paradoxically, the railways are both present and absent in De Aar.[40] Infrastructure, buildings, fenced premises and occasional trains traversing De Aar are a daily reminder of past railway operations. But today's reduced traffic appears dwarfed in comparison with the oversized, ruined infrastructure and seems like a remnant of former glory. Today's residents seem largely indifferent to the railways and their historical importance, and young township dwellers in particular resent the ways in which decaying infrastructure affects their mobility between segregated neighbourhoods. Older generations, in contrast, preserve strong memories of a prosperous past linked to the railways, although black residents unambiguously place SAR at the heart of apartheid. The recollections of white former railway workers, by contrast, are positive and they cherish the railways, even if there is no significant public or private initiative for the preservation of railway heritage in De

Aar.[41] Only an old steam locomotive rests silently on a side track in the difficult-to-access railway yard, appearing somewhat monument-like while at the same time hidden.

*Figure 12.3: Steam locomotive in De Aar railway yard.
(Paul Grendon, 2018; Courtesy of Tina Smith)*

Reimagining Railway Space

The most impressive material remain of the railway past in Usakos are the railway workshop.[42] Once the biggest building in the colony, it today belongs to Namibia's national railway company, TransNamib, and still commands a kind of oppressive majesty. Crumbling though it may be, the workshop looms over a quiet town centre. It is but one of Usakos's railway ruins that are scattered across the urban landscape and that define the town's spatial layout. They include empty administrative buildings, former railway houses and accommodation for migrant workers, and scrap that has been repurposed and turned into everyday implements though still bearing traces of its original use.[43]

Our interest in Usakos stems from the town's preoccupation with reclaiming its past linked to the railways, in a way that attends to the multiplicity of historical experiences and the diversity of local forms and practices of memorialisation. We believe this approach is transformative in that it proposes productive paths towards postcolonial historical imagination. In 2015, an exhibition that used the remarkable photographic collections from Usakos's Old Location, collected and curated by four local women, inaugurated a community museum project. The exhibition was the result of a collaborative project between the women, Usakos municipality, the Museums Association of Namibia, Cape Town-based artists and curators, and scholars from Switzerland.[44] The new museum project tied in with and built on the municipality's previous interest in establishing a local cultural institution, and, importantly, it resonated with young local activists, artists and community members.[45] This combination of interested people is exceptionally productive and shows great promise and potential, especially in a context marked by economic decline, social tension and political gridlock.

Multiple, at times conflicting, interests cluster around the museum's project, but there is a widely shared commitment to establishing a unique museum that acknowledges recent, community-focused and community-sourced pasts. Formulated as a programmatic shift, the envisioned museum distinguishes itself from those parts of the Namibian museum sector that remain deeply rooted in settler historiography. Railway history constitutes one of the key domains in which these historiographical and representational shifts are meant to occur, and thus the numerous relics and ruins inherited from SAR and its German colonial predecessors take centre stage in current discussions about the museum's conception and design. Here, we wish to highlight two concerns that chart the direction these discussions have taken.

The first one relates to a German narrow-gauge steam locomotive situated next to Usakos's neglected train station, which nevertheless remains operational. Henschel Locomotive HD 40 was in use on Namibia's narrow-gauge tracks until the early 1960s. At this stage, key SAR activities were relocated, and the implementation of apartheid urban planning and forced removals deeply changed Usakos's urban fabric. Against the backdrop of fatal economic decline and grave social disruption, the decision of SWA's Monuments Commission to bequeath a locomotive monument as a 'farewell gift' to a sinking community seems almost cynical.[46] The years have taken a toll on locomotive HD 40.[47] This may explain why ideas surrounding the integration of the locomotive in the future museum's collection have focused on restoration.

Figures 12.4: Abandoned Usakos Railway Workshop and parked contemporary train. (Photograph by Raffaele Perniola, 2019)

However, alternative approaches are being formulated as well, since HD 40 constitutes an object of contested and conflictual memorialisation and remembrance that reveals social, racial and representational fault lines. Many black former railway workers express the wish for the restoration of material railway relics in town, the return of materials that moved with the railway, and the repair of the locomotive.[48] They link restoration and return to hopes for economic prosperity and in this way reveal the historical complexity and contemporary resonance of railway modernity.[49] Restoration may in some ways reflect the apartheid regime's obsession with European engineering, but at present it also speaks to railway enthusiasts and former workers alike, and thus sits uncomfortably with distinctions made between black and white, workers and entrepreneurs, profit and deprivation in railway historiography. However, restoration and repair

*Figure 12.5: Cabin of the 'Usakos Locomotive', Henschel Locomotive HD 40.
(Photograph by Raffaele Perniola, 2017)*

most likely run the risk of obliterating signifiers of labour history – among them replacement parts – and deindustrialisation – such as dents and rust – inscribed in the locomotive, and thereby foreclose the potential which the locomotive offers for critical reflection and representation. Attending to these less conspicuous facets of railway materiality could provide the grounds on which the locomotive as object might be situated in material and cultural contexts that transcend the narrow domain of SAR and its constricted history, and hence speak to Usakos's broader memorial landscape in meaningful ways.

Those involved in conceptualising the Usakos Museum have lately shifted their conversations to precisely these complexities and contradictions embodied in local railway heritage. They have considered, for example, artistic reworkings of the locomotive, which retain its current state of decay and situate the object in the context of oral history and memory work that privilege subaltern perspectives – of former railway workers, women, and the broader community. These initiatives are being developed in a context that remains controlled by TransNamib, which still claims ownership over the locomotive and owns much of the surrounding land in the town. Hence the context is still marked by corporate capital and centralised economic and political power located in Namibia's capital, Windhoek.[50] In other words, local and grassroots initiatives in the heritage sector continue to meet with resistance, albeit under a new postcolonial dispensation.[51] Furthermore, there's a shared preoccupation with how curatorial conceptions of the museum and the treatment of railway objects will resonate with different local, national and international constituencies and audiences, given that colonial nostalgic registers remain disturbingly popular among sections of Namibian society and international tourists.[52] The stakes are high, for museums are considered important assets in the tourist sector and accordingly raise expectations of economic development.[53] Local museum activists are aware of the tension between a strategy that orients museum work towards local communities and their concerns, on the one hand, and curatorial concepts that cater to international tastes and expectations, on the other.

The second concern that is currently emerging within local negotiations around an Usakos Museum relates to land and landscape, and ways of positioning the railways' presence in relation to contemporary debates on land reclamation and urban integration. Usakos's urban environment is deeply marked by the railways and histories of colonial dispossession, racial segregation and urban planning. But infrastructural remains and the built environment inherited from SAR also provide a material foundation for understanding the town's urban, social and aesthetic landscape in ways that transcend historical fragmentation along the lines of race and class, and allow for more inclusive visions of Usakos's future, of which the railways remain an integral part. This approach informs ongoing debates about the specific location of railway objects – such as the workshop, the locomotive and the museum building – and their integration in practices and narratives of memorialisation and remembrance, including collecting and curating objects, documenting oral histories, or designing tours around town that engage reclaimed and restored railway buildings, infrastructure, signage and sociality.

Such a productive engagement with the legacy of the railway in the town would fit in with the municipality's efforts to overcome the spatial fragmentation inherited by apartheid. Significantly, the new municipality building opened some years ago was built right in the middle of the former white and black parts of the town, namely on the site of the Old Location, whose inhabitants were forcibly removed in the early 1960s. This area is also at the centre of municipal plans for expanding housing. Should this vision come to fruition, Usakos would have made a significant step towards merging the disparate parts of town, which in many other industrial towns – such as De Aar – remain separated by colonial infrastructure and buffer zones. Comparisons such as this demonstrate the possibilities and limitations in overcoming scarring elements of infrastructural heritage. Peripheries, such as De Aar and Usakos, in particular highlight the financial and political limitations alongside a strong need and will for rejuvenation, as well as a certain spatial freedom in which new possibilities can grow.

Conclusion

South African Railways, the state-owned transport company, was an integral part of South Africa's hegemonic claim to the subcontinent. It was through SAR's sophisticated rail and road transport network that people and goods moved inside and beyond the country's national borders. This network, which both unified the nation and aimed at expanding beyond its borders, created new urban centres that owed their very existence to the railways and associated investments. After the decline of railway transport from the 1960s–1970s onwards, these towns were dramatically transformed, while they concurrently inherited the symbolic and material ruins of a massive imperial enterprise. The railway's decline gave rise to a process of memorialisation that placed at its heart a technology crucial in the making of 20th-century South African modernity.

We argue that railway memorialisation is particularly strong on the network's peripheries, where it predominantly was, and continues to be, celebrated in local settler museums. The chapter retraces the rise and fall of two railway centres, De Aar in South Africa and Usakos in Namibia, and looks at historical differences and diverging current engagements with railway heritage. The memorialisation of the railway is generally focused on technical aspects and modernist achievements, and in South Africa these narratives have made it difficult to uncouple railway history from settler history. Thus, new initiatives to reframe and recontextualise railway history are rare, and often the sheer size and number of ruins left by the railways make it difficult to reclaim spaces and objects in sustainable and meaningful ways.

In De Aar disruptive railway intervention in the town's urban environment has remained unchallenged. De Aar has reimagined itself as a regional administrative hub beyond its railway history. In Usakos, on the other hand, railway pasts and presents remain important, and hopes for a return to former economic prosperity and infrastructural grandeur are substantiated by the persisting presence of the railways as an important landowner. This may explain why residents have pushed for a new engagement with the past and are pursuing a local museum project. The envisioned museum is part of a concerted effort to draw on railway pasts in order to imagine an inclusive future. This is perhaps best encapsulated by the planned museum's logo, which, while emulating the style of tags found on the sides of steam locomotives, does not shy away from highlighting ruination and decay, all the while calling for a celebration of this complicated history.

Figure 12.6: Logo of the Usakos Museu. (Design by Graeme Arendse)

Chapter Thirteen

Usakos Museum and the Re-vision of Colonial Spaces: 'Put Your Hand on Your Forehead'

Florence F. /Khaxas

The Khan River: A place whose water gave them rest

Before colonialism, the natural well along the Khan River in what is today the town of Usakos in Namibia was a place of grazing with plenty of land and water. The wildlife and native people coexisted and moved freely around the vast landscape over the iconic Erongo Mountains. The native inhabitants of the region settled wherever they found a supply of water and grazing land, as they were nomadic people. Even though there are limited written records about the communities who lived in the area before the arrival of European traders, there are documented histories of land leases in the National Archives of Namibia. The Europeans travelled along the main transport route to the interior highlands. Explorers and traders journeying from the coastal Namib Desert would rest for a few days in Usakos to allow their animals to drink water and graze before continuing their journey along the river. The pre-colonial memory exists in oral histories like the untapped beauty of the land in its natural state. The Erongo Mountains that envelop Usakos are the permanent visual memory of this past. The native communities archived the history of pre-colonial south-west Africa through oral histories, folk tales and songs. The memory of Usakos was turned into legendary oral histories that were told from generation to generation.

There is so much power in telling our stories. I am a descendant of the native railway workers of Usakos, a name which derives from the Khoekhoegowab (Damara–Nama) word that means 'put your hand on your forehead'. The Otjiherero name is Okanduu, which speaks of the water found here. According to archival sources, the farm known as Usakos was occupied from 1882, when a German trader called Korner leased the land from the Herero leader (also known as Ovahando) Manasse Tjiseseta for the price of two heifers and a salted (disease-immune) horse.

My ancestors worked under harsh conditions for the Otavi Mines and Railway Company (Otavi Minen- und Eisenbahn-Gesellschaft or OMEG) during the early 1900s. This is the company that gave a new beginning to Usakos, which had started off as a farm and which was soon dramatically transformed by the building of the new railway line between 1903 and 1906. The living conditions of the local inhabitants and workers for the railways were poor, with inadequate housing and no sanitation.

OMEG Railway track

I first visited the railway track after a planning meeting of the Usakos Museum when I became a member of its advisory committee in 2018. I was so fascinated to discover that piece of history. Touching the rails hidden and covered in sand reminded me of the passing of time, that all that we know and use can become ruins. I felt a great sense of appreciation for Namibian history, even its dark past such as the colonial era with its trauma, which is still felt in Usakos.

Train ruins in the Namib

The machine that carried the weight of our resources
Mines of colonialisation
Transport rails of our livelihoods
The ruins of OMEG rails
I touch the iron made of the strength of the migrant workers

FLORENCE F. /KHAXAS

Uncomfortable realisation of destruction
Weapons of war hidden in the sand
The train ruins of the Namib
I touch the iron made as strong as the hope of the locomotive workers
The transport ruins of the OMEG give grace to the mother of this soil, for she cries for the open pits of colonial dominance over natural resources
The train is a ruin now, belonging to nature as a memory of the railway's transport route
!Usa !khos holds evidence of the machines that carried our resources
Transport rails of our livelihoods
Nothing but a distant memory not known to the youth

OMEG Railway workshop

I took this photograph when I lived in Usakos between 2017 and 2020. The building in the far distance used to be a workshop next to the railway line where the trains were repaired. In 2012 the workshop was leased to a Chinese business which continues to operate there today.

The Old Location and Hakhaseb

In 1927, a specific area was designated for African residence; this became known as the Old Location. Under apartheid, a new township called Hakhaseb was established, and in the 1960s residents of the Old Location were forcibly moved or deported over time.

The old location is a vacant space of emptiness which holds a wealth of memories for older community members who lived there before apartheid's forced removals, memories passed on to their living descendants through oral history. Each afternoon I would ride my bicycle while taking my dogs for a run; this was my spiritual connection to the old location. I always imagined what life in the old location was like for this community of rail workers as I walked around and found pieces of broken crockery and other ruins.

FLORENCE F. /KHAXAS

Usakos's ruins

We walk daily on the floors of houses broken down to nothing.
As we play in the mud of the rain that never comes, we connect to the same soil our great grandparents called home.
The ruins of Usakos are the echo of the winds of colonisation; the past is the pain we still feel in the dust of Hakhaseb location.
We did not want to fight them when they forced us to relocate.
The radio warned us of the fate of the blacks in Windhoek.
Bulldozers, gunshots, crying children and running women.
We moved to Hakhaseb in silence.
1961, racial segregation of NE51/6 houses.
We protest against police brutality, 1959.
Why do you force us to leave our homes and memories?
Take your African townships with its bad soil and no sense of dignity.
You took the communal languages we spoke and relocated us according to our ethnicity.
You must pay the rent! they demanded of us, forgetting the loss of our homes of love which they had destroyed.
You threaten to deport us to the reserve.
How do we pay rent for a house we did not even want?
The complete erasure by 1969 of our virtual memory.
The poems of the structures of our homes which are gone.
The kids know nothing.
They walk around and play, not knowing how sacred the land was for us.
The ruins of Usakos give hope to this ever changing landscape.
The only thing that remains is this mountain we call home.

We call Usakos a ghost town because it is home to so many ruins. These are a painful reminder of the deeply rooted inequalities and racism Namibians experienced due to colonisation and apartheid and their legacies in the present. The ruins are also a source of nostalgia for the older generation (who lived through apartheid forced removals) for the communities that were lost in the process. This remembering gives hope to the younger people of Usakos. The Usakos Museum plays an important role in giving voice and meaning to these transgenerational experiences of oppression while also creating room to critique and analyse our current times.

Kaikhoen lokasie

Kaikhoen, #Nûkhoen, elders, black people, railway workers, natives
whose homes gave life to Usakos
Emptiness of nothing
Broken homes under surveillance of the native departments
The voices of uncertainty locating a new home
Rise #Nûkhoe
The machinery that once placed food on our tables
Is left in the ruins
The houses that once hosted locomotives
Left in the ruins
Off to the lokasi ti kaikhoen
We dance to the moments most treasured by our ancestors
Dance with the dust till the storms rise
The youth drown their sorrows
The old location is a site of anger for opportunities lost and grief, the
    constant reminder of our realities at the present moment
Kaikhoen
#Nûkhoe
Rise from the destruction that makes you stumble on the same soil of
    invisible ruins of
Lost heritage
Broken town of the ruins
Houses that hosted locomotives astray
Workers left
Music left as spaces that were once beer halls for the mine workers
The laughter of neighbours
The joy of the kids that once played with wire trucks imitating the glamorous
    future they envisioned
Donkey carts as the trusted means of transportation in the old location
Kaikhoen
They move from, in and through Usakos
Music didn't leave Usakos
The movement of people
Daily commute through the dust left of the old location
Poor sanitation

FLORENCE F. /KHAXAS

The colonial space into the new independence era

I held my hand on my forehead – as in the name Usakos – in awe of how hot Usakos was as a 10-year-old whenever I visited my father from Swakopmund, where I lived with my mother. My father, Micheal Goreseb, was a local teacher from the 1980s and became mayor of Usakos post-independence during the early 2000s. We lived in a house which was originally constructed for the white workers of the OMEG. Usakos's formerly white suburbs were starting to be occupied by a few black civil servants, like my father, including teachers, nurses and police officers. These big houses had abundant space for us children to play: we ran around cheerfully, not knowing the history; not knowing that our great-grandmothers washed the floors of these very same houses.

I played in the slowly degrading urban environment of Usakos. Before Namibia's independence, Usakos's white communities had already started moving out of the suburbs to farms and bigger towns such as Windhoek and Swakopmund. The business of the railway was slowly ending and so was the economy of Usakos. Usakos's black community remained hopeful regardless of the slow decline of the town. Today, Usakos's economic activity is mainly related to public administration.

In 2017, I moved to Usakos from Swakopmund to start my research there, and that is how I became part of the Usakos museum. The museum gave me a home to be involved in the preservation of the history and the building of knowledge of Usakos. I lived for three years in Bo'dorp, a historically white neighbourhood, where I rented a three-bedroom house that was owned by a former Afrikaner mine worker. The neighbourhood was mostly occupied by civil servants and their families. The buildings are slowly degrading except in the case of a few homeowners who maintain their properties. The state of the houses in Bo'dorp is evidence of the economic decline of the town. Many shops are also closing down, and the road and transport infrastructure is in a poor state.

My family live in Hakhaseb township, which was built during the apartheid era when black residents were forcibly removed from Usakos's Old Location. I have seen the state of the apartheid-era houses. Basic services still haven't reached the township. The houses are falling apart, and the fences that act as boundaries between houses are mostly old and non-existent. Most houses have corrugated iron shacks at the back because of the shortage of affordable housing and poverty. The township is faced with social issues such as unemployment, drug abuse and violence. The impact of the colonial project is still being felt in our homes. The continued existence of the backyard toilets continues to remind us of the struggles our forefathers went through.

The black communities in Usakos are venturing into various types of informal businesses, many of which are run from home. There are home-based taverns which sell home-brewed beer, home-based shops that sell basic necessities. Young women sell sweets and food on the streets to generate an income. The youth also organise annual sports tournaments which attract Namibian tourists to Usakos's township. The religious community has also expanded, and there are many pop-up churches that operate from the backyards of houses or in the streets. The most thriving businesses in Hakhaseb are shebeens.

B2 Highway (Windhoek-Swakopmund), Usakos

Usakos is a gateway from Namibia's interior into its coastal towns. The B2 highway that runs through the town connects Windhoek to Swakopmund. The B2 intersection in the photograph marks the perimeter of Usako's Central Business District. On the day government pensions are paid out, many elders come into the business centre of Usakos to do their shopping. In the picture, a woman crosses the road carrying her shopping bag. The B2 highway intersection is also the site of the municipal waterfall, which is a recreational space of leisure and a landmark for locals, who often take their wedding pictures here. In the past, the waterfall held great significance for the farms surrounding Usakos. In 2019 we organised a digital workshop with girls and young women at the nearby youth centre, and I remember that when we asked them to take pictures of Usakos, they went to the waterfall by the B2 highway intersection. As I understood during their photoshoot, the waterfall represents a place of imagination for the young women. In my own experience the B2 intersection and the municipal waterfall is a site of freedom and rest. The scenery helps me relax my mind and the water cools me off. It makes me wonder about the colonial traders who rested at Usakos for water, and how residents and commuters still stop to rest and drink water in Usakos today. Usakos is a transport stop where passengers rest, refresh, and fill fuel before continuing on their journeys to different parts of Namibia. Service stations are one of Usakos's largest businesses.

USAKOS MUSEUM AND THE RE-VISION OF COLONIAL SPACES
292

Water Tower

I used to walk past the tower every day to go to the shops. The water tower is still being used and has great significance for the farms surrounding Usakos. It is also a gathering place for young people in Usakos - providing a place to

rest after the school commute, to play and to chat to friends, and to socialise at night. The graffiti on the tower make it a site of hope and creativity for young people in Usakos (in a context where there are not many opportunities for them), as well as an attraction for tourists and photographers.

Usakos Museum

The museum is a site of storytelling, and the community of Usakos has so many stories to tell. The history of the indigenous people and migrant workers in Usakos exists in the memory of the older generations that lived through the apartheid era and the new independent Namibia. As a site of knowledge production, the museum has the potential to be a site of activism and of economic transformation for the community of Usakos. There is also an urgent need to create a safe space with the museum to document the current realities and lived experiences of the community of Usakos.

All photographs in this chapter were taken by Florence F. /Khaxas.

Contributors

Rui Aristides Lebre is an architect and academic devoted to the study of the social, cultural and political implications of space production. His most recent research has involved examining the history and impact of wartime forced resettlement programmes in Guinea-Bissau, Angola and Mozambique, exploring a multi-method approach combining architectural survey with ethnography and digital mapping. He is currently a lecturer in architecture at the Faculty of Arts, Design and Media at Birmingham City University and a visiting academic at the University of Oxford's African Studies Centre, while keeping his practice as a designer in Colectivo Til (https://www.otil.pt/).

Hiten Bawa is a registered architect, artist and illustrator based in Johannesburg. He is a deaf person with bilateral cochlear implants. He works primarily with acrylic paints, watercolours and inks to express his cultural identity and perspectives of people with disabilities. He holds a Master of Architecture (Professional) degree from the University of Cape Town and runs his own creative practice called Studio HB. Bawa was a finalist for the inaugural SA TAXI Foundation Art Award in 2015 and his work forms part of the prestigious J.P. Morgan Chase Art Collection.

Stefan Chavez-Norgaard is a PhD student in urban planning at Columbia University's Graduate School of Architecture, Planning and Preservation (GSAPP). His research interests include urban and planning theory, local-government and planning law, and mixed-methods research focused on planning practice and urban governance in the related but distinct late-liberal contexts of South Africa and the United States. Stefan is passionate about participatory democracy and in particular how cities' public–private arrangements affect equitable and sustainable urban development. His dissertation examines areas of apartheid-era forced relocation in South Africa and how master plans have been implemented and repurposed in these geographies by residents and planners.

Nuno Coelho is a Porto-based Portuguese designer, artist and curator; professor in the Department of Architecture (DARQ) of the University of Coimbra; and researcher at the Centre for Interdisciplinary Studies (CEIS20). He holds a PhD in contemporary art from the University of Coimbra and a degree in communication design from the University of Porto. He is interested in history, heritage, material culture, digital humanities, and visual semiotics and representation. His work addresses topics related to identity and memory by exploring the politics of image-making and the archives of historic Portuguese trademarks and institutions. He has developed self-initiated projects in the intersection between design and art, mostly on social and political issues. He has curated exhibitions and public programmes; has had two books published; and has edited two others. He has exhibited his work, given talks, participated in conferences, and conducted workshops internationally (www.nunocoelho.net).

Adheema Davis practises as a professional architect and academic, immersed in an inquiry into 'architecture as bearing witness' in her lecturing on design, history, and theory of architecture. Her research interrogating sites of forced removals as monuments of apartheid-coloniality centres her advocacy for justice. She serves as vice-president for the South African Institute of Architects KZN, and on various other architectural platforms concerned with decolonising architecture, education and heritage.

Nabeel A. Essa is a practising architect with a background in fine arts. He graduated with a Bachelor of Architecture degree with distinction from the University of the Witwatersrand. Thereafter he received a master's degree in landscape urbanism from the Architectural Association School of Architecture in London. He participates as guest critic and examiner at numerous South African architectural schools. In 2002 he founded the practice Office 24|7 Architecture, which focuses on unique curatorial and design methodologies in combining spatial understanding with innovative ways of re-interpreting cultural space. The practice works with narrative as a framework for projects that aim to broaden imagination and stimulate engagement. The practice critically and spatially reimagines museums, exhibitions and architectural projects. Through an embodied experience of difference and otherness, and from the margin as vantage, Nabeel curates and designs to engage, empower and, in the making, transform. In 2023 he was an invited participant at the 18th International Architecture Exhibition at the Venice Biennale.

Roland Gunst is a conceptual artist of Belgian-Congolese origin. Through films, performances, installations, objects, photography and mixed media, he researches the potential of fluid identities and Afro-European narratives, inspired by the concept of Afropeanism. Gunst creates disruptive hybrid concepts and forms to reflect on the boundaries that define identity, culture, human condition and history. He is inspired by African and European art history, anthropology, psychology, philosophy and mythology.

Sibonelo Gumede is an urbanist and cultural worker based in Cape Town. A significant aspect of Gumede's practice is engagement with the temporalities of colonial afterlives in order to build a connection between the spatial and relational dimensions of memory and repair. Gumede is a former council member and vice-president of the KwaZulu-Natal Society of Arts and 2021 research fellow at the Center for Arts, Design and Social Research.

Pamila Gupta is research professor at the University of the Free State in Bloemfontein, South Africa, affiliated to the Centre for Gender and Africa Studies (CGAS). She was formerly full professor based at WiSER at the University of the Witwatersrand (2008 22). She holds a PhD in anthropology from Columbia University. Her research and writing interests include Portuguese colonial and Jesuit missionary history in India; diasporas, islands, tourism, heritage and design in the Indian Ocean; photography, tailoring and visual cultures in East Africa; and architecture, infrastructure and affect in South Africa. She is the co-editor of *Eyes across the Water: Navigating the Indian Ocean* (with Isabel Hofmeyr and Michael Pearson, Unisa Press,

2010) and author of three monographs: *The Relic State: St. Francis Xavier and the Politics of Ritual in Portuguese India* (Manchester University Press, 2014); *Portuguese Decolonization in the Indian Ocean World: History and Ethnography* (Bloomsbury Academic, 2019); and *Heritage and Design: Ten Portraits from Goa (India)* (Cambridge University Press, 2022). She has a forthcoming edited volume with Sarah Nuttall, Esther Peeren and Hanneke Stuit entitled *Planetary Hinterlands: Abandonment, Extraction, and Care* that will be published in Palgrave's Series on Globalization, Culture and Society (2023).

Brendan Hart is a part-time lecturer in the history of architecture and urbanism and architectural conservation at the School of Architecture and Planning at the University of the Witwatersrand, Johannesburg. In addition to teaching, Brendan is a founding partner, with Yasmin Mayat, of the multi-award-winning Mayat Hart Architects, a Johannesburg-based architectural and heritage consultancy. The diverse work of the practice focuses on creating and understanding architectural and spatial interventions rooted in context, historical narratives and the complex realities of heritage and identity in contemporary South Africa. Brendan has a master's degree in the conservation of the built environment from the University of Cape Town, and professional architectural degrees from the University of the Witwatersrand and is an Accredited Professional Member of the Association of Professional Heritage Practitioners.

Ali Khangela Hlongwane is a researcher in the History Workshop at the University of the Witwatersrand, and part of the Soweto History and Archives Project (SHAP). He has published on the public histories of the 1976 uprisings: *The Road to Democracy in South Africa*, vol. 7: *Soweto Uprisings: New Perspectives, Commemoration and Memorialisation* (2017). He is co-author of *Public History and Culture in South Africa: Memorialisation and Liberation Heritage Sites in Johannesburg and the Township Space* (2019). His most recent publication is *Lion of Azania: A Biography of Zephania Lekoame Mothopeng (1913–1990)*.

Hilton Judin is an architect in the School of Architecture and Planning at Wits University. He developed the exhibitions *[setting apart]* with

History Workshop in Johannesburg and District Six Museum in Cape Town. He was curator and editor with Ivan Vladislavić of *blank____ Architecture, Apartheid and After* (NAi Publishers, 1998) for the Netherlands Architecture Institute. He was in practice with Nina Cohen on the Nelson Mandela Museum in Mvezo and Qunu and the Living Landscape Project in Clanwilliam. He published *Architecture, State Modernism and Cultural Nationalism in the Apartheid Capital* (Routledge, 2021), and edited the volume *Falling Monuments, Reluctant Ruins: Persistence of the Past in the Architecture of Apartheid* (Wits University Press, 2021).

Florence F. /Khaxas is a feminist writer, indigenous Khoekhoegowab-language poet and storyteller, women's human rights defender, and the founder and executive director of the women's rights organisation called the Young Feminists Movement (Y-Fem Namibian Trust). She is a cultural activist advocating for Horokhoes, the traditional fashion heritage of the #Nūkhoe people in Namibia. She serves as a member of the Usakos Museum Council and on various civil society boards that promote the human rights of indigenous and vulnerable groups in Namibia.

Arianna Lissoni is a researcher in the Wits History Workshop and part of the 'Global Soldiers in the Cold War' project. Her research and publications focus on the history and politics of South Africa's liberation struggle. She is co-editor of *One Hundred Years of the ANC: Debating Liberation Histories Today* (2012), *The ANC between Home and Exile: Reflections on the Anti-apartheid Struggle in Italy and Southern Africa* (2015) and *New Histories of South Africa's Apartheid Era Bantustans* (2017), and co-author of *Khongolose: A Short History of the ANC in the North West Province* (2016).

Giorgio Miescher is the Carl Schlettwein Foundation Senior Lecturer and Research Fellow in Namibian and Southern African Studies at the Centre for African Studies in Basel and an associate researcher of the University of Namibia. He has published widely on the history of Namibia and southern Africa more generally, with a special focus on historical geography and visuality. His ongoing research projects comprise 'Thinking with Empire: Towards an Alternative Geography of South Africa's Imperial Space', 'Usakos – Photographs beyond Ruins: The Old Location Albums, 1920s–1960s', and

'Space in Time: Landscape Narratives and Land Management Changes in the Lower Orange River Cross-Border Region'.

Solam Mkhabela convenes the Master of Urban Design programme at the Wits University School of Architecture and Planning. He is a co-founder of the design collaborative blacklinesonwhitepaper. Professionally, Mkhabela has worked for architectural and urban design studio practices, a local radio station, YFM, and the Market Photo Workshop. He is a recipient of South Africa's National Research Foundation's Thuthuka Research Grant, for his PhD, 'Urban Scripting', on the role of audio-visual storytelling in urban design.

Raffaele Perniola is a PhD candidate in history at the University of Basel. Throughout his undergraduate studies he focused on southern African history. His master's thesis examined how the colonial railway in Namibia is remembered both publicly and privately. He has participated in and co-curated multiple exhibitions on topics surrounding southern African history, photography and popular culture. Currently he is part of the collaborative research project The (In)Audible Past, between the University of Fort Hare, the University of Namibia and the University of Basel with a dissertation project, on the social history of music records in pre-independence Namibia.

Esther Severi is a Belgian dramaturge. She works with artists such as Radouan Mriziga, Thomas Bellinck, Roland Gunst and Einat Tuchman. Inspired by the legacy of dramaturge Marianne van Kerkhoven, she is currently researching the working methods of the Belgian leftist theatre company Het Trojaanse Paard (1970s) to arrive at proposals for political dramaturgies today, in which activism and ideological choices define the nature of the creation process and artistic production.

Greer Valley is a lecturer in the history of art at the Wits School of Arts, University of the Witwatersrand, and an independent curator and writer. She currently serves as chairperson of the Africa South Arts Initiative (ASAI) and as a member of council and vice-president of the KwaZulu-Natal Society of Arts.

Notes

Introduction
1. See W.E.B. DuBois, *The Souls of Black Folk* (1903).
2. Bill Ashcroft, *Post-colonial Transformation* (London: Routledge, 2001), p. 156.
3. See the event 'In Whose Place?' at https://inwhoseplace.witsevents.co.za/.
4. The performance can be viewed at https://www.youtube.com/watch?v=6Ffl-GfUaWQ&t=1s.

Chapter 1: 'Save Our Berea!': Whose Place? Whose Heritage?
1. The notion of the 'rainbow nation' is overused and regarded as a cliché, but as Dubin contends, the phrase 'captured the sense of optimism and anticipation of elemental social transformation' that invigorated public imagination subsequent to the establishment of democracy in April 1994. See Steven Dubin, *Mounting Queen Victoria: Curating Cultural Change* (Johannesburg: Jacana Publishers, 2009), p. 1.
2. Nick Shepherd and Christian Ernsten, 'Good Hope after #RhodesMustFall: Review of Good Hope', 2017, accessed 21 August 2023, https://www.christianernsten.nl/wp-content/uploads/2017/04/Shepherd-Ernsten_review-of-Good-Hope.pdf.
3. For more on this, see Sandy Africa, 'South Africa's Deadly July 2021 Riots May Recur if There's No Change', *The Conversation*, 9 July 2022, accessed 21 August 2023, https://theconversation.com/south-africas-deadly-july-2021-riots-may-recur-if-theres-no-change-186397.
4. Our approach to classifications of race is that race is a socially constructed phenomenon. While the concept of race has material effects that span generations, it has no biological basis. Individuals and social groups are racialised through socio-political systems of power.
5. Bill Freund, 'Is There Such a Thing as a Post-Apartheid City?', *Urban Forum* 21, no. 3 (2010): 7.
6. Khurshid Mohideen, 'Save Our Berea!', *Berea Mail*, 7 November 2013,

accessed 21 August 2023, https://bereamail.co.za/24273/save-our-berea/.
7   Wanda Daly, 'Save Our Berea, Still Making a Difference Three Years On', *Berea Mail*, 5 October 2016, accessed 21 August 2023, https://bereamail.co.za/94304/save-our-berea-still-making-a-difference-three-years-on/.
8   Daly, 'Save Our Berea'.
9   Lauren Walford and Lorna Charles, 'Save Our Berea Says Durban Heritage Needs to Be Preserved', *Berea Mail*, 24 November 2016, accessed 21 August 2023, https://bereamail.co.za/98853/save-our-berea-said-durban-heritage-needs-to-be-preserved/.
10 Walford and Charles, 'Save Our Berea'.
11 Walford and Charles, 'Save Our Berea'.
12 Daly, 'Save Our Berea'.
13 Stuart Hall, 'Whose Heritage? Un-settling "The Heritage": Re-imagining the Post-nation', in *The Politics of Heritage: The Legacies of Race*, ed. Jo Littler et al. (Oxford: Routledge, 2005), pp. 23–36.
14 Hall, 'Whose Heritage?', p. 26.
15 Richard Dyer, *White* (London: Routledge, 1997); and Vron Ware and Les Back, *Out of Whiteness: Color, Politics and Culture* (Chicago: University of Chicago Press, 2002).
16 Gloria Wekker, *White Innocence: Paradoxes of Colonialism and Race* (Durham, NC: Duke University Press, 2016).
17 Prue Mutumi, 'Preservation, Conservation, and Advocacy: A Study of the Parktown Westcliff Heritage Trust (PWHT) in Heritage Management, 1965–2011' (MA thesis, University of the Witwatersrand, 2012).
18 Jeffrey Popke and Richard Ballard, 'Dislocating Modernity: Identity, Space and Representations of Street Trade in Durban, South Africa', *Geoforum* 35, no. 1 (2004): 99–110; and Jeffrey Popke, 'Managing Alterity: Narratives of Race, Space and Labour in Durban, 1870–1920', *Journal of Historical Geography* 29, no. 2 (2003): 248–67.
19 Popke and Ballard, 'Dislocating Modernity'.
20 Ann Stoler, 'Rethinking Colonial Categories: European Communities and the Boundaries of Rule', *Comparative Studies in Society and History* 31, no. 1 (1989): 134–61.
21 Fassil Demissie, *Colonial Architecture and Urbanism in Africa: Intertwined and Contested Histories* (London: Routledge, 2012), p. 1.
22 Popke, 'Managing Alterity', p. 250.
23 Popke, 'Managing Alterity'.
24 Ivan Turok, 'Worlds Apart: Spatial Inequalities in South Africa', in *Confronting Inequality: The South African Crisis*, ed. Michael Smith (Johannesburg: Jacana Media, 2018), pp. 129–51.

25 It is important to note that while census data have limitations, they provide an uniform source of demographic data as collated by Statistics South Africa.
26 AbdouMaliq Simone and Edgar Pieterse, *New Urban Worlds: Inhabiting Dissonant Times* (Hoboken, NJ: John Wiley & Sons, 2018).
27 Mpho Matsipa, 'Woza! Sweetheart! On Braiding Epistemologies on Bree Street', *Thesis Eleven* 141, no. 1 (2017): 31–48.
28 Zama Ngcoya, 'Umbilo Community Crime Awareness Group Calls for By-laws, Town Planning and Zoning Regulations', *Independent Online News*, 2 February 2023, accessed 21 August 2023, https://www.iol.co.za/sunday-tribune/news/umbilo-community-crime-awareness-group-calls-for-by-laws-town-planning-and-zoning-regulations-74531c57-6253-4406-a88f-26460217b9bd.
29 Ngcoya, 'Umbilo Community Crime Awareness Group'.
30 Richard Ballard, *Desegregating Minds: White Identities and Urban Change in the New South Africa* (Swansea: University of Wales, 2002).
31 Mpho Matsipa, *The Order of Appearances: Urban Renewal in Johannesburg* (Berkeley: University of California Press, 2004).
32 Ballard, *Desegregating Minds*, 125.
33 Ballard, *Desegregating Minds*, 125.
34 Kopano Matlwa, *Coconut* (Johannesburg: Jacana Media, 2007).
35 Ballard, *Desegregating Minds*.
36 Daniel Schensul and Patrick Heller, 'Legacies, Change and Transformation in the Post-apartheid City: Towards an Urban Sociological Cartography', *International Journal of Urban and Regional Research* 35, no. 1 (2011): 78–109.
37 Ballard, *Desegregating Minds*.
38 Sizwe Mpofu-Walsh, *The New Apartheid* (Cape Town: Tafelberg, 2021).
39 Peter Johnston and Hyacithia Naidoo, *Durban's Heritage Explored on Walks and Drives Around the City* (Durban: Adams & Co., 1987), p. 3.
40 Tariq Toffa, 'Learning to Speak? Of Transformation, Race and the Colonialities of Architecture', in *Cities, Space and Power*, ed. Amira Osman (Cape Town: AOSIS Scholarly Books, 2020), pp. 65–6.
41 Nick Shepherd, 'Roots and Wings: Heritage Studies in the Humanities', in *Shifting Boundaries of Knowledge: A View on Social Sciences, Law and Humanities in Africa*, ed. Tessa Marcus et al. (Durban: University of KwaZulu-Natal Press, 2005), p. 127.
42 Shepherd, 'Roots and Wings', p. 130.
43 Toffa, 'Learning to Speak?', pp. 52–65.
44 Shepherd, 'Roots and Wings', p. 130.
45 Romila Chetty, 'An Evaluation of the Relevance of Different Theories of

Social Justice to a Particular Ethical Problem, That of the Development of Block AK in the City of Durban' (Master of Regional and Town Planning thesis, University of Natal, 1998), pp. 70–2.
46 South African Institute of Architects (SAIA), www.saia.org.za, accessed 21 August 2023.
47 SAIA KZN, AGM Report, https://www.kznia.org.za/committees-saia-kzn-kznia, accessed 21 August 2023.
48 Itafa Amalinde Heritage Trust, eds, *Durban: Architecture and History: A Guide* (Durban: Itafa Amalinde Heritage Trust, 2010).
49 Len Rosenberg et al., *The Making of Place: The Warwick Junction Precinct, 1870s–1980s* (Durban: Durban University of Technology, 2013), p. 2.
50 Michele Jacobs, R. Harber and B. Kearney, *A Measure of the Past: Measured Drawings of Natal Buildings by Students of the Natal School of Architecture* (Durban: Durban Heritage Trust, 2015).

Chapter 2: Forced Removals: Reflections on Fietas' Photographic Archive, Museum and Heritage Trail

1 Located west of Johannesburg's city centre, Fietas was made up of two suburbs, Pageview and Vrededorp.
2 The Medu Art Ensemble was a collective of cultural workers and artists aligned to southern African liberation struggles that was based in Gaborone, Botswana, between 1978 and 1985.
3 The image on the poster was from a woodcut by Mpikayipheli Faglan, who gave Medu permission to use it in poster form.
4 Anon., 'Smiles Draw Blood Down Here', *Isandlwana Quarterly Journal*, no. 6 (April 1981): 28–31.
5 See Ali Khangela Hlongwane, 'In Search of Everyday Life in Public History: Marabastad, an Exhibition in History, Memory, Place and the Complexities of Land Restitution', in *Public History and Culture in South Africa: The Struggle Continues*, ed. Sifiso Mxolisi Ndlovu and Ali Khangela Hlongwane (Johannesburg: Skotaville Publishing, 2021).
6 Lucille Davie, 'Pageview Hero Stood His Ground for 20 Years', The Heritage Portal, http://www.theheritageportal.co.za/article/pageview-hero-stood-his-ground-20-years, accessed 21 September 2018.
7 Save Pageview Association, *The Renewal of the Area: The Zoning in Terms of the Group Areas Act, the Removal of Residents and the Future Development of Pageview* (Johannesburg: Save Pageview Association, 1981).
8 Davie, 'Pageview Hero'.
9 Eric Itzkin, 'Fietas/Pageview Heritage Trail', Submission to the Gauteng Department of Sport, Recreation, Libraries, Arts and Culture, City of

Johannesburg, 20 August 2018 (copy in author's possession).

10 Quoted in Ufrieda Ho, 'Fietas', *The Star*, 14 August 2012.
11 Brenda Goldblatt interview with Hanifa Patel, n.d. Brenda Goldblatt personal archive.
12 Brenda Goldblatt interview with Hanifa Patel.
13 'Fietas: Fade to Forgotten', *The Star*, 26 October 2013.
14 'Fietas: Fade to Forgotten',
15 Brenda Goldblatt interview with Selma Patel, n.d., Brenda Goldblatt personal archive.
16 Brenda Goldblatt interview with Hanifa Patel.
17 Brenda Goldblatt interview with Hanifa Patel.
18 Davie, 'Pageview Hero'.
19 Alexandra Dodd, *David Goldblatt: The Last Interview* (Göttingen: Steidl, 2019), p. 11.
20 Darren Newbury, *Defiant Images: Photography and Apartheid South Africa* (Pretoria: Unisa Press, 2009), p. 259.
21 Newbury, *Defiant Images*, p. 260.
22 Colin Richards, 'Biting the "Mother Tongue"', *The Star*, 16 June 2001, p. 14.
23 Helena Pohlandt-McCormick, 'Essay: Story of a Photograph – Sam Nzima', in *'I Saw a Nightmare …': Doing Violence to Memory; The Soweto Uprising, June 16, 1976*, p. 1, http://www.gutenberg-e.org/pohlandt-mccormick/pmh01a.html, accessed 25 October 2023.
24 Richards, 'Biting the "Mother Tongue"'.
25 See Njabulo Ndebele, *Rediscovery of the Ordinary: Essays on South African Literature and Culture* (Johannesburg: Congress of South African Writers, 1991); Albie Sachs, 'Preparing Ourselves for Freedom', in *Spring Is Rebellious: Arguments about Cultural Freedom*, ed. Ingrid de Kok and Karen Press (Cape Town: Buchu Books, 1990).
26 Ntongela Masilela, 'The Photographic Vision of Peter Magubane', *AWA-FINNABA: An African Literary Cultural Journal* (West Berlin), no. 11 (March 1988): 44.
27 See Gary Minkley and Phindezwa Mnyaka, 'Seeing Beyond the Official and the Vernacular: The Duncan Village Massacre Memorial and the Politics of Heritage in South Africa', in *The Politics of Heritage in Africa: Economies, Histories, and Infrastructures*, ed. Derek R. Peterson, Kodzo Gavua and Ciraj Rasool (London: International African Institute and Cambridge University Press, 2015), pp. 50–69.
28 Hlongwane, 'In Search of Everyday Life in Public History'.
29 Mark Robbins, Director's Foreword, in *The Rise and Fall of Apartheid: Photography and the Bureaucracy of Everyday Life*, ed. Okwi Enwezor and

NOTES

        Rory Bester (New York: International Centre of Photography and Delmonico Books, 2013), p. 16.

30   Njabulo Ndebele, in *Exchanges: South African Writing in Transition*, ed. Duncan Brown and Bruno van Dyk (Pietermaritzburg: University of Natal Press, 1991), p. 51.

31   Masilela, 'The Photographic Vision of Peter Magubane', p. 44.

32   Diane Smyth, 'Obituary: David Goldblatt, Photographer, 1930–2018', *British Journal of Photography*, 29 January 2020, https://www.bjp-online.com/2018/06/david-goldblatt-full-obituary/, accessed 29 January 2020.

33   Matt Schudel, 'David Goldblatt, Penetrating Photographer of South Africa under Apartheid Dies at 87', *Washington Post*, https://www.washingtonpost.com/local/obituaries/david-goldblatt-penetrating-photographer-of-south-africa-under-apartheid-dies-at-87/2018/06/26/a032cb56-7952-11e8-aeee-4d04c8ac6158_story.html, accessed 29 January 2019.

34   Schudel, 'David Goldblatt'.

35   Denis Herbstein, 'David Goldblatt Obituary', *The Guardian*, 6 July 2018.

36   Don Mattera, 'The Day They Came for Our House', in *Azanian Love Song* (Johannesburg: Skotaville Publishers, 1983), p. 5.

37   Robyn Sassen, 'Mike Feldman at the Bensusan Museum', *ArtThrob* 90 (2005), https://artthrob.co.za/05feb/reviews/bensusan.html, accessed 21 August 2023.

38   Sassen, 'Mike Feldman at the Bensusan Museum'.

39   Tony Campbell, 'Language Appropriation in Resistance and Reconstruction', *The Classic: A Magazine of Creative Writing and Art* 5, no. 1 (1991): 13.

40   Ntongela Masilela, 'Ernest Cole (Kede): In Remembrance', *Isivivane Journal of Letters and Arts in Africa and the Diaspora*, no. 5 (Spring 1992): 23.

41   See Hlongwane, 'In Search of Everyday Life in Public History'.

42   Hlongwane, 'In Search of Everyday Life in Public History'.

43   Fietas Museum Memory In Action, *Background Information*, n.d. (copy in author's possession).

44   Fietas Museum Memory In Action, Background Information.

45   Fietas Museum Memory In Action, Background Information.

46   Don Mattera, *Memory Is the Weapon* (Johannesburg: Ravan Press, 1987).

47   *Sophiatown Removals and Returns, February 1955 – February 2005, 50 Years Commemoration Evening Souvenir Programme*, 18 February 2005 (copy in author's possession).

48   Sophiatown Removals and Returns, February 1955 – February 2005.

49   Sophiatown Removals and Returns, February 1955 – February 2005.

50   Selma Patel, email correspondence to Irene Mafune, Regional Director: Region F, 15 September 2017.

51 Boet Eshuk, *Sunday Times*, 27 March 1977.
52 Manfred Hermer, *The Passing of Pageview* (Johannesburg: Ravan Press, 1978).
53 'Be Wise: Fietas Fiesta First for Fun', *Sunday Times*, 21 September 2003.
54 Inscription on the blue plaque outside Adam Asvat and his wife Khatija's home.
55 *Provincial Gazette Extraordinary* 18, no. 164 (13 June 2012).
56 See Dodd, *David Goldblatt: The Last Interview*.
57 I am indebted to Eric Itzkin, Deputy Director for Immovable Heritage in the City of Johannesburg, for this point.

Chapter 3: Statues Also Die: The Fortress of Cacheu as a Graveyard of the Portuguese Colonial Legacy

1 The Portuguese dictatorship consisted of the military dictatorship from 1926 to 1933, which paved the way for the Estado Novo (New State) from 1933 to 1974; combined, they made Europe's longest dictatorship (48 years).
2 Cacheu is located approximately 100 kilometres north from Bissau.
3 The author would like to acknowledge Ana Lúcia Mendes, Ana Vaz Milheiro, Ariel de Bigault, Claudio Arbore, Fernando Matos Silva, Filipa César, Joana Pontes, José Barahona, Julião Soares Sousa, Pedro Cerdeira, Raúl Mendes Fernandes, Tiago Castela and Welket Bungué for having generously contributed information for this chapter.
4 HPIP – Património de Influência Portuguesa, https://hpip.org/pt.
5 Tiago Castela, 'Empire in the City: Politicizing Urban Memorials of Colonialism in Portugal and Mozambique', in *Whose Tradition? Discourses on the Built Environment*, ed. Nezar AlSayyad, Mark Gillem and David Moffat (London and New York: Routledge, 2017), pp. 188–212.
6 Victor Barros, 'Comemorações da memória do império nas colónias durante o Estado Novo: Usos públicos da história, colonialismo e colonização de imaginários' (PhD diss., University of Coimbra, 2019), http://hdl.handle.net/10316/90761.
7 The first territory invaded and conquered outside Europe by the Portuguese was Ceuta in 1415, which fell under Spanish rule in 1688. The idea of Guinea as the first territory was due to the fact that it was the oldest territory over which Portugal still maintained its rule in the 20th century. During the Estado Novo regime, Portugal ruled over five colonies in Africa (Guinea-Bissau, Cape Verde, São Tomé and Príncipe, Angola and Mozambique) and three others in Asia (Goa, Macau and East Timor).
8 Rodrigues Matias, *Diário da viagem presidencial às províncias ultramarinas da Guiné e Cabo Verde em 1955*, vol. 1 (Lisboa: Agência Geral do Ultramar,

Divisão de Publicações e Bibliotecas, 1957), p. 276.
9 António Lopes Ribeiro, director, *Guiné berço do império 1446–1946*. 1946. 17 min., 29 sec. Film. http://www.cinemateca.pt/Cinemateca-Digital/Ficha.aspx?obraid=3080&type=Video.
10 Carlos Lopes, 'Os limites históricos de uma fronteira territorial: Guiné "Portuguesa" ou Guiné-Bissau', in *Lusotopie, no 1: Géopolitiques des mondes lusophones*, ed. Michel Cahen (Bordeaux: Centre d'Étude d'Afrique Noire, 1994), p. 139, https://www.persee.fr/doc/luso_1257-0273_1994_num_1_1_946.
11 Roger Crowley, *Conquerors: How Portugal Forged the First Global Empire* (London: Faber & Faber, 2015).
12 A. Teixeira da Mota, 'Expansão portuguesa da Guiné', in *Antologia da terra portuguesa, no 16: O ultramar português; Cabo Verde, Guiné, S. Tomé e Príncipe, Macau e Timor*, ed. Luís Forjaz Trigueiros (Lisbon: Bertrand, 1963), p. 115.
13 Amado cited in Joana Gorjão Henriques, *Racismo em Português: O lado esquecido do colonialismo* (Lisbon: Tinta-da-china, 2016), p. 101.
14 Amado cited in Henriques, *Racismo em Português*, p. 102.
15 Manuel Teixeira, 'Cacheu, enquadramento histórico e urbanismo', n.d., Património de Influência Portuguesa Portal, https://hpip.org/pt/Contents/Place/225.
16 Amado cited in Henriques, *Racismo em Português*, pp. 97–8; Joacine Katar Moreira, *Matchundadi: Género, performance e violência política na Guiné-Bissau* (Lisbon: Teatro Praga and Sistema Solar, 2020), p. 48.
17 Amado cited in Henriques, *Racismo em Português*, p. 97; José Manuel Fernandes, *Luso africana: Arquitectura e urbanismo na África portuguesa* (Casal de Cambra: Caleidoscópio, 2015), p. 44.
18 Amado cited in Henriques, *Racismo em Português*, p. 102. The transatlantic slave trade was initiated by the Portuguese in 1444. Slavery within its colonies was only abolished in the late 19th century.
19 Mota, 'Expansão portuguesa da Guiné', pp. 116-17.
20 Ana Vaz Milheiro, *Viagens no 5: Guiné-Bissau* (Porto: Circo de Ideias, 2012), p. 42.
21 Matias, *Diário da viagem presidencial*, p. 273.
22 Fernandes, *Luso africana*, p. 45. The capital was then transferred to Bolama in 1879 and then back to Bissau in 1942.
23 Matias, *Diário da viagem presidencial*, p. 274.
24 Not in the order in which these statues were erected.
25 Milheiro, *Viagens no 5: Guiné-Bissau*, p. 32.
26 The exact location is unknown.

27 Matias, *Diário da viagem presidencial*, p. 44.
28 Gomes Eanes de Zurara, 'Como foi morto Nuno Tristão em terra de Guiné e quais morreram com ele', in *Antologia da terra portuguesa, no 16: O ultramar português; Cabo Verde, Guiné, S. Tomé e Príncipe, Macau e Timor*, ed. Luís Forjaz Trigueiros (Lisbon: Bertrand, 1963), p. 98.
29 A padrão is a stone pillar that the Portuguese explorers planted on the coast to lay claims to the land.
30 Augusto Casimiro, 'Terra ardente, maravilhosa terra ...', in *Antologia da terra portuguesa, no 16: O ultramar português; Cabo Verde, Guiné, S. Tomé e Príncipe, Macau e Timor*, ed. Luís Forjaz Trigueiros (Lisbon: Bertrand, 1963), p. 103.
31 The term 'Política do Espírito' (Politics of the Spirit) was coined by journalist António Ferro in an article published on the front page of the newspaper *Diário de Notícias* of 21 November 1932. It was around this time that the journalist suggested to Portuguese dictator António de Oliveira Salazar, after having interviewed him on several occasions, the need to create an organisation to promote the regime's political propaganda. António Ferro was then called by Salazar to assume the position of director of the SPN (Secretariado de Propaganda Nacional, or Secretariat for National Propaganda), an organisation created in 1933 with the aim of promoting the propaganda and cultural policy of the Estado Novo regime. Nuno Coelho, 'O design de embalagem em Portugal no século XX: Do funcional ao simbólico; O estudo de caso da Saboaria e Perfumaria Confiança' (PhD diss., University of Coimbra, 2013), p. 45, https://eg.uc.pt/handle/10316/23803.
32 Matias, *Diário da viagem presidencial*, p. 39.
33 Matias, *Diário da viagem presidencial*, p. 39.
34 A monument was erected by the Estado Novo at this location marking the place where his fleet landed. 'Guiné 61/74 - P21747: O nosso blogue como fonte de informação e conhecimento (80); Busto do capitão Teixeira Pinto, em Bissau, c. 1943 (Armando Tavares da Silva)'. *Luís Graça & Camaradas da Guiné blog*, 8 January 2021, https://blogueforanadaevaotres.blogspot.com/2021/01/guine-6174-p21747-o-nosso-blogue-como.html.
35 Carlos Manuel Valentim, 'Navegações portuguesas: Diogo Gomes' (Lisbon: Instituto Camões, n.d.), http://cvc.instituto-camoes.pt/navegaport/d24.html.
36 Laura Castro, *Eduardo Tavares* (S. João da Pesqueira: Câmara Municipal de S. João da Pesqueira – Museu Eduardo Tavares, 2003), p. 15.
37 Ironically, the statue overlooked the Pidjiguiti port where a year later, in 1959, a massacre was carried out by the Portuguese after a strike by local sailors and dockworkers. This event provoked the beginning of the armed struggle in Guinea-Bissau four years later, in 1963. Sílvia Roque, 2018. 'Massacre de

Pidjiguiti, Bissau (1959)', in *As voltas do passado: A guerra colonial e as lutas de libertação*, ed. Miguel Cardina and Bruno Sena Martins, 33–9 (Lisbon: Tinta-da-china, 2018); Leonor Pires Martins and José Neves, 'Ataque ao Quartel de Tite: Início da guerra na Guiné (1963)', in *As voltas do passado: a guerra colonial e as lutas de libertação*, ed. Miguel Cardina, and Bruno Sena Martins, 116–20 (Lisbon: Tinta-da-china, 2018).

38 Milheiro, *Viagens no 5: Guiné-Bissau*, pp. 32–3.
39 Camões is widely considered Portugal's greatest poet and the anniversary of his death, 10 June, is Portugal's national day. *The Lusiads*, considered to be his masterpiece, was first published in 1572.
40 Milheiro, *Viagens no 5: Guiné-Bissau*, pp. 32–3.
41 Castro, *Eduardo Tavares*, p. 27.
42 A few years after designing Diogo Gomes's statue, Eduardo Tavares participated in the competition for the statue of Vasco da Gama destined for the Island of Mozambique, which he did not win, receiving a compensation prize only. Castro, *Eduardo Tavares*, p. 31.
43 Mota, 'Expansão portuguesa da Guiné', p. 117.
44 Slavery was only abolished in the Portuguese empire between 1869 and 1875–8.
45 Barreto was involved in the slave trade with his mother. Luís Pedro Nunes, 'O depósito da história', *Expresso*, 30 September 2015, https://expresso.pt/internacional/2015-09-29-O-deposito-da-Historia-1.
46 Mota, 'Expansão portuguesa da Guiné', p. 118.
47 Moreira, *Matchundadi*, pp. 42–3; Henriques, *Racismo em Português*, p. 101.
48 Joana Gorjão Henriques, 'Guiné-Bissau: A colónia onde todas as Fatumata tinham de se chamar Maria', *Público*, 6 December 2015, https://acervo.publico.pt/mundo/noticia/a-colonia-onde-todas-as-fatumata-tinham-de-se-chamar-maria-1716239.
49 Matias, *Diário da viagem presidencial*, p. 275.
50 An expression which is an oxymoron.
51 Mota, 'Expansão portuguesa da Guiné', p. 120.
52 The kingdom of Mussá Molô was defeated in 1892 as well as the Fulas in Gabu. Other campaigns then took place: against Oio-Farim, the first one in 1897; Churo in 1904; and Geba in 1907 and in 1908. Mota, 'Expansão portuguesa da Guiné', p. 120.
53 Where he was nicknamed Kurika, or 'lion' in Kwanyama, a language spoken in southern Angola. Matias, *Diário da viagem presidencial*, p. 70; Albino Undiga Nangurā, 'Estudo de caso: Perspetiva histórica das campanhas de João Teixeira Pinto e Abdul Indjay (1911–1915) na Guiné' (Master's thesis, ISCTE-IUL, 2014), p. 11, http://hdl.handle.net/10071/10179.
54 Bordonaro cited in Moreira, *Matchundadi*, p. 44.

55 Moreira, *Matchundadi*, p. 44. Teixeira Pinto died in combat in Mozambique against the Germans in 1917 during World War I. Matias, *Diário da viagem presidencial*, p. 78.
56 It has not been possible to identify the year of the design project.
57 Matias, *Diário da viagem presidencial*, pp. 67–8.
58 Matias, *Diário da viagem presidencial*, p. 78.
59 It has not been possible to identify its authorship.
60 It has not been possible to identify the materials of which these elements (plinth, laurel wreath and letters) were made. It is likely that the plinth was made of granite, while the others were bronze elements.
61 'Guiné 61/74 – P21747' (blog).
62 It was not possible to verify where the bust was moved to right after being taken down nor the year in which it took place. It is now deposited in Cacheu, but not in the fortress with the four statues. The exact location will be revealed later in the chapter. Regarding other tributes paid to the memory of Teixeira Pinto, in 1947–8 the town of Canchungo, near Cacheu, was named after him while Guinea was under Portuguese rule. Matias, *Diário da viagem presidencial*, p. 272; *Boletim Geral do Ultramar* 31, no. 360 (1955): 87. The town took its former name of Canchungo after the independence of Guinea-Bissau. In a bizarre fashion, Google Maps features today the name Teixeira Pinto, not Canchungo.
63 Castela, 'Empire in the City', pp. 189–90.
64 Castela, 'Empire in the City', p. 188.
65 Galtung cited in Moreira, *Matchundadi*, p. 122.
66 Moreira, *Matchundadi*, p. 123.
67 Ana Vaz Milheiro, 'O Gabinete de Urbanização Colonial e o traçado das cidades luso-africanas na última fase do período colonial português', *Urbe: Revista Brasileira de Gestão Urbana* 4, no. 2 (December 2012): 219, http://hdl.handle.net/10071/13580.
68 Milheiro, *Viagens no 5: Guiné-Bissau*, p. 10.
69 Milheiro, *Viagens no 5: Guiné-Bissau*, p. 10.
70 Fernandes, *Luso africana*, p. 45.
71 Fernandes, *Luso africana*, p. 46.
72 Milheiro, *Viagens no 5: Guiné-Bissau*, p. 18.
73 Fernandes, *Luso africana*, pp. 46–7.
74 Milheiro, *Viagens no 5: Guiné-Bissau*, p. 14.
75 'Monumento ao Esforço da Raça / Monumento aos Heróis da Independência', n.d., Sistema de Informação para o Património Arquitectónico, Sacavém: Direção-Geral do Património Cultural, http://www.monumentos.gov.pt/Site/APP_PagesUser/SIPA.aspx?id=32714.
76 In Bissau, there were other monuments: the one dedicated to Heróis da

Ocupação (Heroes of the Occupation), in the S. José de Amura fortress, built before 1955; and the Monumento Henriquino (Monument to Prince Henry the Navigator) on Avenida Marginal, which in 1960 marked the commemoration of his death five hundred years previously, consisting of a stylised stone sail, similar to the monument by the sculptor Severo Portela, which won a competition at the time in Portugal, and copies of which were erected all over the colonies, in places such as Praia, Bissau, São Tomé, Maputo, Dili and Cacheu, where it still stands today. Fernandes, *Luso africana*, p. 48.

77 Milheiro, *Viagens no 5: Guiné-Bissau*, p. 32.

78 Celeste Fortes and Rita Rainho, 'Início das emissões da Rádio Libertação, do PAIGC', in *As voltas do passado: A guerra colonial e as lutas de libertação*, ed. Miguel Cardina and Bruno Sena Martins (Lisbon: Tinta-da-china, 2018), p. 182.

79 António Lopes Ribeiro, director, *Guiné berço do império 1446–1946*. 1946. 17 min., 29 sec. Film. http://www.cinemateca.pt/Cinemateca-Digital/Ficha.aspx?obraid=3080&type=Video.

80 Ricardo Malheiro, director, *Viagem presidencial à Guiné (1) Bissau*. 1955a. 14 min., 51 sec. Film. http://www.cinemateca.pt/Cinemateca-Digital/Ficha.aspx?obraid=6838&type=Video; Ricardo Malheiro, director, *Viagem presidencial à Guiné 1955 (3) De Farim a Bissau*. 1955b. 10 min., 20 sec. Film. http://www.cinemateca.pt/Cinemateca-Digital/Ficha.aspx?obraid=2152&type=Video.

81 Augusto Fraga, director, *Terra ardente*. 1960. 18 min., 07 sec. Film. http://www.cinemateca.pt/Cinemateca-Digital/Ficha.aspx?obraid=970&type=Video.

82 RTP, producer, *Cidade de Bissau*. 1962. 17 min., 09 sec. Film. https://arquivos.rtp.pt/conteudos/cidade-de-bissau/; RTP, producer, *Bissau*. 1966. 16 min., 49 sec. Film. https://arquivos.rtp.pt/conteudos/bissau/.

83 Fernando Matos Silva, director, *Acto dos feitos da Guiné*. 1980. 1 hr, 21 min. Film.

84 Amílcar Cabral was assassinated on 20 January 1973. On 24 September 1973, Guinea-Bissau unilaterally declared its independence, only to be recognised by Portugal a year later on 10 September 1974.

85 Chris Marker, director, *Sans soleil*. 1983. 1 hr, 44 min. Film.

86 Maria Beatriz Marquilhas, 'Como filmar um clarão num momento de perigo / How to Film a Flash in a Moment of Danger', in *Contemporânea #4: Imagem em movimento / Moving Image*, ed. Celina Brás (Lisbon: Making Art Happen, 2019), p. 176.

87 Marker, *Sans soleil*.

88 Ricardo Ferraz, *Grande guerra e guerra colonial: Quanto custaram aos cofres portugueses?* (Lisbon: Gabinete de Estratégia e Estudos do Ministério da

Economia, 2019), https://www.gee.gov.pt/RePEc/WorkingPapers/GEE_PAPERS_122.pdf.
89 Flora Gomes, director. *Mortu nega*. 1988. 1 hr, 25 min. Film.
90 Marquilhas, 'Como filmar um clarão num momento de perigo, p. 172. After independence, Gomes assisted Chris Marker, when the French director arrived to Guinea-Bissau in 1979 with Sarah Maldoror. Filipa César, director, *Spell Reel*. 2017. 1 hr, 36 min. Film.
91 Gomes, *Mortu nega*.
92 Including the one of Otelo Saraiva de Carvalho, who had a prominent role in the Carnation Revolution.
93 José Barahona, director, *Anos de guerra, Guiné 1963–1974*. 2000. 57 min. Film. https://www.youtube.com/watch?v=mfSwSzRl9bM.
94 Marquilhas, 'Como filmar um clarão num momento de perigo, p. 172.
95 Marquilhas, 'Como filmar um clarão num momento de perigo, p. 170.
96 Marquilhas, 'Como filmar um clarão num momento de perigo, p. 176.
97 Filipa César, director, *The Embassy*. 2011. 37 min., 06 sec. Film.
98 Marquilhas, 'Como filmar um clarão num momento de perigo, p. 172.
99 Filipa César, director, *Cacheu*. 2012. 10 min., 09 sec. Film.
100 This chapter was inspired by this film. I have known of the existence of these statues since watching the film in 2012. Later I was able to visit Cacheu in 2019 for an artistic project I was developing related to the Portuguese slave trade.
101 Marquilhas, 'Como filmar um clarão num momento de perigo, pp. 173–4.
102 Joana Pontes, director, *Visões do Império*. 2020. 1 hr, 33 min. Film.
103 Welket Bunguê, director, *Cacheu CUNTUM*. 2020. 7 min., 26 sec. Film.
104 Bunguê quoted in RTP, 'Novo filme de Welket Bunguê cruza memória da escravatura e futuro da Guiné-Bissau', RTP, 12 January 2021, https://www.rtp.pt/noticias/cultura/novo-filme-de-welket-bungue-cruza-memoria-da-escravatura-e-futuro-da-guine-bissau_n1288762.
105 Bunguê quoted in RTP, 'Novo filme de Welket Bunguê'.
106 Michelle Sales, *À margem do cinema português: Residência artística afroeuropeans* (Coimbra: Colégio das Artes, 2020), p. 9.
107 Milheiro, *Viagens no 5: Guiné-Bissau*, p. 32.
108 Claudio Arbore, pers. comm.; Raúl Mendes Fernandes, pers. comm.; Julião Soares Sousa, pers. comm.
109 In 2020, a heavy truck lost its way, hitting the pedestal. The accident pushed it closer to the limits of the roundabout, where it stands today. Filipa César, pers. comm.
110 Marquilhas, 'Como filmar um clarão num momento de perigo, p. 173.
111 The title of this chapter, 'Statues also die', is a reference to the essay-movie of the same name, from 1953, by Chris Marker, Alain Resnais and Ghislain Cloquet about historical African art and the effects colonialism has had on

how it is perceived. Chris Marker, Alain Resnais and Ghislain Cloquet, directors, *Les statues meurent aussi*. 1953. 30 min. Film. https://www.youtube.com/watch?v=F0y1ZTrql8U. Despite the 'death' of these statues analysed in this chapter, some efforts to 'resurrect' them have been witnessed. In a now deleted comment from 2011 on a blog, reproduced on social media, descendants of Teixeira Pinto expressed their desires to rescue his statue: 'As great-grandchildren of João Teixeira Pinto, my cousin João Maria da Cruz Teixeira Pinto and I Maria Margarida Teixeira Pinto Restani Pinto, we would like to thank those who can help us make contacts to bring the statue to Portugal. If anyone can help us we would be very pleased. Maria Margarida and João.' Curso Teixeira Pinto, 'A saga da estátua do Kurika na Vila Teixeira Pinto', Curso Teixeira Pinto Facebook Page, 31 October 2013, https://www.facebook.com/313614812117255/posts/353281951483874/.

Chapter 4: Building as Artefact: From Prison to Museum

1. Thabo Manetsi, 'Heritage Denunciation and Heritage Enunciation? A Postcolonial Discourse on State Prioritisation on Heritage in South Africa', in *Exchanging Symbols: Monuments and Memorials in Post-apartheid South Africa* (Stellenbosch: Sun Press, 2020), p. 123.
2. Laureates, Pritzker Prize, accessed 21 April 2021, https://www.pritzkerprize.com/laureates.
3. Ursula Rigby, 'Transforming Space and Significance: A Study of the Constitutional Court of South Africa' (Master's thesis, University of Cape Town, 2016), p. 71.
4. Rigby, 'Transforming Space and Significance', p. 191.
5. Rigby, 'Transforming Space and Significance', p. 191.
6. Rigby, 'Transforming Space and Significance', p. 86.
7. Rigby, 'Transforming Space and Significance', p. 89.
8. Lauren Segal, Karen Martin and Sharon Cort, *Number Four: The Making of Constitution Hill* (Johannesburg: Penguin Books, 2006), pp. 79–80.
9. Mark Gevisser and and Sarah Nuttall, 'From the Ruins: The Constitution Hill Project', *Public Culture* 3 (2005): 507–19.
10. Gevisser and and Nuttall, 'From the Ruins', pp. 515–16.
11. Segal, Martin and Cort, *Number Four*, p. 28.
12. Segal, Martin and Cort, *Number Four*, p. 28.
13. Susan Middleton, '"Something Generally Happens": Mapping Young People's Experiences of Constitution Hill' (Master's thesis, University of the Witwatersrand, 2015), p. 75.
14. Segal, Martin and Cort, *Number Four*, p. 29.
15. Segal, Martin and Cort, *Number Four*, p. 147.
16. Segal, Martin and Cort, *Number Four*, p. 59.

17 Segal, Martin and Cort, *Number Four*, p. 59.
18 Gevisser and and Nuttall, 'From the Ruins', p. 509.
19 ICOMOS, *The Burra Charter: The Australia ICOMOS Charter for Places of Cultural Significance.* (Burwood: Deakin University, 2013).
20 Rigby, 'Transforming Space and Significance', p. 84.
21 Segal, Martin and Cort, *Number Four*, p. 59.
22 ICOMOS, *The Burra Charter*.
23 Gevisser and and Nuttall, 'From the Ruins', p. 516.
24 Herbet Prins, Letter to SAHRA, Johannesburg Development Agency, IHAC Minutes, Permits etc.: Con Hill Demolitions, Johannesburg, 2001.
25 Gevisser and and Nuttall, 'From the Ruins', p. 513.
26 ICOMOS, *The Burra Charter*.
27 ICOMOS, *The Burra Charter*.
28 Achille Mbembe, *Out of the Dark Night* (Johannesburg: Wits University Press, 2021), p. 49.
29 ICOMOS, *The Burra Charter*.
30 Arthur Barker and Johan Swart, 'Platforms of Knowledge: Architectural Heritage Practice and the Information Age in South Africa', *Virtual Archeology Review* (2020): 26.
31 ICOMOS, *The Burra Charter*.
32 Peggy Delport, 'Museum or Place for Working with Memory?', in *Recalling Community in Cape Town* (Cape Town: District Six Museum, 2001), p. 11.
33 Homi Bhabha, 'From the Colonial Nation-State to a Decolonized Political Community', Paper presented at the Institute for Advanced Study, University of Johannesburg, 2021.
34 Mbembe, *Out of the Dark Night*, p. 172.
35 Segal, Martin and Cort, *Number Four*, p. 167.
36 Alude Mahali, 'In Whose Name? On Statues, Place and Pain in South Africa', in *Exchanging Symbols: Monuments and Memorials in Post-apartheid South Africa*, ed. Anitra Nettleton and Mathias Alubafi Fubah (Stellenbosch: Sun Press, 2020), p. 74.
37 Karin van Marle, Isolde de Villiers and Eunette Beukes, 'Memory, Space and Gender: Re-imagining the Law', *Southern African Public Law* 2 (2012): 569.
38 Van Marle, De Villiers and Beukes, 'Memory, Space and Gender', p. 573.
39 Gevisser and and Nuttall, 'From the Ruins', p. 518.
40 Mbembe, *Out of the Dark Night*, p. 24.
41 Mbembe, *Out of the Dark Night*, p. 24.
42 Lesley Lokko, 'Bringing the Biennale B(l)ack', African Futures Institute, accessed 9 August 2023, https://www.africanfuturesinstitute.com/bringing-the-biennale-black.

NOTES

Chapter 6: Speculative Desire and Residential Reappropriation: Johannesburg's Ponte City from Apartheid to the Present

1. 'Ponte: The Tallest Residential Building in Africa', *Planning & Building Developments* 17 (1975): 18. Issues of *Planning & Building Developments* from the 1970s are available at the University of the Witwatersrand (Wits) Architecture & Built Environment Library. For more information, visit: https://libguides.wits.ac.za/architectandbuiltenvirolibrary.
2. 'Ponte: The Tallest Residential Building', 18.
3. Anna Hartford, 'Ponte City', *N+1 Magazine*, 14 June 2013, accessed 15 October 2019, https://nplusonemag.com/online-only/online-only/ponte-city/.
4. See, for example, work including Gregory Marinic, 'Adapted Utopia: The Rise, Fall, and Reemergence of Ponte City', in *The African Metropolis: Struggles over Urban Space, Citizenship, and Rights to the City*, ed. Toyin Falola and Bisola Falola (Abingdon: Routledge, 2018), pp. 109–11; Svea Josephy, 'Acropolis Now: Ponte City as "Portrait of a City"', *Thesis Eleven* 141, no. 1 (2017): 67–85; Tanya Pampalone, *The Full Ponte* (Johannesburg: Maverick, 2009); and Denise Lim, 'Remnants of Apartheid in Ponte City, Johannesburg', in *The Politics of Design: Privilege and Prejudice in Aotearoa, New Zealand, Australia and South Africa*, ed. Federico Freschi, Jane Venis and Farieda Nazier (Dunedin, NZ: Otago Polytechnic Press, 2021), pp. 189–211.
5. See, for example, work including Hartford, 'Ponte City'; Benedict Brook, 'Ponte Tower, Johannesburg's "Shanty Town in the Sky", Now Has a Waiting List to Move In', News.Com.AU, 15 August 2016, accessed 3 December 2019, https://www.news.com.au/finance/business/other-industries/ponte-tower-johannesburgs-shanty-town-in-the-sky-now-has-a-waiting-list-to-move-in/news-story/e4d0625c644819af7624c119b5dfc78a; Stephanie Hanes, 'Ponte City – a South African Landmark – Rises Again', *Christian Science Monitor*, 12 February 2008, accessed 24 November 2019, https://www.csmonitor.com/World/Africa/2008/0212/p20s01-woaf.html; and Nickolaus Bauer, 'Ponte's Fourth Coming: An Urban Icon Reborn', *Mail & Guardian*, 20 April 2012, accessed 14 October 2019, https://mg.co.za/article/2012-04-20-pontes-fourth-coming-an-urban-icon-reborn. Writers not associated with an academic or journalistic institution have also written on Ponte and its changing meaning over time, like Suzanne Whitby (who is a facilitator and communication specialist). See Suzanne Whitby, 'Ponte: Tower of Dreams', SuzanneWhitby.com, 23 February 2018, accessed 14 October 2019, https://suzannewhitby.com/ponte-tower-of-dreams/.
6. See, for example, Tanja Winkler, 'Kwere Kwere Journeys into Strangeness: Reimagining Inner-City Regeneration in Hillbrow, Johannesburg' (PhD

diss., University of British Columbia, 2006); Alan Morris, 'The Desegregation of Hillbrow, Johannesburg, 1978–1982', *Urban Studies* 31, no. 6 (1994): 821–43; Alan Morris, 'Tenant-Landlord Relations, the Antiapartheid Struggle and Physical Decline in Hillbrow, an Inner-City Neighbourhood in Johannesburg', *Urban Studies* 36, no. 3 (1996): 509–26; Alan Mabin, 'In the Forest of Transformation: Johannesburg's Northern Suburbs', in *Changing Space, Changing City: Johannesburg after Apartheid*, ed. Philip Harrison, Graeme Gotz, Alison Todes and Chris Wray (Johannesburg: Wits University Press, 2014), pp. 395–418; Ned Temko, 'Hillbrow: Testing Ground for Reform in South Africa: Area of Johannesburg Debates Continuing Illegal Integration', *Christian Science Monitor*, 22 April 1986, accessed 26 April 2022, https://www.csmonitor.com/1986/0422/obrow.html; and Owen Crankshaw and Caroline White, 'Racial Desegregation and Inner City Decay in Johannesburg', *International Journal of Urban and Regional Research* 19, no. 4 (1995): 622–38.

7   This periodisation runs roughly between the end of World War II and the Soweto Uprising and height of the 1970s economic crises. Osmanovic in 'The Retreat of Capitalism in South Africa' looks at GDP over time in South Africa in different sectors of the economy (agriculture and mining; electricity/gas/water, manufacturing and construction; transport/communications and logistics; and financial services) and proposes a compelling periodisation, though somewhat neoclassically grounded, of South African economic arrangements that include an 'apartheid boom' followed by a crisis, one that occurred elsewhere in the global periphery, from which South African economic capitalisation has yet to recover. Writes Osmanovic: 'The "historical success" of Afrikaner Nationalism had a reverse side, namely the exploitation of the African population and its systematic exclusion from social and economic development. Although the African majority clearly bore the brunt of this disadvantage and discrimination, South Africa as a whole eventually paid ... for these imbalances: The exclusion of Black South Africans from social wealth and political power meant that the majority of the labour force remained underqualified – a factor which continues to hamper development in all spheres of society.' See Armin Osmanovic, ed., 'The Retreat of Capitalism in South Africa', in *Transforming South Africa* (Hamburg: Institut für Afrika-Kunde/Institute of African Affairs, 2002), p. 86.

8   As argued by Scott, the decades after World War II saw the operationalising of architects, buildings and spatial plans in service of (often violent) institutional arrangements and paradigms globally. See Felicity Scott, 'Cruel Habitats', in *Outlaw Territories: Environments of Insecurity/Architectures of Counter-Insurgency* (New York: Zone Books, 2016), p. 283.

NOTES

9 Mabin comprehensively documents wealthy white South Africans' movement from neighbourhoods like Hillbrow and Doornfontein to the suburbs well before the 1970s. See Alan Mabin, 'In the Forest'.

10 Mabin, 'In the Forest', p. 404.

11 See Bryan Stringer, 'Cities Divided: The Spatial Legacy of Apartheid' (Honours thesis, Ohio University, 2019), pp. 15, 23. Writes Stringer: 'Johannesburg was transformed under the direction of its city council and engineers to reflect modernist city planning', and luxury modernist design and planning had considerable 'aesthetic influence ... upon the private and commercial developers of Johannesburg. Many of the design and urban theory principles of modernism also found their way into the official planning process of Johannesburg's city council and its engineers.' In short, Stringer looks at the critical role played by private developers and the Johannesburg City Council in promoting Western modernist design, through Ponte but also other projects including the Trust Bank Building (1970), Carlton Centre (1973), and the IBM Tower (1976).

12 For example, the Ponte 'nucleus' shopping centre involved collaboration with the private consultancy D.I. Design, designers of Sandton City. The ambitious complex was never profitable, and required building staff to raise rents on residential tenants. See Rodney Grosskopff, 'The Ponte Saga', *The Heritage Portal*, 11 June 2023, accessed 6 August 2023, https://www.theheritageportal.co.za/article/ponte-saga. For theoretical underpinnings on rent cap and cycles of devaluation, see Neil Smith, 'Gentrification and the Rent Gap', *Annals of the Association of American Geographers* 77, no. 3 (1987): 462–65. For a specific application of rent-gap theory to property development and speculation in Johannesburg, see Martin Murray, *City of Extremes: The Spatial Politics of Johannesburg* (Durham, NC: Duke University Press, 2011). For an embodied account of speculation on Johannesburg's landscape, see Mpho Matsipa, 'The Order of Appearances: Urban Renewal in Johannesburg' (PhD diss., University of California at Berkeley, 2014).

13 Morris, 'The Desegregation of Hillbrow', pp. 821–43.

14 Morris, 'Tenant-Landlord Relations', pp. 509–26.

15 Winkler, 'Kwere Kwere'.

16 Marinic, 'Adapted Utopia', pp. 109–11.

17 A.J. Christopher, 'Introduction', in *The Atlas of a Changing South Africa* (London and New York: Routledge, 2001), pp. 6–8.

18 Jennifer Robinson, 'Inventions and Interventions: Transforming Cities; An Introduction', *Urban Studies* 43, no. 2 (2006): 256.

19 Fabien Cante et al., 'On Urban Re-Arrangements: A Suite in Five Movements', *International Journal of Urban and Regional Research* 47 (2023): 461–70.

20 Edgar Pieterse, 'Building with Ruins and Dreams: Some Thoughts on Realising Integrated Urban Development in South Africa through Crisis', *Urban Studies* 43, no. 2 (2006): 285.

21 Phil Harrison, 'On the Edge of Reason: Planning and Urban Futures in Africa', *Urban Studies* 43, no. 2 (2006): 319.

22 Liza R. Cirolia et al., 'Retrofitting, Repurposing and Re-placing: A Multimedia Exploration of Occupation in Cape Town, South Africa', *plaNext – Next Generation Planning* 11 (2021): 144.

23 Cirolia et al., 'Retrofitting, Repurposing and Re-placing', p. 160.

24 Inspired by a discussion with Thabiso Moyo at the University of the Witwatersrand History Workshop (HW) Seminar, 18 August 2021.

25 Ponte reveals how there are complex – both complementary and contradictory – links between relations in the production of space in affective and political-economic terms. Other similar processes have occurred elsewhere. Neil Smith, using the analogy of the 'frontier', considers changing fortunes for residents and gentrification over time on Avenue B in Manhattan's Lower East Side. Detroit's GM Towers (also known as Renaissance Center and now GMRenCen) bears witness to racist segregation, deindustrialisation, and a changing city workforce. In New York City, the Ford Foundation Building, a late modern testament to mid-century office life, Fordist industrial production and legacy philanthropic surplus generated from such projects, has recently seen a full renovation as a site of social-justice convening. Also in New York City, the apartments at 3333 Broadway, built in 1976 and aesthetically resembling Ponte, have experienced a set of related processes tied to the decline of the NYC West Harlem industrial community and subsequent pressures of gentrification from the Columbia University Manhattanville Campus Expansion. The building was originally constructed under the state-run Mitchell-Lama affordable housing scheme, and is today managed by the private Urban American Management Corporation. See Neil Smith, '"Class Struggle on Avenue B": The Lower East Side as Wild Wild West', in *The New Urban Frontier* (New York: Routledge, 1996), pp. 3–27.

26 Grosskopff, 'The Ponte Saga'.

27 Grosskopff, 'The Ponte Saga'.

28 Grosskopff, 'The Ponte Saga'. MDC was led by Max Miodownik, Ivan Block and Cyril Reid. Vincemus Investments (Pty) Ltd. designed the building: it was Nasbou's wholly owned subsidiary and included Manfred Hermer, Mannie Feldman and Rodney Grosskopff as architects.

29 'Ponte: The Tallest Residential Building', pp. 16–17.

30 Grosskopff, 'The Ponte Saga'.

31 Lim, 'Remnants of Apartheid', pp. 189–90.

32 'Ponte: The Tallest Residential Building', p. 23.
33 Hartford, 'Ponte City'.
34 Grosskopff, 'The Ponte Saga'.
35 Lim, 'Remnants of Apartheid', p. 202.
36 'Ponte: The Tallest Residential Building', p. 23.
37 'Ponte: The Tallest Residential Building', p. 35.
38 'Ponte: The Tallest Residential Building', p. 27.
39 'Ponte: The Tallest Residential Building', p. 27.
40 'Ponte: The Tallest Residential Building', p. 35.
41 Lim, 'Remnants of Apartheid', p. 196.
42 Lim, 'Remnants of Apartheid'. See also Grosskopff, 'The Ponte Saga'.
43 Hartford, 'Ponte City'.
44 Mikael Subotzky, pers. comm., 18 March 2021.
45 'Ponte: The Tallest Residential Building', p. 23.
46 'Ponte: The Tallest Residential Building', p. 23.
47 'Ponte: The Tallest Residential Building', p. 23.
48 Marinic, 'Adapted Utopia', pp. 111–13.
49 Grosskopff, 'The Ponte Saga'.
50 Grosskopff, 'The Ponte Saga'. Grosskopff writes: 'We all subscribed to the tenets of the Bauhaus movement, "Form following function" – Manfred, at its earlier gentler beginning, Mannie, the brutal mainstream, and I, fighting off the brutal extremes at the other end of the movement.'
51 Grosskopff, 'The Ponte Saga'.
52 'Ponte City, A Residential Dream Comes True', promotional advertisement brochure (1973), p. 1.
53 As one example, consider New York City's Ford Foundation building, as described by Felicity Scott. Scott argues how the architectural team led by Kevin Roche, John Dinkeloo and Associates designed a 'garden space … in a conditioned environment … demarking their "little piece of the world"' as a 'calculated and symptomatic response to the social, urban, environmental, and territorial instabilities [Ford Foundation leadership] sought to manage'. See Scott, 'Cruel Habitats', p. 38.
54 Marinic, 'Adapted Utopia', pp. 112–13.
55 Hanes, 'Ponte City'.
56 'Ponte: The Tallest Residential Building', p. 35.
57 Marinic, 'Adapted Utopia', p. 118.
58 Temko, 'Hillbrow: Testing Ground'.
59 See, for instance: 'Hermer, Manfred', *Artefacts*, 2018, accessed 11 November 2019, https://www.artefacts.co.za/main/Buildings/archframes.php?archid=741. Other projects designed and envisioned by Hermer included

downtown Johannesburg's Ballet Theatre and Sappi Park, the Multichoice Auditorium, and the Alexander Theatre. For more, see Doreen Greig, *A Guide to Architecture in South Africa* (Cape Town: Howard Timmins, 1971). See also South African Institute of Architects (SAIA / ISAA), 'The Yearbook of the Institute of South African Architects and Chapter of SA Quantity Surveyors 1958–1959' [Original]: 'Die Jaarboek van die Instituut van Suid-Afrikaanse Argitekte en Tak van Suid-Afrikaanse Bourekenaars 1958–1959', (Johannesburg: ISAA, 1959).

60 'Hermer, Manfred', *Artefacts*, 2018.
61 You can learn and see more of GLH's projects today at http://www.glh.co.za/.
62 See, for example, Hanes, 'Ponte City' and Hartford, 'Ponte City'.
63 Writes Marinic of the neighbourhood: 'Hillbrow [in the early 1970s] provided a space where bohemian whites and blacks mixed ... [It] was an island of cosmopolitan promise within a systematically segregated and staunchly conservative society.' See Marinic, 'Adapted Utopia', p. 112.
64 Hanes, 'Ponte City'.
65 Anonymous former Ponte resident and guide with Dlala Nje, pers. comm., 12 March 2022.
66 Stephen Hobbs, pers. comm., 6 September 2021.
67 Stephen Hobbs, pers. comm., 6 September 2021.
68 Stephen Hobbs, pers. comm., 6 September 2021.
69 Rodney Grosskopff, *Carved in Stone* (Parkview, South Africa: Paper Bag Publishing, 2010), p. 9.
70 Grosskopff, *Carved in Stone*, p. 227.
71 Grosskopff, *Carved in Stone*, p. 238.
72 Clive M. Chipkin, *Johannesburg Style: Architecture and Society, 1880s–1960s* (Cape Town: David Philip Publishers, 1993).
73 Reyner Banham, 'The New Brutalism', *MIT Architectural Review* 136 (2011): 19–28.
74 Stringer, 'Cities Divided', p. 17.
75 Stringer, 'Cities Divided', p. 15.
76 Stringer, 'Cities Divided'.
77 Lim, 'Remnants of Apartheid', p. 190.
78 Clive M. Chipkin, 'The Great Apartheid Building Boom: The Transformation of Johannesburg in the 1960s', in *blank: Architecture, Apartheid and After*, ed. Hilton Judin and Ivan Vladislavić (Rotterdam: Nai Publishers, 1999).
79 See K.S.O. Beavon, 'Sandton City Site Report', Client research prepared for Rapp & Maister property developers, 1970. See also K.S.O. Beavon, 'Critical Factors in the Long Decline of the Johannesburg Central Business District: A Warning for Suburban Shopping Centres', Unpublished paper presented at

the Property Executive Programme conference entitled *The Challenge: Get the Basics Right* (Johannesburg: South African Property Owners' Association, 1997).

80 P.N. Larsen, 'The Changing Status of the Sandton Business District, 1969–2003' (Honours thesis, University of Pretoria, 2005).

81 Timothy Hart, 'The Factorial Ecology of Johannesburg', Occasional Paper no. 5 (Johannesburg: University of the Witwatersrand Urban and Regional Research Unit, 1975).

82 Robert A. Beauregard, 'Edge Cities: Peripheralizing the Centre', *Urban Geography* 16 (1995): 708–21.

83 Brian Larkin, 'Promising Forms: The Political Aesthetics of Infrastructure', in *The Promise of Infrastructure*, ed. Nikhil Anand, Akhil Gupta and Hannah Appel (Durham, NC: Duke University Press, 2018), pp. 176–7.

84 Larkin, 'Promising Forms', p. 177.

85 'Ponte: The Tallest Residential Building', p. 35.

86 James C. Scott, *Seeing Like a State: How Certain Schemes to Improve the Human Condition Have Failed* (New Haven: Yale University Press, 1998), p. 228. See also Leander Schneider, 'High on Modernity? Explaining the Failings of Tanzanian Villagisation', *African Studies* 66, no. 1 (2007): 9.

87 Larkin, 'Promising Forms', pp. 176–7.

88 'Ponte City, A Residential Dream', p. 1.

89 Marinic, 'Adapted Utopia', p. 113.

90 See Mark Werner, 'Storied Ambivalence for Johannesburg's Ponte City Tower, South Africa: The Role of Megaprojects and Vertical Slums in International Planning, Johannesburg, Africa', *Critical Perspectives on International Planning*, 2018, accessed 6 September 2021, https://sites.utexas.edu/internationalplanning/case-studies/storied-ambivalence-for-johannesburgs-ponte-city-tower/.

91 Temko, 'Hillbrow: Testing Ground'.

92 Temko, 'Hillbrow: Testing Ground'.

93 Anonymous former Ponte resident and guide with Dlala Nje, pers. comm., 12 March 2022.

94 Morris, 'Tenant-Landlord Relations', p. 523.

95 Grietjie Verhoef, 'The Dynamics of South African Banking in the 1980s', *South African Journal of Economic History* 9, no. 2 (1994): 84–109, Doi: 10.1080/20780389.1994.10417233.

96 Winkler, 'Kwere Kwere Journeys', p. 41.

97 Morris, 'Tenant-Landlord Relations', p. 523.

98 Anonymous former Ponte resident and guide with Dlala Nje, pers. comm. with author, 12 March 2022.

99 For more on neighbourhood change and 'tipping point' theory, see: Roberto

G. Quercia and George C. Galster, 'Threshold Effects and Neighbourhood Change', *Journal of Planning Education and Research* 20, no. 2 (2000): 146–62. See also Thomas Schelling, 'The Process of Residential Segregation: Neighbourhood Tipping', in *Racial Discrimination in Economic Life*, ed. Anthony H. Pascal (Lexington: D.C. Heath, 1972).

100 Marinic, 'Adapted Utopia', pp. 115–17.
101 Hartford, 'Ponte City'. Hartford notes that not just Ponte, but most buildings in Hillbrow, transitioned to renter-occupied status in the 1980s and 1990s.
102 Crankshaw and White, 'Racial Desegregation', p. 623. Crankshaw and White look at the dramatic demographic turnover in Johannesburg neighbourhoods starting in the late 1970s through 1991, writing: 'the exodus of middle class residents from the inner city led to a change in the nature of the inner city housing market … The urban poor did not have incomes which could ensure the adequate maintenance of the housing stock', leading to overcrowded, unsafe living conditions in formerly middle-class white areas. In short, Ponte, already one of the first buildings in the city to be a de facto integrated space, soon became an informal space, as managing the tower became too expensive.
103 Crankshaw and White, 'Racial Desegregation', pp. 626–8.
104 Writes Suzanne Whitby about this era in Ponte's history: 'The inner core continued to be used as a rubbish dump, filling with waste of all descriptions up to the 14th floor (or the seventh floor, or the fifth – there seems to be some discrepancy on this subject). The building earned the name "Suicide City", apparently because of all the people who leapt to their deaths, and who slowly decomposed in the core. The crime rate escalated and police, who couldn't easily access the flats, apparently flew helicopters around the building trying to track down criminals, who hid by drawing curtains across their windows to prevent detection.' Whitby, 'Ponte: Tower of Dreams'.
105 Whitby, 'Ponte: Tower of Dreams'.
106 Stephen Hobbs, pers. comm. with author, 25 August 2021.
107 Stephen Hobbs, pers. comm. Hobbs learned from building managers in the mid-1990s that they had witnessed up to 60 suicides over the course of the years they had worked at the buildings. Hobbs also learned from the foreman of Natanya Signs, a company contracting with Ponte in 1996 to install the now-infamous rooftop signage (first for Coca-Cola, then Vodacom), that in a span of two months, three people had committed suicide jumping from Ponte's upper storeys. The events inspired him to create his own artistic project, '54-Storeys'. Hobbs argues that 'the building itself as it conceived' was, in effect, a 'death machine': its hollow core and vertical stratification eased morbid proclivities.
108 Stephen Hobbs, pers. comm, and Brook, 'Ponte Tower', p. 2016. Hobbs

noticed a persistent 'transitory, migratory pattern' of Ponte residents in the earlier 1990s, meaning he perceived there were fewer long-term residents amidst more recent arrivals to South Africa. Thus, the true number of residents in the building was likely fluid and changing.

109   Loren Landau, Jean-Pierre Misago and Silindile Mlilo, 'Xenophobia Resources', African Centre for Migration Society (ACMS), 2019, accessed December 1, 2019, http://www.migration.org.za/xenophobia-resources/.
110   Marinic, 'Adapted Utopia', p. 119.
111   Marinic, 'Adapted Utopia', pp. 119–20.
112   Marinic, 'Adapted Utopia'.
113   Tom Keenan, 'Counter-Forensics and Photography', *Grey Room* 55 (2014): 65–6.
114   Eugene Reznik, 'Ponte City: An Apartheid-Era High Rise Mired in Myth', *Time*, 20 May 2013, accessed 22 September 2019, https://time.com/3799611/ponte-city-an-apartheid-era-high-rise-mired-in-myth/.
115   Mikhael Subotzky, pers. comm., 18 March 2021.
116   Mikhael Subotzky, pers. comm.
117   Ed Charlton, 'Trashing Johannesburg: Ponte City-as-Archive of Everyday Loss', *Cultural Geographies* 27, no. 2 (2020): 277–92. See also Josephy, 'Acropolis Now'.
118   Ingrid Martens, *Africa Shafted: Under One Roof*, film, 2016, accessed 1 December 2019, https://www.imoriginal.co/africa-shafted-screenings. Martens films at Ponte entirely, over two and a half years, in the Ponte elevators.
119   'Ponte City Apartments Explained', *Everything Explained*, 2019, accessed 15 November 2019, http://everything.explained.today/Ponte_City_Apartments/#null.
120   Stephen Hobbs, pers. comm., 25 August 2021.
121   Martin Murray, *Taming the Disorderly City: The Spatial Landscape of Johannesburg after Apartheid* (Ithaca, NY: Cornell University Press, 2008). See also Richard Tomlinson and Robert Beauregard, eds, *Emerging Johannesburg: Perspectives on the Postapartheid City* (New York: Routledge, 2003).
122   For more information about the relationship between Kempton and Vincemus, and Kempton's varied South African holdings, see https://kempston.co.za/wp-content/uploads/2017/06/2.-B-BBEE-Vincumus-level-5-exp-June-2018-NEW.pdf.
123   Anonymous Ponte building manager, pers. comm., 13 March 2022.
124   Whitby, 'Ponte: Tower of Dreams'.
125   Pampalone, *The Full Ponte*.
126   Bauer, 'Ponte's Fourth Coming'.
127   Anonymous former Ponte resident and guide with Dlala Nje, pers. comm.,

12 March 2022.

128 Anonymous former Ponte resident and guide with Dlala Nje, pers. comm.

129 Tanya Pampalone, 'Ponte Project Crashes', *Mail & Guardian*, 2008, accessed 22 April 2022, https://mg.co.za/article/2008-12-16-ponte-project-crashes/.

130 Anonymous former Ponte resident and guide with Dlala Nje, pers. comm., 12 March 2022.

131 Bauer, 'Ponte's Fourth Coming'.

132 Murray, *Taming the Disorderly City*, p. 20.

133 Tomlinson and Beauregard, *Emerging Johannesburg*, p. xii.

134 Tomlinson and Beauregard, *Emerging Johannesburg*, p. xiii.

135 Christina Weise, 'Maboneng: Johannesburg's Hipster Island', DW, 7 May 2018, accessed 3 December 2019, https://www.dw.com/en/maboneng-johannesburgs-hipster-island/a-44525787-0.

136 See Lynsey Chutel, 'Johannesburg's Hipster Gentrification Project Is at Risk of Crumbling', *QZ Africa*, 9 April 2019, accessed 4 August 2021, https://qz.com/africa/1589532/how-maboneng-ended-up-being-auctioned-in-liquidation-sale/. For a masterful and descriptive account of Maboneng today, see Tselio Monaheng, 'Maboneng: A Place and Its Lights', *Okay Africa*, 16 March 2021, accessed 4 August 2021, https://www.okayafrica.com/maboneng-a-place-and-its-lights/.

137 Gwen Ansell, 'Inner-City Joburg and Maboneng: A Tale of Two Cities', *News24 – Arts24*, 4 May 2021, accessed 4 August 2021, https://www.news24.com/arts/culture/inner-city-joburg-and-maboneng-a-tale-of-two-cities-20210504.

138 Adjaye has since taken his name off the building.

139 Ponte, in this regard, is a 'heterotopia', a concept fruitfully explored by Foucault and applied to Ponte by Marinic. See Michel Foucault, '11 January 1978', in *Security, Territory, Population: Lectures at the Collège de France, 1977–1978*, trans. Graham Burchell (New York: Palgrave, 2007), pp. 1–27. See also Marinic, 'Adapted Utopia', p. 122.

Chapter 7: Political Evolution of a Building Type: Community Centres at the End of Apartheid

1 Belinda Bozzoli, 'Class, Community and Ideology in the Evolution of South African Society', in *Class, Community and Conflict: South African Perspectives*, ed. Belinda Bozzoli (Johannesburg: Ravan Press, 1987), pp. 34–5.

2 Rafael Moneo, 'On Typology', *Oppositions* 13 (Summer 1978): 44.

3 'Steinkopf: A Response to the Problems of a Rural Community', *Architect and Builder* (June 1978): 18.

4 Joel Bregman, 'Land and Society in the Komaggas Region of Namaqualand'

NOTES

      (Master's diss., University of Cape Town, 2010), pp. 83–8.

5   Haig Beck, ed., 'Southern Africa', *UIA/International Architect Magazine* 8 (1985): 12.

6   'Steinkopf', p. 22.

7   'Steinkopf', p. 22.

8   See sketches in loose documents and drawings of 'The Hall within Its Context,' BC 1264 H19.11, Uytenbogaardt Papers, University of Cape Town Libraries Special Collections.

9   Roelof Uytenbogaardt and Norbert Rozendal, 'Minor Community Hall, Erica Ext 9, Belhar, Cape', *Architecture SA* (July/August 1986): 36.

10   See the chapter on 'Belhar Housing: "Coloured" Publics and "Urban Problems"', in Noeleen Murray, 'Architectural Modernism and Apartheid Modernity in South Africa' (PhD diss., University of Cape Town, 2010).

11   Beck, 'Southern Africa', (1985): 34.

12   Interview with Jo Noero, 15 June 2021. See John Allan, '1938: Finsbury Health Centre, London', 100 Buildings 100 Years, C20 *Twentieth Century Society*, 16 June 2021, accessed 20 June 2021, https://c20society.org.uk/100-buildings/1938-finsbury-health-centre-london.

13   An interesting riposte at the time was made by architect Graham Owen in which he questioned such good intentions given 'the inadvertent symbolism of the west elevation in effect, a stripped Classical portico, a universal Western image of entrance, that appears to have been bricked up completely'. Graham Owen, 'Forget Europe, Forget America: Architecture and Apartheid', *Journal of Architectural Education* 42, no. 3 (Spring 1989): 13–14. For Noero, it was importantly the memory of the historical lecture slides he prepared for the head of the Architecture School at Wits University, Pancho Guedes, that had brought Renaissance Italy to life. Online interview with Jo Noero, 15 June 2021.

14   Architect Jo Noero's notes to author following interview and email communication: 'Ipelegeng Community Center – Jabavu, White City, Soweto', 25 June 2020.

15   Online interview with Jo Noero, 15 June 2021.

16   See Werner Oechslin. 'Premises for the Resumption of the Discussion of Typology', *Assemblage* 1 (1986).

17   Quatremère de Quincy, 'Type', in *Oppositions Reader*, ed. K. Michael Hays (Princeton: Princeton University Press, 1998), p. 618.

18   Giulio Carlo Argan, 'On the Typology of Architecture', *Architectural Design* (December 1963): 565.

19   Anthony Vidler, 'The Third Typology', reprinted in *Oppositions Reader*, ed. K. Michael Hays (Princeton: Princeton University Press, 1998), p. 14.

20   Vidler, 'The Third Typology', 15.

21 See Chapter 13, 'Architecture and Revolution in Russia', in Jean-Louis Cohen, *The Future of Architecture since 1889* (London: Phaidon Press, 2012), pp. 162–72.

22 Manfredo Tafuri, *Architecture and Utopia: Design and Capitalist Development*, trans. Barbara Luigia La Penta (Cambridge, MA: MIT Press, 1976), p. 178.

23 See, for example, the article by Henry Sanoff, from North Carolina State University, following his lectures in major centres as a guest of the Institute of South African Architects (ISAA). Henry Sanoff, 'Designing with Community Participation', *Architecture SA* (September/October 1986): 24–6.

24 See the section on 'Low-Cost and Alternative Housing', in Diane Ghirardo, *Architecture after Modernism* (London: Thames and Hudson, 1996), pp. 146–56. See also Paul Davies, 'Lucien Kroll', *Architectural Review*, 28 August 2018, accessed 1 May 2021, https://www.architectural-review.com/essays/reputations/lucien-kroll-1927.

25 See 'The Fragment and the City: Research and *Exempla* of the Seventies', in Manfredo Tafuri, *History of Italian Architecture, 1944–1985* (Cambridge, MA: MIT Press, 1989), pp. 119–20.

26 De Carlo had to cancel his trip at the last moment and had his paper 'What Is Housing?' read at the conference. Michael Lazenby, ed., *Housing People: Proceedings of the Housing 75 Conference* (Johannesburg: Ad Donker, 1977). Erskine interestingly discussed in his 'Housing and Community Planning' one of his projects for a new community in the Canadian Arctic, the transport base at Resolute Bay, for an integrated community of southern Canadians and 'Eskimo' [Inuit and Yupik] men.

27 Iain Low, 'Building and Self-Reliance', in *blank___Architecture, Apartheid and After*, ed. Hilton Judin and Ivan Vladislavić (Rotterdam: NAI Publishers, 1998): F7.

28 See Chapter 4 on 'Emerging Traditions: The Vernacular in "Separate Development"', in Hilton Judin, *Architecture, State Modernism and Cultural Nationalism in the Apartheid Capital* (London: Routledge, 2021), pp. 84–91.

29 CS Studio Architects, 'Our Philosophy', accessed 2 September 2019, https://csstudio.co.za/Philosophy.html.

30 See 'Founding SCAT' and their mission statement on ongoing projects, decades after their establishment in 1984, accessed 7 August 2023, https://www.scat.org.za.

31 John Sharp and Emile Boonzaier, 'Ethnic Identity as Performance: Lessons from Namaqualand', *Journal of Southern African Studies* 20, no. 3 (1994): 412–13.

32 See Joel Bregman, 'Land and Society in the Komaggas Region of

Namaqualand' (Master's diss., University of Cape Town, 2010).
33. Cost was a primary factor with funding from SCAT to a modest amount of R320,000 at the time. Online interview with Carin Smuts, 17 June 2021.
34. The steel frame structure was familiar to the architect having worked previously on a number of such industrial structures which had reinforced the cost effectiveness, efficiency and ease of construction that would be significant in a project in such a remote location. Online interview with Smuts, 17 June 2021.
35. CS Studio, 'Our Philosophy'.
36. Architecture as a social mission became central to Carin Smuts, as she described it, through the influence of Günter Behnisch. His socially responsive architecture, or 'Situationsarchitektur', focus on school buildings in Stuttgart and landscape place-making were important counter-arguments to the international rational and technical systems building then prevalent. Online interview with Carin Smuts, 17 June 2021.
37. Sharp and Boonzaier, 'Ethnic Identity as Performance', pp. 413–14.
38. Michal Lyons, Carin Smuts and Anthea Stephens, 'Participation, Empowerment and Sustainability: (How) Do the Links Work?', *Urban Studies* (July 2001): 1249.
39. Interview with Carin Smuts, 7 August 2023.

Chapter 8: The Rescripting of the Johannesburg West Dutch Reformed Church

1. As racially classified and segregated by the apartheid state.
2. Schalk Le Roux, 'Church to Mosque: A Short History of the Recycling of the Pretoria West Dutch Reformed Church', *South African Journal of Art History* 22, no. 2 (2007).
3. The Dutch East India Company or VOC
4. Herman Giliomee, *The Afrikaners* (Cape Town: Tafelberg, 2003), p. 5; Gerald Pillay, 'Church, State and Apartheid', in *Perspectives on Christianity: 1948+50 Years; Theology, Apartheid and Church, Past, Present and Future*, series 5, vol. 1, ed. J.W. Hofmeyer et al. (Pretoria: University of Pretoria, 2001), p. 53.
5. Giliomee, *The Afrikaners*, p. 5.
6. Giliomee, *The Afrikaners*, p. 41.
7. J.C. Krüger, *Lest We Forget: The History of the Dutch Reformed Church in South Africa* (Kempton Park: Bitouw, 1984), p. 5.
8. Giliomee, *The Afrikaners*, p. 123.
9. George Rossouw, 'Essentials of Apartheid', in *Perspectives on Christianity: 1948+50 Years; Theology, Apartheid and Church, Past, Present and Future*,

       series 5, vol. 1, ed. J.W. Hofmeyer et al. (Pretoria: University of Pretoria, 2001), p. 95.
10   Giliomee, *The Afrikaners*, pp. 320, 321.
11   Luli Callinicos, *A Place in the City: The Rand on the Eve of Apartheid* (Johannesburg: Ravan Press, 1993), p. 10.
12   Keith Beavon, *Johannesburg: The Making and Shaping of the City* (Pretoria: Unisa Press, 2004), p. 110.
13   Rossouw, 'Essentials of Apartheid', p. 96.
14   Giliomee, *The Afrikaners*, p. 269.
15   Giliomee, *The Afrikaners*, p. 384.
16   Rossouw, 'Essentials of Apartheid', p. 97.
17   The ruling party of apartheid South Africa.
18   Giliomee, *The Afrikaners*, pp. 454, 458.
19   Giliomee, *The Afrikaners*, p. 463.
20   Christo Lombard, 'The Bible in the Apartheid Debate', in *Perspectives on Christianity: 1948+50 Years*; Theology, Apartheid and Church, Past, Present and Future, series 5, vol. 1, ed. J.W. Hofmeyer et al. (Pretoria: University of Pretoria, 2001), p. 71.
21   Giliomee, *The Afrikaners*, p. 459.
22   J.J. Lubbe, 'A Tale of Fear and Faith', *in Perspectives on Christianity: 1948+50 Years*; Theology, Apartheid and Church, Past, Present and Future, series 5, vol. 1, ed. J.W. Hofmeyer et al. (Pretoria: University of Pretoria, 2001), p. 46.
23   Giliomee, *The Afrikaners*, p. 621; Piet Meiring. 'Faith Communities and Their Apartheid Past', in *Perspectives on Christianity: 1948+50 Years*; Theology, Apartheid and Church, Past, Present and Future, series 5, vol. 1, ed. J.W. Hofmeyer et al. (Pretoria: University of Pretoria, 2001), p. 108.
24   Le Roux, 'Church to Mosque', p. 100.
25   Our own church building style.
26   Le Roux, 'Church to Mosque', p. 100; Schalk Le Roux, 'Die soeke van drie argitekte na 'n planvorm vir Afrikaanse Gereformeerde kerkbou', *South African Journal of Cultural History* 22, no. 2 (2008): 23.
27   Roger Fisher, 'The Third Vernacular', in *Architecture of the Transvaal*, ed. Roger Fisher et al. (Pretoria: Unisa Press, 1998), p. 124.
28   Le Roux, 'Die soeke van drie argitekte'.
29   Fisher, 'The Third Vernacular', p. 132.
30   Church Buildings for South Africa.
31   Irma Vermeulen, *Man en monument: Die lewe en werk van Gerard Moerdijk* (Pretoria: J.L. van Schaik, 1999), p. 38. Author's translation from Afrikaans.

32   Vermeulen, *Man en monument*.
33   Fisher, 'The Third Vernacular', p. 132,
34   Le Roux, 'Die soeke van drie argitekte', pp. 24, 28.
35   Fisher, 'The Third Vernacular', p. 130.
36   Le Roux, 'Die soeke van drie argitekte', pp. 24.
37   Le Roux, 'Die soeke van drie argitekte', pp. 38–40.
38   Z.A. Cajee, 'Islamic History and Civilisation in South Africa: The Impact of Colonialism, Apartheid, and Democracy (1652–2004)', *Journal of the Islamic Medical Association* 11, no. 4 (2004): 5.
39   Achmat Davids, '300 Years: The Cape Muslims and Cape Architecture', *Architecture SA* (July/August 1994): 17.
40   Cajee, 'Islamic History and Civilisation in South Africa', pp. 5–7.
41   Pillay, 'Church, State and Apartheid', p. 56.
42   Cited in Callinicos, *A Place in the City*, p. 115.
43   Giliomee, *The Afrikaners*, p. 101.
44   Uma Dhupelia-Mesthrie, ed., *From Cane Fields to Freedom: A Chronicle of Indian South African Life* (Cape Town: Kwela Books, 2001), pp. 10–11.
45   Cajee, 'Islamic History and Civilisation in South Africa', pp. 7–8.
46   Cajee, 'Islamic History and Civilisation in South Africa', p. 8.
47   Peter Randall and Yunus Desai, *From 'Coolie Location' to Group Area: A Brief Account of Johannesburg's Indian Community* (Johannesburg: SAIRR, 1967), pp. 1–5.
48   Cajee. 'Islamic History and Civilisation in South Africa', p. 9.
49   Cajee. 'Islamic History and Civilisation in South Africa', p. 11.
50   Eric Itzkin, *Gandhi's Johannesburg: Birthplace of Satyagraha* (Johannesburg: WUP, 2001), pp. 1–3; Peter Kallaway and Patrick Pearson, *Johannesburg: Images and Continuities; A History of Working Class Life through Pictures, 1885–1935* (Johannesburg: Ravan Press, 1986), p. 95.
51   Itzkin, *Gandhi's Johannesburg*, p. 9.
52   Davids, '300 Years', p. 17; Schalk Le Roux, 'The Transvaal Mosque: Towards a Theory of Precedent,' *Architecture of the Transvaal*, ed. Roger Fisher et al. (Pretoria: Unisa Press, 1998), p. 99.
53   Le Roux, 'The Transvaal Mosque', p. 99.
54   Le Roux, 'The Transvaal Mosque', p. 113.
55   Dogan Kuban, *Muslim Religious Architecture, Part II: Development of Religious Architecture in Later Periods* (Leiden: E.J. Brill, 1985), p. 14.
56   Le Roux, 'The Transvaal Mosque', pp. 114, 115.
57   Le Roux, 'The Transvaal Mosque', pp. 114, 115.
58   J.J. Lubbe, 'The Story of 1948', in *Perspectives on Christianity: 1948+50 Years*; Theology, Apartheid and Church, Past, Present and Future, series 5, vol. 1, ed. J.W. Hofmeyer et al. (Pretoria: University of Pretoria,

2001), p. 12.
59 Geers & Geers, Artefacts (2012), www.artefacts.co.za/main/Buildings/archframes.php?archid=568&countadd=1.
60 Geers, Geurt Marinus Jacobus, Artefacts (2012), www.artefacts.co.za/main/Buildings/archframes.php?archid=566&countadd=1.
61 Beavon, *Johannesburg*, p. 213.
62 Claire Pickard-Cambridge, *The Greying of Johannesburg: Racial Desegregation in the Johannesburg Area* (Johannesburg: SAIRR, 1988), p. 4.
63 Pickard-Cambridge, *The Greying of Johannesburg*, p. 213.
64 Yasmeen Dinath, '"Lifting the Veils" on Urban Ritual Spaces in the Multicultural City' (MTRP diss., Wits University, 2002), pp. 114, 118.
65 2012 interview.
66 Dogan Kuban, *Muslim Religious Architecture, Part I: The Mosque and its Early Development* (Leiden: E.J. Brill, 1974), pp. 1, 12.
67 Botho Molosankwe, 'Holy War for One of City's Oldest Churches', *The Star*, 15 April 2012.
68 SAPA, 'NG Church Becomes Muslim School', News24 (2012), http://www.news24.com/SouthAfrica/News/NG-church-becomes-Muslim-school-20120415.
69 Botho Molosankwe, 'Islamic Institution Surprised by Anger over Church Sale', *The Star*, 2 May 2012.
70 2012 interview.
71 Bill Ashcroft et al., eds, *The Post Colonial Studies Reader* (New York: Routledge, 2006), pp. 1, 5.
72 Helen Tiffin, 'Post-colonial Literatures and Counter Discourse', in *The Post Colonial Studies Reader* (New York: Routledge, 2006), p. 99.
73 Ashcroft et al., *The Post Colonial Studies Reader*, p. 138.
74 Homi Bhabha, 'Cultural Diversity and Cultural Differences', in *The Post Colonial Studies Reader*, p. 155.
75 Nezar AlSayyad, ed., *Hybrid Urbanism* (London: Praeger, 2001), p. 7.
76 Bhabha, 'Cultural Diversity and Cultural Differences', p. 155.
77 AlSayyad, *Hybrid Urbanism*, pp. 3, 6, 7.
78 Ashcroft et al., *The Post Colonial Studies Reader*, p. 137.
79 AlSayyad, *Hybrid Urbanism*, p. 4.
80 Ashcroft et al., *The Post Colonial Studies Reader*, p. 117.
81 Salman Rushdie, 'Imaginary Homelands', in *The Post Colonial Studies Reader* (New York: Routledge, 2006), p. 431.
82 Kirsten Holst Peterson and Anna Rutherford, 'Fossil Psyche', in *The Post Colonial Studies Reader* (New York: Routledge, 2006), p. 142.

Chapter 10: Notes for a Visual Essay on the Experience of Art Deco in South Africa

1. Geoff Dyer, *Yoga for People Who Can't Be Bothered to Do It* (New York: Vintage Books, 2003), Chapter 7, 'The Despair of Art Deco', p. 87.
2. Dyer, *Yoga for People Who Can't Be Bothered to Do It*.
3. By happenstance, I also recently visited Miami on 21–25 January 2022 and had Dyer's essay in the back of my mind as I experienced its Art Deco on foot. I was caught unaware by how many Art Deco buildings there were in the South Beach neighbourhood, with row after row of them appearing as I walked in the city. This visual experience in some ways helped me make sense of Dyer's essay and how historically distinct Art Deco movements were in places like New York City and Miami as compared to the South African case.
4. Pamila Gupta, *Portuguese Decolonization in the Indian Ocean World: History and Ethnography* (London: Bloomsbury Academic, 2019), Chapter 7, 'Renovating in Beira', pp. 127–4.
5. Pamila Gupta, 'Blue Johannesburg', in *Planned Violence: Post/Colonial Urban Infrastructures, Literature and Culture*, ed. Elleke Boehmer et al. (London: Palgrave Macmillan, 2018), pp. 213–30.
6. Here I would like to thank Hilton Judin for pressing me to think more about the analytical role of my photographs in shaping my arguments, including my foci on Art Deco detailings and façades. Discussant comments, 'In Whose Place? Confronting Vestiges of the Colonial Landscape in Africa' Conference, Wits University, Johannesburg (online), 21 May 2021. I would also like to thank all three editors (Hilton Judin, Arianna Lissoni and Ali Hlongwane) for their insightful comments during the revision process.
7. Francis Nyamnjoh, 'Incompleteness: Frontier Africa and the Currency of Conviviality', *Journal of Asian and African Studies* 52, no. 3 (2017): 253–70.
8. Dyer, *Yoga for People*, p. 87.
9. Keith Beavon, *Johannesburg: The Making and Shaping of the City* (Pretoria: Unisa Press, 2004).
10. Art Deco was an international design movement from the 1920s through the 1940s (and endured longer in the colonies). Its inspiration was technological modernity, commerce and speed, and drew on a variety of themes: archaeology, the machine age, aviation, the skyscraper, and employed streamlined images, repetition, symmetry, geometry, and used lacquer, inlaid wood, aluminium and stainless steel in its architectural detailing. http://www.visual-arts-cork.com/history-of-art/art-deco.htm, accessed 15 April 2018.
11. Beavon, *Johannesburg*, p. 94. Foremost architects include Anifantakis for the Springs Fire Station (1938), Obel and Obel for Astor Mansions (1931) in

Joburg and Crofton and Benjamin Architects for Durban's waterfront (1955–64).

12 Federico Freschi, 'Art Deco, Modernity, and the Politics of Ornament in South African Architecture', in *The Routledge Companion to Art Deco*, ed. Bridget Elliott et al. (New York: Routledge, 2019), p. 260.

13 Freschi, 'Art Deco'; Arianna Lissoni and Roshan Dadoo, 'Indian Trading, Art Deco and Urban Modernity in a Segregated Town: Jubilee House in Krugersdorp', in *Falling Monuments, Reluctant Ruins: The Persistence of the Past in the Architecture of Apartheid*, ed. Hilton Judin (Johannesburg: Wits University Press, 2021), pp. 150–72.

14 Beavon, *Johannesburg*, pp. 94–5.

15 Lissoni and Dadoo, 'Indian Trading', p. 162.

16 Clive Chipkin, *Johannesburg Style. Architecture & Society, 1880s–1960s* (Cape Town: David Philip, 1993), p. 314.

17 I would like to thank Hilton Judin for elaborating this point.

18 David Eng and David Kazanjian, eds, *Loss: The Politics of Mourning* (Berkeley: University of California Press, 2002). Also see Federico Freschi, 'Art Deco, Modernism and Modernity in Johannesburg: The Case for Obel and Obel's "Astor Mansions" (1932)', *De Arte* 32, no. 55 (1997): 21–35; Federico Freschi, 'The Politics of Ornament: Modernity, Identity, and Nationalism in the Decorative Programmes of Selected South African Public and Commercial Buildings, 1930–1940' (PhD diss., University of the Witwatersrand, 2006); and Freschi, 'Art Deco'.

19 Dyer, *Yoga for People*, p. 85.

20 The 'we' included myself, Wits City Institute director Noeleen Murray, Joburg writer Ivan Vladislavić, geographer Jill Weintroub, architect Alexander Opper (based at the University of Johannesburg), and Wits (City Institute) postdoctoral fellow Jonathan Cane; we all squeezed into a hired rental car for the day.

21 The City of Springs boasts the largest number of small-scale Art Deco buildings in the world, outside Miami in the United States. See https://springsadvertiser.co.za/188007/art-deco-sightseeing-in-springs-town/, accessed 10 June 2022.

22 I would like to thank Ivan Vladislavić for pointing me in the direction of Dyer's essay as it helped me formulate my own set of notes on Art Deco in SA and inspired my title.

23 The 'we' this time round was almost the same motley crew (minus Vladislavić), but added on were two new researchers, Johan Lagae (a Belgian urban planner based at Ghent University, visiting Wits) and former WiSER PhD student Ruth Sacks, who graciously led our experience through the Italianate

Johannesburg City Library with its interior Art Deco (1935) before we ended up at her own Art Deco flat in the Anstey's Building (1937).

24 The 'we' this last time around included myself and Jonathan Cane, mentioned on previous tours.

25 On Sunday, 14 November 2021, I went on an organised Art Deco tour of Killarney hosted by the Johannesburg Heritage Foundation and entitled 'Art Deco Meets African Riviera' (www.joburgheritage.co.za). I learned so much about the history of both my own neighbourhood and Joburg through its focus on Art Deco. More recently, on 31 May 2022, I visited the heritage Art Deco waterworks building, which now houses the Environmental Centre for Delta Park in Joburg.

26 Gupta, 'Blue Johannesburg'.

27 Jeremy Foster, *Washed with Sun: Landscape and the Making of White South Africa* (Pittsburgh: University of Pittsburgh Press, 2008); Jeremy Foster. 'From Socio-nature to Spectral Presence: Re-imagining the Once and Future Landscape of Johannesburg', *Safundi* 10, no. 2 (2009): 175–213.

28 Peter Merriman, 'Driving Places: Marc Auge, Non-Places and the Geographies of England's M1 Motorway', *Theory, Culture and Society* 21, nos. 4/5 (2004): 146.

29 Dyer, *Yoga for People*, p. 84.

30 The Arcades Project, conceived in Paris and written between 1927 and 1940 as a form of musings on city life from the perspective of its materialities, was also an unfinished work – it was still in progress when Benjamin fled the Occupation in France in 1940 and then committed suicide crossing the border into Spain. His writings also coincide with the time frame of the Art Deco movement in South Africa.

31 Howard Eiland and Kevin McLaughlin, 'Translators' Foreword', in Walter Benjamin, *The Arcades Project*, trans. H. Eiland and K. McLaughlin (Cambridge, MA: Harvard University Press, 2002), p. xii.

32 Ivan Vladislavić quoted in Foster, 'From Socio-nature to Spectral Presence', p. 175.

33 Dyer, *Yoga for People*, p. 87.

34 Ming Wei, 'Hidden in Plain Sight: Everyday Aesthetics and Capital in Chinese Johannesburg', Unpublished paper, presented at WISH Seminar, 5 October 2015, University of the Witwatersrand, 2015, p. 9.

35 Here I am exploring a relationality of aesthetics for Art Deco and hair salons in a manner parallel to the way I have previously explored the relationality of tailoring and photography as professions (where the camera becomes 'the scissors for seeing') for a set of Goan Zanzibari fathers and sons. See Pamila Gupta, 'Being (Goan) Modern in Zanzibar: Mobility, Relationality, and the

Stitching of Race', in *Luso-tropicalism and Its Discontents: The Making and Unmaking of Racial Exceptionalism in the Portuguese-speaking World*, ed. Warwick Anderson et al. (New York: Berghahn Books, 2019), pp. 265–86. As well, the entrepreneurial spirit behind the opening up of hair salons in South Africa is also a factor, as a kind of business that requires very little start-up money and allows for individuals to thrive as 'frontier Africans' (Nyamnjoh, 'Incompleteness'), opening up salons in leftover spaces inside Art Deco buildings that were once also sites of entrepreneurial success. See Justin Lin and Celestin Monga, *Beating the Odds: Jump-starting Developing Countries* (Princeton: Princeton University Press, 2017). In some sense, I am replacing their intriguing question 'Why so many beauty salons in a township?' with my own: 'Why so many hair salons inside Art Deco buildings?'

36 Dyer, *Yoga for People*, p. 85.
37 Gupta, *Portuguese Decolonization*.
38 Springs is the most important stop on the South African Art Deco heritage circuit, with frequent tours available year-round. As well, the Fire Station features prominently in the tour and is a protected monument. See https://www.theheritageportal.co.za/, accessed 13 June 2022.
39 While in the recent past there were multiple Art Deco tours of Joburg on offer, it was less the case during the pandemic, but fortunately the Johannesburg Heritage Foundation has resumed its walking tours as of December 2021. https://joburgheritage.org.za/, accessed 10 June 2022.
40 In Durban, there is a larger history of Art Deco tours run by the Durban Art Deco Society. See http://www.durbandeco.org.za/, accessed 10 April 2019. I thank Lindy Stiebel for providing me with a downloaded version of their latest catalogue for their Durban Art Deco walking tours.
41 Laurence Hughes, *Johannesburg: The Cosmopolitan City* (Johannesburg: Delta Books, 1983).
42 Sarah Nuttall and Achille Mbembe, eds, *Johannesburg: The Elusive Metropolis* (Johannesburg: Wits University Press, 2008).
43 Lindsay Bremner, *Writing the City into Being: Essays on Johannesburg, 1998–2008* (Johannesburg: Fourthwall Books, 2010).
44 Pamila Gupta, 'Consuming the Coast: Mid-century Communications of Port Tourism in the Southern African Indian Ocean', *Comunicação, Mídia e Consumo* (São Paulo) 12, no. 35 (2015): 149–70.
45 Dyer, *Yoga for People*, p. 84.
46 Steve Graham and Simon Marvin, *Splintering Urbanism: Networked Infrastructures, Technological Mobilities and the Urban Condition* (New York: Routledge, 2001).
47 Italo Calvino quoted in William Bissell, *Urban Design, Chaos and Colonial*

Power in Zanzibar (Bloomington: Indiana University Press, 2011), p. 8.
48 Nyamnjoh, 'Incompleteness'.
49 AbdouMaliq Simone, *Improvised Lives: Rhythms of Endurance in an Urban South* (Cambridge: Polity Press, 2019).
50 Bettina Malcomess and Dorothy Kreutzfeldt, *Not No Place: Johannesburg; Fragments of Space and Time* (Johannesburg: Fanele, 2013).
51 Steven Jackson, 'Rethinking Repair', in *Media Technologies: Essays on Communication, Materiality and Society*, ed. Tarleton Gillespie et al. (Cambridge, MA: MIT Press, 2014), pp. 221–40.
52 Dyer, *Yoga for People*, p. 90.
53 I would like to thank scholar Bill Freund, who took the time to speak to me by phone after I missed visiting him in Durban and during a short visit of his to Joburg. Our phone conversation/interview took place on 4 March 2019. I feel fortunate to have had the opportunity to speak with him, and gain his insights into his own Art Deco experience, particularly given his untimely death on 17 August 2020.
54 Nyamnjoh, 'Incompleteness'.
55 Simone, *Improvised Lives*.

Chapter 11: Garden of Ruins: The Urban Production of Colonial Bissau and the History of a Dilapidated Present

1 Maria Kaika, 'Autistic Architecture: The Fall of the Icon and the Rise of the Serial Object of Architecture', *Environment and Planning D: Society and Space* 29, no. 6 (1 December 2011): 968–92, https://doi.org/10.1068/d16110.
2 Philip Meuster and Adil Dalbai, eds, *Architectural Guide: Sub-Saharan Africa*, 7 vols (Berlin: DOM publishers, 2020). Despite the plurality of voices and openness of the discussion on what can constitute African architecture enabled by this guide, it nevertheless suggests this reading of modernist architecture in Africa. This is the case in specific regional sections, such as those representing Guinea-Bissau, Angola and Mozambique in particular.
3 Hannah le Roux, 'Comfort, Violence, Care: Decolonising Tropical Architecture at Blida, 1956', *ABE Journal: Architecture beyond Europe*, no. 17 (2 September 2020), https://doi.org/10.4000/abe.8197; Ayala Levin, 'Ruins of Modernity That Never Was', in *Timing Is Everything: The Exhibition of a Necessary Incompleteness* (Exhibition brochure, University Art Gallery, University of California, 2013), pp. 1–17.
4 Levin, 'Ruins of Modernity That Never Was'.
5 Ana Vaz Milheiro, *Nos trópicos sem Le Corbusier: Arquitectura luso-africana no estado novo* (Lisbon: Relógio d'Água, 2012); Ana Vaz Milheiro, *Guiné-Bissau, 2011* (Porto: Circo de Ideias, 2012); Ana Tostões, *Arquitectura*

  moderna em África: Angola e Moçambique (Lisbon: Caleidoscópio, 2014).

6 André Gunder Frank, *Dependent Accumulation and Underdevelopment* (London: Palgrave Macmillan, 1978); Samir Amin, *Unequal Development: An Essay on the Social Formations of Peripheral Capitalism* (New York: Monthly Review Press, 1976); Jason Moore, *Capitalism in the Web of Life: Ecology and the Accumulation of Capital* (London: Verso, 2014).

7 I am using the triad of capital, power and life in the sense elaborated by Jason Moore, *Capitalism in the Web of Life*, and as a dialectical interdependency between capitalist development, social organisation and ecological transformation.

8 Ann Laura Stoler, 'Imperial Debris: Reflections on Ruins and Ruination', *Cultural Anthropology* 23, no. 2 (2008): 191–219.

9 Olúfémi Táíwò, *Against Decolonisation: Taking African Agency Seriously* (London: Hurst & Co., 2022).

10 Edgar Pieterse, *City Futures: Confronting the Crisis of Urban Development* (London and New York: Zed Books, 2008).

11 Some recent eminent examples are the following: Miles Larmer, *Living for the City: Social Change and Knowledge Production in the Central African Copperbelt* (Cambridge: Cambridge University Press, 2021); António Tomás, *In the Skin of the City: Spatial Transformation in Luanda* (Durham, NC: Duke University Press, 2022); Mpho Matsipa et al., 'African Mobilities Exhibition: African Mobilities', 2018, https://archive.africanmobilities.org/african-mobilities-exhibition/; Garth Myers, *African Cities: Alternative Visions of Urban Theory and Practice* (London and New York: Zed Books, 2011).

12 Stoler, 'Imperial Debris'.

13 Alfred Crosby, *Ecological Imperialism: The Biological Expansion of Europe, 900–1900* (Cambridge: Cambridge University Press, 2004); Guillermo Kuschel, ed., *Biogeography and Ecology in New Zealand*, vol. 27, Monographiae Biologicae (The Hague: Dr W. Junk Publishers, 1975).

14 Because of the Guinean civil war in the 1990s, Guinea's national archives at INEP (Instituto Nacional de Estudos e Pesquisa) are very incomplete and mostly uncatalogued. This is mainly due to the fact they were ransacked during the civil war. Thus, several references from this archive here used consist mainly of document title and date when possible. On the state of Guinea-Bissau's national archives, see Mustafah Dhada, 'The National Historical Archives in Guinea-Bissau after the Military Intervention of 1998', *International Journal of African Historical Studies* 51, no. 3 (2018): 487–95. Other relevant archives for the research here presented include the Historical Military Archive and Historical Overseas Archive in Lisbon, and the Military

Museum in Porto, where research was conducted from 2019 to 2021.
15   Ann Laura Stoler, *Along the Archival Grain: Epistemic Anxieties and Colonial Common Sense* (New Jersey: Princeton University Press, 2008).
16   Research of the Portuguese forced villagisation programme presented here was developed as part of the funded research project 'Regulating the Rural', in which I was involved. For an initial historical review of this programme, see Rui Aristides Lebre and Tiago Castela, 'Aldeamento de guerra no colonialismo português na Guiné-Bissau', *e-cadernos CES*, no. 37 (15 June 2022), https://doi.org/10.4000/eces.7122.
17   Crosby, *Ecological Imperialism*.
18   John Iliffe, *Africans: The History of a Continent* (Cambridge: Cambridge University Press, 2007); Toby Green, *A Fistful of Shells: West Africa from the Rise of the Slave Trade to the Age of Revolution* (London: Penguin, 2020).
19   René Pélissier, *Les campagnes coloniales du Portugal, 1844–1941* (Paris: Pygmalion, 2004).
20   Judith A. Carney, *Black Rice: The African Origins of Rice Cultivation in the Americas* (Cambridge, MA: Harvard University Press, 2001).
21   Charles R. Boxer, *Four Centuries of Portuguese Expansion, 1415–1825: A Succinct Survey* (Berkeley and Los Angeles: University of California Press, 1970); João de Barros, *Ásia: Dos feitos que os Portugueses fizeram no descobrimento e conquista dos Mares do Oriente* (Lisbon: Imprensa Nacional Casa da Moeda, 1932).
22   Marina Padrão Temudo, 'A narrativa da degradação ambiental no Sul da Guiné-Bissau: Uma desconstrução etnográfica', *Etnográfica: Revista do Centro em Rede de Investigação em Antropologia* 13, no. 2 (1 November 2009): 237–64, https://doi.org/10.4000/etnografica.1341.
23   António Monteiro Filipe, 'S. Tomé e Guiné Agrícolas', *Acção Colonial: Jornal de Informação e Propaganda das Colónias*, 1934.
24   Carlos Craveiro, 'Da Guiné Portuguesa, Bolama ou Bissau?', *Acção Colonial: Jornal de Informação e Propaganda das Colónias*, 1934.
25   Until 1941, Bolama was the colonial capital. Making Bissau the new capital corresponded to both a concrete and symbolic change of colonial approach, as Bissau allowed better connections inland. For a graphic introduction to Quinhones's plan, see Milheiro, *Guiné-Bissau*.
26   Ana Vaz Milheiro, *African Colonial Architecture at the End of the 'Portuguese Empire'* (Lisbon: Relógio d'Água, 2017).
27   This is commonly referred to in Portuguese architecture historiography as 'Português Suave'; see José Manuel Fernandes, *Português Suave: Arquitetura do Estado Novo* (Lisbon: IPPAR, 2003); Milheiro, *African Colonial Architecture at the End of the 'Portuguese Empire'*.
28   Anthony D. King, *The Bungalow: The Production of Global Culture* (Oxford:

Oxford University Press, 1984).

29 For a study of the uses of the 'garden' metaphor for urban colonial government in Mozambique, see Tiago Castela, 'Imperial Garden: Planning Practices and the Utopia of Luso-tropicalism in Portugal/Mozambique, 1945–1975', *Traditional Dwellings and Settlements Working Paper Series: Architecture, Tradition, and the Utopia of the Nation-State*, 2010, pp. 75–98.

30 Manuel Maria Sarmento Rodrigues, 'Discurso de abertura da conferência anual de administradores coloniais', 27 November 1947, INEP.

31 Michel Foucault, *Discipline and Punish: The Birth of the Prison* (London: Penguin, 1991).

32 'Relatório da reunião de administradores coloniais' (Governo da Colónia da Guiné, 28 November 1947), INEP.

33 'Relatório da reunião de administradores coloniais'.

34 Eduardo Matos Guerra, 'Punição' (Câmara Municipal de Bissau, 1962), Box 71, INEP. Although most measures concerned disciplining Guinean men and women, a considerable number of measures concerned disciplining Portuguese to similar standards.

35 Frederico Ágoas and Cláudia Castelo, 'Social Sciences, Diplomacy and Late Colonialism: The Portuguese Participation in the Commission for Technical Co-operation in Africa South of the Sahara (CCTA)', *Estudos Históricos (Rio de Janeiro)* 32 (5 September 2019): 409–28, https://doi.org/10.1590/S2178-14942019000200005. The literature is thin on the formation and role of CIAO in the immediate post-Second World War reorganisation of colonial government. It is clear, however, that these conferences created a network for knowledge-sharing that served the practical arts of governing colonial fields and bodies.

36 Comité Permanente das CIAO, 'Relatório sobre a preparação da CIAO II', 1945, A6/A22.1306, INEP.

37 José Pereira Zagallo, 'Ofício nº1/confidencial de 25/1/1941' (Serviços de Obras Públicas, 15 January 1941), Box 'Diversos (Confidencial)', INEP.

38 Zagallo, 'Ofício nº1/confidencial de 25/1/1941'. *Contos* was the Portuguese currency before the adoption of the euro in 1999.

39 Zagallo, 'Ofício nº1/confidencial de 25/1/1941'.

40 Zagallo, 'Ofício nº1/confidencial de 25/1/1941'.

41 Zagallo, 'Ofício nº1/confidencial de 25/1/1941'.

42 Eduardo Fonseca Pousada, 'Memória descritiva para as ruas de Macau, Estado da Índia, Governador Sousa guerra e ladeia do cemitério' (Serviços de Obras Públicas, 19 November 1971), INEP.

43 By 1959 there were various liberation movements, but by the war's start, in 1963, PAIGC combined all anti-colonial efforts and causes. PAIGC stands for Partido Africano para a Independência da Guiné e Cabo Verde (African

Party for the Independence of Guinea and Cape Verde). For a succinct and informative introduction to the liberation movement in Guinea-Bissau, see Immanuel Wallerstein, 'The Lessons of the PAIGC', *Africa Today* 18, no. 3 (July 1971): 62–8.

44   Câmara Municipal de Bissau, 'Plano Orçamental para 1974', November 1973, 14/2045, INEP.

45   'Mapa de Obras Públicas' (Secção Permanente de Obras Públicas, 13 April 1945), 'Doc.Ñ Iniv. Obras Públicas', INEP.

46   'Anteprojecto Provincial do III Plano de Fomento', n.d., A6/A12.768, INEP. The 'Planos de Fomento' were born in the 1960s from Marshall-inspired post-war development and were used by the dictatorship as a palliative for the colonial war and the general misery of Portugal and its imperial possessions. What is remarkable about the study is not its recognition of the impossibility of implementing the plan, but how little had been achieved by 1968 to make Guinea the agribusiness colony dreamt of in 1934.

47   On the exportation of 'Europes' as a major socio-ecological force of European colonialism, see Crosby, *Ecological Imperialism*.

48   J.C. Ferreira and V.S. da Veiga, 'Estatuto dos indígenas portugueses das províncias da Guiné, Angola e Moçambique' (1957); Maria Paula G. Meneses, 'O "indígena" africano e o colono "europeu": A construção da diferença por processos legais', *e-cadernos CES*, no. 07 (1 de março de 2010), https://doi.org/10.4000/eces.403. The legislation was first formulated with the colonial labour law of 1928, then the Colonial Act of 1930, legally integrated in 1933 with the constitution of the dictatorship, reviewed in 1954 and only finally abolished, in its original 1928 indigenous labour law format, in 1961, when the wars for liberation started.

49   Avelino Teixeira da Mota, *A habitação indígena na Guiné portuguesa* (Bissau: Centro de Estudos da Guiné Portuguesa, 1948).

50   This idea of governing through assimilation using architecture and urban planning was an established professional proposition for colonial architects in the 1960s such as Mário de Oliveira. He argued that the solution for the colonial situation was the promotion of 'structures of conviviality' and 'influence', within the Luso-tropical horizon of a multiracial Portuguese empire. As we move later in the decade and deeper into the war, Portuguese architects become more and more attached to the Luso-tropical discourse as a way to both place themselves critically and to recreate professional cultural capital. Mário de Oliveira, *Urbanismo no ultramar: Problemas essenciais do urbanismo no ultramar; Estruturas urbanas de integração e convivência* (Lisbon: Agência Geral do Ultramar, 1962).

51   Fernando Varanda, 'Um estudo de habitação para indígenas em Bissau',

Geographica, no. 15 (July 1968): 22–44.
52   Oliveira, *Urbanismo no ultramar*.
53   In Guinea-Bissau, besides Santa Luzia there was only the Ajuda neighbourhood in the late 1960s. This pattern was common to Angola and Mozambique, where most housing efforts by the colonial state were directed at the white settlers, while African populations lived in 'suburbs'. See Tiago Castela Meneses Maria Paula, 'Naming the Urban in Twentieth-Century Mozambique: Towards Spatial Histories of Aspiration and Violence', in *Urban Planning in Lusophone African Countries* (Routledge, 2015).
54   Instituto do Trabalho, Previdência e Acção Social, 'Missiva Urgente 7/1971', 24 August 1971, INEP.
55   Comissão para o Estudo do Problema Demográfico de Bissau, 'Relatório confidencial da reunião no 4', 30 August 1971, INEP.
56   Lebre and Castela, 'Aldeamento de guerra no colonialismo português na Guiné-Bissau'; Gerald J. Bender, *Angola under the Portuguese: The Myth and the Reality* (Berkeley and Los Angeles: University of California Press, 1978).
57   James C. Scott, *Seeing Like a State: How Certain Schemes to Improve the Human Condition Have Failed* (New Haven and London: Yale University Press, 1998).
58   Oliveira, *Urbanismo no ultramar*.
59   Stephen Cairns and Jane M. Jacobs, *Buildings Must Die: A Perverse View of Architecture* (Cambridge, MA: MIT University Press, 2014); Jonathan Hill, *The Architecture of Ruins: Designs on the Past, Present and Future* (London: Routledge, 2019); Le Roux, 'Comfort, Violence, Care'.
60   Levin, 'Ruins of Modernity That Never Was'.

Chapter 12: Reclaiming South African Railway Spaces: Ruination and Remembrance in the Former Southern African Railway Centres of De Aar and Usakos

1   See Dag Henrichsen, Giorgio Miescher, Ciraj Rassool and Lorena Rizzo, 'Rethinking Empire in Southern Africa', *Journal of Southern African Studies* 41, no. 3 (4 May 2015): 431–5, as well as the whole special edition of *JSAS* in which this article is published. This look at the railways as an integral part of the South African imperial project is also part of an ongoing research and forthcoming publication project. See Giorgio Miescher, *Thinking with Empire: South African Railways and the Formation of an Imperial Space*, 2024.
2   The establishment of South African Railways was part of the South Africa Act of 1909. See Kenneth E. Wilburn, 'Engines of Empire and Independence:

Railways in South Africa, 1863–1916', in *Railway Imperialism*, ed. Clarence B. Davis, Kenneth E. Wilburn and Ronald Edward Robinson, Contributions in Comparative Colonial Studies, no. 26 (New York: Greenwood Press, 1991), p. 37. See also Jeremy Foster, '"Land of Contrasts" or "Home We Have Always Known"? The SAR&H and the Imaginary Geography of White South African Nationhood, 1910–1930', *Journal of Southern African Studies* 29, no. 3 (2003): 661. The company's official name changed in 1980 to South African Transport Services.

3   This particular role beyond profit was explicitly stated in the South Africa Act of 1909, which formed the legal basis of the Union.

4   Ronald Hyam and Peter Henshaw, *The Lion and the Springbok: Britain and South Africa since the Boer War* (Cambridge: Cambridge University Press, 2003), pp. 77–101, https://doi.org/10.1017/CBO9780511523915.

5   The number of staff exceeded 100,000 for the first time in 1929, and over half of the employees were classified as European. See South African Railways & Harbours, Annual Report 1929, p. 184. The company reached the highest number of staff in 1982 with 275,000 employees. See South African Transport Services, Annual Report 1981–82, p. 91.

6   Foster speaks of South African Railways being seen as 'government within a government'. See Foster, 'Land of Contrasts', p. 661.

7   SAR's control over road motor transport was exceptional in an African context even if compared with other colonies with similar regulations. Notably there were also colonies like Ghana where motor transport was hardly regulated and was especially open to African entrepreneurship. See, for example, Brian J. Turton, 'The Road Motor Services of Rhodesia, 1927–38', *Journal of Transport History* 18, no. 1 (1 March 1997): 1–15, https://doi.org/10.1177/002252669701800102.

8   In both cases, the railway company started to integrate new transport technologies at an early stage, namely in 1912 in the case of road transport and 1931 in the case of aviation.

9   See Giorgio Miescher, 'Arteries of Empire: On the Geographical Imagination of South Africa's Railway War, 1914/1915', *Kronos*, no. 38 (2012): 22–46.

10 See Martin Chanock, *Unconsummated Union: Britain, Rhodesia and South Africa, 1900–45* (Manchester: Manchester University Press, 1977), pp. 161–2 in particular.

11 The role of SAR in the making of an imperial South African space is part of the ongoing book project. See Miescher, *Thinking with Empire: South African Railways and the Formation of an Imperial Space*.

12 See in particular the work by Gordon Pirie: 'Racial Segregation on South African Trains, 1910–1928: Entrenchment and Protest', *South African Historical Journal* 20, no. 1 (1 November 1988): 75–93, https://doi.

org/10.1080/02582478808671637; 'Race, Class and Comfort on Rural Buses, 1925–1955', *Contree* 27 (April 1990): 5–11; 'Rolling Segregation into Apartheid: South African Railways, 1948–53', *Journal of Contemporary History* 27, no. 4 (1992): 671–93.

13 See *Report of the Commission of Inquiry into the Road Transportation Bill*, 1977.

14 Parallel research on the two towns started a decade ago and has resulted in several publications on the respective histories. See Paul Grendon, Giorgio Miescher, Lorena Rizzo and Tina Smith, eds, *Usakos Photographs beyond Ruins: The Old Location Albums, 1920s–1960s* (Basel: Basler Afrika Bibliographien, 2015); Giorgio Miescher, 'The NE 51 Series Frontier: The Grand Narrative of Apartheid Planning and the Small Town', *Journal of Southern African Studies* 41, no. 3 (4 May 2015): 561–80, https://doi.org/10.1080/03057070.2015.1030900; Raffaele Perniola, 'Tsuku Tsuku Says the Black Train: Remembering the Railway in Namibia' (Master's thesis, University of Basel, 2020), https://edoc.unibas.ch/78844/; Giorgio Miescher, *De Aar: Lines of Architecture in the Making of a South African Town, 1902–1977* (Pretoria: ESI-Press University of Pretoria, 2023). This chapter marks the first attempt to discuss the two towns together.

15 Photography and railway shared similarities in that both technologies surfaced at roughly the same time. Both technologies regulated and reordered time and space, which made photography and railways 'natural allies in the creation and definition of new political territories'. See Foster, 'Land of Contrasts', quote from p. 600. Lorena Rizzo described this relationship specifically for Namibia, stating that in Namibian colonial landscape photography a discernible subgenre can be found of photographs documenting the appropriation of resources and land in terms of the 'conquest and indexing of the colony'. See Lorena Rizzo, 'Faszination Landschaft: Landschaftsphotographie in Namibia', BAB Working Papers, Basel, February 2014, quote from p. 8.

16 The topic of railway remembrance in the specific case of Namibia, both in official propaganda and in other media, has been analysed in more depth in Raffaele Perniola's master's thesis. See Perniola, 'Tsuku Tsuku'.

17 See Adelheid Wessler, 'Von Lebendabgüssen, Heimatmuseen und Cultural Villages: Museale Repräsentation des Selbst und des Anderen im (De-)Kolonisierungsprozess Namibias' (Doctoral dissertation, University of Cologne, 2007), pp. 116–20; Andree-Jeanne Tötemeyer, *Museums Report: Report on the Survey 'The State of Museums in Namibia and the Need for Training for Museum Services'*, The State of Information Services in Namibia and the Need for Training for Information Services, vol. 5 (Windhoek: University of Namibia, Dept. [of] Information and Communication Studies,

1999), pp. 58–64 for a discussion of how struggles over cultural hegemony between German-speaking and Afrikaner settlers brought about a split in the museum scene of Namibia in the 1960s, leading to German-initiated museums being extremely sceptical of government aid.

18 See Wessler, 'Lebendabgüsse, Heimatmuseen und Cultural Villages', pp. 203–4, 218–19. Wessler also shows that in Namibia these institutions remain predominantly German in character and content.

19 See Wessler, 'Lebendabgüsse, Heimatmuseen und Cultural Villages', pp. 97–102, 205–9.

20 See 'Kommissie: Notule – 1949–1954', 1949–1954, Box: RNG 4. File: H.M.K. 1/10, National Archives of Namibia.

21 It has to be noted, however, that in the early years of the commission's existence, the focus lay on natural sites – which it can be argued were also being 'whitewashed' by being claimed in the name of the settler regime. A few railway-related monuments were also discussed. The notable exception to these efforts at creating symbols of settlement was a handful of 'native monuments' that were discussed for declaration, most notably the grave of the founder of Windhoek, Jan Jonker Afrikaner (/Haramumab). See 'NAN. Box: RNG 4. File: H.M.K. 1/10'.

22 See 'Komiteesake: Notule van die Dagbestuur RNG', 1956–1976, Box: RNG 4. File: 1/10/1, National Archives of Namibia. The reports in this file show how the musealisation of railway monuments picks up in the 1970s, and at times railway monuments make up the majority of monuments discussed for the South West African territory. For the other regions in the Union railway monuments are discussed, but they never take up as prominent a position as in South West Africa.

23 See Miescher, 'Arteries of Empire'.

24 In the cases of Swakopmund station, Lüderitz station and Okahandja station, there are archival sources that document discussions between SAR&H and the Monuments Commission and detail the struggles over the different goals pursued by the two institutions. See 'Railway Station: Swakopmund', 1970–1976, Box: RNG 43. File: 3/s/S-d/4, National Archives of Namibia; 'Station Lüderitz', 1974–1984, Box: RNG 41. File: 3/s/L-z/2, National Archives of Namibia; 'Station Okahandja', 1980–1982, Box: RNG 42. File: 3/s/O-a/2, National Archives of Namibia.

25 Introduction by the curator to *Museu dos CFM*, the official brochure by the museum, n.d. For a careful discussion of how far the museum can keep up to this promise, see the contribution by Osvaldo Luis to this conference.

26 A good example is South Africa's biggest railway museum, the Outeniqua Transport Museum, in George. The museum is part of the Transnet Heritage

Foundation. For a short, although slightly outdated overview of railway heritage in South Africa, see Robert C. de Jong, 'South Africa: Railway Heritage at Risk', *Heritage at Risk* (2003): 184–6, https://doi.org/10.11588/hr.2003.0.21206.

27   See, for instance, the DRISA (Digital Railway Images of South Africa), which was formally launched in 2016, and which aims to make accessible the holdings of the Transnet Heritage Library. The project is run and funded by volunteers. See also the freely accessible publication Nicholas J. Clarke and Roger C. Fisher, 'NZASM Footsteps along the Tracks: The Identified Extant Built Residue of the Nederlandsche Zuid-Afrikaansche Spoorweg-Maatschappij, 1887–1902', Report (Visual Books, 2016), https://repository.up.ac.za/handle/2263/57875.

28   Railway museums throughout the world tend to focus on displaying machines, while adding purely technical information or focusing on the economic impact of railways. For a specific example see Lucy Taksa, 'Machines and Ghosts: Politics, Industrial Heritage and the History of Working Life at the Eveleigh Workshops', *Labour History*, no. 85 (2003): 65–88. In this text Taksa details her struggles as a historian with integrating workers' histories in a state- and industry-initiated railway museum in Australia, while also reflecting more broadly on the need to integrate human, history-from-below narratives in such displays of modern machinery and industry.

29   See E.A. Venter, *De Aar: Town of the Future, 1902–1952* (De Aar: De Aar Municipality, 1952), pp. 1–2.

30   Quoted after Lawrence G. Green, *When the Journey's Over*, 1st edn (Cape Town: Howard Timmins, 1972), p. 9.

31   The Friedlander brothers started to auction the plots in 1902, and that year became known as the founding year of the town, although the municipality of De Aar was only proclaimed in 1904. See Government Proclamation no. 159, 20 May 1904.

32   See 'De Aar: Establishment of Municipality, 1903–1904', 1903–1904, Depot: KAB Source: PAS volume no.: 2/175 Reference: L25C, National Archives of South Africa.

33   For population figures for the early years, see 'Report of Systematic Health Inspections of De Aar on 12th March 1928 by Dr. E.H. Chluver, Assistant Health Officer Pretoria (from File De Aar Municipality. Establishment of Location and Hostels: Regulation Therefore)', 1928, Depot: SAB Source: NTS volume no.: 4309 Reference: 162/313, National Archives of South Africa. For the 1960s, see 'Sekretaris van Kleurlingbetrekkinge: Woongebiede: Afbakening en Beplanning: De Aar: Kaap', 1961–1969, Depot: KAB Source:

KUS volume no.: 1/38 Reference: 5/2/1/F73, National Archives of South Africa.

34   For a concise history of Usakos until the 1970s, see Giorgio Miescher, 'Usakos' Urban Past: Traces in the Archives', in *Usakos Photographs beyond Ruins. The Old Location Albums, 1920s–1960s*, ed. Paul Grendon et al. (Basel: Basler Afrika Bibliographien, 2015), pp. 26–61.

35   See 'Usakos Local Authorities: Minutes of Meetings, 1927–1946', 1927–1946, Box: LOC 50 File: SWA 2/7/15 (vol. 1), National Archives of Namibia.

36   Juma Murar, Carol Smith and Theresa Thompson, Discussion round with De Aar residents, interview by Paul Grendon and Giorgio Miescher, 21 June 2018; information in this case given by Carol Smith.

37   De Aar is the seat of the Pixley ka Seme District Municipality, one of five districts of the Northern Cape.

38   This is based on information received from the municipality.

39   Murar, Smith and Thompson, Discussion round with De Aar residents; information in this case given by Theresa Thompson.

40   On this topic, see Lars Meier, Lars Frers and Erika Sigvardsdotter, 'The Importance of Absence in the Present: Practices of Remembrance and the Contestation of Absences', *Cultural Geographies* 20, no. 4 (1 October 2013): 423–30, https://doi.org/10.1177/1474474013493889; as well as the whole special edition of *Cultural Geographies* on 'Absence, Materiality, Embodiment, Resistance' in which this article is published.

41   This information stems from interviews with De Aar residents (Murar, Smith and Thompson, Discussion round with De Aar residents) as well as personal communication between Giorgio Miescher and Tobie van der Westhuizen in 2012 and 2018. For details, consult the author.

42   This section concerning Usakos and its planned museum was made possible by a close collaboration with the Usakos Museum Advisory Council, which allowed us to sit in on discussions on multiple occasions and especially exchanges and discussions with Usakos museum activist Chalden Sabab, who also accompanied Raffaele Perniola's oral history research in Usakos in 2019.

43   An interviewed resident, who was the son of a white former railway worker, told us that people looted the railway facilities after SAR's move to Windhoek in search of materials for their homes. He himself had fenceposts made out of rails as well as an old railway hammer. Another interviewee in Usakos's township Hakaseb instead built a cutter for metal sheets out of scraps modelled after a similar object he knew from his time at the railway, and had an anvil made out of rail. This culture of recycling is quite common throughout Usakos. Information from P.J.G., Interview with son of former Usakos railway worker, interview by Raffaele Perniola and Chalden Sabab,

7 August 2019; and D./A., Interview with former Usakos railway worker, interview by Raffaele Perniola and Chalden Sabab, 22 July 2019. The names of interviewees from Usakos and surroundings have been abbreviated to their initials as interviewees only gave permission for their full names to be used in Raffaele Perniola's master's thesis while giving permission for the interviews themselves to be used for further research and papers.

44 See Grendon et al., *Photographs beyond Ruins*, the publication that accompanied the exhibition for more details.

45 See NBC News, *Usakos Museum* (Namibian Broadcasting Association, 2014), https://www.youtube.com/watch?v=4MCsIC2KHUM. In this news story the then mayor details the plans for the museum in 2014.

46 In the Afrikaans original: "'n soort afskeidsgeskenk van die S.A.S.&H. aan Usakos'. 'Antieke Voorwerpe: Spoorweglokomotief – Usakos', 1955–1959, Box: RNG 13, File 7/1/7, National Archives of Namibia. Translation by the authors.

47 Most notably, the locomotive was hit by a truck in 2008. It is also heavily rusted in places and has been tagged and partially graffitied. See Piet Conradie, 'Usakos, Namibia, Steam Locomotive at Station Building', *Old Steam Locomotives in South Africa* (blog), 24 November 2007, http://steam-locomotives-south-africa.blogspot.com/search/label/*%20Usakos%20%28Namibia%29. This blog by a railway enthusiast details (and laments) the decay of the Usakos locomotive.

48 Information from K.G., Interview with former Usakos railway worker, interview by Raffaele Perniola and Chalden Sabab, 20 July 2019; A.//G. et al., Group interview with former Usakos railway workers, interview by Raffaele Perniola and Chalden Sabab, 15 August 2019.

49 Especially in one interview, the only group interview done in the context of Raffaele Perniola's research of Usakos's history (//G. et al., Group interview with former Usakos railway workers), one of the interviewees fetched a book about the railway by an amateur historian and railway enthusiast, which the interviewees used to show us the machines they had worked on and to discuss their fascination with some of these machines. Other interviewees also showed a fascination for the materials and technology of the railway and shared some of the ideas about prosperity through modern industry that are so common in enthusiast literature and settler museums.

50 Usakos municipality has even publicly complained about TransNamib's continued control over much of the town's land and sought help from the government. See 'TransNamib Owns Huge Tract of Usakos', *New Era Live* [online magazine of *New Era* newspaper], 24 July 2018, https://neweralive.na/posts/transnamib-owns-huge-tract-of-usakos.

51 Recent development efforts in Usakos have always entailed projects which would manifest in or near the railway's land, and thus reshape this area into an economic centre as it used to be in the 1950s and 1960s. See, for an undergraduate study, sponsored by TransNamib, concerned with the potential of bringing back a railway workshop to Usakos: Aidan Burn, Constantine Scaperdas and Yiğit Uyan, 'Defining TransNamib's Engineering Future: A Study on the Establishment of a New Motive Power and Rolling Stock Repair Workshop in the Usakos-Erongo Region of Namibia' (Bachelor's thesis, Worcester Polytechnic Institute, 2016), https://web.wpi.edu/Pubs/E-project/Available/E-project-050616-083932/unrestricted/TransNamib_-_Final_Paper.pdf. This project was later considered by TransNamib but came to an impasse, see Isabel Bento, 'Usakos Yearns for Speedy Resolution on Locomotive Project', *The Namibian*, 26 February 2019, sec. Business.

52 Namibian tourism has a long tradition of catering to German tourists, who long for or at least are interested in colonial nostalgia. See Philipp Rodrian, *Das Erbe der deutschen Kolonialzeit in Namibia im Fokus des 'Tourist Gaze' deutscher Touristen*, Würzburger Geographische Arbeiten (Würzburg: Selbstverlag des Instituts für Geographie der Universität Würzburg, 2009), pp. 43–5, 155–60.

53 Members of the municipality as well as some of the activists hope that the museum will spark interest in the town and lead visitors to stay and visit local shops and restaurants.

Index

Page numbers in italics indicate figures

A

Abrahams, Peter 48
Actstop 179
Adjaye, David 153
African architecture 34, 87, 185, 296,
African National Congress *see* ANC
Afrikaans *120*, *123*, 181, 183–186
Afrikaner nationalism 182–184
Afropunk music festival 108
Alexandra, Johannesburg 7, 113–*114*, *118*, *120*, *122*, *123*
Amafa (KwaZulu-Natal Amafa and Research Institute) 30–32
ANC 25, 33, 50, 96, *119*, 165, 168
Anglican church 166–*167*, 185
Anglo American Corporation 161
Anglo-Boer War 142, 183, 187
apartheid colonialism 38, 57
appropriation 50, 142, 154, 235, 240, 252, 257
Aranya housing scheme, Indore 172
Arcades Project 220
Architects Against Apartheid 168
Architecture and Utopia 170
Argan, Giulio Carlo 169
art brut 176
Art Deco 8, 185, 191, 215–218, 220–221, 226–229
    buildings 212, 215, 217, 221–223, 226
    features 221, 224–226, 228
    heritage 217, 222, 226
    movement 211–212, 214
    style 71, 212, 217, 222–225
Ashcroft, Bill 3, 199
Asvat, Aboobaker 48
Asvat, Adam 52–54
ATB 90–*94*, 96–98, 100–101, 108–109
Auwal mosque 188
Avenida Amílcar Cabral 65, 71–72
Avenida da República 65, 70–71, 72–73, 75
Avenida de Cintura (Bordering Avenue) 71
Awaiting Trial Block 88, 90, 93, 95, 100, *101 see also* ATB
Ayyoub, Noor Addine 150–151
Azanian People's Organisation (AZAPO) 157

B

B2 Highway 289
Ballard, Richard 22, 26–28
Banham, Reyner 142
Bantfu netindzawo 113
bantustans 4–5, 157
Barahona, José 78
Barreira, Maria 68
Barreto, Honório Pereira 60, 67–68, 72–73, 75–76, 81–82
Barrios, Joana 79
Barros, Victor 61
Basha Uhuru youth festival 108

INDEX

Bauer, Nickolaus 148, 150
Bay of Natal 17
Beavon, Keith 214
Beinart, Julian 172
Belgian Congo 8, 202
Belhar 162, 164
Belhar Minor Community Hall 163
Benjamin, Walter 220, 228
Berea, Durban 16–20, 22–23, 25–29, 31, 34, 130–131, 141, 143, 145, 223 see also Save Our Berea
Berlin Conference (1884–1885) 62, 69, 116, 237–238
Bhabha, Homi Kharshedji 106, 198–199
Bissau 8, 59–60, 63–68, 70, 74–75, 81–82, 233, 235, 239–240, 241, 242–257
colonial 8, 231, 255, 258
New Bissau 40, 240, 243, 256
Bissau Velho (Old Bissau) 71–72
Black Consciousness Movement 37, 48, 157
Bozzoli, Belinda 156
Bretton Woods, Johannesburg 229
bricolage 177
British colonial rule 18, 85
Brixton Gereformeerde Church 195
Brixton Hervormde Church 194
Brown, Audrey 106
Built Environment Support Group (BESG) 179
Bungué, Welket 80
Bureau of Archaeology 30
Burra Charter 89, 100–101, 104–105
Byker Wall, Newcastle upon Tyne 171

C
Cabral, Amílcar 76–77
Cabral, Luís 81
Cacheu, fortress of see fortress of Cacheu
Calvinism 182
Campbell, Tony 47
Cane, Jonathan 221, 226
Cape Town 5, 38, 43, 47, 87, 91–92, 133, 140, 142, 179, 188, 265, 271
Cardoso, Manuel Lopes 62
Carlton Centre 142
Carved in Stone 142
Casimiro, Augusto 64, 74
Castela, Tiago 61
Catholic University of Leuven, Woluwe-Saint-Lambert 171
CAVE (Centro de Audiovisuais do Exército, or the Portuguese Army Audiovisual Archive) 78
Celliers, Elma and Danie 150
Central Business District (CBD) 22, 26–27, 113, 120, 143
César, Filipa 61, 78–79
Che Guevara Square 68, 72–73
Chipkin, Clive M 142–143, 215
Church of Norway 175
Cinegraphic Mission to the Colonies of Africa 74
City of Johannesburg (COJ) 49–52, 56, 85, 134, 137
Coconut 27
colonial spaces 9, 205–206, 279, 288
Colonial Superior School, Lisbon 243
Colonial War (Portugal) 76–78
Coloured Persons Communal Reserves Act 161
Coloured Persons Reserve 161
Coloureds 25, 27, 39, 156–157, 162, 175–177, 191
commemoration 57, 61, 64, 97, 100
Commission for Technical Cooperation in Africa South of the Sahara (CCTA) 243
communal house 170
community development initiatives (CDIs) 33, 35
Conférence Internationale des Africanistes Occidentaux (CIAO) 243
Constitution Hill 6, 85–90, 93, 96–97, 104–108, 110
cultural significance 89, 90, 92, 101, 104–105
Human Rights Festival 108

Constitution Hill Development Company 88, 110
Constitutional Court 85–90, 93–94, 97–98, 107
Correia, António Mendes 243
Covid-19 pandemic 5, 16
Crankshaw, Owen 146
CS Studio 175–178
cultural difference 198
cultural diversity 186, 198

D

Da Conceição, Vasco Pereira 68
Dadoo, Yusuf 48
Davis, John Henry 117
De Aar 8–9, 259, 262, 265–268, 275–276
    railway station 260
    railway yard 269–270
De Beers Consolidated Mines 161, 176
De Carlo, Giancarlo 171–172
De Castro, Ponce 71
De Quincy, Quatremère 168
decolonisation 2, 5, 15, 33, 76, 231, 243–244, 263
Delport, Peggy 106
Delta Park, Johannesburg 219
Demisse, Fassil 23
Democratic Republic of Congo (DRC) 201–202, 205
Department of Community Development 159
Development Action Group 179
Discipline and Punish 242
District Six Museum 38, 47, 106
Dlala Nje 133, 141, 145, 147, 151
Dokrat ruin 54, 55
Doshi, Balkrishna 172
Durban 16–17, 21–27, 29, 31, 33–35, 140, 211, 213–215, 218, 221–228
Durban Arcades 213
Durban Heritage Trust 33
Durban Port 227
Durban University of Technology 26
Durban's Heritage Explored on Walks and Drives around the City 29
Dutch settlers 182, 186
Dyer, Geoff 211–212, 215, 217, 220–221, 223–224, 226, 228

E

Eerste Treetjies (First Steps) Community Centre 174–175, 177
Erskine, Ralph 171–172
Essop, Ahmed 48
Estado Novo 59, 63–64, 66, 68, 73, 82
eThekwini 16, 18–19, 25–26
European Union National Institutes for Culture (EUNIC) 5
Exchanging Symbols: Monuments and Memorials in Post-apartheid South Africa 88–89

F

Feldman, Mannie 135, 140–143
Feldman, Mike 6, 46–47, 57
Fietas, Johannesburg 38–41, 43, 44–45, 46–49, 51, 57
    Heritage Trail 6, 51, 56
    museum 6, 46–50, 56, 57
    reflections on 37
Fietas Memory in Action Museum 38, 41
Filipe, António J.M. 238
films produced after Guinea-Bissau's independence 73, 75
    Acto dos feitos da Guiné (Act of the Achievements of Guinea) 75
    Anos da guerra, Guiné (Years of War, Guinea 1963–1974) 77
    Cacheu 78–79
    Cacheu CUNTUM 80
    Mortu nega (Death Denied, or Those Whom Death Refused) 77, 79
    Sans soleil (Sunless) 76, 79
    The Embassy 78–79
    Visões do império (Visions of Empire) 80
films produced during Portuguese rule 73

Bissau 75
Cidade de Bissau (Town of Bissau) 75
Guiné, berço do império (Guinea, Cradle of the Empire 1446–1946) 74
Terra ardente (Ardent Land) 74
Viagem presidencial à Guiné (Presidential Visit to Guinea) 74
First World War 237
forced removals 6, 24, 31, 37–38, 40, 46–47, 51–53, 141, 164, 271, 283
fortress of Cacheu 6, 59–62, 63–64, 74–75, 77, 79, 81, 83
Foucault, Michel 242–243
Fourier, Charles 170
Fraga, Augusto 74
Free State Institute of Architects (FSIA) 140
Freschi, Federico 214
Freund, William Mark (Bill) 16, 222, 225–226, 228
Friedlander brothers 266

G
Gabinete de Urbanização Colonial (Colonial Urbanisation Office) 71–72
Gandy, Joseph M 232
Garden of Ruins 8, 231
Geers and Geers 190
Geers, Geurt Marinus Jacobus 191
Geers, Leendert Marinus 191
Gevisser, Mark 88, 93, 102, 107
Ginzburg, Moisei 170
Goldblatt, David 6, 41, 43, *44–45*, 47, 57
Goldfinger, Ernö 143
Gomes, Diogo 60, 66–68, 71, 72, 75, 77, 81
Gomes, Flora 77, 79
Gosani, Bob 95, 98
Green, Ralph Wesley 140
Grosskopff, Rodney 134–135, 137, 139–142
Group Areas Act 24, 27, 30, 39, *44–45*, 53–54, *121*, 141, 187, 191
Guevara, Che 68, 72–73, 81–82
Guinea-Bissau 6, 59, 61, 64–65, 69–73, 75–80, 83, 233–236, 238, 243, 245–246, 254

H
Hakhaseb township, Usakos 283, 286, 288–289
Hallmark House, Johannesburg 153
Henschel Locomotive HD 40 271–272, 273
heritage 2, 5–6, 9, 15, 28–33, 35, 42, 52, 61, 90, 111, 176,
architectural 6, 17, 20, 23, 29–34, 87, 98
conservation 21, 30, 86, 90, 92, 97–98, 105
consultants 7, 87, 93
definition 21, 29
practice 21, 87, 89, 104, 110
practitioners 2, 89, 92–93, 97, 105
resources 30, 32
sites 8, 19, 51, 87–89, 217
trail 6, 37–38, 49, 51, 56–57
Hermer & Grosskopff Architects 140
Hermer, Manfred 51, 135, 140–141
Hillbrow, Johannesburg 85, 92, 102, 131, 141, 143–146
Historical Monuments Commission (HMC) 29, 263
Hlongwane, Ali Khangela 50
Hobbs, Stephen 133, 141–142, 147, 150
Huddleston, Trevor 166
hybridity 198–199

I
IBM Tower 142
Independence War, Guinea-Bissau 75–76, 81
Infant of Sagres 75
Institute Français d'Afrique Noir (IFAN) 243
Institute of South African Architects (ISAA) 172
Institute of Work, Welfare and Social Action (ITPAS) 253
Instituto Nacional de Cinema e Audiovisual (INCA) 76
Integrated Urban Development Framework

(IUDF) 25
International Conference of Western Africanists 243
International Council on Monuments and Sites (ICOMOS) 88
Ipelegeng Community Centre 166
Islam 182, 186, 188, 196, 190, 200
Islamic architecture 188, 196, 200

J

Jabavu (White City), Soweto 165, *167*
Japha, Vivienne and Derek 87, 91–92, 98, 99
Jassat, Abdulhay 48
Jassat, Essop 48
Jewish Community Centre, Trenton, New Jersey 161
Johannesburg Heritage Foundation (JHF) 22, 53
Johannesburg Style 215
Johannesburg West Dutch Reformed Church 181
Johannesburg West NGK 181, *189*, 190, *192*, 193, 200 *see also* Mayfair West Dutch Reformed Church
Johnston, Peter 29
Jubilee House, Krugersdorp 214
Juma Masjid 190

K

Kahn, Louis 161–162, 164
Kaikhoen, Usakos 287
Kate Otten Architects 102
Kearney, Brian 31, 32
Keenan, Tom 147
Kempston Group 150–151, *152*
Killarney, Johannesburg 215, 218, 229
Khan River 279
Kleinzee 176
Koeberg nuclear power plant 5
Komaggas *174*–176
Kreutzfeldt, Dorothy 225
Kroll, Lucien 171

KwaZulu-Natal (KZN) 15–16, 26, 30–31

L

Lacaton, Anne 90
Land Policy Act of 1997 30
Legacy Project 33
Lenasia 39–40, 187
Lesotho 172
liberation struggle 41, 48, 92, 106
Liebman, Jonathan 153
Lim, Denise 142
Lokko, Lesley 110
Lona, Armando 78–79
Lopes, Adolfo Norberto 74
Lopes, Craveiro 74, 69
Louw, Wynand 184
Low, Iain 172
Lubetkin, Berthold 166
Lyons, Michael 177

M

Madikida, Churchill 96
Magubane, Peter 48
Malay Location (Fietas) 38
Malay Mosque, 23rd Street 53–54
Malcomess, Bettina 225
Malheiro, Ricardo 74
Mandela, Nelson Rolihlahla 15, 96
Mandinga house *250*
Manetsi, Thabo 89
Mangunza, James 147
Marabastad, Pretoria 38, 47
Marais, Pieter Jacobus *115*, *117*
Marker, Chris 76–78
Martinez, José 243
Masilela, Ntongela 42–43
Masjid-ul-Islam *189*–190, 193, 197–200
Matlwa, Kopano 27
Matsipa, Mpho 27
Matteotti Quarter, Terni 171
Mattera, Don 46, 49
Mayfair West, Johannesburg 7, 181, 190, 192, 198, 200

Mayfair West Dutch Reformed Church 7, 190
Mbembe, Achille 104, 106–107
Medu Art Ensemble 37, 38
Meer, Fatima 102
Melnikov, Konstantin 170
Mémé Medical School student dormitories 171
Memorial da Escravatura e do Tráfico Negreiro (Memorial to Slavery and the Slave Trade) 63, 80
Memory Is the Weapon 49
Mentone Court, Johannesburg 215
Merriman, Peter 218
Milandu 8, 206–208
Minor Community Hall 162, *163*
Mnyele, Thami 38
Moerdijk, Gerard Leendert Pieter 184–186, 191
Moloi, Godfrey 96
Moneo, Rafael 158
Monod, Théodore 243
Monumento ao Esforço da Raça (Monument to the Effort of the Race) 71
Morris, Alan 131, 145
Mortu nega 77, 79
Moscow 170
Mosojada, Janina 96
Mphahlele, Rebecca 48
Mpofu-Walsh, Sizwe 28
Murray, Martin 151
Musée de l'Homme 243
Museum Africa 46–47
Museum of the Constitution 87, 109
Muslim community 186–188, 190, 196, 199
    Cape 186, 188
    Indian 54, 187–188
    Johannesburg 181, 190
    Natal 187–188
    Transvaal 187–188
Muslims 54, 197
    immigration 187–188, 199–200

N

Naidoo, Hyacinthia 29
Nama 176–177, 280
Namaqualand 161, 175
Namibia 9, 260–261, 263–264, 267, 270–271, 274
Nana, Suleiman 48
Narkomfin Communal House 170
narratives of oppression 96, 108
National and Historical Monuments Act 29
National Forum 157
National Heritage Council Act 30
National Heritage Resources Act 30–31, 90
National Monuments Council (NMC) 30, 90, 92, 98
Native Location Act 23
Native Trust and Land Act 24
Natives Land Act 4, 24
Ndebele 172
Ndebele, Njabulo 42
Nederduits Gereformeerde Kerk *see* NGK
neo-Byzantine style 185, 191
New Apartheid, The 28
New Bissau 240, 243, 256 *see also* Bissau
New Brutalist buildings 143
Newbury, Darren 41
Newcastle upon Tyne 171
NGK 181–183, 185–186, 188, 190, 193, 196, 199
    architecture 182, 184, 186
    buildings 182, 184–185, 190, 193, 199
    Langlaagte 193, 196
Nguni *114*, 172
Nkwe, David 166
Noero, Jo 158, 166, *167*, 168, 178
Nova Cidade de Bissau (New City of Bissau) 70, 239
Number Four prison 100, 109
Nuttall, Sarah 88
Nzima, Sam 166

O

O'Regan, Kate (Justice) 96

O'Toole, Sean 43
Old Location, Usakos 9, 271, 275, 283, 288
Oliver, Diana 175
OMEG 266, 280–282, 288
OMM Design Workshop 87
Orange Free State Provincial Institute of Architects (OFSPIA) 140
Oriental Plaza, Fordsburg 40, 57
Otavi Mines and Railway Company *see* OMEG

P

Pageview 50–51, *120*, 141
Pampalone, Tanya 151
Papenfus, Herbert B *118*
Parktown and Westcliff Heritage Trust (PWHT) 22 *see also* Johannesburg Heritage Foundation
Partido Africano para a Independência da Guiné e Cabo Verde (PAIGC) 76–77
Passing of Pageview, The 51, 141
Patel, Hanifa 39–40
Patel, Selma 38–41, 47–50, 57
Phalanstère 170
Photographic Society of South Africa 46
Pidjiguiti massacre 252
Pieterson, Hector 166
Pinto, João Teixeira 60–61, 68–70, 72, 73–76, 79–81
Plan of the site, 2021 *103*
Planact 168, 179
Pohlandt-McCormick, Helena 42
Ponte City 7, 127, *128–129*, 130–132, 134, 139–144, 147–148, *149*, 154
Ponte City, films featuring
 Africa Shafted: Under One Roof 148
 Chappie 148
 Ponte Tower 148
 District 9 148
 Dredd 148
 Resident Evil: The Final Chapter 148
Popke, Jeffrey 22

Portuguese
 colonial legacy 6, 59, 83
 colonial statues *60*, 70, 83
 revolution (Carnation Revolution) 77, 80
Portuguese Colonial Exhibition 238
Portuguese Empire 61–62, 64, 80, 83, 236, 257
Portuguese Guinea 59, 61, 68 *see also* Guinea-Bissau
post-traumatic stress disorder (PTSD) 203
Praça do Império (Empire Square) 71, 72, 75,
Praça dos Heróis Nacionais (National Heroes Square) 71, 72
Prince Henry the Navigator (Infant of Sagres) 75
Prins, Herbert 87, 92–93, 101
Propertuity 153

Q

Quinhones, José Guedes 70–71, 239–240, 242, 244, 248, 252, 255

R

Radio Televisão Portuguesa (RTP) 74–75
railway heritage 262, 264–265, 269, 274–276
rainbow nation 29, 97, 106
reappropriation 7, 133–134, 141–142, 144–145, 147–148, 154
 definition 132
 residential 7, 127–128
Reconstruction and Development Programme (RDP) 25
Red Ants 150–151
Regional Heritage Committee 92
Reitz, Francis William 142
resistance 5, 40–41, 47, 54, 64, 69, 75, 78, 96, 102, 104, 106, 110, 155, 159, 164, 171–172, 178–179, 191, 205, 243, 246, 274
 acts of 3, 165, 187
 to colonisation 5, 234, 237

INDEX

history of 38, 64
legacy of 6, 37
and struggle, 9, 42
residential reappropriation 7, 127
Revised Listing of the Important Places and Buildings of Durban, A 31
Rhenish Missionary Society 176
Rhodes Must Fall 2, 15, 88
Ribeiro, António Lopes 74
Rigby, Ursula 88
Rodrigues, Manuel Sarmento 61, 64, 240, 242–244, 248
Royal Photographic Society 46
Rozendal, Norbert 162
ruination 232–234, 257, 259–262, 276
ruins, architectural 231–234, 255, 257, 286
Rusakov Workers Club 170

S

Sachs, Albie 42
SAIA KZN 30–33
Salazar, Oliveira 238
Saloojee, Molvi 48
Santa Luzia 248–249, 251–252, 255–257
São José de Amura, fort of 67, 70, 72
SASOL oil refinery 5
Sassen, Robyn 46
Save Our Berea (SOB) 6, 15, 18–22, 26, 28, 30, 32–33
Save Pageview Association 40, 53–54, 57
School of Architecture and Planning, University of Witwatersrand 5, 110
Scott, James 144, 256
Second World War 239–240, 244
segregation 2–4, 16, 22–24, 137, 141, 153, 156, 165, 181, 183, 191, 266
racial 181, 205, 262, 268, 275, 286
spatial 2, 23, 268
Seidman, Judy 38
Selvan, David 150–151
sense of presence 159, 162
Silva, Fernando Matos 75–76
Silver, Paul 147
Simões, João 71

Smuts, Carin 158, 173–174, 177–178
Soane, John 231–232, 257
social change 16, 157, 175, 178, 191, 199
Social Change Assistance Trust (SCAT) 175
Social Realism 170
Socio-Economic Rights Institute (SERI) 153
Sophiatown 49, 53, *120*, 141
Sophiatown Heritage and Cultural Centre 46, 49
South African Heritage Resources Agency (SAHRA) 90
South African Institute of Architects KwaZulu-Natal Region *see* SAIA KZN
South African Native National Congress (SANNC) *119*
South African Railways (SAR) 9, 259, 261–268, 271, 274–275
South African Railways and Harbours (SAR&H) 261
Soviet Union 170
Soweto 39, 96, 165, 168
Soweto 1976 student uprising 108, *123*, 131, 155, 166
spatial architecture 88, 201, 205
spatial transformation 34, 97, 131–132
spatial violence 70, 155
speculative desire 127, 131–132, 154
Springs 211, 214–218, 222–226, 228
Springs Fire Station *216*
St Anthony's Church, Krause Street 54
St Paul's Anglican Church, Soweto 165–166, *167*
Stacey, Jeff 93
Stalinism 170
State of Emergency 155, 158
Steinkopf 161
Steinkopf Community Centre *160*
Stephens, Anthea 177
Stoler, Ann 233–234
Streek, Barry 175
Stringer, Bryan 142
Subotzky, Mikhael 133, 137, 148
Surtees/Kays Fashion Building 56

T

Tafuri, Manfredo 170
Tavares, Eduardo 66–67
Tell Freedom 48
Temko, Ned 144
Training for Self-Reliance Project, Lesotho 172
Transvaal Scottish Regiment 98
Tristão, Nuno 59, 64–65, 70–72, 74–75, 77–79, 81
Tropical Bungalow 8, 201–203, 206–207
Trust Bank Building 142
Tutu, Desmond 166
typologies
    architectural 156, 168, 251
    of Art Deco buildings 212, 223
    of dissonance 178–179

U

United Democratic Front (UDF) 157
University of Cape Town 161
Urban Foundation 156
Urban Lime 28, 33
Urban Problems Research Unit (UPRU) 161
urbanisation 23, 25, 30, 63, 67, 71–72, 183, 190, *241*, 248
Urban Solutions (architects and urban designers) 87
Usakos 259–260, 262, 265–267, 270–271, 274–276, 279–280, 286–289, 292–294
    Museum 9, 274, 277, 279, 281, 286, 288, 294
    railway workshop 272
utopian socialism 170

Uytenbogaardt, Roelof 158, *160*, 161–162, *163*, 164, 178

V

Vassal, Jean-Philippe 90
Vaz, Euclides 69
Venice Biennale 110
Vidler, Anthony 169
Vieira, Nino 81
Vladislavić, Ivan 217, 220
VOC (Dutch East India Company) 186
Vrededorp 39, 48, 51

W

Walton, James 172
water tower 292
Waterhouse, Patrick 133, 148
Wekker, Gloria 21
Welleman Construction 164
West Rand (Bantu) Administration Board (WRAB) *123*, 159
Western Native Township *120*, 172
White Innocence: Paradoxes of Colonialism and Race 21
white settlers 23, 29–30, 34, 224, 229, 263
White, Caroline 146
Whitehall Court, Johannesburg 215
Winkler, Tanja 131

X

xenophobia 147, 151

Y

Yeoville, Johannesburg 130, 141, 145
Yoga for People Who Can't Be Bothered to Do It 217